Mathematical Aspects

of

Scheduling and Applications

International Series in
MODERN APPLIED MATHEMATICS AND COMPUTER SCIENCE

General Editor: E. Y. RODIN

Volume 4

Other titles in the Series

COOPER & COOPER
Introduction to Dynamic Programming

SAATY & ALEXANDER
Thinking with Models

SURI
Resource Management Concepts for Large Systems

Some Pergamon Titles of Interest

GREENSPAN
Arithmetic Applied Mathematics

GREENSPAN
Computer-oriented Mathematical Physics

LAKSHMIKANTHAM
Nonlinear Differential Equations in Abstract Spaces

ZACKS
Parametric Statistical Inference

Journals*

Computer and Mathematics with Applications

Mathematical Modelling

Topology

* Free specimen copy available on request

Mathematical Aspects

of

Scheduling and Applications

by

R. BELLMAN

University of Southern California
Los Angeles, USA

A. O. ESOGBUE

Georgia Institute of Technology
Atlanta, USA

and

I. NABESHIMA

University of Electro-Communications
Tokyo, Japan

PERGAMON PRESS

OXFORD · NEW YORK · TORONTO · SYDNEY · PARIS · FRANKFURT

UK	Pergamon Press Ltd., Headington Hill Hall, Oxford OX3 0BW, England
USA	Pergamon Press Inc., Maxwell House, Fairview Park, Elmsford, New York 10523, U.S.A.
CANADA	Pergamon Press Canada Ltd., Suite 104, 150 Consumers Road, Willowdale, Ontario M2J 1P9, Canada
AUSTRALIA	Pergamon Press (Aust.) Pty. Ltd., P.O. Box 544, Potts Point, N.S.W. 2011, Australia
FRANCE	Pergamon Press SARL, 24 rue des Ecoles, 75240 Paris, Cedex 05, France
FEDERAL REPUBLIC OF GERMANY	Pergamon Press GmbH, 6242 Kronberg-Taunus, Hammerweg 6, Federal Republic of Germany

First edition 1982

Library of Congress Cataloging in Publication Data
Bellman, Richard Ernest, 1920–
Mathematical aspects of scheduling and applications.
(International series in modern applied mathematics
and computer science; v. 4)
Includes bibliographies.
1. Scheduling (Management)   I. Esogbue, Augustine O.
II. Nabeshima, Ichiro, 1921–   III. Title.   IV. Series.
TS157.5.B44 1982   658.5′3   81–15809

British Library Cataloguing in Publication Data
Bellman, R.
Mathematical aspects of scheduling and applications
(International series in modern applied
mathematics and computer science; v. 4)
1. Scheduling (Management)—Mathematics
I. Title   II. Esogbue, A. O.   III. Nabeshima, I.
IV. Series
658.5′3   TS157.5

ISBN 0–08–026477–8 Hardcover
ISBN 0–08–026476–X Flexicover

Printed in Great Britain by A. Wheaton & Co. Ltd., Exeter

Preface

THROUGHOUT the two major epochs in human history, in both the mechanical age and now the systems age, mankind has been beset with the arduous problem of optimal utilization of the usually limited resources in accomplishing the variegated tasks or objectives. The problem is thus not new although contemporary manifestations of this problem in forms such as the energy crisis or inflation may proffer it that coloration. Further, the problem appears recurrent and eternal. An attempt to cope with such problems demands that one develop some plan or schedule. The analysis and study of such plans particularly, with respect to their optimality and other properties under various scenarios of objectives and constraints, constitutes an exciting field known as Scheduling Theory. This theory thus deals with a concretization of continuing human experience.

The purpose of the book is, however, not a prosaic rendition of history. Rather, it is an attempt to syphon out of both the mechanical age (when man was building machines to analyze and do work) and the systems age (when the synthesis of the total problem and interrelationships are the focus of attention) certain pervasive problems that occur and are important enough to warrant the focus of our attention. We then present the kernel of these problems in mathematical terms and devise mathematical solutions to them. As always, we study their intrinsic properties and, whenever we can, generalize to other situations. Similar objectives appear in numerous works in the field. What we have done that is unique is to integrate our experiences of over two decades of research work in the field, from different vistas of experience with problems and techniques into one compendium.

The book is particularly timely. First, as we said, the problem of scheduling is a perennial one and nearly as old as history. Second, mankind is currently going through a special period in which critical shortages of important resources needed to continue civilization have been flung to the limelight. The plea to conserve is not only a plea to schedule one's consumption. It is more than that. It is also a plea for efficient utilization of available resources including optimal combinations of resources. These are issues of central interest in scheduling theory. Third, the existing books in the field are either considerably outdated or are severely limited in their scope of treatment. Fourth, the problem of optimal systems design and control bears striking interdependence with that of optimal scheduling.

We have attempted to capture the essential problems in scheduling as well as treat them via the most effective techniques. We have introduced material in this book that are considerably current, novel, and well researched. Sometimes, these techniques and problems have not even appeared in the open literature. Other times, they may have only appeared in the form of technical reports of some research institute or in scientific journals. Further, we have exploited our familiarity with the literature of such fields as mathematics, economics, operations research, management science, computer science, engineering and medicine, to motivate our problems and methods of attack.

This book does not and is not intended to discuss everything there is to know about scheduling. For example, dynamic problems involving stochastic arrival times of jobs are not considered. Inclusion of such topics here would have led to a much lengthier book than this one or to the sacrifice of the depth of coverage of each of the topics in this book. We decided to err on the side of depth than breadth.

This book is intended as a graduate text or reference work in a course usually entitled Scheduling Theory or Control Theory in most universities' departments of mathematics, operations research, management science, computer science or engineering. It will also be useful to economists and planners. It gives an almost didactic treatment of the subject. The central techniques employed can be picked up along the way although previous familiarity with dynamic programming and integer programming is useful particularly with the advanced algorithms. The reader will find the exercises at the end of each chapter instructive and challenging. The comments and bibliography section will be useful in pursuing an in-depth study of the material covered in each chapter.

The book consists of twelve chapters. It begins with network problems—a very special subgroup of mathematical programming problems. The shortest-path problem, one of the fundamental problems in mathematics, is the problem of tracing a path of shortest length through a finite network. This problem occurs in many fields and we devote the first two chapters to it. In Chapter 1, we show how a simple dynamic programming argument yields a fundamental nonlinear equation. Thus, dynamic programming converts a combinatorial problem into an analytic one. Simple approximate techniques yield upper and lower bounds for the solution of this equation. These bounds can be easily interpreted in terms of approximate policies. We also exploit such bounds and other fathoming criteria suggested by branch and bound strategies to solve large-scale traveling-salesman problems. Applications to control theory and other parts of the calculus of variations are also discussed. In Chapter 2 we show that this problem can be used to treat many problems in artificial intelligence and that many popular mathematical games can be interpreted in these terms. The role and use of computers is stressed.

In Chapter 3 we classify scheduling problems and briefly discuss their solution approaches. The machine scheduling problem is the problem of processing n items on m machines in an efficient manner. The problem is remarkably difficult. We discuss the many methods that can be applied, and give many examples. Among these methods are the branch and bound method, backtrack programming, dynamic programming, and various combinatorial methods.

The only analytic result known is due to Selmer Johnson for the case of two machines. If there are more than two machines, it is quite likely that no simple analytic result exists. However, for the permutation flow-shop problem with makespan objective, there have been many efficient analytic results under some restricting conditions, as described in Chapter 7.

Since these are finite problems, it might be thought they could be handled by enumeration, particularly with the speed of the digital computer. This is not the case, mathematical analysis is definitely needed, to identify and/or extend the solvable cases. Also we require an approximation method with guaranteed accuracy, or with simple efficient heuristics.

To see this, two numbers are convenient to keep in mind. First of all, $10! = 3,628,800$; secondly, a year has approximately 3×10^7 seconds.

Consequently, if each case takes one second to examine, we see that $10!$ cases takes about a month. Since $20!$ is more than $10^{10} \times 10!$, we see that $20!$ cases cannot be examined by enumeration. Even if each case requires only a microsecond, it is not feasible to examine $20!$ cases. In combinatorial problems of this type, it is not uncommon to meet numbers such as $100!$ or $1000!$. Thus mathematical analysis, whenever possible, helps us reduce the computational drain tremendously.

Chapters 4 through 6 discuss different problems and techniques of machine sequencing. Chapter 5 discusses capacity expansion problems and introduces the new technique of imbedded state space dynamic programming for reducing dimensionality so that larger problems can be solved. Chapter 6 considers an important class of network problems with nonserial phase structures and exploits dimensionality reduction techniques such as the pseudo-stage concept, branch compression and optimal order elimination methods to solve large-scale nonlinear network scheduling problems.

In Chapters 7 through 11 we consider the flow-shop scheduling problem under different objectives and constraints. We present several novel analytic results and employ various ingenious techniques of branch and bound including backtrack programming, lexicographical search method and unified multi-stage combinatorial algorithms. Applications to the increasingly important area of parallel processing are discussed. Approximate solutions for these interesting cases are also presented. In Chapter 11 we address machine scheduling problems involving sequence-dependent set-up times and present novel efficient dynamic programming formulations especially for the three-machine problem.

The book is concluded with a chapter on the job-shop-scheduling problem. Using the disjunctive graph viewpoint and the techniques of **BAB, EXTBAB**, dynamic programming, important analytical and computational results are derived.

What we have attempted in this work is to present a unified treatment of the many problems and techniques of solution. We want to point out how many problems exist in these domains and what opportunities there are. These are new parts of applied mathematics. What is particularly interesting about these problems is that they require a blend of analysis, algebra, topology, computer science, and a knowledge of how the problems arise.

We are grateful to a long list of friends, colleagues, and graduate students who have collaborated with us in various phases of our research efforts. In particular, we acknowledge the contributions of Burton Corwin and Thomas Morin.

RICHARD BELLMAN
Santa Monica, California

AUGUSTINE ESOGBUE
Atlanta, Georgia

ICHIRO NABESHIMA
Chofu-shi, Tokyo, Japan

Contents

x   *Contents*

CHAPTER 1

Network Flow, Shortest Path and Control Problems

1.1. Introduction

In this chapter we wish to discuss briefly an interesting class of problems with wide ramifications. On the one hand, they can be viewed as abstractions and natural generalizations of a control process. Furthermore, they provide us with an entry into the rugged terrain of scheduling processes and into the study of some other types of decision processes of combinatorial type, such as pattern recognition and numerous other problems arising in the field of artificial intelligence. The application of these ideas to artificial intelligence will be given in Chapter 2. Finally, in our continuing quest for feasible computational procedures, they furnish considerable motivation for the creation of sophisticated decomposition techniques based upon topological considerations. We will do this in Section 1.16 when we make an application of these techniques to the calculus of variations. Let us also mention that questions of this nature occur more and more frequently in connection with the execution of complex computer problems.

In abstract terms, we are interested in a discrete control process of the following type: Let p be a generic element of a finite set S and $T(p, q)$ be a family of transformations with the property that $T(p, q) \in S$ whenever $p \in S$ and $q \in D$, the decision space, again taken to be discrete. We wish to determine a sequence of decisions, $q_1, q_2, \ldots$, which transform p, the initial state, into p_N, a specified state, in an optimal fashion.

We are really interested in questions of feasibility. However, in order to handle this imprecise concept we narrow our sights and consider optimization.

A problem of great contemporary interest, the "routing problem", is a particular case of the foregoing. We will use it as our leitmotif.

1.2. The Routing Problem

Consider a set of N points, numbered $1, 2, \ldots, N$, with N the terminal point, as shown in Fig. 1.1.

1

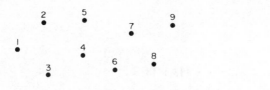

FIG. 1.1

We suppose that there exists a direct link between any two points i and j which requires a time t_{ij} to traverse, with $t_{ii} = 0$, $i = 1, 2, \ldots, N$. In all that follows we take $t_{ij} \geq 0$. What path do we pursue, starting at 1, passing through some subsets of the points $2, 3, \ldots, N-1$, and ending at N, which requires a minimum time?

Two possible paths are shown in Figs. 1.2 and 1.3. The first goes directly to N; the second goes through every point always moving from a lower order number to a higher order one before reaching N.

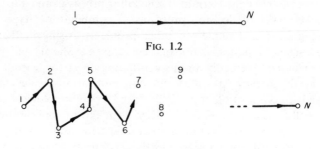

FIG. 1.2

FIG. 1.3

Analytically, we are required to minimize the expression

$$T(i_1, i_2, \ldots, i_k) = t_{1i_1} + t_{i_1 i_2} + \ldots + t_{i_k N}, \tag{1.1}$$

where $(i_1, i_2, \ldots, i_k)$ is some subset of $(2, 3, \ldots, N-1)$.

Exercises

1. Does a minimizing path ever contain a loop, i.e. pass through the same point twice?

2. How many different admissible paths are there?

3. Can the problem presently be solved by direct enumeration with a digital computer for $N = 100$? Assume that we can enumerate and compare paths at the rate of one per microsecond.

1.3. Dynamic Programming Approach

To treat this problem by means of dynamic programming, we imbed the original problem within the family of problems consisting of determining the optimal path from i to N, $i = 1, 2, \ldots, N-1$. Let

$$f_i = \text{minimum time to go from } i \text{ to } N, \quad i = 1, 2, \ldots, N-1, \qquad (1.2)$$

and set $f_N \equiv 0$. Then the principle of optimality yields the relation

$$f_i = \min_{j \neq i} [t_{ij} + f_j], \quad i = 1, 2, \ldots, N-1, \qquad (1.3)$$

with the "boundary condition" $f_N = 0$.

This functional equation is different in form from the usual dynamic programming equation, being implicit rather than explicit. Further, we note its dependence on one (the current node) variable rather than two (the stage and state) variables. The unknown function occurs on both sides of the equation which means that the solution cannot be obtained by any direct iteration. Consequently, some interesting analytic questions arise:

(a) Does (1.3) possess a solution?
(b) Does it possess a unique solution?
(c) Provided that it does possess a unique solution, how can the equation be used to provide the optimal path?
(d) How can the solution be obtained computationally?

The question of computational feasibility is, as usual, the thorniest one and one that forces us to consider new and alternate methods. Some aspects of this question will be discussed now; others will be described in the references.

Exercises

1. In some cases we are interested not only in the path of shortest time, but also in the next best path and generally the kth best path. Let $f_i(2)$ be defined as time required to go from i to N following a second best path. Obtain a functional equation similar in form connecting $f_i(2)$ and f_i.

2. Similarly, obtain a functional equation for $f_i(k)$, the time associated with the kth best path.

3. Obtain a functional equation corresponding to (1.3) for the case where the time to go from i to j depends upon the "direction" in which i is entered, which is to say upon the point from which i is reached.

4. What is the form of the equation if we cannot go from every point to every other point?

1.4. Upper and Lower Bounds

Prior to a demonstration of the existence and uniqueness of the solution of (1.3), let us show how easy it is to obtain upper and lower bounds for the solution (or solutions) of (1.3). An "experimental proof" of uniqueness is thus available in any particular case if we can show computationally that the upper and lower bounds coincide.

Let the sequence $\{\phi_i^{(r)}\}, r = 0, 1, 2, \ldots$, be defined for each i in the following fashion:

$$\phi_i^{(0)} = \min_{j \neq i} t_{ij}, \quad i = 1, 2, \ldots, N-1, \quad \phi_N^{(0)} = 0,$$

$$\phi_i^{(r+1)} = \min_{j \neq i} [t_{ij} + \phi_j^{(r)}], \quad i = 1, 2, \ldots, N-1, \quad \phi_N^{(r+1)} = 0. \quad (1.4)$$

Let us recall that we are assuming that $t_{ij} \geq 0$.

It is clear that $\phi_i^{(r)} \geq 0$ and thus that

$$\phi_i^{(1)} = \min_{j \neq i} [t_{ij} + \phi_j^{(0)}] \geq \min_{j \neq i} t_{ij} = \phi_i^{(0)}. \quad (1.5)$$

Hence, inductively,

$$\phi_i^{(0)} \leq \phi_i^{(1)} \leq \ldots \leq \phi_i^{(r)} \leq \phi_i^{(r+1)} \leq \ldots. \quad (1.6)$$

Let us now show inductively that

$$\phi_i^{(r)} \leq f_i, \quad (1.7)$$

where f_i is any nonnegative solution of (1.3). We have

$$\phi_i^{(0)} = \min_{j \neq i} t_{ij} \leq \min_{j \neq i} [t_{ij} + f_j] = f_i, \quad (1.8)$$

whence (1.7) follows from (1.4) via an induction.

Since the sequence $\{\phi_i^{(r)}\}, r = 1, 2, \ldots$, is uniformly bounded and monotone increasing, we have convergence for each i. Let

$$\phi_i = \lim_{r \to \infty} \phi_i^{(r)}. \quad (1.9)$$

Then (1.7) yields

$$\phi_i \leq f_i, \quad (1.10)$$

and (1.4) shows that ϕ_i is itself a solution. Hence, ϕ_i is a lower bound for any solution.

To obtain an upper bound, let us introduce the sequence $\{\psi_i^{(r)}\}$ where

$$\psi_i^{(0)} = t_{iN}, \quad i = 1, 2, \ldots, N,$$

$$\psi_i^{(r+1)} = \min_{j \neq i} [t_{ij} + \psi_j^{(r)}], \quad i = 1, 2, \ldots, N. \quad (1.11)$$

Then

$$\psi_i^{(0)} = t_{1N} \geq \min_{j \neq i} [t_{ij} + f_j] = f_i, \quad (1.12)$$

and again an induction establishes

$$\psi_i^{(0)} \geq \psi_i^{(1)} \geq \ldots \geq \psi_i^{(r)} \leq f_i. \quad (1.13)$$

Hence, the monotone decreasing sequence $\{\psi_i^{(r)}\}$, $r = 1, 2, \ldots$, converges to a limit function ψ_i which is itself a solution. Thus, for any nonnegative solution of (1.3), we have

$$\phi_i \leq f_i \leq \psi_i, \quad i = 1, 2, \ldots, N, \tag{1.14}$$

where ϕ_i is a "lower solution" and ψ_i an "upper solution".

Exercises

1. Will the paths that determine $\psi_i^{(r)}$ ever possess any loops?

2. What is a geometric significance of $\psi_i^{(r)}$, and on this basis why is (1.13) obvious without calculation?

3. Show that $\psi_i^{(r)}$ converges in at most $N - 2$ steps.

4. Will the paths that determine $\phi_i^{(r)}$ ever possess any loops? If so, show that at most a finite number can occur if $t_{ij} > 0$. Obtain an upper bound for the number of possible loops in terms of N and $d = \min_{i,j} t_{ij}$.

5. What is the geometric significance of $\phi_i^{(r)}$?

6. Show that $\phi_i^{(r)}$ converges in a finite number of steps. Obtain an upper bound for this number of steps in terms of N and d.

7. Does the sequence $f_i^{(n)} = \min_{j \neq i} [t_{ij} + f_j^{n-1}]$, $n \geq 1$, $f_j^{(0)} = c_i$, $i = 1, 2, \ldots, N-1, N$, converge for any nonnegative sequence $\{c_i\}$ with $c_N = 0$?

8. Show that we can increase the rate of convergence by using the best estimates to date "updating".

1.5. Existence and Uniqueness

The existence of a solution of the functional equation

$$f_i = \min_{j \neq i} [t_{ij} + f_j], \quad i = 1, 2, \ldots, N-1,$$

$$f_N = 0, \tag{1.15}$$

is immediate. There is a shortest path from i to N, since there are only a finite number of admissible paths, namely those containing no loops. The time required to traverse this path (which need not be unique) defines a function $g_i, = 1, 2, \ldots, N-1$, with $g_N = 0$.

Since a path of minimum length must go to some other point, say k, we have

$$g_i = t_{ik} + g_k \tag{1.16}$$

for some k. This value of k must be a value which minimizes the righthand side. Otherwise, we would contradict the definition of g_i. Hence,

$$g_i = \min_{k \neq i} [t_{ik} + g_k], \tag{1.17}$$

which is to say, the g_i constitute a nonnegative solution of (1.15).

A proof of uniqueness requires a bit more effort, but we shall give a proof for the sake of completeness. As we shall soon see, however, we have no need of this result for the purposes we have in mind.

Let us show that there cannot be two distinct solutions of (1.15). In order to do this, we shall assume that $g_i (i = 1, 2, \ldots, N)$, and $h_i (i = 1, 2, \ldots, N)$, are two solutions, and we shall prove that $g_i = h_i (i = 1, 2, \ldots, N)$.

We know that $g_N = 0$ and $h_N = 0$. If $g_i = h_i$ for every i, there is nothing to be proved. Hence, we start with the hypothesis that there is at least one value of i for which g_i and h_i are different. Looking at all values of i for which $|g_i - h_i|$ is different from zero (if any), we now pick out the index i for which this difference is largest. By changing the numbering of the vertices, if necessary, we can suppose that $i = 1$ gives the largest difference, and by interchanging the names of g_i and h_i for every i, if necessary, we can suppose that $g_i - h_i > 0$. We now have

$$g_1 - h_1 \geqq g_i - h_i, \quad i = 2, 3, \ldots, N. \tag{1.18}$$

On the other hand, from (1.1) we see that

$$g_1 = \min_{j \neq 1} (t_{1j} + g_j),$$

$$h_1 = \min_{j \neq 1} (t_{1j} + h_j). \tag{1.19}$$

Let us suppose that a value of j giving the minimum in the second equation is 2 which we can arrange by renumbering the vertices 2 to N if necessary. Then we have

$$g_1 \leqq t_{1j} + g_j, \quad \text{for } j = 2, 3, \ldots, N,$$

$$h_1 = t_{12} + h_2, \quad h_1 \leqq t_{1j} + h_j \quad \text{for} \quad j = 3, 4, \ldots, N. \tag{1.20}$$

These relations lead us to

$$g_1 - h_1 \leqq (t_{12} + g_2) - h_1 = g_2 - h_2. \tag{1.21}$$

Combining this inequality with (1.18), we see that $g_1 - h_1 = g_2 - h_2$.

Now we repeat this argument. We have

$$g_2 = \min_{j \neq 2} (t_{2j} + g_j),$$

$$h_2 = \min_{j \neq 2} (t_{2j} + h_j). \tag{1.22}$$

The value of j giving the minimum in the second equation cannot be $j = 1$, since

$$t_{21} + h_1 = t_{21} + t_{12} + h_2 > h_2. \tag{1.23}$$

We can therefore suppose that it is $j = 3$ (renumbering the vertices 3 to N if necessary). Then we have

$$g_2 \leqq t_{2j} + g_j, \quad j = 1, 2, \ldots, N,$$
$$h_2 = t_{23} + h_3, \quad h_2 \leqq t_{2j} + h_j \quad \text{for} \quad j = 1, 2, \ldots, N. \tag{1.24}$$

Hence,

$$g_1 - h_1 = g_2 - h_2 \leqq t_{23} + g_3 - h_2 = g_3 - h_3. \tag{1.25}$$

Using (1.18), we therefore see that $g_1 - h_1 = g_3 - h_3$. Thus, $g_1 - h_1 = g_2 - h_2 = g_3 - h_3$.

By continuing in this manner for $N - 1$ steps, we arrive at the continued equation $g_1 - h_1 = g_2 - h_2 = \ldots = g_i - h_i$ ($i = 1, 2, \ldots, N - 1$), thus proving that the two solutions are in fact identical.

We have previously shown that the desired minimal times comprise a solution of (1.15). Thus it follows from the uniqueness just proved that if we can by any method whatsoever find a solution $f_1, \ldots, f_{N-1}$ of (1.15) then this solution provides us with the desired minimal times.

EXAMPLE 1. For the network depicted in Fig. 1.4, determine a shortest path from the node 1 to the node 8 by applying the successive approximation methods of two types in Section 1.4 respectively.

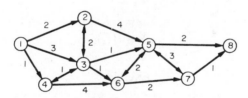

FIG. 1.4

Solution. 1. The sequence $\{\varphi_i^{(r)}\}$, $r = 0, 1, 2, \ldots$, giving a lower bound solution, can be calculated successively as shown in Table 1.1. Since we have $\varphi_i^{(3)} = \varphi_i^{(4)}$ for all i, we can determine $f_i = \varphi_i^{(3)}$, $i = 1, 2, \ldots, 8$.

TABLE 1.1						TABLE 1.2					
i	$\varphi_i^{(0)}$	$\varphi_i^{(1)}$	$\varphi_i^{(2)}$	$\varphi_i^{(3)}$	$\varphi_i^{(4)}$	i	$\psi_i^{(0)}$	$\psi_i^{(1)}$	$\psi_i^{(2)}$	$\psi_i^{(3)}$	$\psi_i^{(4)}$
1	1	2	3	5	5	1	∞	∞	6	5	5
2	2	3	5	5	5	2	∞	6	5	5	5
3	1	3	3	3	3	3	∞	3	3	3	3
4	1	2	4	4	4	4	∞	∞	4	4	4
5	2	2	2	2	2	5	2	2	2	2	2
6	2	3	3	3	3	6	∞	3	3	3	3
7	1	1	1	1	1	7	1	1	1	1	1
8	0	0	0	0	0	8	0	0	0	0	0

2. The sequence $\{\psi_i^{(r)}\}$, $r = 0, 1, 2, \ldots$, giving an upper-bound solution, can be calculated successively as shown in the Table 1.2. Since we have $\psi_i^{(3)} = \psi_i^{(4)}$ for all i, we can determine $f_i = \psi_i^{(3)}$, $i = 1, 2, \ldots, 8$.

Exercise

1. Suppose that not all points i and j are connected by a link. Show that we can reduce this more common case to the foregoing case, for computational purposes, by assuming that there exists a link with a large time associated whenever no link exists in the original network, and give a value for this "large time".

1.6. Optimal Policy

Once we have established uniqueness of the solution of (1.15), we can use this solution to determine the optimal policy, a function $j(i)$ which tells us what point (or points) to go to from i. It may be obtained by minimizing the quantity $t_{ij} + f_j$ with respect to j.

An optimal path is then given by

$$[i, j_1, j_2, \ldots, j_k, N], \tag{1.26}$$

where

$$
\begin{aligned}
j_1 &= j(1), \\
j_2 &= j(j_1), \\
&\;\;\vdots \\
j_k &= j(j_{k-1}), \\
N &= j(j_k).
\end{aligned}
\tag{1.27}
$$

Exercises

1. Determine the forms of some approximate policies.

2. What is the form of the equation if we have a terminal set rather than a terminal point?

1.7. Approximation in Policy Space

The equation

$$
\begin{aligned}
f_i &= \min_{j \neq i} [t_{ij} + f_j] \quad i = 1, 2, \ldots, N-1, \\
f_N &= 0,
\end{aligned}
\tag{1.28}
$$

can be solved by means of successive approximations as we have indicated. If N is large, the choice of an initial approximation can be crucial in determining the time required for the calculation.

In many cases, a great deal is known about the underlying process, which means that various types of approximate policies exist. It may then be far better to approximate in policy space than in function space.

Let $j_0(i)$ be a policy which enables us to go from i to N and let $f_i^{(0)}$ be calculated using this policy,

$$f_i^{(0)} = t_{ij_0} + f_j^{(0)} = t_{ij_0} + \ldots, \qquad (1.29)$$

where the dots indicate the terms obtained by iterating the relation. This furnishes an initial approximation which can be used as a starting point for the method described above.

An interesting and important question is whether we can obtain monotone approximation in policy space. Given any initial policy $j_0(i)$ we want a systematic way of obtaining a new policy which yields times no larger than the original, and smaller if the original policy is not an optimal policy. One way of doing this is the following: With $f_i^{(0)}$ determined as in (1.29) determine j to minimize the expression $t_{ij} + f_j^{(0)}$. Call this function $j_1(i)$. We assert the function $f_i^{(1)}$ calculated using the policy $j_1(i)$ satisfies the relation $f_i^{(1)} \le f_i^{(0)}$.

This follows from the relations

$$\begin{aligned} f_i^{(0)} &= t_{ij_0} + f_j^{(0)} \ge t_{ij_1} + f_{j_1}^{(0)}, \\ f_i^{(1)} &= t_{ij_1} + f_j^{(1)}. \end{aligned} \qquad (1.30)$$

Observe how the technique of approximation in policy space is tied in with the theory of positive operators.

1.8. Computational Feasibility

Let us now examine the computational feasibility of the methods of successive approximation given in Section 1.4. Let us consider the second method,

$$\psi_i^{(0)} = t_{iN},$$

$$\psi_i^{(r+1)} = \min_{j \ne i} [t_{ij} + \psi_i^{(r)}], \quad i = 1, 2, \ldots, N. \qquad (1.31)$$

To calculate the set of values $\{\psi_i^{(r+1)}\}$, $i = 1, 2, \ldots, N$, we require the previous set $\{\psi_i^{(r)}\}$ and the matrix (t_{ij}). If N is large, e.g. $N = 10^4$, storage of the matrix (t_{ij}) involving $N^2 = 10^8$ values puts an unbearable strain on rapid-access storage. Observe, however, that the situation is a good deal better than it first appears because to calculate $\psi_i^{(r+1)}$, for a particular value of i, requires only that the column

$$t_i = \begin{bmatrix} t_{i1} \\ t_{i2} \\ \vdots \\ t_{iN} \end{bmatrix} \qquad (1.32)$$

and $\{\psi_i^{(r)}\}$, $i = 1, 2, 3, \ldots, N$, be available in rapid-access storage. Naturally, we pay a cost in time for this shifting of data back and forth from core, but this is bearable compared with the cost of not being able to treat the problem at all. If, for example, $N = 10^{10}$, the algorithm as it stands is not feasible at the present time even with this artifice.

Exercise

1. Is there any advantage in time or storage in picking the K first points to minimize over, $K \geq 2$?

1.9. Storage of Algorithms

In the previous section we indicated that severe difficulties were encountered if we insisted upon the values t_{ij} being immediately accessible. Suppose that the situation is such that we can calculate t_{ij} as needed using an algorithm which requires very few instructions. It will, in general, require a certain amount of time to calculate t_{ij} as opposed to looking it up in a table. This means that we are trading time, which we possess, for rapid-access storage capacity on which there is an absolute upper bound.

As an example of this, consider the case where the ith point is specified by Cartesian coordinates (x_i, y_i) and where the time to traverse the distance between i and j is directly proportional to this distance. Taking this factor of proportionality to be unity, we have

$$t_{ij} = [(x_i - x_j)^2 + (y_i - y_j)^2]^{1/2}. \tag{1.33}$$

If N is small, we can calculate these numbers in advance; if N is large, it may be better to generate them as they are needed. This technique enables us to handle routing processes of high dimension with very little demand on rapid-access storage or core.

1.10. Alternate Approaches

The routing problem has attracted a great deal of attention as a consequence of an almost unique combination of intrinsic simplicity of statement and widespread application. As a consequence, a number of ingenious and effective techniques now exist based on principles quite different from those expounded above.

The dynamic programming approach is useful because it can handle the stochastic case where chance events occur, as well as the adaptive case where the properties of the network have to be determined as one goes along. It can also treat the "fuzzy" case. Further, it can be used in conjunction with other procedures to treat otherwise intractable problems.

1.11. "Traveling-salesman" Problem

Let us now discuss an interesting example of a combinatorial problem where the introduction of suitable state variables allows us to use the foregoing approach to the routing problem. In place of asking for a path of minimal time from 1 to N, let us now seek to determine a path starting at 1, passing through each point 2, 3, . . . , N in some order, and returning to 1, which consumes the least time. It is clear why this is called the "traveling-salesman" problem.

We see that at each point in the tour it is necessary to know either where we have been, or where we have not yet been. It is not sufficient, as in the previous process, to keep track only of the current position.

Let us then introduce a multistage decision process in which the state of the system at any time is denoted by

$$P = [i_1 i_2, \ldots, i_{k-1} i_k] \tag{1.34}$$

where $i_1, i_2, \ldots, i_{k-1}$ denotes points already visited starting from the origin the point 1, and where i_k is the current point; see Fig. 1.5.

FIG. 1.5

We have drawn the diagram (Fig. 1.5) to emphasize the fact that the order in which $i_1, i_2, \ldots, i_{k-1}$ appear in (1.34) is of no importance. Once we are at i_k, it suffices to know that we have already visited $i_1, i_2, \ldots, i_{k-1}$ in some order. This turns out to be an essential feature as far as computational feasibility of the following method is concerned.

The principle of optimality yields the functional equation

$$f(i_1, i_2, \ldots, i_k) = \min_j [t_{i_k j} + f(i_1, i_2, \ldots, i_k, j)], \tag{1.35}$$

where

$$f(i_1, i_2, \ldots, i_k) = \text{time required to tour the remaining points}$$
$$\text{and return to 1 using an optimal policy.} \tag{1.36}$$

When $i_k = N$ and $i_1, i_2, \ldots, i_{k-1}$ represent 2, 3, . . . , $N-1$ in some order, we have

$$f(i_1, i_2, \ldots, i_k) = t_{i_k 1}. \tag{1.37}$$

Computational feasibility will be briefly treated in the exercises. Here we were principally concerned with the idea of an induced routing process. We will see the applications of this model to sequencing and scheduling problems particularly of the variety discussed in Chapter 11.

Exercises

1. What rapid-access storage will be required to solve an N-point "traveling-salesman" problem, assuming that at the proper stage we change over from keeping track of where we have been to keeping track of where we still have to go?

2. What slow-access storage (core) would be required to treat the foregoing problem for the case where the points are the fifty state capitals?

3. Are there any advantages to choosing the K first points in the path, solving the remaining $(N - K)$-point traveling-salesman problem and then maximizing over the K first points?

4. Devise some methods of successive approximation which would allow one to obtain reasonable estimates of the minimum time required for the case $N \gg 1$ assuming "time" is equal to distance.

5. A tourist wants to visit N points of interest, seeing no more than M on a particular day and returning to his hotel each night. What is an efficient way of doing this?

6. The assignment problem. Suppose it is necessary to assign N men to N jobs and we are given the value of assigning the ith man to the jth job. We assume that the total value is additive. Obtain a functional equation similar to that above for this problem.

7. How large a value of n can we treat?
(This problem can be treated by other methods and very large values of n can easily be handled.)

Miscellaneous Exercises

1. Let x_i be either an a or b and consider expressions of the form $x_1 x_2, \ldots, x_N$. *Suppose that these have the property that* $(x_1 x_2, \ldots, x_N)(x_1 x_2, \ldots, x_N)$ reduces to an identity element. Show that the only expressions that cannot be condensed are $1, a, b, ab, ba, aba, bab$.

2. Consider the same situation where $(x_1 x_2, \ldots, x_N)^3 = 1$. Are there a finite or infinite number of non-equivalent expressions?

3. Let $f_N(a)$ be the length of the "word" of maximum length starting with a when at most N multiplications are allowed. Show that $f_N(a) = 1 + \max_x f_{N-1}(ax)$, $n \geqslant 2$, with a similar expression for $f_N(b)$.

4. Discuss the feasibility of the foregoing as a computational scheme for determining $f_N(a)$. (The foregoing is stimulated by the Burnside conjecture in group theory.)

1.12. Reducing Dimensionality via Bounding Strategies

Solution of problems of moderate size ($N \geq 20$ nodes) via the direct invocation of the approaches we have outlined thus far is inhibited by the excessive high-speed computer memory requirement. However, we can reduce this drain by recourse to ingenious relaxation and bounding strategies using some of the results developed in Section 1.4 and the approaches of Section 1.7. As an example, let us see how we can use branch and bound strategies to fathom certain states in the traveling-salesman problem. This approach enables us to solve larger problems than otherwise possible via a solo application of the conventional dynamic programming formulation given in Section 1.11.

EXAMPLE 2. Consider the following example of a directed network of five nodes whose internodal transversal times are given by the matrix:

TABLE 1.3

$$T_{ij} \quad \begin{array}{c} \\ 1 \\ 2 \\ 3 \\ 4 \\ 5 \end{array} \begin{array}{ccccc} 1 & 2 & 3 & 4 & 5 \\ \left[\begin{array}{ccccc} \infty & 10 & 25 & 25 & 10 \\ 1 & \infty & 10 & 15 & 2 \\ 8 & 9 & \infty & 20 & 10 \\ 14 & 10 & 24 & \infty & 15 \\ 10 & 8 & 25 & 27 & \infty \end{array}\right] \end{array}$$

Let the set of vertices $S \subseteq \{1, 2, 3, 4, 5\}$ with $j, k \in S$. Further let f_i = path of minimum time starting in node i, visiting all nodes $k \in S$ in some fashion and terminating in node $j \in S$. It is obvious that for all $k \in S \neq \phi$, the null set,

$$f_i(S) = \min \{t_{ij} + f_j(S - i) | k \in S - i\} \tag{1.38}$$

with

$$f_0(0) = 0, \tag{1.39}$$

If we define ϕ_i and ψ_i as the lower and upper bounds on (1) respectively then the following fathoming criterion can be proposed:

If $f_i + \phi_i > \psi_i$, then any tour $t \in T$ which contains a path between nodes 1 and i that connects all nodes in $S - i$ cannot be a path of minimum time. (1.40)

The use of (1.38) and (1.39) to generate the minimum time path of 62, i.e. $\{1, 5, 2, 3, 4, 1\}$ is standard and will not be shown here. We, however, sketch how to use (1.38) and (1.39) in conjunction with the fathoming criterion (1.40) to produce a more efficient computational procedure.

The upper bound $\psi_i = 62$, i.e. the minimum of the travel time (65) of the path $(1, 2, 3, 4, 5, 1)$ and the travel time (62) of a "nearest neighbor" path $(1, 5, 2, 3, 4, 1)$. The lower bounds ϕ_i are calculated by solving the assignment problem relaxation. For $|S| = 1$

TABLE 1.4

(S, i)	$f_i(S)$	k'	$\phi_i(S)$	$f_i + \phi_i$
$(\{2\}, 2)$	10	1	55	$65 > \psi_2$
$(\{3\}, 3)$	25	1	42	$67 > \psi_3$
$(\{4\}, 4)$	25	1	40	$65 > \psi_4$
$(\{5\}, 5)$	10	1	50	$60 < \psi_5$

From these calculations $f_i + \phi_i > \psi_i$ for the following tours: $\{(\{2\}, 2), (\{3\}, 3), (\{4\}, 4)\}$. Thus to calculate $f_i(S)$ for $|S| = 2$ we need only $f_5\{5\}$ stored in rapid access implying a maximum of one location as opposed to four locations required in a conventional DP application.

Further, descendant nodes of fathomed states are eliminated from further search i.e. we can fathom the following states: $\{ (\{2, 3\}, 2), (\{2, 3\}, 3), (\{2, 4\}, 2),$ $(\{2, 4\}, 4), (\{2, 5\}, 5), (\{3, 4\}, 3), (\{3, 4\}, 4), (\{3, 5\}, 5), (\{4, 5\}, 5)\}$ before evaluating either $f_i(S)$ or $\phi_i(S)$. Thus, for $|S| = 2$ only 3 of the 12 possible states remain. We list the calculations for this stage below:

(S, i)	$f_i(S)$	k^*	$\phi_i(S)$	$f_i + \phi_i$
$(\{2, 5\}, 2)$	18	5	44	$62 = \psi_2$
$(\{3, 5\}, 3)$	35	5	31	$66 > \psi_2$
$(\{4, 5\}, 4)$	37	5	28	$65 > \psi_2$

Once again we can fathom nodes 3 and 4 right away resulting in a maximum high-speed storage of only one location when calculating $f_i|3|$ as opposed to twelve locations required in the conventional DP approach.

We leave the completion of this problem as an exercise to the reader. The point we make is that adroit combinations of structure, intelligent bounds, etc., with the DP approach enable us to drastically reduce dimensionality so often a nuisance in the use of DP to solve large problems.

Exercises

1. Consider the traveling-salesman problem given in the network of Example 2. Show that the optimal tour of the salesman is $\{1, 5, 2, 3, 4, 1\}$ and that the minimum time is 62.

2. Using bounding strategies and the fathoming criterion discussed in the text, complete the optimal tour search for the salesman.

3. For this problem, compare and contrast the two approaches particularly with respect to (a) maximum high-speed storage requirement, (b) total low-speed storage requirement and (c) total computer time requirement.

1.13. Stochastic Traveling-salesman Problem

The problem we treat here is essentially the same as that treated in Section 1.11 with the important difference that in a stochastic version the internodal travel times are not deterministic but random. Thus our objective is to find a tour that maximizes the probability of completion of node visits within some specified time period.

The deterministic assumption of the classical model is defied by certain practical phenomena. For example, in flow-shop scheduling problems involving sequence dependent setup times (see Chapter 11) it may be the case that wide variability in setup times occurs from job to job. Such large variabilities in set-up times or internodal travel times will usually be present in scenarios that have large human component. When internodal travel times are random variables with large variances, then the approximate deterministic models or variations built around the criterion of minimizing expected total time are inadequate. Let us then outline a formulation and a solution approach based on preference order dynamic programming.

Let the t_{ij} of Section 1.11 be independent random variables with distribution function F_{ij} defined on $R^+ = [0, \infty)$. For a given tour t, let $T(t)$, also a random variable, be the total travel time. Clearly,

$$T(t) = \sum_{(i,j) \in t'} t_{ij} \text{ with } t' = [(0, i_1), (i_1, i_2), \ldots, (i_{n-1}, i_n), (i_n, 0)]$$

as the ordered pair representation of t. An optimal solution is a tour that maximizes Prob $(T(t) \le \tau)$ with τ a specified constant. For an optimal subtour yielding the maximum probability that τ or less time units will be utilized by the salesman, $f_k(i, S_k)$, let the distribution function of the corresponding total time be denoted by $G_k(i, S_k)$. We note that

$$f_k(i, S_k) = [G_k(i, S_k)(\tau)] \quad \forall i, k \in S, \tag{1.41}$$

By the principle of optimality

$$G_k(i, S_k) = \underline{1}_{j \in S_k}\{F_{ij} O G(j, S_k - j)\} \tag{1.42}$$

$$i = 1, 2, \ldots, n$$

with $G_0(i, \phi) = F_{i0}, i = 1, 2, \ldots, n$ and $k \in \{1, 2, \ldots, n-1\}$ and $G_n(0, S_n) = \underline{1}_{j \in S_n}\{F_0 O G(j, S_n - j)\}$ and O, the compositor operator. The preference order operator $\underline{1}$ is a mapping which chooses the i^*th order distribution function Ω_{i*} from the set of distribution functions $\{\Omega_1, \Omega_2, \ldots, \Omega_l\}$ via the criterion

$$[\Omega_{i*} Z](\tau) \ge [\Omega_i O Z](\tau) \quad \forall i \in \{1, 2, \ldots, l\} \tag{1.43}$$

with Ω_i, $Z \in \xi$– the set of all distribution functions.

The preference order dynamic programming proposed by Mitten (1974) has an appeal which has been exploited by Kao (1978) in solving the stochastic traveling salesman problem formulated here.

Exercises

1. Consider the TVS problem of Example 2 but assume now that the travel times between cities are independent normal variates with means μ_{ij} and variances σ_{ij} given by

$$\{\mu_{ij}\} = \begin{array}{c} \\ 1 \\ 2 \\ 3 \\ 4 \\ 5 \end{array} \begin{bmatrix} \infty & 10 & 25 & 25 & 10 \\ 1 & \infty & 10 & 15 & 2 \\ 8 & 9 & \infty & 20 & 10 \\ 14 & 10 & 24 & \infty & 15 \\ 10 & 8 & 25 & 27 & \infty \end{bmatrix}$$

	1	2	3	4	5
1	∞	10	25	25	10
2	1	∞	10	15	2
3	8	9	∞	20	10
4	14	10	24	∞	15
5	10	8	25	27	∞

$; \{\sigma_{ij}\} =$

	1	2	3	4	5
1	∞	2.4	9.0	9.0	2.4
2	0.2	∞	6.0	2.0	0.9
3	2.0	1.0	∞	12.0	4.0
4	9.0	4.0	2.0	∞	4.0
5	4.0	1.0	9.0	10.0	∞

Find the tour which maximizes the probability of completion with 70 time units, i.e. $\tau = 70$.

2. Solve the above problem using ordinal or preference order dynamic programming in conjunction with fathoming and bounding strategies discussed in Section 1.12.

1.14. Applications to Control Theory

In Section 1.1, we pointed out how the shortest-path problem could be applied to control theory – a branch of applied mathematics useful in scheduling. By a suitable interpretation of state, we can think of the problem of transforming a system from one state to another at minimum cost.

Many problems in control theory can be reduced to the minimization of an integral. If the duration is short, it is easy to supply a constructive method. If the duration is large, a simple use of functional analysis establishes the existence of a solution. However, the determination of this solution is not simple.

In the following sections we wish to show how the shortest-path problem can furnish a useful approximation to the solution. Sometimes, this approximation is all we want. In other cases, it furnishes a useful initial approximation.

1.15. Stratification

In general, regardless of the power of the computer available in the foreseeable future, complex processes cannot be handled without making use of intrinsic structural features. It is thus the recognition and exploitation of structure that is the art of mathematics. Our aim here is to utilize this structure to reduce dimensionality difficulties, to lift the "curse of dimensionality".

As an example of the way in which the structure of the process can greatly simplify our task, consider the case where the set of points has the appearance in Fig. 1.6.

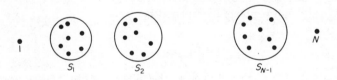

FIG. 1.6

The point of the figure is to indicate the fact that starting at 1, we must go to some point in S_1, from this point to some point in S_2, and so on; from a point in S_{N-1} we must go to N. Rather than treat this in the foregoing general fashion, we introduce a sequence of functions

$$f_i(p) = \text{minimum time from the point } p \in S_i \text{ to } N, \ i = 1, 2, \ldots, N-1.$$

$$(1.44)$$

Then we readily obtain the recurrence relations

$$f_i(p) = \min_{p_1 \in S_{i+1}} [t(p, p_1) + f_{i+1}(p_1)],$$ (1.45)

for $i = 1, 2, \ldots, N-1$, with

$$f_{N-1}(p) = t(p, N),$$ (1.46)

with $t(p, p_1)$ the time to go from p to p_1.

If f_1 is as before, the minimum time to go from 1 to N, we have

$$f_1 = \min_{p \in S_1} [t(1, p) + f_1(p)].$$ (1.47)

It is clear that the demands on rapid-access storage have been significantly reduced by means of this decomposition or stratification, as we shall call it. In a number of important processes, time automatically yields this stratification. By this we mean that the set S_k will be the set of admissible states at time k.

When there is no variable corresponding to time, or when the dimensions of the sets S_k are themselves overwhelming, the process of stratification becomes much more complex and represents a new type of topological-algebraic problem. As might be expected, the type of stratification possible depends critically upon the nature of the underlying control process.

1.16. Routing and Control Processes

Let us now turn to an examination of the application of the foregoing ideas to control processes and, particularly, to their computational treatment. Consider the example, the problem of minimizing the functional

$$J(u) = \int_0^T (u'^2 + 2g(u)) \, dt,$$ (1.48)

where $u(0) = c$ and g is convex. As we know, for any $T > 0$ the minimizing function exists and is specified as the unique solution of the Euler equation

$$u'' - g'(u) = 0, \quad u(0) = c, \quad u'(T) = 0.$$ (1.49)

Specified yes, but is it constructively determined?

Crude successive approximation techniques will work when $T \ll 1$ and a more sophisticated technique based upon quasilinearization will be effective provided we can obtain a plausible initial approximation. Other techniques based upon direct and sophisticated search techniques exist. Let us now present a quite different approach based upon a combination of the routing algorithm and the calculus of variations.

If $T \ll 1$, as just mentioned, we can determine the minimizing function. We thus possess efficient techniques for obtaining local solutions. Can we piece together local solutions, $T \ll 1$, in some fashion to determine global solutions, $T \gg 1$? It turns out that we can. We can use the calculus of variations to obtain these local solutions and dynamic programming to combine these local solutions and thus locate the global solution or, at least, its desired approximation. This is a nice example of the importance of combining different methods.

1.17. Computational Procedure

Let us sketch briefly how we might proceed. We begin with a grid in the (c, T)-plane, as in Fig. 1.7. Suppose that at the times $T_1, T_2, \ldots, T_k$, where $0 < T_1 < T_2 < \ldots < T_k < T$, we allow only the states $c_1, c_2, \ldots, c_r$.

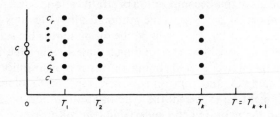

FIG. 1.7

By this we mean that if the state is c_i at time T_k, it is required that the state of the system become c_j at times T_{k+1}. This is a suboptimization technique. Furthermore, we require that the path from c_i to c_j be a "geodesic" in the sense that it minimizes the functional

$$J(T_k, T_{k+1}, c_i, c_j; u) = \int_{T_k}^{T_{k+1}} (u'^2 + 2g(u))dt, \qquad (1.50)$$

with u subject to the constraints

$$u(T_k) = c_i, \qquad u(T_{k+1}) = c_j. \qquad (1.51)$$

When $T_{k+1} = T$, there is no terminal constraint.

If $T_{k+1} - T_k$ is not too large and if $|c_i - c_j|$ is not too large, we know successive approximations, of either simple or complex type, will yield the quantity

$$t_{ij} = \min_u J(T_k, T_{k+1}, c_i, c_j; u). \qquad (1.52)$$

We can ensure this by introducing a "nearest-neighbor" constraint. We allow only those values of j for which $|c_i - c_j| \ll 1$. In other words, we are looking for a reasonably smooth trajectory.

Once the matrix of these fundamental times has been determined, we can apply the shortest-path algorithm to determine an optimal path of the foregoing nature over $[0, T]$. This path will have, in general, the appearance of Fig. 1.8.

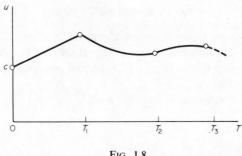

FIG. 1.8

We now use this as an initial approximation for quasilinearization applied to the Euler equation over $[0, T]$, and we proceed to obtain a more accurate representation of the minimizing function.

Exercise

1. How would we go about smoothing this initial approximation to obtain one with a continuous derivative at T_1, T_2, etc.? Is this necessary for the quasilinearization method?

1.18. Feasibility

Let us take a closer look at what is required for a successful application of the foregoing method. To begin with, it is necessary to have a reasonable idea of the part of state space of interest. In some cases, there exist *a priori* bounds on the domain of the state of the system, either established analytically or on the basis of physical considerations, which furnish this information. Secondly, there is the question of determining the allowable steps in time and the grid in state space.

As usual, we are on the horns of a dilemma, or perhaps polylemma. If the timestep is small, we can guarantee the calculation of t_{ij}. This decrease in $|t_{i+1} - t_i|$, however, is at the expense of increasing the time of the entire calculation. Furthermore, even if the timestep is small, we have to worry about abrupt changes of state. In other words, as previously indicated, it may be wise to impose some bounds on the change of state, which would again be a restriction of either analytic or physical origin. This means that in minimizing over p_1 in the relation (1.35), we want to impose a restriction $p_1 \in R(p)$ where $R(p)$ consists of states near p in an appropriate norm. This is a "nearest-neighbor" constraint: In short time intervals we can only go to nearby points in state space. Restrictions of this type speed up the calculation to a great extent, greatly facilitate the determination of the t_{ij}, and usually represent meaningful constraints on the type of control that is allowable.

1.19. Perturbation Technique

In many cases, we possess an initial approximation to the minimizing function, say u_0. Sometimes, we want to obtain more and more refined approximations: sometimes we merely want to know whether the approximation is a reasonable one.

One way to proceed is as follows: We write

$$u = u_0 + w,$$

$$g(u) = g(u_0 + w) = g(u_0) + wg'(u_0) + w^2/2g''(u_0) + \dots, \qquad (1.53)$$

and consider the minimization of the quadratic functional

$$J_1(w) = \int_0^T [(u_0' + w')^2 + 2g(u_0) + 2wg'(w_0) + w^2 g''(u_0)]dt. \qquad (1.54)$$

This is equivalent to applying quasilinearization to the Euler equation. If the minimizing w is small, we have the desired improvement; if it is large, we have been warned that u_0 is not a good choice. There are many ways of treating the quadratic variational problem in (1.54).

An alternate approach is to draw a tube around the initial approximation and then proceed as we have to stratify state space; see Fig. 1.9.

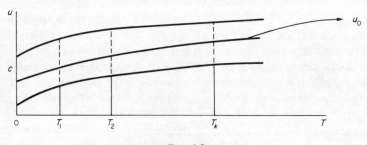

FIG. 1.9

We hope that the routing algorithm yields a result of the type in Fig. 1.10.

If, on the other hand, the routing algorithm yields a solution which keeps hitting the boundary of the tube, as in Fig. 1.11, we can conclude that u_0 was not a good initial approximation.

Let us again emphasize that there is nothing routine about determining optimal policies in realistic control processes. If we hope to obtain optimal

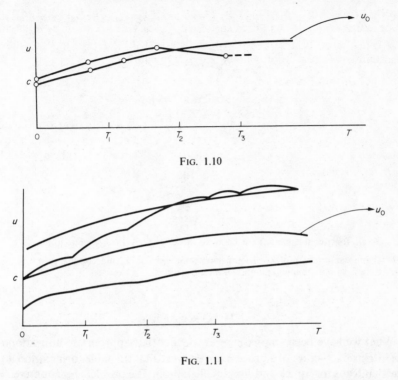

FIG. 1.10

FIG. 1.11

policies, we must enter the fray armed with an arsenal of weapons and be psychologically prepared for the use of various combinations of methods. Successful computing is an adaptive control process.

1.20. Generalized Routing

In some cases, we encounter in place of the process originally associated with Fig. 1.1, a process where from a point in S_i we can go either to another point in S_i or to S_{i+1}. A transformation of the first type we call recurrent; one of the second type is transitive. In place of (1.54) we obtain the occurrence relation

$$f_i(p) = \min \left[\min_{p_1 \in S_i} [t(p, p_1) + f_i(p_1)], \min_{p_2 \in S_i} [t(p, p_2) + f_{i+1}(p_2)] \right]. \quad (1.55)$$

In other cases, the situation is still more complex. We encounter a situation where the set of points has the form in Fig. 1.12. We have a branching of states and of sets. Once again, a point may be transformed into another point in the same set or into one of the succeeding sets.

Provided that there is not too much branching, we can use the routing algorithm to determine the optimal paths. In general, the task of constructing a decomposition of this type is not an easy one.

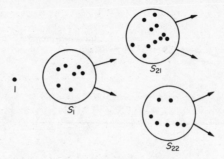

FIG. 1.12

Exercises

1. Obtain functional equations analogous to those of (1.55) corresponding to Fig. 1.12.

2. As an example of a process where the branching gets out of hand, consider the problem of calculating 2–with a minimum number of multiplications.

1.21. Discussion

What we have been emphasizing is the fact that appropriate utilization of the intrinsic structure of a process can convert an intractable formulation into one that leads to a quick and simple calculation. The problems encountered in this type of endeavor are highly algebraic and topological. Essentially what is required is a semi-group theory of structures. Some few tentative steps have been taken in this direction, but almost everything remains to be done.

Miscellaneous Exercise

1. Use the shortest path algorithm to obtain an approximation to a geodesic on a surface.

Bibliography and Comments

Section 1.1
  Detailed discussions and many additional references may be found in
R. BELLMAN, K. L. COOKE, and J. LOCKETT, *Algorithms, Graphs, and Computers*, Academic
  Press, New York, 1970.
  See also
R. BELLMAN and K. L. COOKE, "The Königsberg bridges problem generalized", *J. Math. Anal.
  Appl.* **25** (1969), 1–7.
  For the theory of control processes, see
R. BELLMAN, *Introduction to the Mathematical Theory of Control Processes*, Vol. I, Academic
  Press, Inc., New York, 1968.
R. BELLMAN, *Introduction to the Mathematical Theory of Control Processes*, Vol. II, Academic
  Press, New York, 1971.

Section 1.2
For some economic applications see
R. RADNER, "Paths of economic growth that are optimal with regard to final states: a 'turnpike theorem'", *Rev. Econ. Stud.* **28** (1961), 98–104.

Section 1.3
The method was first presented in
R. BELLMAN, "On a routing problem", *Quart. Appl. Math.* **16** (1958), 87–90.
See also
R. BELLMAN and R. KALABA, "On k-th best policies", *J. Soc. Indus. Appl. Math.* **8** (1960), 582–588.

Section 1.7
See the book
R. HOWARD, *Dynamic Programming and Markovian Decision Processes*, M.I.T. Press, Cambridge, Mass., 1965
where the "policy improvement" method is discussed in detail, and
G. J. MINTY, "Monotone networks", *Proc. Roy. Soc. London*, Ser. A, **257** (1960), 194–212.
For the theory of dynamic programming, see the books cited above, and
R. BELLMAN and S. DREYFUS, *Applied Dynamic Programming*, Princeton University Press, Princeton, New Jersey, 1962.
S. DREYFUS and A. M. LAW, *The Art and Theory of Dynamic Programming*, Academic Press, Inc., New York, 1977.

Section 1.8
A detailed discussion of computational procedures in dynamic programming will be found in the book cited above, *Applied Dynamic Programming*.

Section 1.10
A careful and thorough analysis and comparison of a number of different methods was first presented in
S. DREYFUS, "An appraisal of some shortest path algorithms", *Operations Research*, RAND Corporation, RM-5433-PR, 1967.
See also the book cited in Section 1.1.
See also the book
E. LAWLER, *Combinatorial Optimization: Networks and Matroids*, Holt, Rinehart & Winston, New York, 1976.
For a discussion of stochastic and adaptive cases, see
R. BELLMAN, *Adaptive Control Processes: A Guided Tour*, Princeton University Press, Princeton, New Jersey, 1961.
For an application of dynamic programming to the case where the criterion function is fuzzy see
R. BELLMAN and L. ZADEH, "Decision-making in a fuzzy environment", *Management Science*, **17**, No. 4 (1970), 141–164.

Section 1.11
The method was first presented in
R. BELLMAN, "Dynamic programming treatment of the travelling salesman problem", *J. Ass. Comput. Mach.* **9** (1962), 61–63.
See also
R. BELLMAN, "Combinatorial processes and dynamic programming", *Proc. Ninth Symp. Appl. Math.*, American Mathematical Society, 1960.
V. N. BURKOV and S. E. LOVETSKII, "Methods for the solution of extremal problems of combinatorial type" (Review), *Autom. and Remote Control*, No. 11 (1968), 1785–1806.
For use of these ideas in the field of pattern recognition see
K. S. FU, *Sequential Methods in Pattern Recognition and Machine Learning*, Academic Press, New York, 1968.

When the number of points becomes large, $N \geq 50$, various approximate methods must be employed. An excellent survey of the problem is given in

M. BELLMORE and G. L. NEMHAUSER, "The travelling salesman problem: A survey", *Operations Research*, **16** (1968), 538–558.

The traveling-salesman problem has important practical applications particularly to sequencing problems involving sequence dependent setup times. See, for example,

M. HELD and R. M. KARP, "A dynamic programming approach to sequencing problems", *J. SIAM*, **10** (1962), 196–210.

and

M. HELD and R. M. KARP, "The travelling salesman problem and minimum spanning trees, Part II", *Mathematical Programming*, **1** (1971), 6–25.

B. D. CORWIN and A. O. ESOGBUE, "Two machine flow shop scheduling problems with sequence dependent set up times: a dynamic programming approach", *Naval Research Logistics Quarterly*, **21**, No. 3 (Sept. 1974), 515–524.

Section 1.12

That bounding schemes can be used to minimize the usual excessive storage requirements in dynamic programming has been stressed in this chapter as well as various writings of Bellman, Esogbue and others.

The use of bounding and fathoming strategies within dynamic programming was explicated by:

F. PROSCHAN and T. BRAY, "Optimal redundancy under multiple constraints", *Operations Research*, **13** (1965), 800–814.

H. M. WEINGARTNER and D. N. NESS, "Methods for the solution of the multi-dimensional 0/1 knapsack problems", *Operations Research*, **15** (1967), 83–103.

The fathoming criteria and relaxations discussed here in the context of the traveling-salesman problem were proposed by:

T. L. MORIN and M. E. MARSTEN, "Branch and bound strategies for dynamic programming", *Operations Research*, **24**, No. 4 (1976), 611–627.

Section 1.13

The theory of preference order dynamic programming was proposed by

L. G. MITTEN, "Preference order dynamic programming", *Management Science*, **21** (1974), 43–46.

For an application to stochastic assembly line balancing problems, see

E. P. C. KAO, "A preference order dynamic program for stochastic assembly line balancing", *Management Science*, **22** (1976), 1097–1104.

The model discussed here was presented in:

E. P. C. KAO, "A preference order dynamic program for a stochastic travelling salesman problem", *Operations Research*, **26**, No. 6 (1978), 1033–1045.

In certain applications of the traveling-salesman problem, such as routing, the profit function may vary with time as well as distance.

For a discussion of these interesting cases, using both dynamic programming and branch and bound procedures see:

W. J. FELTS, "Solution techniques for stationary and time-varying travelling salesman problems", Ph.D. Dissertation, Vanderbilt University, 1971.

and

W. J. FELTS and P. D. KROLAK, "The travelling salesman in time", unpublished manuscript, 1971.

Section 1.14

For the theory of control processes see

R. BELLMAN, *Introduction to the Mathematical Theory of Control Processes*, Vol. I, Academic Press, Inc., New York, 1968.

R. BELLMAN, *Introduction to the Mathematical Theory of Control Processes*, Vol. II, Academic Press, Inc., New York, 1971.

Section 1.15

The concept of stratification is discussed in

R. BELLMAN, *Dynamic Programming and Markovian Decision Processes with Particular Applications to Baseball and Chess, Applied Combinatorial Mathematics*, Wiley, New York, 1964, pp. 221–236,

R. BELLMAN, "Stratification and the control of large systems with application to chess and checkers", *Inform. Sci.* **1** (1968), 7–21,

with applications to the determination of optimal play in chess and checkers.

See also

R. LARSON, *State Increment Dynamic Programming*, Elsevier, New York, 1968.

E. L. LAWLER, "Partitioning methods for discrete optimization problems", in *Recent Mathematical Advances in Operations Research*, E. L. LAWLER and G. MINTY (eds.), Univ. of Michigan, Ann Arbor, 1964.

Section 1.16

See

J. F. SHAPIRO, *Shortest Route Methods for Finite State Space, Deterministic Dynamic Programming Problems*, Tech. Rep. Operations Research Center, M.I.T., Cambridge, Mass., 1967.

Section 1.19

See the book

D. H. JACOBSON and D. Q. MAYNE, *Differential Dynamic Programming*, Elsevier, New York, 1970

for a systematic discussion of this method.

Section 1.21

See

H. HAPP, *The Theory of Network Diakoptics*, Academic Press, New York, 1970.

B. K. HARRISON, "A discussion of some mathematical techniques used in Kron's method of tearing", *J. Soc. Indus. Appl. Math.* **11**, 1963.

G. KRON, "Tearing and interconnecting as a form of transformation", *Quart. Appl. Math.* **13** (1955), 147–159.

G. KRON, "A set of principles to interconnect the solution of physical systems" *J. Appl. Phys.* **24** (1953), 965–980.

J. P. ROTH, "An application of algebraic topology, Kron's method of tearing", *Quart. Appl. Math.* **17** (1959), 1–14.

W. R. SPILLERS and N. HICKERSON, "Optimal elimination for sparse symmetric systems as a graph problem", *Quart. Appl. Math.* **26** (1968), 425–432.

D. V. STEWART, "Partitioning and tearing systems of equations", *J. Soc. Indust. Appl. Math.*, Numer. Anal., **2** (1965), 345–365.

CHAPTER 2

Applications to Artificial Intelligence and Games

2.1. Introduction

In this chapter we shall discuss decision-making problems outlined in Chapter 1 but with emphasis on the use of the computer. We could talk in general terms. However, we feel that it is better to illustrate the methods that are used and the difficulties that occur by means of a particular example. This example seems quite special. Actually, it turns out to be a prototype of many decision processes, particularly those occurring in scheduling problems and their applications.

Let us review the fundamental steps:

1. Some forms of thinking can be considered decision-making.
2. Some forms of decision-making can be interpreted as tracing a path through a network.
3. The problem of tracing a path through a network, as we know, can be converted into solving a nonlinear functional equation.

The interlinkages are clear. Combining these, we have a method for doing some forms of thinking by computer.

2.2. An Operational Point of View

We shall take an operational point of view, "the proof is in the program". Let us then discuss some particular problems and see if we can get the computer to exhibit intelligence, according to our definition of what we mean by this term. This intelligence will be helpful in generating solutions to the various mathematical models and algorithms which we discuss in this book.

2.3. Description of a Particular Problem

We begin with a particular problem. Actually, it represents a very general process, which we have discussed in Chapter 1, Section 1.2.

Consider a set of states given in Fig. 2.1.

FIG. 2.1

The objective is to start at 1, the initial point, and trace a path to the final point which requires the shortest time. We are given the time array $[t_{ij}]$ which tells us the time required to go from state i to state j in a direct link. One path, for example, is $1N$, which is to say we go directly from the initial state to the terminal state. Another path is $127N$, and so forth.

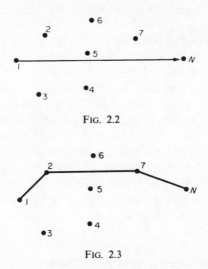

FIG. 2.2

FIG. 2.3

The procedure that we follow is not the best in all cases. This problem has been studied by many people, and many ingenious techniques have been discovered, because this problem occurs in many contexts. However, the method that we will follow has many advantages. In the first place, it is easy to understand and to implement, either by hand or by computer. In the second place, it generalizes to many cases, particularly where chance events are concerned.

2.4. Imbedding

We use a very powerful technique to study this problem. We imbed the particular problem within a family of problems. In addition to studying the original problem, we determine the time to go from any state to the terminal state.

At first sight, it seems very inefficient to solve these additional problems. It turns out that it is easy to get an equation for all the members of the family at the same time.

Obviously this imbedding may be done in many ways. Any particular problem can be studied by various means. We want to stress that anything that can be done one way usually can be done another way.

2.5. A Fundamental Equation

Let us then define a function, the minimum time to go from any state i to the terminal state. The time required to go from any state to the terminal state obviously depends upon the state at which we start. The mathematical translation of "depends upon" is the concept of function. Let us agree to call this function f_i.

The next step is to get an equation for this function, and in order to get an equation we ask for some intrinsic property of the process and convert that property into an equation.

Let us then consider the problem of going from any state i to state N in minimum time. The first question is, "How do we determine the function f_i?" Now we begin to feel much happier because we have changed the original combinatorial problem over to the problem of determining a certain function. We are now on familiar ground. The way we determine a function is we obtain an equation for this function, the standard way. Thus, the next question is, "Can we find an equation which will determine the function f_i?"

Of course, we have two problems. We want not only to determine the function but we want also to find the method for determining the optimal path. These two problems are not the same. It might turn out that we could find some method which would give us the time for the minimal path without telling us how to find the minimal path. This is, after all, a very common situation in mathematics. We may not get all the information we need from one equation.

The first problem then is can we find an equation for f_i? In order to find an equation, we say "Is there some intrinsic property of the process which we can use to get an equation?" The answer fortunately is, "Yes". Looking at the problem, if we start at state i, we have to go someplace. The first observation to make is that we have to go from i to some state j. We do not know what j is, but we have to go to some j. Now the second observation is that if f_i is the minimum time from i to N, then no matter what state j we go to, we must go from j to N in the shortest time. This is obvious, and a simple proof is by contradiction.

If the original path from i to N were a minimal path, then the part of the path from j to N must be a path of minimum time too, because if it were not we could convert it into the path of minimum time and make the total time shorter, which it cannot be, because f_i is the minimum time by definition of the function.

This is an essential intrinsic property of the process: the tail of the process, the end of the process, is always a path of shortest length. What does that mean as far as the equation is concerned? It means this: If f_i is going to be the time required to go from i to N along the shortest path, it will consist of t_{ij}, the time required to go from i to j (we do not know what j is yet), plus f_j, the shortest time from j to N for some j. Now the question is, "What j do we choose?" We choose the j which minimizes the sum $[t_{ij} + f_j]$. We get then the equation

$$f_i = \min_{j \neq i} [t_{ij} + f_j], f_N = 0, i = 1, 2, \ldots, N - 1. \qquad (2.1)$$

This is a fundamental equation. It is the equation which extends to all kinds of applications. We have discussed this equation in detail in Chapter 1.

2.6. Geometric Ideas

What we have done is convert a geometric problem into an analytic problem. Frequently, in applications it is important to go in the other direction to convert an analytic problem into a geometric problem. In general, one has to use both techniques, analytic and geometric. This is where mathematical ingenuity and training are important. The more one knows, the better one is at attacking problems.

We have stressed the analytic approach here because the digital computer does arithmetic. If we had a device which could do geometry as well as a digital computer does arithmetic, we would use a geometric approach.

2.7. Conversion of a Decision Process into an Equation

We have used a fundamental device. We have converted a decision process into an equation. Obviously, there are many equations which can be used. In other words, there are many ways of doing this. How we do this depends upon ingenuity. There is no getting around the fact that mathematics requires ingenuity. We try to use general methods, and this is very desirable.

When we teach, we very seldom describe how a method was really discovered. Partly we do this because it is easier to give a logical method; partly we do it because it would usually be embarrassing to describe how we really found something.

2.8. The Concept of a Solution

This, of course, does not complete the problem. It is, however, the beginning of the second phase. What we have to show is that this is a useful equation. It may turn out that it is a tautology, an intrinsic part of the process that does not tell us anything which can be used to determine the function f_i.

We have changed the original decision problem into a problem involving a nonlinear equation for the unknown function. There are four questions which we can think of immediately.

1. Does a solution exist?
2. Is the solution unique?
3. How can it be determined?
4. What is the connection between the solution and the original problem?

It might very well be that there is no connection at all between the solution of the equation and the original decision problem. This is a standard problem that one always has in science. When we change a scientific problem into a mathematical problem, we may have lost a great deal in the process. Let us, therefore, discuss this last question first. It is the most important at the moment. The first two are just technique; the third is a different kind of problem.

What does equation (2.1) determine? It determines two things: first of all it determines the minimum time; secondly, it determines the minimal path, because the question that we ask ourselves at i is what state should we go to next. There are two questions then:

1. What is the minimal time?
2. What is the minimal path?

This last question can be answered in two ways. One is to say: We start at i then we go to some state i_1, then i_2, i_k and then N.

This is our minimal path. Another way of answering the question is to say: That isn't the way we want to give instructions as to how to proceed. All we want to do at every state i is to furnish a rule as to where to go next, that is to say, if we are at state i, we go to j according to the function $j(i)$.

Thus, there are two forms of the solution: One is the actual set of indices, the actual set of numbers $[i, i_1, i_2, \ldots, i_k, N]$; the other is a rule, a policy, which tells us in terms of where we are now, what to do next. We see the connection with decision-making. This, of course, can be interpreted as a decision. What we are saying is that we are looking at this as a multi-stage decision process.

What is interesting is that the set of indices $[i, i_1, \ldots, i_k, N]$ is the conventional mathematical approach, the conventional approach of mathematical analysis. The function $j(i)$ is the approach of dynamic programming, a new mathematical theory, but it is also the intuitive approach. If we were not educated mathematically, this is the way we would think of it.

Again let us point out that equation (2.1) has been discussed in detail in Chapter 1.

2.9. Determination of the Solution

Let us now see if we can determine the answers to the two questions, the determination of the function f_i and the optimal path, at the same time.

Equation (2.1) really determines two functions. It is obviously an equation for f_i, but it is also an equation for $j(i)$. If we have the function f_i, then the j which minimizes tells us what state to go to next. Thus, we have one equation that determines two functions. This is strange at first sight, but it's what we want. We want an equation which determines the actual minimal time, but we also want an equation which determines the policy—the optimal policy.

Now, which is more fundamental? Is the function more fundamental or is the policy more fundamental? We would say that the policy is more fundamental because the concept of minimum time does not carry over to situations in which there is no ordering. If we do not have complete ordering, if we do not have a concept of the best or the worst, we cannot talk about a variational problem. But if we have a situation where we have to make decisions, where we have a multi-stage decision process, we can still think in terms of policies. Thus, the more fundamental concept which carries over to many different fields of decision-making is the concept of policy.

2.10. Determination of a Number

In using digital computers for making decisions, what we expect is a policy. We have converted this problem of decision-making by computer to the problem of determining a policy. The determination of a policy will involve a number and it is important to realize that the problem of decision-making has been converted into a problem of generating a number. This is why digital computers can be used for certain types of decision-making. If we cannot reduce a problem to numbers we have great difficulty in using computers. The new theory of fuzzy systems due to Lotfi Zadeh can be used in certain cases, but little has been done in this direction using computers. Consequently, we will say nothing about this theory here.

2.11. Decision-making by Computers

Let us now review how we are going to tackle decision-making by computers. What we are going to try and do is to take a particular problem and show that it can be considered to be a multistage decision process, and furthermore a multistage decision process of essentially the type we have been talking about. If we can show that a particular problem is a multistage decision process of this type, then we can get an equation for the function f_i. If we can get an equation for the function f_i, we can, theoretically at least, determine the optimal policy. If we can determine the optimal policy, then we have a way of solving this problem by means of computers.

Now, in order to solve the problem by means of a digital computer, we have to show that there is an arithmetic algorithm which can be used. If we look at equation (2.1), we see that it is nonlinear but that the operations are arithmetic.

We have a sum and we have a minimum over a finite set. Both of these operations can be readily carried out using a computer. The difficulty, however, is that we have the unknown function on both sides. What we have to do is to convert the equation into a recursive algorithm; we have to introduce iteration, an operation which the digital computer performs very well, in some fashion.

In this case, iteration means that we have to employ successive approximations in some way. There are many ways in which successive approximations can be used. Any application of successive approximations requires that we examine the storage question. What we want to do is to hold one approximation in fast storage while we calculate the next. Thus, the method will be analytically sound in all cases, but if the storage requirements are too great we cannot employ the computer. There are many ways that we can reduce the storage requirements. However, we shall not discuss them here since that requires a considerable digression.

Successive approximations can be used in many ways. Not only do we have the storage problem but we also have to establish convergence and convergence to the solution which we want.

We have discussed several methods of successive approximations in Chapter 1.

2.12. Enumeration

There are several ways of solving the particular routing problem using the computer. The simplest method, and the most sensible, is enumeration. If we have a digital computer, why not just explore all possible paths?

Let us discuss enumeration. How many different paths are there? It is easy to convince ourselves that there are at least $(N-2)!$. We can go from the first state to any of the other $N-1$ states, then to any of the other $N-2$, and so on. Hence, we have at least $(N-2)!$ paths. These are the paths that go through every possible state. We also have to consider those that omit one state, two states, etc., but let us ignore these. This number $(N-2)!$ is an interesting number. It gets large rather quickly. Ten factorial is a convenient unit of how large factorials are. That is only 3,628,800 possibilities. With a modern digital computer, it is not unreasonable to say we will look through 3,628,800 possibilities. Consider, however, 20!. We see that it is obviously larger than $10^{10} \times 10!$. If we had a good, efficient way of enumerating and we wanted a time scale, we would say: whatever time it took to search through 10! possibilities, 20! possibilities would take us at least 10^{10} times as long.

Another very good unit is one year, equal to approximately 3×10^7 seconds. If we want to have some idea of how long it takes us to perform a certain number of operations, and each operation takes one second, then 3×10^7 seconds is one year. If we change the seconds to microseconds, and then multiply by 10^{10} and so on, we get a very large number of years. Think now of how large 100! is. It is a number beyond belief, yet that is still a consequence of only a very small network. Consider where the question involves 1000! . . . 10,000!. These are numbers beyond imagination.

Enumeration remains the best way to solve problems, if we can do it. Of course, mathematicians do not like to solve problems by enumeration, (technological unemployment!) but if we have a fast digital computer, why not solve problems by enumeration? The answer is that most problems cannot be tackled by enumeration because you rather easily start getting into numbers like 1000! or 10,000!. These are small numbers compared to some encountered in combinatorial problems. We can easily get numbers like $2^{100!}$ or $2^{1000!}$ in pattern recognition.

Thus, we cannot say. "We can always solve problems by enumeration." It is just not true.

Even when enumeration is possible, we have to worry about error build up. Thus, a solution by enumeration may be theoretically possible, but practically impossible.

2.13. Writing a Program

The point we want to indicate, without going into details, is that by these methods of successive approximation we end up solving a feasible equation, and that is an arithmetical operation. Thus, it is an operation that can easily be carried out on a digital computer. We think we can see that the computer program required to solve an equation of this type is a very simple one. It can be written by a beginner; a person who has just learned something about Fortran programming in a couple of hours could write a computer program for that equation.

With a little bit more experience, we can write a little bit better program, but there is no need for any sophistication or expertise. We might also say that for $N \le 100$ or so, it is a hand calculation. We have had people test this for about a hundred different states. This would take about an hour, using a hand calculator. If one can do the calculation by hand in one hour, a digital computer could do it in one second or something like that.

2.14. Storage

There is one interesting question of feasibility – the question of storage. We are talking about ordinary, commercial digital computers. How do we store the distance array? There are several aspects to this question. If it is an actual geographical problem, where the times t_{ij} represent ordinary distances, then we do not have to store them at all. We just store the set of states and an algorithm for computing the distance given each two states. This is given by

$$t_{ij} = [(x_i - x_j)^2 + (y_i - y_j)^2]^{1/2}.$$

In other words, we generate rather than store. In any particular problem, it is a very interesting question whether it is more efficient to generate rather than store. Here is where experience and mathematical knowledge counts. Often, a problem is feasible only if certain functions are generated rather than stored.

It is interesting to note that to solve problems involving, say, certain trigonometric functions on paper, we commonly look up values in tables stored in handbooks. To determine the same value using a digital computer, a stored library program may be called upon to generate the answers (usually by means of a power series formula). If we wish to know a sequence of adjacent answers, instead of using a power series (polynomial), we may instead solve a differential equation.

2.15. Dimensionality

The second point is that, in general, $t_{ij} = \infty$. That is to say, if we have a network, it is not possible to go from one state to every other state in one stage. We can only go from one state to other nearby states. Thus, most of the time t_{ij} is going to be ∞. Therefore, when we are storing the matrix t_{ij} we only have to store the non-infinite elements with the convention that, if we cannot find a value, it must have the value infinity. These are some of the local tricks and devices which we use when we are trying to solve high-dimensional problems.

If we were to ask: What is the principal difficulty of applying these analytic techniques to problems of decision-making? (problems of problem solving), the answer is dimensionality. There is no difficulty in applying this formalism to all kinds of problems in the field of artificial intelligence and decision-making.

The difficulty is that, in general, it does not yield a feasible approach. Just as enumeration was not feasible for the routing problem, so this type of approach will not be feasible for problems of very high dimension, because we get into storage and time difficulties. These are new and formidable mathematical problems.

2.16. Structure

What saves the day in many cases is that the network has structure. How this structure is used is a matter of mathematical ingenuity.

In some cases, we do not want to examine the structure. Thus, for example, we have said above that it is not possible in general to go from every state to every other state. Thus, the equation should read

$$f_i = \max_{j \in S(i)} (t_{ij} + f_j). \tag{2.2}$$

The set $S(i)$ tells us what states to examine. This information will considerably reduce the search. However, it requires a preliminary examination of the network. If we do not want to do this, it is practical to use a very large number for forbidden paths. Either we can use the largest number available in the computer, or we can determine a number from an approximate policy. This avoids any geometric consideration of the network. As we said above, sometimes we want to do it and sometimes we do not. It is nice to have a choice.

In Chapter 1 we gave an example of how structure can be used.

2.17. Heuristics

If the storage capacity of the digital computer is exceeded, we have to use approximate policies. These approximate policies, particularly in artificial intelligence, are called "heuristics". The determination of these approximate policies is not easy. Often we are guided by experience with the actual process.

In general, many interesting problems arise in the determination of these approximate policies. The determination of these approximate policies depends upon the structure of the process and how we wish to describe it.

2.18. Discussion

In the previous pages, we have shown how a digital computer can be used for decision-making in certain cases. One of the tasks of a mathematician is to recognize that a given problem is of this form. What would be desirable would be a computer method which would recognize a problem. At present, we seem far from this.

Consequently, at the moment we need the mathematician to formulate the problem for the computer. Even if we solve the problem of computer recognition, and there are signs that we shall, we need the mathematician to determine which problems are worth solving. Artificial intelligence needs more human intelligence, not less. The computer requires more mathematicians, not less.

We have spent a considerable amount of time on this problem for several reasons. In the first place it illustrates many important points about the use of digital computers. In the second place, the same method can be used for quite general systems. Naturally, the method cannot be used automatically. It requires that a great deal be known about the system.

Let us summarize the essence of the method. We must describe the system by means of numbers, state variables, and the possible constraints on decisions; then we must describe the effect of a decision, action, upon these state variables; finally we must state the objective, the criterion function, explicitly.

2.19. Application to Game Playing

Let us now apply the *method* of the shortest path. Puzzle-solving is one of the attributes of human intelligence. Consequently, it is important to show how a digital computer may be used to solve these puzzles. We shall consider two classical puzzles, the wine-pouring problem and cannibals and missionaries. In addition, we shall consider a very amusing game invented by Lewis Carroll and the Chinese fifteen puzzle. Finally, we shall say a few words about chess and checkers. Through these fundamental examples, the relationships to scheduling will be clear.

2.20. Mathematical Abstractions

We want then to use the power of mathematics, of mathematical abstraction.

We gave the routing problem in terms of tracing a path through a network when, in actuality, what we were talking about was N states. We called these N states the numbers 1 to N, just for convenience. We could also have called them $p_1, p_2, \ldots p_N$ and so on, and we could have used Greek letters or German letters, etc. These are dummy symbols. It does not make any difference what symbols we use.

What we are really talking about is the problem of transforming a system in state space from some initial state to some terminal state. The problem then is, in any particular case, how to determine the state space and how to determine the transformations. This is where mathematical ability and experience comes in. We have this mathematical abstraction at our disposal but any particular realization is a trick. In any particular case, we have to look at the problem and determine what the states are, what the space is, and what the transformations are.

2.21. Intelligent Machines

Hence, when we are talking about intelligent machines and artificial intelligence, there really are many levels of problems. One problem is to say, we as mathematicians will teach a computer; we will tell a computer how to solve this problem. Another problem which, at the moment, is completely beyond our ability is how to read this problem in ordinary English speech with a program which would tell the computer how to convert this problem into a dynamic programming problem. We do not think we are that far away from this at the present time, but it is a different problem. It is important that we realize the levels of problems.

2.22. The Wine-pouring Problem

Let us now turn our attention to a puzzle which has amused and bemused people for hundreds of years.

Two men have a jug filled with eight quarts of wine which they wish to divide equally between them. They have two empty jugs with capacities of five and three quarts respectively. These jugs are unmarked and no other measuring device is available. How can they accomplish the equal division?

We shall show how the techniques of the shortest-path problem are applicable.

2.23. Formulation as a Multistage Decision Process

In stating the pouring problem, several assumptions were made tacitly. Let us see if we can make them explicit. First, we assume that no liquid is spilled (a conservation requirement), that none is lost due to evaporation, and that none is drunk (a prohibition requirement).

The fact that no measuring device is available means that the only operation that is allowed at any time is that of pouring wine from one jug to another. The pouring is stopped when one jug is empty, or the other is full, whichever event happens first.

Thus, for example, the first operation might be to pour five quarts from the full jug into the previously empty five-quart jug, or it might be to pour three quarts from the full jug into the previously empty three-quart jug. No other initial operation is possible.

It remains to identify the process, by which we mean to have to choose state variables. Let us agree that the amounts of wine in each jug will specify the process. Next, we must see how decisions, actions, affect these state variables. It is easy to see the effect of various pourings.

Let us now examine how a digital computer can be used. In the first place, we want to examine the storage requirements. We see that there are four possibilities for the first jug, six for the second, and nine for the third, a total of $4 \times 6 \times 9 = 216$. This is a modest requirement for a digital computer.

EXAMPLE 1. For simplicity we consider the pouring problem in which the containers hold 4, 3, and 1 quarts. Then the state of our system at a given stage is indicated by (x, y, z), where x, y, and z represent the amounts of wine in the 4, 3, and 1-quarts jugs respectively. Determine the only possible states (x, y, z) which can be reached starting from the initial state $(4, 0, 0)$.

Solution. By examining a tree diagram constructed by branching from $(4, 0, 0)$ to all possible states, the only possible states (x, y, z) are the next eight states:

$$(4, 0, 0) \quad (3, 0, 1) \quad (2, 1, 1) \quad (1, 3, 0) \quad (0, 3, 1)$$
$$(3, 1, 0) \quad (2, 2, 0) \quad (1, 2, 1)$$

However, this figure may be considerably reduced. Let us observe that it is efficient to specify the amount of wine in two jugs. Since the total amount stays the same, it is sufficient to specify any two jugs. Naturally, we will choose the smaller. Thus, we have a total of twenty-four possibilities plus a small calculation. This is a very important reduction in many cases.

EXAMPLE 2. For the problem in Example 1, since $x + y + z$ is equal to 4 for any state, we can consider only the state (y, z) at any stage, where the integers y and z satisfy $0 \leqq y \leqq 3$, $0 \leqq z \leqq 1$.

Once we have determined the state variables we can have the computer print out the results of one pouring, two pourings, etc. We can have the computer stop when no new states are generated. This will automatically determine what states are reachable. If we do not want to proceed that way, we can introduce a distance function. In other words, we can convert the original problem to that of getting as close as possible. This is quite a common device by which in many cases we avoid the difficult problem of determining whether a certain operation is possible.

What we have sketched above is essentially a solution by enumeration. If we do not want to employ this method we can use the functional equation approach of Chapter 1.

EXAMPLE 3. In the problem in Example 1, instead of the time t_{ij} to move from the point i to the point j defined in Chapter 1, we can define the "cost" of performing any transition from one state $i = (y_1, z_1)$ to another state $j = (y_2, z_2)$ to be one unit, i.e. $t_{ij} = 1$. Then determine the related cost matrix.

Solution. From the tree diagram as in the Example 1, the cost matrix becomes as in Table 2.1.

TABLE 2.1 *Cost Matrix* (*Containers* 4, 3, 1)

From	(0,0)	(0,1)	(1,0)	(1,1)	(2,0)	(2,1)	(3,0)	(3,1)
(0,0)		1					1	
(0,1)	1		1					1
(1,0)	1	1			1		1	
(1,1)		1	1		1			1
(2,0)	1			1		1	1	
(2,1)		1			1		1	1
(3,0)	1					1		1
(3,1)		1					1	

EXAMPLE 4. For the problem, let us define $f(y, z)$ to be the minimum number of pourings required to reach the desired state (y_d, z_d), starting in state (y, z), then show the functional equation for the pouring problem in Example 1.

Solution. We have the following equation (cf. (1.3) in Chapter 1).

$$f(y, z) = \min_{(u, v) \in A(y, z)} [1 + f(u, v)] \tag{2.3}$$

with the boundary condition $f(y_d, z_d) = 0$, where $A(y, z)$ is the set of all states accessible from (y, z) (cf. Table 2.1).

EXAMPLE 5. By combining the following approximation method with (2.3) for the desired state $(2, 0)$ (cf. Section 1.4):

$$f^{(0)}(y, z) = 1, \ (y, z) \neq (2,0); \ f^{(0)}(2, 0) = 0,$$
$$f^{(r+1)}(y, z) = \min_{(u, v) \in A(y, z)} [1 + f^{(r)}(u, v)], \ (y, z) \neq (2, 0), \ r = 0, 1, 2,$$
$$f^{(r+1)}(2, 0) = 0,$$

determine the shortest path from the state $(0, 0)$ to the state $(2, 0)$.

Solution. We have Table 2.2.

TABLE 2.2 *Successive Approximation*

State (y, z)	$f^{(0)}(y,z)$	$f^{(1)}(y,z)$	$f^{(2)}(y,z)$	$f^{(3)}(y,z)$
$(0, 0)$	1	2	3	3
$(0, 1)$	1	2	3	3
$(1, 0)$	1	2	2	2
$(1, 1)$	1	1	1	1
$(2, 0)$	0	0	0	0
$(2, 1)$	1	1	1	1
$(3, 0)$	1	2	2	2
$(3, 1)$	1	2	3	3

Since $f^{(2)}(y, z) = f^{(3)}(y, z)$ holds for every (y, z), we have $f(y, z) = f^{(2)}(y, z)$ for all (y, z). The shortest path is $(0, 0) \rightarrow (3, 0) \rightarrow (2, 1) \rightarrow (2, 0)$. Note that we can assume that, for example, $f^{(0)}(y, z) = \infty$ for $(y, z) \neq (2, 0)$ and $f^{(0)}(2, 0) = 0$, or $f^{(0)}(y, z) = 0$ for all (y, z).

2.24. Cannibals and Missionaries

In this section, we wish to consider the following classical conundrum: "A group consisting of three cannibals and three edible missionaries seeks to cross a river. A boat is available which will hold at most two people, and which can be navigated by any combination of cannibals and missionaries involving one or two people. If the missionaries on either side of the river, or in the boat, are outnumbered at any time by cannibals, dire consequences which may be guessed at will result. What schedule of crossings can be devised to permit the entire group of cannibals and missionaries to cross the river safely?"

Our experience with the wine-pouring puzzle suggests the desirability of looking at this puzzle, too, as a succession of transitions from one state, or condition, to another, and indeed such an interpretation is possible.

2.25. Formulation as a Multistage Decision Process

Let us follow the same procedure used in the wine-pouring problem.

We first introduce state variables. In this case, the numbers of cannibals and missionaries on each bank and in the boat can be used as state variables. This yields a small number of possibilities. However, once again, we observe that we have a conservation condition which can be used to reduce dimensionality. The number of cannibals and missionaries stays constant. Consequently, we can use either the numbers on each bank, or the number on one bank and the number in the boat. Again, this is an important reduction in dimensionality.

The effect of a decision upon these state variables is readily determined.

Again, we have the problem of determining whether the original puzzle can be solved. Either of the methods sketched before may be used.

Exercise

1. Let $(x_1, y_1; x_2, y_2)$ be the state at any stage, where x_1 and y_1 are the numbers of the cannibals and missionaries respectively on the first bank and x_2 and y_2 show the respective numbers at the opposite bank, then, as in the Examples 4 and 5 in Section 2.23, show the functional equation for the problem and determine the minimal time for all persons to cross the river safely.

2.26. Chinese Fifteen Puzzle

Let us now turn to the Chinese fifteen puzzle. This is a disease which becomes epidemic every once in a while (see Fig. 2.4 below).

1	2	3	4
5	6	7	8
9	10	11	12
13	14	15	X

FIG. 2.4

We have sixteen squares with a number in each and a blank space X into which we can put a nearby square. For example,

1	2	3	4
5	6	7	8
9	10	11	X
13	14	15	12

FIG. 2.5

The problem is to manipulate the blank space in such a way that the fourteen and fifteen are reversed. One possible configuration is given in Fig. 2.6. This of course does not solve the problem.

1	2	3	4
5	6	7	8
9	10	11	12
13	14	X	15

FIG. 2.6

Occasionally in newspaper advertisements, you see somebody offering a prize of ten thousand dollars to anybody who can do it. They are very safe because we can prove mathematically that it is impossible. Simple theoretical considerations will show which configurations are possible and which ones are not. Suppose then we take this task as a puzzle and say that we want a computer to solve this type of problem. Let us take a very simple version of it, and then we will explain why we cannot solve the original puzzle at this time using dynamic programming in any direct fashion.

Suppose then we take a three by three version. We have the numbers 1, 2, 3, 4, 5, 6, 7 and 8, originally given in this order:

1	2	3
4	5	6
7	8	X

FIG. 2.7

The question is: Can we slide the sections around so that we get the numbers 8 and 7 reversed? This would be a test of decision-making.

2.27. The Puzzle Again

Now, let us look at the puzzle. One of the numbers denotes the blank space. Each one of these corresponds to a state. What are the allowable transformations? Wherever the blank is, we can change one of the states into at most four adjoining states, depending upon where the blank is. Sometimes there are only two or three adjoining states. Can you show this configuration in a diagram? We can see that every transformation takes us from the original state to one of four at most nearby states. What is the "time" required?

2.28. Feasibility

We originally asked the question, "Can it be done?", which is actually a harder problem than saying, "What is the shortest way of doing it?" Hence we solve the problem of, "Can it be done?", by saying, "What is the minimum number of operations?" Of course, one gets into such difficulties as, "How does one know whether it can be done at all?"

Let us assume that we are in an initial state which can be converted into the desired state. Then we can safely ask, "What is the minimum number of operations?" Given any initial position, using the algorithm we mentioned above, we have a way of determining how one shifts the blank around to get the desired final position. We assume that we do not cheat, that we give a position that can be transformed into the final position.

2.29. Doable Positions

The second part of the problem is, how do we know which are the positions which can be transformed? There are several ways of doing this. One way is to look at the time. We can get an upper bound on the time required. We did not mention this, but when we have N points, it turns out that N is an upper bound for the number of iterations required when we use an appropriate method of successive approximations. Hence, if we count the number of possible positions of this type, and set the program going, if the calculation takes more than N time units, we know it is impossible to solve the original problem.

2.30. Associated Questions

Another way of approaching this, avoiding this problem of whether it is feasible or not, is to ask a different question. Instead of asking for the minimum time, we could ask: How close can we come to a given position? One of the ways we can measure distance is to say, we look at the number of symbols that are not correct. We want to get as close as possible to the specified configuration. This is a very important consideration in pattern recognition. We want to get one pattern to represent another as closely as possible.

We can use this technique in many puzzles to avoid the question of whether a puzzle can be done in its original form.

2.31. The Original Puzzle

Why can we not use the foregoing methods on the Chinese fifteen puzzle? We are stymied by storage considerations. A single calculation shows that there are 16! possible states. There are 15! states having the blank in the lower-right corner, but 16! states into which the blank can move. Hence, it is easy to write down the relevant functional equation. However, we cannot use existing computers to resolve it. This dimensionality difficulty is typical of many combinatorial problems. It is easy to write down equations, but we cannot use digital computers to treat these equations routinely. It is essential to reduce the dimensionality by using the structure of the process. In other words, we must use mathematical training.

2.32. Lewis Carroll's Game of Doublets

Lewis Carroll invented the game of "Doublets". The idea of the game is to construct a chain of English words connecting two given words subject to the condition that each word differs from the preceding word by the change of exactly one letter.

There is no difficulty in writing down an appropriate functional equation using the method given above. To resolve a given problem we may need an unabridged dictionary. Obviously, there will be a different problem for each language.

2.33. Chess and Checkers

Let us say a few words about chess and checkers. Unfortunately, the two are often lumped together. As we shall see, they should not be since there is a vast difference in dimensionality between checkers and chess.

Let us begin with checkers. If we regard each position as a state, we see that the effect of a move is to change one state into another. Consequently, there is no difficulty in writing down an equation depending upon whether it is white's move or black's move. The basic question in using a digital computer is that of storage.

This means that checkers is a solvable puzzle. If we use the structure of the process, we can lower the storage requirements considerably.

Let us turn to chess. There is no difficulty as before in writing down the relevant functional equation. However, the number of states, positions, is so great, that this is not a feasible procedure, either now or in the near future.

How then does a chess master play chess? How does he recognize a favorable position and determine a good move? We wish we knew. Some people are born with the magical ability to play chess well. We can train people to play chess much better than they do, but we cannot make a chess genius.

The question is that of gestalt. If we understood this, we would know how to perform pattern recognition and language translation. At present, and most probably forever, we cannot use a computer to recognize structure. However, there is no proof of this conjecture, and it may well be possible that tomorrow someone will find a way to use a computer for this purpose. If we can make this structure explicit, there is no difficulty. This means that we have considerable difficulty in using a computer for interviewing or for reading tissue smears for cancer.

2.34. Solving Puzzles by Computer

What we want to indicate here is that we have very systematic ways for solving puzzles. We can, of course, object on many grounds. We can say, we give a method of solving puzzles by mathematics. Is this the way a human being would solve puzzles? We reply that we do not care. This is not the problem that interests us. In the first place, we do not care and, in the second place, we do not know how humans solve problems. One good reason we do not care is because we do not know.

2.35. Discussion

In the preceding pages we have discussed some puzzles using the methodology we have developed. We want to stress again that there are many other ways of attacking these puzzles. Again, we do not know how the human mind solves these puzzles. What we have given here is a mathematical method which can be used on a computer in some cases.

Bibliography and Comments

Section 2.1
A detailed discussion of these matters will be found in
R. BELLMAN, *An Introduction to Artificial Intelligence: Can Computers Think?*, Boyd & Fraser Publishing Co., San Francisco, 1978.
We are employing the theory of dynamic programming in what follows. The reader who wants to learn more about the theory may wish to consult the following books:
R. BELLMAN, *Introduction to the Mathematical Theory of Control Processes*, Vol. I, Academic Press, Inc., New York, 1968.
R. BELLMAN, K. COOKE and J. LOCKETT, *Algorithms, Graphs, and Computers*, Academic Press, Inc., New York, 1970.
S. DREYFUS and AVERILL LAW, *The Art and Theory of Dynamic Programming*, Academic Press, Inc., 1977.
A basic question in structural theory in all fields of culture concerns the reconstruction of evolutionary or cladistic trees on pathways by inferences from the characteristics of organisms, systems, or data surviving at the present time. Let us cite the fields of biology and anthropology, the use of fossils in the case of archeology, and the domain of philology.
In recent years, methods have been developed for deducing trees which satisfy the condition of requiring a minimal number of evolutionary steps or changes in characters to explain the evolutionary history of the set of existing structures. See
W. H. WAGNER, Jr., "Problems in the classification of ferns. In *Recent Advances in Botany*, University of Toronto Press, Toronto, 1961, 841–844.
J. H. CAMIN and R. R. SOKAL, "A method for deducing branching sequences in phylogeny", *Evolution*, **19** (1965), 311–326.
J. A. HENDRICKSON, "Clustering in numerical cladistics: A minimum-length directed tree problem", *Mathematical Biosciences*, **3** (1968), 371–381.
A. G. KLUGE and J. S. FARRIS, "Quantitative phyletics and the evolution of Anurans", *Syst. Zool.* **18** (1969), 1–32.
For a theoretical approach, see
G. F. ESTABROOK, "A general solution in partial orders for the Camin-Sokal model in phylogeny", "*Journal of Theoretical Biology*, **21** (1968), 421–438.
D. SANKOFF, "Matching sequences under deletion/insertion constraints", *Proceedings of the National Academy of Science, U.S.A.* **69**, No. 1 (1972), 4–6.
The principle of minimum evolution or "parsimony" is generally assumed in these papers as a suitable hypothesis in the absence of empirical laws of evolution. General algorithms for these "most parsimonious" trees have not been completely studied, although algorithms for close approximations called "Wagner trees" do exist. See

J. S. FARRIS, "Methods for computing Wagner trees", *Syst. Zool.* **19** (1970), 83–92.
Other conceptually related trees are studied in
R. BELLMAN, K. L. COOKE and J. LOCKETT, *Algorithms, Graphs, and Computers*, Academic Press, Inc., 1970.
A very interesting algorithm for reconstructing phylogenetic relationships from protein amino acid sequence data under some restrictions about all distance measures is given by
W. A. BEYER, M. L. STEIN, T. F. SMITH and S. M. ULAM, "A molecular sequence metric and evolutionary trees", *Mathematical Biosciences*, **17** (1973), 444–461.
A source of reference is
R. BELLMAN and S. DREYFUS, *Adaptive Dynamic Programming*, Princeton University Press, 1961.

Section 2.4
We have used the concept of imbedding in many contexts. In mathematical physics it can be used widely. See
R. BELLMAN and G. M. WING, *An Introduction to Invariant Imbedding*, John Wiley & Sons, Inc., New York, 1975.

Section 2.7
It is very interesting to observe a given behavior and see whether this behavior can be interpreted in terms of some optimal policy. This leads to many interesting problems which are often called "inverse problems". See, for example, the papers
R. BELLMAN and J. M. RICHARDSON, "A note on an inverse problem in mathematical physics", *Quarterly Journal of Applied Mathematics*, **19** (1961), 269–271.
R. BELLMAN, H. KAGIWADA and R. KALABA, "Numerical inversion of Laplace transforms and some inverse problems in radiative transfer", *Journal of the Atmospheric Sciences*, **23**, No. 5 (1966), 555–559.
R. BELLMAN, "Inverse problems in ecology", *J. Theoret. Biol.* **11** (1966), 164–167.
R. BELLMAN, "Dynamic programming and inverse optimal problems in mathematical economics", *Journal of Mathematical Analysis and Applications*, **29**, No. 2 (1970), 424–428.
R. BELLMAN, B. KASHEF and R. VASUDEVAN, "The inverse problem of estimating the heart parameters from cardiograms", *Mathematical Biosciences*, **19** (1974), 221–230.
Many further references are given in these papers.
Often, a particular equation can be considered as minimization equation. In this way, we get upper and lower bounds which are very valuable. See, for example,
R. COURANT and D. HILBERT, *Methods of Mathematical Physics*, Vols. I and II, Wiley, New York, 1953, 1962, and 1974.
See
R. BELLMAN, *Methods of Nonlinear Analysis*, Vol. II, Academic Press, Inc., New York, 1973.

Section 2.8
See
R. BELLMAN and P. BROCK, "On the concepts of a problem and problem solving", *American Mathematical Monthly*, **67**, No. 2 (1960), 119–134.
The conventional approach described in the text in the continuous version is that of the calculus of variations. For a discussion of these matters, see
R. BELLMAN, *Introduction to the Mathematical Theory of Control Processes*, Vol. II, Academic Press, New York, 1971.
The approach of dynamic programming is a dual approach to that of the calculus of variations. The calculus of variations regards a curve as a locus of points. Dynamic programming regards a curve as an envelope of tangents.
We can use the computer by means of a very simple program, to convert one solution into the other.

Section 2.9
In this case, the equivalence between a policy and the function f_i is the fundamental duality of Euclidian space. The locus of points is the same as the envelope of tangents. In the stochastic case, this equivalence does not hold.

Section 2.10
See
L. A. ZADEH, "The linguistic approach and its application to decision analysis", *Proceedings of Conference on Directions in Decentralized Control, Many-person Optimization and Large-scale Systems*, Y. C. HO and S. K. MITTER (eds.), Plenum Press, New York, 1975.
See also
R. BELLMAN and L. ZADEH, "Decision-making in a fuzzy environment", *Management Science*, **17**, No. 4 (1970), 141–164.

Section 2.18
The method can also be used to locate "missing links". It has application in many fields. In philology, see
A. KAUFMAN and R. FAURRE, *Introduction to Operations Research*, Academic Press, Inc., New York, 1968.
The general problem of finding a logical path from one phenomenon to another leads to many interesting mathematical problems. See the paper,
E. MARCHI and R. I. C. HANSELL, "Generalizations on the parsimony question in evolution", *Mathematical Biosciences*, **17** (1973), 11–34.
In addition to general decision-making problems, numerous specialized problems in artificial intelligence (e.g. pattern recognition) can be solved using the same methods. See
K. S. FU, *Sequential Methods in Pattern Recognition and Machine Learning*, Academic Press, New York, 1968.
The method can also be applied when the state variables are sets. See, for example,
R. BELLMAN and B. GLUSS, "On various versions of the defective coin problem", *Information and Control*, **4** (1961), 118–131.
R. BELLMAN, "An application of dynamic programming to the coloring of maps", *ICC Bull.* **4** (1965), 3–6.
R. BELLMAN, "A note on cluster analysis and dynamic programming", *Mathematical Biosciences*, **18**, Nos. 3, 4 (1973), 311–312.

Section 2.19
For details, see the book
R. BELLMAN, K. COOKE and J. LOCKETT, *Algorithms, Graphs, and Computers*, Academic Press, Inc., New York, 1970.
Many popular puzzles are discussed there.
The same method can be used for other puzzles. See
R. BELLMAN, "An application of dynamic programming to the coloring of maps", *ICC Bull.* **4** (1965), 3–6.
R. BELLMAN and K. COOKE, "The Konigsberg Bridges problem generalized", *Journal of Mathematical Analysis and Applications*, **25**, No. 1 (1969), 1–7.
Many puzzles can be analyzed completely using mathematical methods; see the book cited above. See also the journal *American Mathematical Monthly* and the column by Martin Gardener in the *Scientific American*, and
D. D. SPENCER, *Game Playing with Computers*, Revised 2nd Edition, Hayden Book Co., Inc., Rochelle Park, New Jersey, 1975.
See also the book
W. ROUSE BALL, *Mathematical Recreations*, London, Macmillan, 1922.

Section 2.32
See
R. BELLMAN, "Dynamic programming and Lewis Carroll's game of doublets", *B. Inst. Math. and its Appl.*, 1968.

Section 2.33
See
R. BELLMAN, "On the application of dynamic programming to the determination of optimal play in chess and checkers", *Proc. of the National Academy of Sciences*, **53** (1965), 224–247.

R. BELLMAN, "Stratification and the control of large systems with applications to chess and checkers", *Information Science*, **1** (1968), 7–21.

For a discussion of early checker and chess-playing computer programs, see EDWARD A. FEIGENBAUM and JULIAN FELDMAN, *Computers and Thought*, New York, McGraw Hill, 1963.

Present-day programs are much better, and can defeat "average" human players. Dimensionality problems are reduced by incorporating "learning" mechanisms.

CHAPTER 3

Scheduling Problems and Combinatorial Programming

3.1. Introduction

In this chapter, we want to present some of the fundamental problems in scheduling theory and some of the fundamental methods.

In the references, there will be found papers where further discussion is contained.

3.2. Classification of Scheduling Problems

The scheduling problem is the problem which arises inevitably whenever we want to make a daily routine for any planned work.

As basic problems which are now the object of the study in operations research and related literature we can list the following three problem classes:

1. The sequencing problem, or job-shop scheduling problem.
2. The project scheduling problem.
3. The assembly-line balancing problem.

In this chapter we briefly describe each of these problems.

3.3. Sequencing Problem

This problem is also called the job-shop scheduling problem and is concerned with deciding the order for the items to be serviced such as in the manufacturing process described below.

When n jobs or n items are processed by m machines, under a given ordering that is, given the machine order to process each job, and given processing times of each job on each machine, the problem is to determine the sequence of n jobs on each machine in order to minimize a given objective function (performance measure). This objective function is generally any nondecreasing function of the completion time of each job which includes total elapsed time (makespan) to complete the processing of all jobs, weighted mean completion time, weighted mean lateness or tardiness under the given due date for each job, machine idle time or total waiting times of n jobs to be processed and so on.

48

This problem can be divided into the following two types in case there are more than one machine:

1. *Flow-shop type.* This is the case where each job has identical ordering. This type can be classified into the next two types by the sequence of n jobs on each machine:

   (a) No passing is allowed. This means that the sequence of n jobs on each machine is the same. Sometimes the problem of interest here is called the permutation flow-shop problem.

   (b) Passing is allowed. In this case the sequence of n jobs on each machine may be different.

Obviously the analysis for the former is easier than for the latter and therefore almost all analytical results for the sequencing problem are for the former type.

2. *Job-shop type.* This is the case where generally the ordering for each job may not be identical and therefore is considered to include the flow-shop type as a special case.

Concerning the solution method, although simulation by using priority rules has been used for a long time, theoretical results have begun from the determination of a sequence deciding criteria for the min-makespan problem for the two-machine case and in a special three-machine case by S. M. Johnson and R. Bellman in 1954.

These results were generalized for the m machine case where no passing is allowed. The general solution method to determine the optimal schedule for the three-machine case without any restraint was presented by Z. A. Lomnicki, E. Ignall and L. Schrage in 1965 by applying branch and bound methods introduced by D. C. Little *et al.* in 1963 for the resolution of the traveling-salesman problem. This method was successfully applied for the general M ($M \geqslant 3$) machines case. Also B. Roy presented a general method by using S.E.P. (separation et enumeration progressive) which has a procedure similar to the branch and bound method.

Combinatorial programming is applied to determine the optimal schedule. Generally, the process for determining the optimal schedule becomes a multistage decision process where in each stage a suitable criterion or rule is used in order to exclude the state with less possibility to produce the optimal schedule thereafter. Specifically this includes dynamic programming, branch and bound methods or S.E.P., backtrack programming, and the lexicographical search method. These methods are implicit enumeration methods that avoid complete enumeration of all feasible schedules. When we formulate the problem as mathematical programming, integer linear programming or 0-1 programming implicit enumeration can be applied.

Analytical results, for example, simple criterion, can be obtained by using heuristic methods or dynamic programming type procedures. In some particular real-life situations, as faced in an engineering or planning office, these techniques may not be as practical as those based on some search procedures. We will discuss one such search technique in Chapter 5. Also we refer to some polynomially solvable cases in Chapter 8 and heuristic methods such as EXTBAB algorithm in Section 3.10. We discuss many approximate algorithms in the subsequent Chapters.

3.4. Project Scheduling Problem

This is also called the coordination problem and is concerned with the planning which consists of activities that must be processed by following the given precedence relation with or without the resource constraints (manpower, material, equipment, funds and so on). In general, let us consider the following two types:

1. *PERT type.* This type is based on the Program Evaluation Review Technique, looks for the schedule which minimizes the objective function such as project time (total elapsed time), that is, it determines the start and completion times of each activity.

2. *CPM type.* This type, based on the Critical Path Method, looks for the schedule with minimum cost in a definite period of time in the case where the cost is associated with each activity.

PERT type problems that relate to resources are classified into the following two kinds:

(a) Resource-leveling (balancing) problem. This problem levels or balances the resource requirement at each period in a schedule with definite project time.

(b) Resource allocation problem. This problem is to allocate each required resource to each activity in order to minimize the objective function under each resource constraint, that is, under limited availability of each resource at each period.

PERT and CPM were developed in the late 1950s and were extended to PERT/Cost, RAMPS and so on and these are now applied to many project scheduling problems in construction planning, production developing and system developing and so on. The project scheduling problem requires the most advanced computer programming among all scheduling problems. These problems can be solved as a shortest-route problem, critical-path problem or flow problem on a network. Also, they are formulated as integer linear programming, 0–1 programming or parametric linear programming, and dynamic programming problems.

It can now be seen why we began this book with a discussion of network and shortest-route problems.

The problems with resource constraints can be treated also by combinatorial programming.

3.5. Assembly-line Balancing Problem

There has been interest in this problem since the early 1950s. The purpose of the problem is to decide the minimum number of work stations that are assigned to work elements with some precedence relations, or to minimize the cycle time, that is, the maximum among total working time at each station, under the given number of work stations.

Dynamic programming, branch and bound methods and heuristic methods are applied to its solution.

3.6. Mutual Relations

Mutual relations between the above three basic scheduling problems are summarized as shown in the following:

1. Multiproject scheduling problem with resource constraints as a resource allocation problem includes obviously the PERT which is a single project scheduling problem with unlimited resources and, moreover, includes the general sequencing problem since the following correspondence holds between them:

Multiproject scheduling problem with resource constraints	General sequencing problem
Project	Job
Activity	Operation (each job on each machine)
Precedence relation	Ordering
Resource	Machine
Resource availability	Number of identical machines
Resource requirements by each activity	Number of identical machines that can process each operation

2. The single-project scheduling problem with single resource constraint is closely related to the assembly-line balancing problem since there exists the following correspondence between them with one exception explained afterwards:

Single project scheduling problem with single resource constraint	Assembly-line balancing problem
Unit period	Work station
Activity	Work element
Precedence relation	Precedence relation
Resource availability	Cycle time
Resource requirement by each activity	Work time of each work element

The only difference between them is that process time of each activity expands to many periods and, on the other hand, each work element is assigned to one work station. Hence, if we divide each activity i with processing time p_i assumed integer into p_i tasks each of them has a unit processing period, then both correspond completely.

From the above, the resource allocation problem has close relations with the other two scheduling problems. This scheduling problem will be considered in Chapter 12.

3.7. Summary of Combinatorial Programming as a Solution Technique

As already mentioned, combinatorial programming is applied for the solution of scheduling problems and further for efficient approximate solutions of the problems, combined with heuristics and/or search methods. In this section its content will be explained briefly. Further details can be found in subsequent chapters.

Scheduling problems are contained in combinatorial optimization problems or discrete optimization problems. These problems look for an optimal solution within a large number of feasible solutions. Many such problems are formulated as integer programming but their efficient solution uses combinatorial programming.

Although some types of these problems can be solved by discrete dynamic programming, generally they become multistage decision problems that are calculated sequentially in forward fashion and therefore any optimal solution at a former stage is not necessary for the optimal solution at the present stage. Hence, we must establish a method which has a procedure for excluding any feasible solution which cannot lead to the desired optimal solution. This procedure will be called the principle of domination. The principle of optimality in dynamic programming is a special case. The fundamental process embedded in the branch and bound method, backtrack programming and dynamic programming as the the techniques in combinatorial programming is state transformation processes explained below.

3.8. State Transformation Process

This process makes a decision at each state to transform the set of states to its subset, in which each state has a possibility of leading to the final optimal state. By approximation in state space, by means of the principle of domination, we have the fundamental state equation. That is, this process consists of the following terminologies and procedures:

Let $\{S_k\}$ be the set of vectors S_k at state k ($k = 1, 2, 3, \ldots$) in a multistage decision process, then for each $S_k \in \{S_k\}$ the following are defined: to be definite see Sections 10.2 and 10.6 in Chapter 10.

Let $\{P(S_k)\}$ be the set of state vectors $P(S_k)$ defined for S_k, and $f(S_k)$ be the set of $P(S_k)$ in $\{P(S_k)\}$ which is capable of yielding an optimal state only by information at stage k when an optimal policy is applied subsequently where optimal state means the state at the final stage giving an optimal solution.

A state transformation at each stage results from the following principle of domination: for each S_k and for any two state vectors $P_1(S_k)$, $P_2(S_k)$ in $\{P(S_k)\}$, we define that $P_1(S_k)$ dominates $P_2(S_k)$ in case that $P_2(S_k)$ never yields an optimal state unless $P_1(S_k)$ yields an optimal state, or generally the possibility of yielding an optimal state is diminished when $P_2(S_k)$ is considered instead of $P_1(S_k)$ at stage k.

Since the case may occur where the above dominance relation between two states in $\{P(S_k)\}$ does not hold, let $\mathrm{ND}\{P(S_k)\}$ be the set of $P(S_k)$ never dominated by any other $P(S_k)$ in $\{P(S_k)\}$. Then a transformation G of $\{P(S_k)\}$ on its subset $\mathrm{ND}\{P(S_r)\}$ is defined and this is a decision at stage k.

Hence, the equation holds for each S_k in $\{S_k\}$.

$$f(S_k) = G(\{P(S_k)\}) \equiv \mathrm{ND}\{P(S_k)\}, S_k \in \{S_k\}, k = 1, 2, 3, \ldots \quad (3.1)$$

Next we set the restraint (R) which must be satisfied by a state transformation process in order to determine the set $\mathrm{ND}\{P(S_k)\}$ $(k \neq 1)$. Let i be any subset of the set S'_k defined by depending on S_k, then the restraints 1, 2 must be satisfied:

1. The next relation must hold:

$$\{P(S_k)\} = H(\{\{P(S_k - i)\}, i)\}, i), k = 2, 3, \ldots$$
$$i \in S'_k \qquad\qquad (3.2)$$
$$\{S_k - i\}$$

where $S_k - i$ is a vector at a former stage which is obtained from S_k by excluding i, and H is a transformation which transforms the set of state vectors $\{P(S_k - i)\}$ and i on $\{P(S_k)\}$ by considering all i in S'_k and all $S_k - i$ for each i.

2. The subset $\mathrm{ND}\{P(S_k)\}$ of the set $\{P(S_k)\}$ defined by the right side of (3.2) can be constructed by taking $\mathrm{ND}\{P(S_k - i)\} = f(S_k - i)$ for $\{P(S_k - i)\}$ in (3.2).

Hence, if the state set $\{P(S_k)\}$ satisfies the restraint (R) for each vector S_k in $\{S_k\}$ $(k \neq 1)$, then the next fundamental state equation (F.S. equation) holds from (3.1) and (3.2):

$$f(S_k) = G[H(f(S_k - i), i)], S_k \in \{S_k\}, k = 2, 3, \ldots$$
$$i \in S'_k$$
$$\{S_k - 1\} \qquad\qquad (3.3)$$
$$f(S_1) = G(\{P(S_1)\}), S_1 \in \{S_1\}$$

where $f(S_k - i) = f(S_{k-1})$ if $S_k - i = S_{k-1}$, but generally $f(S_k - i) = f(S_q)$ when $S_k - i = S_q (q = 1, 2, \ldots, k - 1)$.

The F.S. equation (3.3) is a recurrence relation which transforms a desirable state set $f(S_q)$ at a stage q ($q = 1, 2, \ldots, k-1$) into a desirable state set $f(S_k)$ at stage k.

Finally, when we have $\{S_{N+1}\} = \phi$ (empty) or $\{S_{N+1}\} \equiv \{S_N\}$ at stage $(N+1)$, $f(S_N)$ is the set of optimal states or its subset.

Recurrence relation (3.3) gives us an algorithm for the related combinatorial optimization problem.

By suitably defining the elements in this state transformation process: S_k, $P(S_k)$, $f(S_k)$, G, S'_k, i, H, it can be shown that discrete dynamic programming, the branch and bound methods and backtrack programming and so on satisfy the restraint (R). Also, this technique can be applied to unify the multistage combinatorial algorithm (Sections 10.2, 10.6) and parallel scheduling for a finite number of stations with identical resources.

3.9. Branch and Bound Method (BAB Method)

The BAB method is a typical technique of the implicit enumeration method or tree search method which can find an optimal solution by systematically examining the subsets of feasible solutions. This procedure is depicted in a solution tree or a scheduling tree with nodes that correspond to these subsets. For combinatorial optimization problems to minimize an objective function f, the BAB method successively applies the branching and bounding and by these operations excludes the subsets which are found not to include any optimal solution and then finally leads to at least one optimal solution. Lower bound (LB) of the values of f of feasible solutions contained in each subset decides the priority of the corresponding node and usually a node with least LB is branched in order to decompose the related subset into its subsets. On the other hand, we need an upper bound of the minimum f_0 of the objective function f. This upper bound is usually defined as the minimum f^* of the values f of all feasible solutions found up to date. If we do not know any feasible solution, in the beginning f^* is taken to be infinity until the first feasible solution is found.

After the search ending at a subset, which gives a feasible solution, we backtrack to the nearest incompletely searched node with lower bound less than the present f^*. This node is again branched to new nodes (subsets) where incompletely searched nodes are defined as nodes which are not branched or partially branched up to the present. Hence, elimination (exclusion) of the subsets with no optimal solution is made by excluding any node (subset) with LB not less than the then upper bound f^* which means the pruning of the corresponding node and its successors (cf. Theorem 1). Backtracking in the solution tree causes the branching of an incompletely searched node only in case there exists a node with LB less than the then f^*, and if LBs of the newly created nodes are greater than or equal to the then f^*, then again backtracking is made in order to search another incompletely searched node.

Then finally when lower bounds of all incompletely searched nodes in the solution tree are greater than or equal to the then f^*, a feasible solution with this f^* is an optimal solution (cf. Theorem 2).

In this BAB method the following theorems hold:

THEOREM 1. *If we have* $S_j \subset S_i$ *for any two subsets* S_i, S_j *of all feasible solution sets, then* $LB[S_j] \geqq LB[S_i]$ *holds where say* $LB[S_j]$ *represents the lower bound for* S_j.

Proof. The result obviously follows from the fact that S_j contains a part of the set of feasible solutions in S_i.

THEOREM 2. *The BAB method can determine an optimal solution after the search of a finite number of subsets (nodes).*

Proof. The number of nodes created in the solution tree is finite since the original problem has a finite number of feasible solutions and each node in the solution tree is branched to at most a finite number of nodes. Then by the branching under the condition $LB < f^*$, finally lower bounds at all incompletely searched nodes become greater than or equal to the then f^*. All lower bounds of the nodes branched from such incompletely searched nodes are also greater than or equal to that f^* by Theorem 1. Hence, a feasible solution with that f^* becomes an optimal solution with f_0, that is, $f^* = f_0$ after the search of a finite number of nodes.

Precautions in applying BAB methods are the following:

1. The way of selection of the criterion to branching the subset successively starting from all feasible solution sets determines the efficiency of the BAB algorithm (cf. Section 9.6).

2. The more precise the lower bound of the subset is, the fewer the number of the nodes to be searched. Since the total computation time becomes large under complicated lower bounds we must be careful of the trade offs between preciseness and complication of the lower bound (cf. Section 9.8).

3. When any subset represents one feasible solution it is desirable that its lower bound be equal to the value of f of this feasible solution (cf. the specific examples in Chapter 9).

4. If elimination of the subsets can be made by a certain dominance relation in addition to the criterion: $LB \leqq f^*$, then generally the number of the nodes to be searched in the solution tree diminishes (cf. Section 9.14).

3.10. Relative Error of Approximate Value and Heuristic Algorithm for Deciding a Reliable Approximate Solution (Extended BAB Method)

In this section it is assumed that the values of the objective function f and lower bound LB of any subset in the BAB method are positive. This assumption holds for any objective function which does not include lateness where lateness of job i is defined to be the completion time of job i minus its due date.

The percentage of relative error (PRE) of f^* to an unknown optimal (minimal) value f_0 when we select a feasible solution with the then f^* as an approximate solution is expressed as

$$\text{PRE} = \frac{f^* - f_0}{f_0} \times 100\,(\%). \tag{3.4}$$

We can find a lower bound $\underline{f_0}$ of f_0 if necessary by looking for a lower bound of f_0 under additional subsets. For example, the minimal value of lower bounds for all nodes constructed by branching once the first (root) node becomes $\underline{f_0}$.

From $\underline{f_0} \leqq f_0$ and (3.4), we have

$$\text{PRE} \leq \frac{f^* - \underline{f_0}}{\underline{f_0}} \times 100\,(\%) \equiv \alpha\,(\%). \tag{3.5}$$

We can determine the upper bound α of PRE of f^* to f_0. If an approximate solution with PRE $\leqq \alpha(\%)$ under a prescribed value of α can be constructed for a large problem, this approximate solution is a reliable approximate solution in the sense that its PRE to the unknown minimal value f_0 is less than or equal to $\alpha(\%)$.

The following theorem shows an important procedure in the extended branch and bound method (EXTBAB Method) which determines a reliable approximate solution.

THEOREM 3. *In any BAB method if the revised elimination condition*

$$\text{LB} \geqq \frac{f^*}{1 + \dfrac{\alpha}{100}}\ (< f^*) \tag{3.6}$$

is applied instead of the condition LB $\geq f^*$ whenever new f^* is obtained, then by this EXTBAB method a feasible solution with the then f^* in the case where lower bounds of all incompletely searched nodes are greater than or equal to the value of $f^*/(1 + (\alpha/100))$ becomes a reliable approximate solution with PRE $\leqq \alpha(\%)$. When $\alpha = 0$, this reduces to the original BAB method.

Proof. It is obvious that the expression (3.6) holds for all incompletely searched nodes at the final stage of this EXTBAB method as in the proof of Theorem 2. Since all LB are positive, (3.6) is equivalent to

$$\frac{f^* - LB}{LB} \times 100 \leqq \alpha\,(\%). \tag{3.7}$$

The expression (3.7) shows that expression (3.5) holds for the same f^* by means of branching and elimination in the EXTBAB method and Theorem 2. Hence, the conclusion results. Particularly for $\alpha = 0$, we have the original BAB method.

By enlarging the range of admissible feasible solutions under $\alpha > 0$ for large problems, the number of eliminated nodes increases since we have $f^*/(1 + (\alpha/100)) < f^*$. We can obtain an approximate solution with PRE $\leqq \alpha(\%)$ in less computation time, resulting from the search of a smaller number of nodes (subsets) than in the case by the original BAB method. Moreover, generally we can obtain an approximate solution with smaller PRE by calculating the right side of (3.5) after the termination of the EXTBAB method. Specific applications of the EXTBAB method are found after Chapter 9.

If there exists a BAB method which gives f^* near f_0 in a short time, the PRE calculated by (3.5) is sometimes rather smaller than α even if a somewhat large value of α, say $\alpha = 20 \sim 40$, was taken beforehand. Also, if the original BAB method gives a first feasible solution with f^* near f_0 then the effect of the EXTBAB method increases.

As an application of the EXTBAB method, we have the sequential EXTBAB method. This method specifies a computation step or computation time T in advance and then the EXTBAB method is applied with a varying value of α which is taken, say, such that $\alpha = 0$ for the first $(1/2)T$, $\alpha = 5$ for the second $(1/2^2)T$, etc., and generally $\alpha = 5(k-1)$ for the kth $(1/2^k)T$. Since $\sum\limits_{k=1}^{\infty} (1/2^k) = 1$ the process terminates within T and the value of α at the termination gives an upper bound of PRE of a determined approximate solution.

The following theorem holds concerning the EXTBAB method.

THEOREM 4. *An optimal solution can be determined by the following steps in applying the EXTBAB method:*
1. *Obtain first a feasible solution under $\alpha = 0$.*
2. *Obtain a better feasible solution under positive $\alpha\,(\alpha = 10, 20$ or larger).*
3. *Terminate under $\alpha = 0$.*

Proof. The conclusion follows since no node with LB less than f of a second feasible solution obtained at step 2 is eliminated.

3.11. Backtrack Programming and Lexicographical Search Method

Backtrack programming uses the procedures that search each node in a definite order as shown in Fig. 3.1 in a search tree which is a prototype of a solution tree for the BAB method; we compare the lower bound at each node with the upper bound f^*, eliminate the subtree having the node as its root if LB $\geq f^*$, at this node and then proceed to the next node. Hence, a feasible solution with the last f^* after all nodes were searched is an optimal solution.

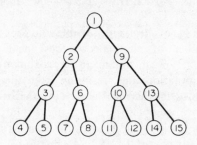

FIG. 3.1. Node search order in search tree by backtrack programming. (Nodes are searched in numerical order.)

Since only the value of each f^* is to be stored, backtrack programming needs smaller storage than the BAB method for which lower bounds of all incompletely searched nodes and the value of f^* are stored. On the contrary much computation time is required for backtrack programming generally. Also, backtrack programming can be recognized as lexicographical search procedure which searches a sequence of subsets according to a prescribed lexicographical order (cf. Sections 9.9 and 9. 14).

By following a procedure similar to the EXTBAB method, we can formulate extended backtrack programming and sequential extended backtrack programming.

Bibliography and Comments

Section 3.3
   For simulation research by priority rules in 1950s, see
R. L. SISSON, "Methods of sequencing in job shops—a review", *Opns. Res.* **7**, No. 1 (1959), 10–29.
   For the early analytic results, see
S. M. JOHNSON, "Optimal two- and three-stage production schedules with setup times included".
   Nav. Res. Log. Quart. **1**, No. 1 (1954), 61–68; Chap. 2, *Industrial Scheduling*, J. F. MUTH and
   G. L. THOMPSON (eds.), Prentice-Hall, 1963.
R. BELLMAN and S. DREYFUS, *Applied Dynamic Programming*, Princeton Univ. Press, 1962,
   Chapter 3, Sections 42–47.
   Branch and bound methods for the three-machine case are found in the following papers:
Z. A. LOMNICKI, "A branch-and-bound algorithm for the exact solution of the three machine
   scheduling problem", *Opnl. Res. Quart.* **16**, No. 1 (1965), 89–100.

E. IGNALL and L. SCHRAGE, "Applications of the branch and bound technique to some flow-shop scheduling problems", *Opns. Res.* **13**, No. 3 (1965), 400–412.
For S.E.P. method see, for example,
B. ROY and B. SUSSMAN, "Les problemes d'ordonnancement avec constrainte disjunctives", *SEMA*, Note, D.S. No. 9, 1964.

Section 3.6
For mutual relation between multiproject scheduling problem with resource constraints and general sequencing problem, see

E. BALAS, "Project scheduling with resource constraints", *Applications of Mathematical Programming Techniques*, E. M. L. BEALE (ed), The English Univ. Press, 1970, 187–200.
The solution method for the assembly-line balancing problem was applied to the single project scheduling problem with single resource constraint in the paper:
E. W. DAVIS and G. E. HEIDORN, "An algorithm for optimal project scheduling under multiple resource constraints", *Mgt. Sci.* **17**, No. 12 (1971), B.803–B.816.

Section 3.7
Several topics in combinatorial optimization techniques are found in, say,
A. J. SCOTT, *Combinatorial Programming, Spatial Analysis and Planning*, Methuen, 1971.
N. CHRISTOFIDES, A. MINGOZZI, P. TOTH and C. SANDI (eds.), *Combinatorial Optimization*, Wiley, 1979.
E. HOROWITZ and S. SAHNI, *Fundamentals of Computer Algorithms*, Computer Science Press, 1978.

Section 3.8
The state transformation process has been presented in
I. NABESHIMA, "Dynamic programming and state transformation process in Discrete optimization problems", *Part I, Rep. Univ. Elect-Comm.* **23**, (1967), 61–68.
I. NABESHIMA, *Dynamic Programming* (in Japanese), Math. Library 7, Morikita Shuppan, 1968, Chapter 8.

Section 3.9
Detailed explanations of the branch-and-bound method are found in
N. AGIN, "Optimum seeking with branch and bound", *Mgt. Sci.* **13**, No. 4 (1966), B.176–B.185.
E. L. LAWLER and D. E. WOOD, "Branch-and-bound methods: A survey", *Opns. Res.* **14**, No. 4 (1966), 679–719.
E. BALAS, "A note on the branch-and-bound principle", *Opns. Res.* **16**, No. 2 (1968), 442–445.
L. G. MITTEN, "Branch-and-bound methods: General formulation and properties", *Opns. Res.* **18**, No. 1 (1970), 24–34.
See also
L. G. MITTEN, Errata, *Opns. Res.* **19** (1971), 550.
A. H. G. RINNOOY KAN, "On Mitten's axioms for branch-and-bound", *Opns. Res.* **24**, No. 6 (1976), 1176–1178.
T. IBARAKI, "Theoretical comparisons of search strategies in branch-and-bound algorithms", *Int. J. Computer Inf. Sci.* **5** (1976), 315–344.
T. IBARAKI, "Computational efficiency of approximate branch-and-bound algorithms, *Math. of Opns. Res.* **1**, No. 3 (1976), 287–298.
T. IBARAKI, "The power of dominance relations in branch-and-bound algorithms", *J. Ass. Comp. Mach.* **24**, No. 2 (1977), 264–279.

Section 3.10
An extended branch and bound method approach was given in
I. NABESHIMA, "A backtrack programming algorithm and reliable heuristic programs for general scheduling problem", *Rep. Univ. Elect.-Comm.* **24**, No. 1 (1973), 23–36.
I. NABESHIMA, "Extended branch and bound algorithm and its application to biobjective problem", *Rep. Univ. Elect.-Comm.* **28**, No. 1 (1977), 67–74.
A similar technique is found in

W. H. KOHLER and K. STEIGLITS, "Exact, approximate, and guaranteed accuracy algorithms for the flow shop problem $n/2/F/\bar{F}$", *J. ACM.* **22**, No. 1 (1975), 106–114.

E. G. COFFMAN, Jr. (ed.), *Computer and Job-Shop Scheduling Theory*, John Wiley, New York, 1976, Chapter 6, Section 6.4.8.

For ε-approximate algorithm as a general technique, see the following paper and the papers cited in its reference:

A. SAHNI, "General techniques for combinatorial approximation", *Opns. Res.* **25**, No. 6 (1977), 920–936.

Related papers and books are

M. R. GAREY, R. L. GRAHAM and D. S. JOHNSON, "Performance guarantees for scheduling algorithms", *Opns. Res.* **26**, No. 1 (1978), 3–21.

T. GONZALEZ and S. SAHNI, "Flowshop and jobshop schedules: complexity and approximation", *Opns. Res.* **26**, No. 1 (1978), 36–52.

P. BRUCKER, "NP-complete operations research problems and approximation algorithms", *Zeitsch. Für Oper. Res.* **23** (1979), 73–94.

M. R. GAREY and D. S. JOHNSON, *Computers and Intractability: A Guide to the Theory of NP-Completeness*, Freeman, 1979, Chapter 6.

E. HOROWITZ and S. SAHNI, *Fundamentals of Computer Algorithms*, Computer Science Press, 1978, Chapter 12.

Section 3.11

For backtrack programming see, for example,

I. NABESHIMA, "A backtrack programming algorithm and reliable heuristic programs for general scheduling problem", *Rep. Univ. Elect-Comm.* **24**, No. 1 (1973), 23–36.

S. W. GOLOMB and L. D. BAUMERT, "Backtrack programming", *J. ACM.* **12**, No. 4 (1965), 516–524.

A. J. SCOTT, *Combinatorial Programming, Spatial Analysis and Planning*, Methuen & Co. Ltd., London, 1971.

CHAPTER 4

The Nature of the Sequencing Problem

4.1. Introduction

The sequencing problem, that is, the job-shop scheduling problem, is stated as a model in the manufacturing industry. It relates to the following scheduling problems and their variations:

1. Schedule of motorcars (jobs) for the equipment (machines) in a repair shop.
2. Schedule of classes (jobs) for the lecture rooms (machines) in a school.
3. Schedule of patients (jobs) to be examined (machines).
4. Schedule of ships (jobs) to be anchored (machines) in a harbor.
5. Schedule of programs (jobs) for the processors (machines) of a computer.

When the machine order to process each job for n jobs and m machines M_q, $q = 1, 2, \ldots, m$ and the processing time of each job on each machine are known, if it is necessary to schedule all jobs on all machines, that is, to decide the starting time of the processing of each job on each machine, in order to optimize, given the objective function, then a sequencing problem occurs.

Let any job be processed on each of m machines only once, then the order of machines $M_{q\gamma}, \gamma = 1, 2, \ldots, m$, to process each job i is called the ordering for job i and is represented by $T_i = (iq_1, iq_2, \ldots, iq_m)$ and an ordering matrix is defined as an $n \times m$ matrix with T_i as its ith row.

The case where ordering for all jobs is identical is called the flow-shop scheduling problem.

The time to process each job i on each machine M_q is called the processing time of job i on machine M_q and is expressed by $p_{i,q}$. A sequence of processing times $P_i = (p_{i,1}, p_{i,2}, \ldots, p_{i,m})$ corresponds to each job i and a processing time matrix is defined as an $n \times m$ matrix with P_i as its ith row.

Processing of job i on machine M_q is called an operation and is expressed by operation iq.

Hence, the sequencing problem is a problem which decides the order of all jobs on each machine and determines the starting time of each operation in order to optimize an objective function with a given ordering matrix and processing time matrix for n jobs and m machines. The order of all jobs on machine M_q is called job ordering on machine M_q and expressed S_q. A job-

61

ordering matrix is defined as an $m \times n$ matrix with S_q as its qth row. Sometimes a set of job orderings on all machines is called a sequence.

In the flow-shop scheduling problem, if the job ordering is the same on any machine, we say that no passing is allowed since any job is not allowed to pass any former job.

On the contrary, if it is allowed that the job ordering on each machine may be different, then the case where passing is allowed occurs. The flow-shop scheduling problem where no passing is allowed is sometimes called the permutation flow-shop problem.

The scheduling problem with one machine is called the single-machine scheduling problem and it can be easily analyzed contrary to the problems with many machines. The traveling-salesman problem can be transformed to a single-machine problem (cf. Chapter 1).

By classifying the sequencing problem according to the number of machines, ordering and job ordering becomes as in Fig. 4.1.

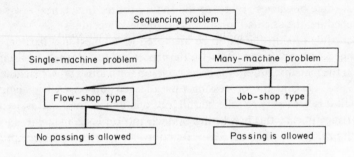

FIG. 4.1. Classification of sequencing problem.

The other macro classifications are shown below:

1. *Static and dynamic.* Static means that as described in the above scheduling problem, the processing of any job in n jobs is ready to be done. On the other hand, dynamic means the scheduling problem where jobs are done one by one as in the queuing problem. Analytical results and algorithms to determine an optimal schedule are limited to the static case and in the dynamic case we can apply the techniques for the static case provided the arrival time of each job is known, but otherwise results by simulation are now obtained by applying, say, the technique in the queuing problem.

There exist many static cases in practice and experience for the static problem leads to understanding and insight into the dynamic problem. Since it is necessary to decide the order of jobs at the carrying stage, even in the case where jobs are assigned to each period, as in period planning, the static sequencing problem plays an important role.

Also, the solution methods for the static sequencing problems help our understanding of the techniques in combinatorial programming. The sequencing problem in this book is limited to the static case.

2. *Deterministic and stochastic.* The deterministic case is the case where all elements of the problem such as the state of the arrival of the jobs in the shop, due-dates of jobs, ordering, processing times and availability of machines and so on do not include stochastic factors and so are determined beforehand. The stochastic case refers to the case where at least one of those elements includes stochastic factors. Almost all results for sequencing problems are obtained for the deterministic case. On the contrary, results in the stochastic case are limited to simple cases such as a single-machine scheduling problem with independent distributions of processing times and/or due-dates and two-machine flow-shop problems with independent exponential distributions of processing times, and so on.

This book considers deterministic cases only.

4.2. Assumption and Objective Functions

Usual assumptions for jobs, machines and processing times in (static) job-shop scheduling problems are the following:

1. *Assumptions on jobs*
   1.1. All n job-sets can be available in the beginning.
   1.2. No processing of any operation can be done by more than one machine.
   1.3. Any operation starting to be processed is not interrupted by the other operations and is continued to its completion.
   1.4. Each job is processed according to a given serial ordering.
   1.5. There exist no priority orders within jobs and each job has the same degree of importance.
   1.6. Each operation can wait its processing if the former operation continues its processing. That is, inventory in process or intermediate waiting time is allowed.
   1.7. A definite due-date can be assigned to each job.
   1.8. Each job can be processed by each machine only once.
   Generally, each job may be processed by a part of a machine-set and may be processed by the same machine more than once.

2. *Assumptions on machines*
   2.1. All m machines can be available at the outset. Breakdown or repair of any machine does not occur during the planning period.
      Any machine can process any job.

    2.2. There exists one machine of each type and machines are independent of each other.

    2.3. Each machine can process at most one operation at the same time.

3. *Assumptions on processing times*

    3.1. Processing time of each operation is given at the outset and is constant regardless of its order of processing.

    3.2. If not mentioned otherwise, processing time includes set-up times, that is, transportation time of related jobs between machines and arrangement time to process related jobs.

By relaxing some of these assumptions, we have job-shop problems of another type. For example, concerning the assumptions on jobs, the case where arrival times of n jobs are known beforehand in assumption 1.1 can be treated as in the usual case. Results are obtained even for the case where start lags and stop lags of the processing by the following machines for the job-lots are prescribed and simultaneous processing by many machines is allowed in assumption 1.2 (cf. Section 8.17). In assumption 1.3, the case where interruptions of the operations are allowed are also treated. In assumption 1.4 the case with ordering of network type, that is, partition and assembling of each job, can be treated in the same way (cf. Section 12.22). Also the case where no inventory in process or no intermediate waiting time of each job exists can be treated (cf. Misc. Exercise 6 in Chapter 10).

Next in assumption 2.2 on machines, the case where many machines of the same kind exist can be treated as a scheduling problem with resource constraints (cf. Section 12.22). In assumption 3.2 on processing times, the case where explicit setup times are considered in addition to the processing time is treated (cf. Sections 10.9 and Chapter 11).

4.3. Objective Function (Measure of Performance)

Let $W_{i,j}$ be the waiting time of job i counting from the completion time of its $(j-1)$th operation to the starting time of its jth operation, then the total waiting time W_i of job i is

$$W_i = \sum_{j=1}^{g_i} W_{i,j}$$

where g_i is the total number of operations of job i. $W_{i,1}$ is a waiting time of the first operation of job i.

Hence, let the completion time C_i of job i be the completion time of its last operation, r_i be the arrival time of job i where usually it is assumed that $r_i = 0$ for any job $i, i = 1, 2, \ldots, n$, $t_{i,j}$ be the processing time of the jth operation of job i, and t_i be the total processing time of job i, then we have

$$C_i = r_i + \sum_{j=1}^{g_i} t_{i,j} + \sum_{j=1}^{g_i} W_{i,j} = r_i + t_i + W_i. \tag{4.1}$$

If we put F_i the flow time of job i, that is, total elapsed time by job i in the shop, then we have

$$F_i = \sum_{j=1}^{g_i} t_{i,j} + \sum_{j=1}^{g_i} W_{i,j} = t_i + W_i = C_i - r_i. \qquad (4.2)$$

Hence, under the simultaneous arrival of all jobs, we have $F_i = C_i$. Next let L_i be the lateness of job i, that is, the algebraic difference of the completion time C_i of job i and due-date d_i of job i, we have

$$L_i = C_i - d_i = F_i - a_i \qquad (4.3)$$

where $a_i = d_i - r_i$ is the allowable time of the job in the shop. Also, let T_i be the tardiness of job i, that is, the difference between completion time and due-date for the delay of job i, then we have

$$T_i = \max(L_i, 0) = \max(C_i - d_i, 0). \qquad (4.4)$$

As objective functions for the sequencing problem, we take the means of the above waiting time, completion time, flow time, lateness and tardiness: $\bar{W}, \bar{C}, \bar{F}, \bar{L}, \bar{T}$, and their maxima: $W_{max}, C_{max}, F_{max}, L_{max}, T_{max}$, and also their weighted means by considering the degree of importance of each job are considered.

Generally, the minimization of the objective function of the completion time, which is called normal objective function, means the minimization of a nondecreasing function $f = f(C_1, C_2, \ldots, C_n)$ of completion times $C_i (i = 1, 2, \ldots, n)$ of n jobs and thus it includes all objective functions defined above. In particular, the maximum of the completion times, $C_{max} = \text{Max}(C_1, C_2, \ldots, C_n)$, is called total elapsed time or makespan. Although almost all papers select makespan as their objective functions, optimal schedules for one objective function are not necessarily optimal for the other objective functions.

EXAMPLE 1. In the flow-shop problem with three jobs $(i = 1, 2, 3)$, two machines (M_1, M_2), processing time matrix as shown in the table below:

i	M_1	M_2
1	2	1
2	4	3
3	2	3

and ordering M_1, M_2, an optimal schedule for makespan C_{max} becomes a sequence $321 (C_{max} = 10)$ by the Johnson criterion (cf. Section 7.11) where mean completion time $\bar{C}$ of this sequence is $(5 + 9 + 10)/3 = 8$. However, the $\bar{C}$ of a sequence 132 is $(3 + 7 + 11)/3 = 7$ and so the sequence 321 is not optimal for the objective function $\bar{C}$.

However, there exists a class of objective functions leading to the same optimal schedules. That is to say the following theorem holds.

THEOREM 1. *In the sequencing problem, a schedule which is optimal for any one of the objective functions: mean waiting time $\bar{W}$, mean completion time $\bar{C}$, mean flow time $\bar{F}$ and mean lateness $\bar{L}$ is also optimal for the other objective functions.*

Proof. From (4.1) we have

$$\bar{C} = \sum_{i=1}^{n} r_i/n + \sum_{i=1}^{n} t_i/n + \bar{W} \equiv \bar{r} + \bar{t} + \bar{W}$$

where the first two terms on the right hand are constant. Hence, $\bar{C}$ and $\bar{W}$ have the same optimal schedules. Also from (4.2) and (4.3) we have

$$\bar{C} = \bar{F} + \bar{r} = \bar{L} + \bar{d}$$

where $\bar{r}$ and $\bar{d}$ are constant. Hence, $\bar{C}$, $\bar{F}$ and $\bar{L}$ have the same optimal schedules.

4.4. Objective Functions of the other Type

The above objective function for completion time relates to every job. In practical problems sometimes it may be useful to consider the maximization of facility utilization or the minimization of work-in-process inventory as an objective function for the whole shop.

Facility utilization is defined to be the ratio of the time which is used for processing by machines and available time of all machines which is assumed to be the length of the interval from the arrival time of the first job: $\min_i r_i$, to the completion time of the last job: C_{max}. Usually, since simultaneous arrivals of all jobs, that is, all $r_i = 0$ are assumed and the above length of interval is $F_{max} = C_{max}$. Hence, in this case, facility utilization and mean utilization are represented respectively by

$$U = \sum_{i=1}^{n} t_i/F_{max}, \quad \bar{U} = \sum_{i=1}^{n} t_i/(mF_{max})$$

and so they are inversely proportional to the maximum flow time, that is, makespan. In this case, minimization of the makespan is equivalent to maximization of the facility utilization. However, it must be remarked that if explicit setup times exist and vary by depending on the following job then the value of the numerator of utilization changes.

Next, there exist two types in the definition of work-in-process inventory. One defines it as the amount of work in the shop. Namely, we put $N(t) = N_p(t) + N_q(t)$ as the amount of work in the shop at time t where $N_p(t)$, $N_q(t)$ are the number of jobs in process, and the number of jobs waiting for processing respectively. Also, by putting

$$\bar{N}(t_1, t_2) = \int_{t_2}^{t_2} N(t)dt/(t_2 - t_1)$$

as the mean number of jobs in the shop during the time interval from t_1 to t_2. The next theorem holds from the assumption of simultaneous arrival.

THEOREM 2. *In the sequencing problem, the ratio of mean number of jobs to maximum number n of jobs in the shop is equal to the ratio of mean flow time or mean completion time to maximum flow time or makespan. Also, in a fixed schedule interval, the mean number of jobs in the shop is proportional to mean flow time or mean completion time.*

Proof. The mean number of jobs in the shop is $\bar{N}(0, F_n)$ where $F_n = F_{max}$. As easily seen from Fig. 4.2, since

$$\bar{N}(0, F_{max}) = \{nF_1 + (n-1)(F_2 - F_1) + (n-2)(F_3 - F_2) + \cdots + (n - (n-1))(F_n - F_{n-1})\}/F_{max}$$

$$= \sum_{i=1}^{n} F_i / F_{max}.$$

We have $\qquad \dfrac{\bar{N}(0, F_{max})}{n} = \dfrac{\bar{F}}{F_{max}} \qquad$ from $\displaystyle\sum_{i=1}^{n} F_i / n = \bar{F}$

and then the conclusion follows.

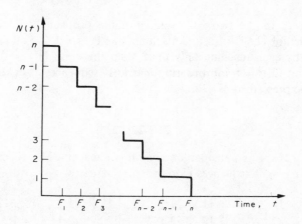

FIG. 4.2. Graphs of number of jobs.

Next another definition of the work-in-process inventory is to consider work content as the sum of the processing times of all operations of all jobs.

By partitioning it into the sum of (a) operations already completed, (b) operations now in process, (c) operations not yet started, the mean of (a) is used in the case where work-in-process inventory is estimated by money and the mean of (c) shows actual work backlog.

Finally, in the case where cost is taken as an objective function, we can consider operating cost, machine-idle cost, in process inventory cost, penalty cost in the case where there are job delays over its due-date and so on. However, since it may be difficult to solve the problem with the cost objective which is not a nondecreasing function of the completion times of all jobs, if not otherwise mentioned, any objective function is defined to be a normal objective function described in Section 4.3.

4.5. Classification of Sequences and Non-numerical Judgement

When ordering of each job and processing time of each operation are prescribed in the sequencing problem, determination of job ordering on each machine yields a schedule. Such a schedule may be feasible or infeasible.

We want to obtain a feasible schedule. To simplify the problem, in the case where each job is processed by each machine only once there are $(m!)^n$ combinations of possible orderings of n jobs and $(n!)^m$ sequences, that is, $(n!)^m$ combinations of possible job orderings on m machines.

A classification of a sequence which is independent of the value of processing times is the following:

A feasible sequence is a sequence where a precedence relation of operations is compatible with a precedence relation of operations by the given ordering.

EXAMPLE 2. In the two-jobs, three-machine problem (2×3 sequencing problem), let jobs be $i = 1, 2$ and machines be M_q, $q = 1, 2, 3$ and each job be processed by each machine only once, then there are $(3!)^2 = 36$ ordering matrices and $(2!)^3 = 8$ job ordering matrices (sequences). Let the ordering matrix T be prescribed as

$$T = \begin{bmatrix} 12 & 13 & 11 \\ 21 & 22 & 23 \end{bmatrix}$$

where, say, 12 expresses an operation of job 1 on machine M_2. We can consider the following eight sequences (job ordering matrices):

$$S_1 = \begin{bmatrix} 11 & 21 \\ 12 & 22 \\ 13 & 23 \end{bmatrix}, \quad S_2 = \begin{bmatrix} 11 & 21 \\ 12 & 22 \\ 23 & 13 \end{bmatrix}, \quad S_3 = \begin{bmatrix} 11 & 21 \\ 22 & 12 \\ 13 & 23 \end{bmatrix}, \quad S_4 = \begin{bmatrix} 11 & 21 \\ 22 & 12 \\ 23 & 13 \end{bmatrix},$$

$$S_5 = \begin{bmatrix} 21 & 11 \\ 12 & 22 \\ 13 & 23 \end{bmatrix}, \quad S_6 = \begin{bmatrix} 21 & 11 \\ 12 & 22 \\ 23 & 13 \end{bmatrix}, \quad S_7 = \begin{bmatrix} 21 & 11 \\ 22 & 12 \\ 13 & 23 \end{bmatrix}, \quad S_8 = \begin{bmatrix} 21 & 11 \\ 22 & 12 \\ 23 & 13 \end{bmatrix}.$$

If we place six operations in two rows along the jobs by following the precedence relation decided by T, we have the graph in Fig. 4.3.

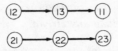

FIG. 4.3. Graph by T.

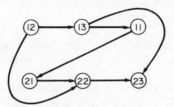

FIG. 4.4. Graph by T and S_1.

If we select a sequence S_1, a graph depicted in Fig. 4.4 which is decided by the ordering matrix T and a sequence S_1 shows that precedence relations of operations determined by them are compatible with each other. Namely, we have $12 < 13 < 11, 21 < 22 < 23$ by ordering where, say, $12 < 13$ means that an operation 12 precedes an operation 13 and by adding the precedence relation decided by the sequence S_1 finally we have $11 < 21 < 22 < 23$, $12 < 22 < 23$, $12 < 13 < 23$ which shows no contradiction. Hence, the sequence S_1 is a feasible sequence.

Next, if we select a sequence S_2, a graph depicted in Fig. 4.5 is constructed. In this case we have $11 < 21 < 22 < 23$, $12 < 22 < 23$, $23 < 13 < 11$ and so we have $11 < 23$, $23 < 11$ simultaneously, that is, there exists, in a graph in Fig. 4.5, a circuit $11 \to 21 \to 22 \to 23 \to 13 \to 11$, which is a contradiction. Hence, the sequence S_2 is an infeasible sequence. In the same way, we can conclude that the sequences S_1, S_5, S_6, S_7, S_8 are feasible sequences and S_2, S_3, S_4 are infeasible sequences.

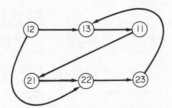

FIG. 4.5. Graph by T and S_2.

4.6. Judgement for Determination

The following theorems hold:

THEOREM 3. *In the general sequencing problem any sequence is a feasible sequence if and only if a directed graph constructed by the prescribed orderings and a sequence does not include any circuit.*

Proof. If there exists a circuit, any two operations have two precedence relations oppositely directed and so they are not practicable. Also, if no circuit exists all operations can be carried out by following the precedence relation on the graph under any processing times.

THEOREM 4. *In the flow-shop scheduling problem any sequence is a feasible sequence.*

Proof. Since orderings of all jobs are identical only vertically directed precedence relations by sequence exists in the graph and no circuit occurs.

There are three types of procedures resulting from Theorem 3 for judging the feasibility from a direct precedence relation table as shown in the following:

DETERMINATION OF FEASIBILITY I (PROCEDURE TO ELIMINATE
THE OPERATIONS NOT ON CIRCUIT)

1. Make a direct precedence relation table like Fig. 4.6. Its (a, b) element becomes 1 only when an operation a on the left side directly precedes an operation b on the right side.

2. Since any operation on the row with no 1 does not directly precede the other operation and so is not on any circuit. Also any operation on the column with no 1 is not on any circuit. Eliminate the operations on these rows and columns.

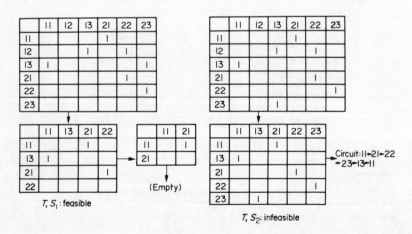

FIG. 4.6. Judgement of Feasibility I.

3. Repeat step 2 for the reduced table.

4. If all operations on all rows and columns are eliminated, the sequence is feasible. Otherwise the last reduced table gives a circuit and so the sequence is infeasible.

Example of the sequences S_1, S_2 in Example 2 is shown in Fig. 4.6.

DETERMINATION OF FEASIBILITY II (THE DEPENDENCE TREE OF ALL OPERATIONS)

Although this technique is similar to the method indicated in Example 2, it constructs a dependence tree which shows precedence relations determined by orderings T and a sequence S. Starting from node 0, next follow the operations that have no preceding operations under T and S or, if such operations do not exist, the first operations of every job. After this, operations directly following the operations already placed by following T and S are connected with the latter.

If the tree terminates, then this sequence S is feasible. On the contrary, if operations are continued forever then the same operation occurs on a certain path and the same sequence of operations is repeated which shows the existence of a circuit. Then the sequence S is infeasible.

The dependence trees for the sequences S_1, S_2, S_3 in Example 2 become as shown in Fig. 4.7.

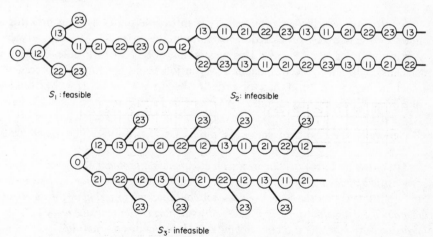

S_1 : feasible S_2: infeasible

S_3: infeasible

FIG. 4.7. Dependence tree.

DETERMINATION OF FEASIBILITY III (BOOLEAN ALGEBRA)

We explain this method for the two-job three-machine case in Example 2. Let the notation q or number 1 mean that in a certain sequence job 1 precedes job 2 on machine M_q and notation $\bar{q}$ or 0 means that job 2 precedes job 1 on machine M_q where the two jobs are numbered 1 and 2 and three machines are M_1, M_2, M_3. Then eight sequences $S_1, S_2, \ldots, S_8$ are expressed as in Table 4.1 or Table 4.2.

TABLE 4.1

Sequence		S_1	S_2	S_3	S_4	S_5	S_6	S_7	S_8
	1	1	1	1	1	$\bar{1}$	$\bar{1}$	$\bar{1}$	$\bar{1}$
Machine	2	2	2	$\bar{2}$	$\bar{2}$	2	2	$\bar{2}$	$\bar{2}$
	3	3	$\bar{3}$	3	$\bar{3}$	3	$\bar{3}$	3	$\bar{3}$

TABLE 4.2

Sequence		S_1	S_2	S_3	S_4	S_5	S_6	S_7	S_8
	1	1	1	1	1	0	0	0	0
Machine	2	1	1	0	0	1	1	0	0
	3	1	0	1	0	1	0	1	0

As already described, a sequence S_2 is infeasible under a given ordering matrix T when job 1 is processed by machines in the order M_2, M_3, M_1 and job 2 is in the order M_1, M_2, M_3. This means that both $\bar{3}$ and 1 (Table 4.1) hold while machine M_3 precedes machine M_1 in job 1 and machine M_1 precedes machine M_3 in job 2 and then job ordering becomes $13 < 11, 21 < 23$ from T and $23 < 13, 11 < 21$ from $\bar{3}$ and 1 which yields $13 < 11 < 21 < 23 < 13$, that is, $13 < 13$.

Generally, the next theorem holds in the case of two jobs and m machines.

THEOREM 5. *In the two job m machine sequencing problem where each job is processed by each machine, a necessary and sufficient condition for a sequence S to be feasible is that the sequence does not contain a job ordering $\bar{u}v$ for any two machines u, v for which job 1 is processed by machine v after machine u and job 2 is processed by machine u after machine v both in the given orderings.*

Proof. Proof of necessity. If a feasible sequence includes the job ordering $\bar{u}v$ for two machines u, v, we have $2u < 1u, 1v < 2v$. From the assumptions: $1u < 1v, 2v < 2u$ and $\bar{u}v$, we have a precedence relation: $1u < 1v < 2v < 2u < 1u$, that is, $1u < 1u$ which is a contradiction. Hence any feasible sequence does not include such $\bar{u}v$.

Proof of sufficiency. Similarly a contradictory proposition which states that infeasible sequence S includes $\bar{u}v$ for some two machines u, v is proved. Since S is infeasible there exist operations $1u, 2v$ that cannot be executed first in respective orderings of jobs 1, 2 because execution of all operations of any one job yields that of another job. This case for $1u$ occurs only when operation $2u$ follows operation $2v$ since otherwise $2u$ is executed and then $1u$ can be executed and also S includes $\bar{u}$ since otherwise $1u$ can be executed. Similarly, that case for $2v$ occurs only when operation $1v$ follows operation $1u$ and S includes v. Hence, the conclusion follows.

This theorem is applied to the above Example 2 as shown below.

By asking for the orders, within two machines: M_2M_3, M_2M_1 and M_3M_1 in ordering of job 1, that are in the reverse order in ordering of job 2, we have M_2M_1 and M_3M_1, since we have M_1M_2 and M_1M_3 respectively in the ordering of job 2. Hence, only the sequences with job orderings $\bar{2}\cdot 1$ and/or $\bar{3}\cdot 1$ are infeasible by Theorem 5. By excluding them we have feasible sequences S_1, S_5, S_6, S_7, S_8.

As shown in Table 4.3, let the sequence which does not include each of $\bar{2}\cdot 1$, $\bar{3}\cdot 1$, that is, without $\bar{2}\cdot 1$ and without $\bar{3}\cdot 1$ be 1, respectively, and the other sequence be 0, then the sequences with logical product 1, 0 become feasible sequences, infeasible sequence respectively.

Without proof the following generalization of Theorem 5 to the n job case will be described.

TABLE 4.3

Sequence	S_1	S_2	S_3	S_4	S_5	S_6	S_7	S_8
Without $\bar{2}.1$	1	1	0	0	1	1	1	1
Without $\bar{3}.1$	1	0	1	0	1	1	1	1
Logical product	1	0	0	0	1	1	1	1

THEOREM 6. *In the n job m machine sequencing problem where machines are expressed by letters $a, b, c, \ldots, z$ and each job is processed by each machine only once, a necessary and sufficient condition for a sequence to be feasible is that the sequence does not contain a job ordering l: $A(2 < 1)B(3 < 2)C(4 < 3) \ldots Y(\alpha < \alpha - 1)Z(1 < \alpha)$, where, say, $A(2 < 1)$ means that job (2) is processed before job (1) on machine a, for any loop existing in orderings of α jobs $(2 \leq \alpha \leq n)$:*

$$
\begin{array}{lll}
(1) \text{ --------------} & a_1 & \text{----------------} \quad z_1 \quad \text{-----------------} \\
(2) \text{ --------------} & b_2 & \text{----------------} \quad a_2 \quad \text{-----------------} \\
(3) \text{ --------------} & c_3 & \text{----------------} \quad b_3 \quad \text{-----------------} \\
\end{array}
$$

$$
\begin{array}{lll}
(\alpha - 1) \text{ -----------} & y_{\alpha - 1} & \text{--------------} \quad x_{\alpha - 1} \quad \text{--------------} \\
(\alpha) \text{ -----------} & z_\alpha & \text{----------------} \quad y_\alpha \quad \text{-------------------}
\end{array}
$$

where, say, a_1 means an operation of job (1) on machine a.

Remark. In the case of two jobs ($\alpha = 2$), we have $y = a$ and then the loop shows that machine a precedes machine z in the ordering of job 1 and its reversed order holds for job 2 and the condition becomes $\bar{a}z$. Hence, Theorem 6 coincides with Theorem 5 for two jobs.

4.7. Generation of Feasible Sequences

We explain the procedure to generate a feasible sequence under given orderings by using Example 2.

Since orderings in Example 2 are M_2, M_3, M_1 for job 1 and M_1, M_2, M_3 for job 2, the set of operations that can be processed at the first stage is $\{12, 21\}$ and one of these operations is processed. After processing of, say, operation 12, the set of operations to be processed at the second stage is $\{21, 13\}$ which includes an operation 13 which follows 12 directly, instead of 12. In the same way, we can obtain a feasible sequence.

4.8. Potentially Optimal Sequence and Nonoptimal Sequence

The fact whether a sequence is feasible or infeasible is determined according to whether a graph determined by this sequence and orderings contains no circuit or circuit respectively and does not depend upon the normal objective functions. We divide the set of feasible sequences into the following two subsets.

A potentially optimal sequence is a feasible sequence which can be an optimal sequence for a certain processing timetable. And the set of such sequences contains an optimal sequence for any processing timetable.

On the contrary, a nonoptimal sequence is a feasible sequence which cannot be an optimal sequence for any processing timetable.

In the next section, we examine the determination of these sequences for the two-job problem with makespan as its objective function.

4.9. Determination of Potentially Optimal Sequences and Nonoptimal Sequences

The Gant chart of a feasible sequence S_1 of the two job three machine problem with ordering $M_2 M_3 M_1$ for job 1 and $M_1 M_2 M_3$ for job 2 in Example 2 is shown in Fig. 4.8 by selecting processing times suitably.

Since obviously S_1 starts the processing of job 2 after the processing of job 1, S_1 cannot be optimal under any processing timetable. For example, a feasible sequence S_5 finishes sooner than S_1 (cf. Fig. 4.9). If we compare S_1 with S_5, in S_1 two operations, 11, 21, are continuously processed on machine M_1 and, moreover, the other machines are idle during the interval of this processing. Hence, an operation which is processed immediately after this interval is an

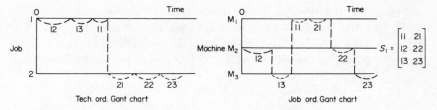

FIG. 4.8. Gant chart of feasible sequence S_1.

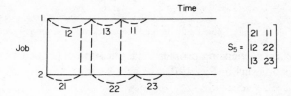

FIG. 4.9. Gant chart of S_5.

operation of job 2 on another machine which follows the operation 21, for example an operation 22 for S_1. If we transfer to S_5 with inverted job ordering on machine M_1, then the operation 22 finishes sooner and then S_5 finishes sooner than S_1.

Like machine M_1 in the above case, if there exists a machine which processes continuously two operations during a certain interval where all other machines are idle, this machine is called a free machine.

The next theorem shows that only the feasible sequence which does not cause any free machine is a potentially optimal sequence.

THEOREM 7. *In the min-makespan problem with two jobs and m machines a necessary and sufficient condition for a feasible sequence S to be a potentially optimal sequence is that this sequence does not cause any free machine.*

A necessary and sufficient condition is also given by the next theorem.

THEOREM 8. *In the same problem as in Theorem 7, a necessary and sufficient condition is that if for each machine M_v there exist in the ordering,*

(a) *Machines M_u, M_w such that* $\dfrac{\text{---}1u\ 1v\text{-----}1w\text{-----}}{\text{---}2u\text{------}2v2w\text{-----}}$, *then a feasible sequence S does not contain uvw. Here when $1v$ is the first operation, M_u is excluded and when $2v$ is the last operation, M_w is excluded.*

(b) *Machines M_u, M_w such that* $\dfrac{\text{----}1u\text{------}1v\ 1w\text{----}}{\text{----}2u\ 2v\text{------}2w\text{----}}$, *a feasible sequence S does not contain $\bar{u}v\bar{w}$. Here when $2v$ is the first operation, M_u is excluded and when $1v$ is the last operation, M_w is excluded.*

EXAMPLE 3. If we apply the rules of Theorem 8 to the feasible sequences S_1, S_5, S_6, S_7, S_8 in the simple Example 2, in which we consider three cases where (b) $v = 1$, (a) $v = 2, w = 3$ and (a) $u = 2, v = 3$, then we find that S_5 and S_8 are potentially optimal sequences and S_1, S_6 and S_7 are nonoptimal sequences.

Exercise

1. In the min-makespan problem with two jobs and three machines and ordering matrix:

$$T = \begin{bmatrix} 11 & 13 & 12 \\ 23 & 21 & 22 \end{bmatrix}$$

determine feasible sequences, potentially optimal sequences and nonoptimal sequences.

In the general sequencing problem, classification of sequences under given orderings becomes as in Fig. 4.10.

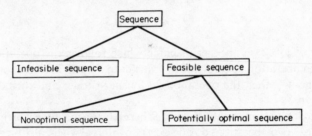

FIG. 4.10. Classification of the sequences under given orderings.

4.10. Classification and Generation of Schedules

Since a sequence is an allocation of all jobs on all machines under given orderings alone without taking into account processing times, the sequence gives no information of the processing periods of each operation and idle time of each machine. A schedule is defined as a feasible sequence in which start and finish times of every operation are determined. Here, it must be remarked that in a scheduling problem with given precedence relation such as the general project scheduling problem, the problem is to decide the start and finish times of each activity directly. There exist both feasible schedules and infeasible schedules, which is contrary to the fact that any schedule is feasible in a sequencing problem as defined above.

Any schedule in the sequencing problem means a feasible schedule and the Gant chart of its sequence classified by machine is used as its graphical representation. Once a feasible sequence is determined, it may happen that the idle times of machines between the processings of consecutive operations and, moreover, successive enlargements of these idle times yield another feasible schedule. Hence, infinitely many schedules result from each feasible sequence.

However, since we take into consideration only normal objective functions, it is desirable that we should obtain a schedule which processes each operation as soon as possible.

Thus schedules are classified in the way shown in Fig. 4.11.

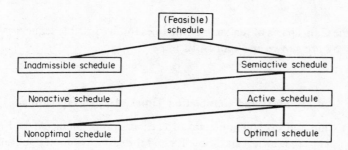

FIG. 4.11. Classification of schedules.

4.11. Semiactive Schedule and Inadmissible Schedule

A schedule which is constructed by processing a feasible sequence as quickly as possible and satisfying the given orderings is called a semiactive schedule and the other schedules constructed by that feasible sequence are called inadmissible schedules.

We can obtain a corresponding semiactive schedule by shifting each operation of any inadmissible schedule to the left as far as possible for a given ordering and sequence. In order to minimize any normal objective function it is sufficient to consider only the set of semiactive schedules.

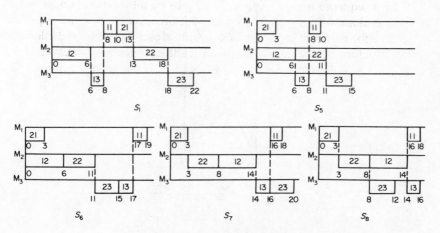

FIG. 4.12. Semiactive schedules of Example 4.

EXAMPLE 4. For the ordering matrix T in Example 2 (2×3 problem), let the processing time matrix P be

$$P = \begin{bmatrix} p_{11} & p_{12} & p_{13} \\ p_{21} & p_{22} & p_{23} \end{bmatrix} = \begin{bmatrix} 2 & 6 & 2 \\ 3 & 5 & 4 \end{bmatrix} \text{ where } T = \begin{bmatrix} 12 & 13 & 11 \\ 21 & 22 & 23 \end{bmatrix}$$

Then the Gant charts of semiactive schedules for five feasible sequences S_1, S_5, S_6, S_7, S_8 are shown in Figure 4.12.

4.12. Start and Completion Times of Each Operation

Start time and completion time of each operation depicted in Fig. 4.12 correspond to the earliest start time ES and the earliest completion (finishing) time EF respectively of the corresponding node, that are obtained by critical path calculations in a directed flow graph G defined as below. The graph G has precedence relation of operations which is determined by related feasible sequence and by ordering and its nodes consist of each node which shows each operation and a dummy source node 0 which has directed arcs with length 0 to the nodes denoting the first operations of every job and a dummy sink node E which accepts directed arcs from the nodes denoting the last operations of every job (cf. Fig. 4.13).

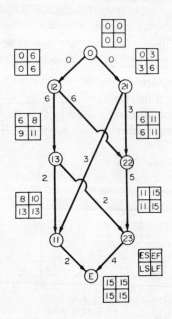

FIG. 4.13. Flow graph G for a feasible sequence S_5.

Generally, an earliest start time ES_i of an operation i is defined by

$$ES_0 = 0, \quad ES_i = \max_{(j,i) \in A} (ES_j + P_{(j)}) \tag{4.5}$$

where A is the set of all directed arcs and $P_{(j)}$ is the processing time of an operation j. ES_i can be successively calculated by the above relation starting from the source node 0. Also an earliest completion time EF_i of operation i is determined by $EF_i = ES_i + P_{(i)}$. Then $ES_E \equiv EF_E = \lambda$ at the sink node E shows the makespan of this schedule.

As in the PERT or critical path method, we can have a latest start time LS_i of operation i at which the operation i must start at latest in order to complete the schedule at λ and also a latest completion (finishing) time LF_i at which the operation i must complete at latest under schedule completion time λ. These are calculated by proceeding backward from the sink node E and time λ. That is, each latest start time can be calculated successively by

$$LS_E \equiv ES_E = \lambda, \quad LS_i = \min_{(i,j) \in A} (LS_j - P_{(i)}) \tag{4.6}$$

and each latest completion time can be obtained by

$$LF_i = LS_i + P_{(i)}. \tag{4.7}$$

Figure 4.13 shows ES_i, EF_i, LS_i, LF_i of each operation i in schedule S_5.

Among the paths that start at the source node 0 and end at the sink node E, a path on which relation $ES_i = LS_i$, or equivalently $EF_i = LF_i$, holds for every node i is a critical path and any operation on the critical path is a critical operation which cannot be delayed in order to complete the schedule at time λ. Thus it is an important operation for management purposes. A critical path in Fig. 4.13 is a path $o \longrightarrow \textcircled{\scriptsize 12} \longrightarrow \textcircled{\scriptsize 22} \longrightarrow \textcircled{\scriptsize 23} \longrightarrow E$.

An operation i for which $LS_i > ES_i$ holds does not delay the schedule completion time λ even if its starting time is delayed $TF_i \equiv LS_i - ES_i = LF_i - EF_i > 0$ time units from its earliest starting time ES_i. This $TF_i \equiv LS_i - ES_i = LF_i - EF_i$ is called the total float of the operation i. In a schedule in Fig. 4.13 total floats of the operations 21, 11, 13 are $3 - 0 = 3$, $13 - 8 = 5$, $9 - 6 = 3$, respectively, and total floats of the critical operations are obviously zero.

In this case, even if the processing of the operation 21 starts at its latest starting time 3 it does not influence the earliest starting times of every successive operation, that is, the earliest starting time 8 of the operation 11, the time 6 of the operation 22 and the time 11 of the operation 23 are not delayed. Therefore, a float of an operation i which can be carried out without any influence on the earliest starting times of every successive operation is called a free float of the operation i and denoted by FF_i. FF_i is calculated by

$$FF_i = \min_{(i,j) \in A} (ES_j - EF_i) \tag{4.8}$$

and $0 \leq FF_i \leq TF_i$ holds by definition.

In a schedule in Fig. 4.13 free floats of the operations 21, 13 and 11 are 3, 0 and 5 respectively. $FF_i = TF_i = 0$ holds for any critical operation i.

4.13. Active Schedule and Nonactive Schedule

The semiactive schedule was constructed by shifting each operation on every machine to the left as far as possible under a given ordering and a predetermined sequence. Furthermore, we can obtain an active schedule by shifting every operation to the left as far as possible when it is allowed for any operation to pass the operations that precede it on the same machine, which means the modification of a given sequence under given ordering. That is to say, an active schedule is a schedule on which any idle time on any machine is shorter than the processing time of a processable operation under a given ordering. Here every operation is processed as soon as it is processable under a given ordering and a modified sequence, that is, this schedule is restricted to be semiactive. The other semiactive schedules that are not active schedules are called nonactive schedules.

Among five semiactive schedules shown in Fig. 4.12, S_1 is a nonactive schedule since an operation 21 can be processed during the idle time prior to the processing of an operation 11 on M_1 and then operations 22, 23 can be shifted to the left respectively which leads to a schedule S_5. S_5 is an active schedule since the left shift of any operation is not possible under an ordering. S_6 is a nonactive schedule since an operation 13 can be processed at time 6 by shifting it in front of an operation 23 on M_3 and then an operation 11 can be shifted to the left which leads to a schedule S_5. S_7 is a nonactive schedule since an operation 23 can be processed at time 8 by shifting it in front of an operation 13 on M_3 and S_8 follows. S_8 is an active schedule since no more left shift is possible.

As is clear from the above, any nonactive schedule among all semiactive schedules constructed when the ordering and a sequence are given can be modified to a certain active schedule by altering its sequence. This fact makes it possible to decrease in the wide sense the value of any normal objective function. Hence, it is sufficient for us to consider only the active schedules, that is, at least one optimal schedule is contained in the set of active schedules.

Remark. Generally there exist a fairly large number of active schedules. The case occurs where we take into consideration the non-delay schedules as a subset of the set of active schedules for the purpose of obtaining a good schedule approximately.

A non-delay schedule is an active schedule in which there exists no operation processable under an ordering at any time within any idle time on every machine, that is to say, it is an active schedule in which any processable operation under an ordering is not delayed by the idleness of a machine.

In Fig. 4.12 only the S_5 is a non-delay schedule. Another active schedule S_8 is not a non-delay schedule since an operation 12 is delayed though it can be processed at time 0 on M_2.

Generally speaking, the set of non-delay schedules does not always contain the optimal schedule as shown in Fig. 4.14.

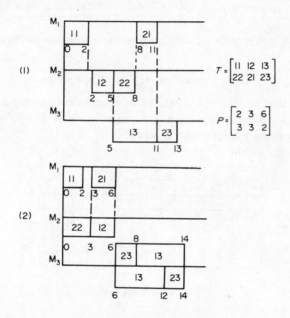

FIG. 4.14. (1) (delay) is shorter than (2) (non-delay).

4.14. α-Optimal Schedule and Non-α-optimal Schedule

While an optimal schedule can be looked for in the set of active schedules, even the number of active schedules becomes high in large-scale problems. Thus, as a practical problem one way of keeping away from the above difficulty is to satisfy by selecting an approximate schedule taking as objective value with relative error which is less than or equal to α (%) to the minimal objective value under a prescribed value of α. This kind of schedule will be called α-optimal schedule.

Then the classification of active schedules for large-scale problems becomes as shown in Fig. 4.15. Obviously any optimal schedule is included in the set of α-optimal schedule: An α-optimal schedule can be determined by applying the extended BAB method, or extended backtrack programming (cf. Sections 3.10, 3.11). Note that another important practical way is to determine an approximate schedule by applying any efficient approximate algorithm using suitable heuristic and/or search methods.

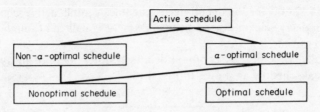

Fig. 4.15. Classification of active schedules in large-scale problems.

4.15. Generation of Active Schedules

All active schedules can be generated by successively making an entry in a work table which has job columns on each machine block, as shown in Fig. 4.16, by using the following procedure:

M_1				M_2				....				M_m			
1	2	···	n	1	2	···	n	1	2	···	n	1	2	···	n

Fig. 4.16. Work table.

Step 1. Write at the related first row the completion time of each operation which is processed first on each machine block under a given ordering. (These completion times may be changed afterwards.)

Step 2. Let the minimum of the completion times so entered be T.

Step 3. In each machine block with the operation completed at time T determine the class of all operations which includes (a) the operations completed at time T and (b) the operations that complete after T and also are simultaneously processed with each operation in (a). This class of operations is called conflict.

Step 4. Select each operation from the conflict consisting of γ operations ($\gamma \geqq 1$ where a special case $\gamma = 1$ means an operation in (a)). Let the completion time of that operation be T' which is determined by shifting it to the left if possible and in case $\gamma = 1$ proceed to step 5. When $\gamma \geqq 2$ further change the completion time of the other operation j in the conflict to the sum of the processing time of j and the maximum value between T' and the starting time of j. Let each of these values be T'. (The completion time of any operation not in the conflict is not changed.)

Step 5. Find a machine (if any, otherwise step 6) which next processes a job of each operation i assigned at step 4 and write at the next operation row the sum of the completion time of the operation i and the processing time on the next machine.

(1) If completion time T' of the new operation is smaller than T go back to step 3.

(2) Otherwise, proceed to step 6.

Step 6. If T is not the maximum among all entries, put $T = T'$ where T' is next larger than T and go back to step 2.

Otherwise, the procedure terminates and then T is the makespan of the related active schedule.

Remark 1. T shows the time at which the scheduling was accomplished and after which conflict may occur.

Remark 2. The above procedure can be modified for the cases, such as the case where there exist several machines of the same type, the case where there exist explicit setup times and the case where simultaneous processing of the operation is possible.

The fact that all active schedules are generated by the above procedure is shown by the following theorem. Also, the BAB algorithm which follows the above procedure is shown in Sections 8–11, Chapter 12.

THEOREM 9. *The above procedure generates all active schedules.*

Proof. Any schedule constructed by the procedure satisfies the given ordering by the steps 1 and 5. Also by step 4 all conflicts are resolved and by the steps 3, 5 and so on every operation is assigned on the machine always when this machine can process the job. Hence, any schedule generated is active. Conversely, it is shown next by induction that any active schedule is generated. The first operation of any active schedule S is assigned at time 0 by the steps $1 \sim 4$. Then assume that the operations of S are assigned until time t. If there exists no new operation which was assigned to S at time t, then since S is active this is a case where the procedure has no operation for selection at time t. Otherwise this new operation is certainly assigned by the steps 4 and 5. Hence by induction each operation assigned to S is certainly assigned at the assigned time by the procedure.

EXAMPLE 5. All active schedules of the 2 × 3 problem in Example 4 will be generated by the above procedure as shown in the following. Related ordering and processing times shown in the parentheses are

$$T = \begin{bmatrix} 12(6) & 13(2) & 11(2) \\ 21(3) & 22(5) & 23(4) \end{bmatrix}$$

The result using the procedure is given in Table 4.4. At No. 1 completion times 6 and 3 of the first operations 12 and 21 are written. At $T = 3$ we have $\gamma = 1$ and then it becomes $T = 6$ after writing the completion time $3 + 5 = 8$ of the next operation 22 after the operation 21. Operations 12 and 22 cause a conflict. If we select the operation 12 we go to No. 11 and if we select the operation 22 we go to No. 12. In the same way, from No. 11 we proceed successively to Nos. 111, 1111 and No. 1111 gives an active schedule S_5 and also from No. 12 we reach No. 1211 which gives an active schedule S_8.

Remark. There exist the methods of generation of semiactive schedules and non-delay schedules.

TABLE 4.4

No.	M_1		M_2		M_3		
	1	2	1	2	1	2	
1		3	6	8			
11		3	6	11	8		
12		3	14	8		12	
111	10	3	6	11	8		
121		3	14	8	16	12	
1111	10	3	6	11	8	15	S_5
1211	18	3	14	8	16	12	S_8

Exercise

1. Generate all active schedules of the 3 × 3 sequencing problem with following ordering and processing times shown in the parentheses.

$$T = \begin{bmatrix} 11(2) & 12(3) & 13(4) \\ 22(4) & 21(3) & 23(5) \\ 33(6) & 32(5) & 31(4) \end{bmatrix}$$

Bibliography and Comments

Section 4.1

General statements of the sequencing problem are found in

J. F. MUTH and G. L. THOMPSON (ed.), *Industrial Scheduling*, Prentice-Hall, Englewood Cliffs, New Jersey, 1963.

R. W. CONWAY, W. L. MAXWELL and L. W. MILLER, *Theory of Scheduling*, Addison-Wesley, Reading, Massachusetts, 1967.

S. ASHOUR, *Sequencing Theory*, Springer-Verlag, New York, 1972.

K. R. BAKER, *Introduction to Sequencing and Scheduling*, John Wiley, New York, 1974.

S. S. ELMAGHRABY, "The machine sequencing problem—Review and extensions", *Nav. Res. Log. Quart.* **15**, No. 2 (1968), 205–232.

M. S. BAKSHI and S. R. ARORA, "The sequencing problem", *Mgt. Sci.* **16**, No. 4 (1969), B247–263.

J. N. D. GUPTA, "M-stage scheduling problem – a critical appraisal", *Int. J. Prod. Res.* **9**, No. 2 (1971), 267–281.

S. EILON, "Production scheduling," *OR '78*, K. B. HALEY (ed.), North-Holland, 1979, pp. 237–266.

R. L. GRAHAM, E. L. LAWLER, J. K. LENSTRA and A. H. G. RINNOOY KAN, "Optimization and approximation in deterministic sequencing and scheduling: a survey", in *Discrete Optimization* II, *Annales of Discrete Mathematics*, Vol. 5, 1979.

Also, refer to the subsequent books.

The dynamic case is treated in Conway *et al.*'s book.

For the stochastic cases see, for example, the following papers and their References:

B. P. BANERJEE, "Single facility sequencing with random execution times", *Opns. Res.* **13**, No. 3 (1965), 358–364.

T. B. CRABILL and W. L. MAXWELL, "Single machine sequencing with random processing times and random due-dates", *av. Res. Log. Quart.* **16**, No. 4 (1969), 549–554.

A. A. CUNNINGHAM and S. K. DUTTA, "Scheduling jobs, with exponentially distributed processing times, on two machines of a flow shop", *Nav. Res. Log. Quart.* **20**, No. 1 (1973), 69–81.

Also refer to

Z.-SING SU and K. C. SEVICK, "A combinatorial approach to dynamic scheduling problems", *Opns. Res.*, **26**, No. 5 (1978), 836–844.

A summary on complexity of the sequencing problem is found in

A. H. G. RINNOOY KAN, *Machine Scheduling Problems, Classification, Complexity and Computations*, Martinus Nijhoff, The Hague, 1976.

E. G. COFFMAN, Jr. (ed.), *Computer and Job-shop Scheduling Theory*, John Wiley, New York, 1976.

J. K. LENSTRA, *Sequencing by Enumerative Methods*, Mathematisch Centrum, 1977.

Section 4.2

For the interruptions of the operations see

L. SCHRAGE, "Solving resource-constrained network problems by implicit enumeration—preemptive case," *Opns. Res.* **20**, No. 3 (1972), 668–677.

S. SAHNI, "Preemptive scheduling with due dates", *Opns. Res.* **27**, No. 5 (1979), 925–934.

E. G. COFFMAN, Jr. (ed.), *op. cit.*

For no inventory in process, see

S. S. REDDI and C. V. RAMAMOORTHY, "On the flow-shop sequencing problem with no wait in process", *Opnl. Res. Quart.* **23**, No. 3 (1972), 323–331.

Also, concerning the multiple processors, see the next papers and their References:

E. G. COFFMAN, Jr. and J. LABETOULLE, "Flow-time sequencing of independent tasks on multiple processors", *INFOR*, **15**, No. 3 (1977), 289–307.

M. PINEDA and G. WEISS, "Scheduling of stochastic tasks on two parallel processors", *Nav. Res. Log. Quart.* **26**, No. 3 (1979), 527–535.

Section 4.5

For the summary on the classification, see

M. S. BAKSHI and S. R. ARORA, "The sequencing problem", *Mgt. Sci.* **16**, No. 4 (1969), B247–B263.

Section 4.6
For the summary, see
M. S. BAKSHI and S. R. ARORA, "The sequencing problem", *Mgt. Sci.* **16**, No. 4 (1969), B247–
   B263.
Judgement of feasibility I is found in
R. B. MARIMONT, "A new method of checking the consistency of precedence matrices", *J. ACM*, **6**
   (1959), 164–171.
Judgement of feasibility III is found in
S. B. AKERS and J. FRIEDMAN, "A non-numerical approach to production scheduling problems",
   Opns. Res, **3**, No. 4 (1955), 429–442.

Section 4.7
For a detailed statement see
J. HELLER and G. LOGEMANN, "An algorithm for the construction and evaluation of feasible
   schedules", *Mgt. Sci.* **8**, No. 2 (1962), 168–183.
Also, for a practically simple and controllable technique, see
P. P. BESTWICK and K. G. LOCKYER, "A practical approach to production scheduling", *Int. J.
   Prod. Res.* **17**, No. 2 (1979), 95–109.

Section 4.9
For a detailed discussion of the Theorems 7 and 8 see
S. B. AKERS and J. FRIEDMAN, "A non-numerical approach to production scheduling problems",
   Opns. Res. **3**, No. 4 (1955), 429–442.

Section 4.12
For the critical path analysis see, for example,
J. D. WIEST and F. K. LEVY, *A Management Guide to PERT/CPM*, Prentice-Hall, Englewood
   Cliffs, New Jersey, 1969 (second edition, 1977).
   This analysis is akin to the shortest-path problem in Chapter 1, and since the network contains
no circuits, i.e. acyclic, the equations (4.5) are simpler than were the equations (1.3) in Chapter 1.

Sections 4.13 and 4.15
For the generations of active schedules and non-delay schedules, see
R. W. CONWAY, W. L. MAXWELL and L. W. MILLER, *Theory of Scheduling*, Addison-Wesley,
   Reading, Massachusetts, 1967.
For the generations of semiactive schedules and non-delay schedules see
S. ASHOUR, *Sequencing Theory*, Springer-Verlag, New York, 1972.
For the generation of active schedules and detailed discussions, see
R. GIFFLER and G. L. THOMPSON, "Algorithms for solving production scheduling problems",
   Opns. Res. **8**, No. 4, (1960), 487–503.

CHAPTER 5

Sequencing Involving Capacity Expansion

5.1. Introduction

The management of capital expenditure planning encounters problems that tempt the planner to use complete enumeration, the so-called "brute force" approach. Yet, the magnitude of such problems often defies the use of these direct methods. The literature of optimization theory, operations research, and management science is rich in the exposition of theoretical foundations of tools that may prove useful in these problem areas. However, direct transfer is neither feasible nor wise. Consequently, the establishment of a strong analytic base for this transfer is both necessary and useful. In this regard the concepts developed in Chapter 4 are useful background material.

In this chapter we discuss methods, mostly of the dynamic programming variety, for the analysis and optimization of models arising in sequencing problems particularly those involving capacity expansion. Problems of this genre assume great importance in industry, water resources and developing economies where management must expand facilities to meet growing market demands. The problem can be analysed using such methodological approaches as recurrent or generative sequences, differential calculus, search, integer programming and dynamic programming.

5.2. A Simple Expansion—Sequencing Problem—the One-dimensional Version

The simplest form of this problem consists of determining how to sequence (time) the construction completion dates of each of a finite set of N projects in order to always meet resource demands while minimizing the discounted costs of these N projects. To introduce this problem, we define the following. Let

r = annual (discrete) interest rate;
N = number of feasible projects;
C_i = capital cost of construction of the ith project at its completion date;
Q_i = capacity of the ith project;
$D(t)$ = demand requirement at time t;

87

T = length of the planning horizon.

We further assume the following project characteristics:

(a) the investment cost C_i incurred at the time the project is completed, does not vary with time;

(b) the full capacity Q_i is available for use instantaneously upon project completion;

(c) project capacity once created has infinite life and does not change during the planning horizon;

(d) variable operating and distribution costs are proportional to the amount actually produced and identical for all projects;

(e) demand must be met from current production.

Total capacity $Q(t)$ at time $t \geq 0$ composed of initial capacity plus the sum of individual project capacities undertaken up to time t.

Then the one-dimensional sequencing problem may be stated as: Find $(t_1, t_2, \ldots, t_N)$ so as to:

$$\min \sum_{i=1}^{N} C_i (1+r)^{-\langle t_i \rangle} \tag{5.1}$$

subject to

$$\sum_{i=1}^{N} Q_i(t) = D(t), \quad \forall t \in [0, T] \tag{5.2}$$

where $\langle x \rangle$ denotes the smallest positive integer $\geq x$ and $Q_i(t) = 0$ or Q_i according to whether t is less than t_i or greater than or equal to t_i.

The scheduling problem, on the other hand, includes both the problem of project selection decision and project construction timing decision. Thus, if we let:

$$S_l = (p_{[1]}, p_{[2]}, \ldots, p_{[l]}) \text{ where } p_{[i]} \in (1, 2, \ldots, N) \tag{5.3}$$

and $p_{[i]} \neq p_{[j]} \, \forall i, j = 1, 2, \ldots, l$, denote an

$$l - \text{project sequence, with } l \leq N, \tag{5.4}$$

then the one-dimensional scheduling problem is: Find $\{(p_{[1]}, t_{[1]}), (p_{[2]}, t_{[2]}), \ldots, (p_{[l]}, t_{[l]})\}$ so as to:

$$\min_{K_l \in S} \sum_{i \in K_l} C_i (1+r)^{-\langle t_i \rangle} \tag{5.5}$$

subject to

$$\sum_{i \in K_l} Q_i(t) \geq D(t), \quad \forall i \in [0, T] \tag{5.6}$$

where the brackets denote a project's position in the sequence and S is the set of $\sum_{l=0}^{N} \binom{N}{l} l!$ possible sequences composed of N or fewer projects.

A scheduling problem reduces to a sequencing problem whenever all N projects must be constructed to meet the demand requirements over the planning horizon; i.e. if $D(t)$ is monotonically nondecreasing on $[0, T]$, a one-dimensional scheduling problem reduces to a one-dimensional sequencing problem whenever

$$D(T) \in \left(\sum_{i \in \hat{K}_{N-1}} Q_i, \sum_{i \in \hat{K}_N} Q_i \right) \tag{5.7}$$

where $\hat{K}_{N-1} \subset \hat{K}_N$ and $\hat{K}_N$ is an N-project sequence in which the projects appear in nondecreasing order of their capacities. Hence, whenever (5.7) holds, l must equal N, and therefore we have a one-dimensional sequencing problem.

5.3. Why Dynamic Programming?

One approach to the capacity expansion sequencing problem is complete enumeration. However, in an N project problem, there are $N!$ possible sequences each of which might require N discount calculations. For example, if $N = 10$, i.e. a 10-project problem, we may have to examine 3,628,800 possible sequences. On the other hand, if we use dynamic programming—even the most conventional formulation—we have only to consider $N(2)^{N-1}$ discount calculations for a complete solution. This means that for the 10-project problem, we only need to perform 5120 discount calculations in order to select the best sequence. The obvious computational advantage becomes more dramatic when larger size expansion sequencing problems are being considered. Thus, we will present for the most part dynamic programming formulations for this problem.

5.4. Conventional Dynamic Program (DPI) for the One-dimensional Sequencing Problem

Consider a problem situation with the following cost functional $g^i(q)$ defined for $i = 1, 2, \ldots, N$ as

$$g^{(i)}(q) = 0, \qquad \forall q \in (-\infty, 0]$$
$$g^{(i)}(q) = C_i, \qquad \forall q \in (0, Q_i] \tag{5.8}$$
$$g^{(i)}(q) = \infty, \qquad \text{otherwise.}$$

Then if we introduce the functional $f_n^{k_n}(q)$ defined as the minimum present cost of providing a capacity of at least q units to meet demand by a sequence k_n of n or fewer projects, we obtain the following functional equation for the conventional dynamic programming algorithm.

For $n = 1, 2, \ldots, N$

$$f_n^{k_n}(q) = \min \left[g^i(q_n)(1+r)^{-\psi(q-q_n)} + f_{n-1}^{k_{n-1}}(q - q_n) \right] \tag{5.9}$$
$$0 \leq q_n \leq q, \quad i \notin k_{n-1}$$

where r is the annual interest rate and $\psi(q - q_n)$ is the smallest integral time t for which $D(t) \geq q - q_n$. This project timing function $\psi(\cdot)$ may be redefined for a more general demand function as:

$$\psi(q) = \left\langle \sup_{t \in [0,t]} [t \mid \max_{\tau \in [0,t]} \{D(\tau)\} \leq q] \right\rangle \tag{5.10}$$

$$\forall q \in \Omega$$

where Ω is the state space of all cumulative capacity levels.

The boundary condition is

$$f_0^{k_0}(q) = 0, \quad q \leq 0,$$

$$f_0^{k_0}(q) = \infty, \quad \text{otherwise.} \tag{5.11}$$

The solution procedure is as follows. We recursively solve the functional equation backward starting at $n = 0$ with equation (5.11). Then we solve equation (5.9) for $n = 1, 2, \ldots, N$ successively, recording k_n as we proceed backward and terminating once $f_N^{k_N}[D(T)]$ has been calculated. The minimum present cost is $f_N^{k_N}[D(T)]$ and the projects selected and their sequence are given by k_N. This is the conventional DP formulation and as we shall see later it has certain noteworthy drawbacks.

5.5. The Imbedded States Space Dynamic Program (DP2) for the One-dimensional Sequencing Problem

Before presenting the more efficient dynamic programming algorithm for the sequencing problem, DP2, developed by Morin and Esogbue (1971), we will develop the basic theorem on which our algorithm is based. Define a permutation schedule k_N^* as a schedule formed by taking a permutation of the numbers $1, 2, \ldots, N$ and sequencing the project according to this permutation, a project being completed only when the cumulative capacities of the previous projects are totally used. Figure 5.1 illustrates this permutation schedule graphically. The permutation schedule is expressed mathematically by

$$t_{[j]}^* = D^{-1}\left(\sum_{i=1}^{j-1} Q_{[i]} \right) \tag{5.12}$$

$$j = 1, 2, \ldots, N$$

where $D^{-1}(\ )$ is the inverse function of demand and the brackets denote the order in the sequence, i.e. $[j] = i$ denotes project i is the jth position of the sequence. We can show rather easily that the following theorem holds for this problem.

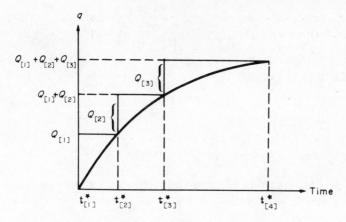

FIG. 5.1. Demand versus time curve showing permutation points in the time horizon.

THEOREM 1. *If there is a feasible solution to the sequencing problem, then all* $N!$ *permutation schedules are feasible, and furthermore at least one permutation schedule is optimal.*

Proof. The theorem will be proved by considering first the feasibility and then the optimality of schedules.

Feasibility. The completion times for any permutation schedule are given by equation (5.12).

$$t_{[j]}^* = D^{-1} \left(\sum_{i=1}^{j-1} Q_{[i]} \right)$$ (5.13)

$$j = 1, 2, \ldots, N$$

which implies capacity at time $t \geq D(t)$ for all $t \in [0, T]$. Therefore all permutation schedules are feasible.

Optimality. Let $T = \{t_{[1]}^*, t_{[2]}^*, \ldots, t_{(N)}^*\}$ be the set of completion times for the permutation schedule S_N^* with the lowest discounted cost of the $N!$ permutation schedules. Assume to the contrary that S_N^* is not optimal but that there is another schedule composed of N projects S_N' that is optimal (if the schedule had fewer than N projects, it could not be feasible because of equation (5.2)). Since S_N' differs from S_N^*, then there is at least one $[j]$ for which $t_{[j]}' \neq t_{[j]}^*$; i.e. either

$$t_{[j]}' > D^{-1} \left(\sum_{i=1}^{j-1} Q_{[i]} \right)$$ (5.14)

or

$$t'_{[j]} < D^{-1} \left(\sum_{i=1}^{j-1} Q_{[i]} \right).$$ (5.15)

Consider the first case. If

$$t'_{[j]} > D^{-1} \left(\sum_{i=1}^{j-1} Q_{[i]} \right)$$

then

$$\sum_{i=1}^{j-1} Q_{[i]} < D(t_{[j]}).$$ (5.16)

Figure 5.2 illustrates this relationship graphically. Capacity at time t is less than or equal to $D(t)$ for all

$$t \in \left[D^{-1} \left(\sum_{i=1}^{j-1} Q_{[i]} \right), t'_{[j]} \right].$$ (5.17)

Therefore S'_N could not even be feasible, much less optimal.

Consider the second case.

$$t'_{[j]} < D^{-1} \left(\sum_{i=1}^{j-1} Q_{[i]} \right) = t^*_{[j]}.$$

Without any loss of generality, let $[j] = p$. Then the present cost of S'_N is

$$\mathrm{PV}(S'_N) = \sum_{\substack{i=1 \\ i \neq p}}^{N} C_i (1+r)^{-\langle t'_i \rangle} + C_p (1+r)^{-\langle t'_p \rangle}$$ (5.18)

Where $\langle x \rangle$ equals the smallest integer $\geq x$. The present cost of S^*_N is

$$\mathrm{PV}(S^*_N) = \sum_{\substack{i=1 \\ i \neq p}}^{N} C_i (1+r)^{-\langle t^*_i \rangle} + C_p (1+r)^{-\langle t^*_p \rangle}.$$ (5.19)

But $t^*_i = t'_i$ for all $i \neq p$ and

$$\langle t'_p \rangle \leq \langle t^*_p \rangle \quad \therefore \quad t'_p < t^*_p.$$

Therefore

$$C_p (1+r)^{-\langle t'_p \rangle} \geq C_p (1+r)^{-\langle t^*_p \rangle}.$$ (5.20)

Hence

$$\mathrm{PV}(S'_N) \geq \mathrm{PV}(S^*_N)$$ (5.21)

which is a contradiction since S'_N was assumed to be optimal. Therefore S^*_N is optimal.

The reasoning behind the theorem is that since it is cheaper in terms of present cost considerations to construct a project as far in the future as possible, then the project should be constructed as late as possible without

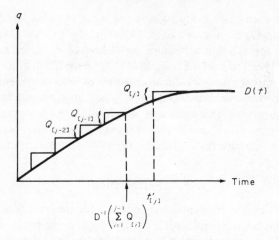

FIG. 5.2. Demand versus time curve for $t_{[j]'} > t_{[j]^\bullet}$.

violating the demand requirement over the planning horizon. A similar result concerning permutation schedules can be proved for the scheduling problem. The special structure of the sequencing problem is considered in the following discussion.

5.6. Discussion

Equation (5.2) holds for the sequencing problem. Therefore all N projects must be constructed if the demand requirements are to be met over the entire planning horizon. Also, the cumulative capacities of the N projects will be entirely used by the end of the planning horizon. Furthermore, T is a permutation point that satisfies equation (5.12) for $j = N + 1$, and by our theorem at least one permutation schedule is optimal. Consider the calculation of $f_N^{k_N}[D(T)]$. Since only permutation schedules need to be considered, the minimum of equation (5.9) over q_N occurs at $q_N = Q_i$ for some $i \notin k_{N-1}$; otherwise k_N could not be a permutation schedule. Now $D(T) - Q_i$ also corresponds to a permutation point, and therefore the minimum of the functional $f_{N-1}^{k_{N-1}}[D(T) - Q_i]$ for a capacity exactly equal to $D(T) - Q_i$ occurs at $q_{n-1} = Q_j$ for some $j \notin k_{N-2}$ and $j \neq i$, and so on. Therefore the minimization operation over q_n in equation (5.9) can now be deleted. Furthermore, the cost functional $g^i(q_n)$ can be replaced by C_i, since from equation (5.8), $g^i(Q_i) = C_i$. This approach substantially reduces computational effort.

Rather than calculate $f_n^{k_n}(q)$ for a large number of q over fixed increments in the state space Ω, we can use the imbedded state space approach and further reduce computational effort. Since it is sufficient to consider only permutation schedules, it may not be necessary to calculate $f_n^{k_n}(q)$ for all the fixed-state increments at each stage n. Consider a sequence of point sets $\Omega_1, \Omega_2, \ldots,$ $\Omega_N \subset \Omega$, where Ω_n represents the point set of the $\binom{N}{n}$ possible cumulative capacities of permutation schedules consisting of n projects. Morin and Esogbue (1971) call this set the imbedded state space. Then at the nth stage of the recursion, rather than consider an entire set of fixed increments defined on Ω, we need to consider only those $q \in \Omega_n$, since only permutation schedules have to be considered. This approach, which is distinct from state increment dynamic programming (Larson, 1968) in that it exploits the specific structure of the class of combinatorial problems, can vastly reduce computational effort.

5.7. Formulation

Let us now develop the functional equation for the imbedded states space dynamic programming formulation for this sequencing problem.

Define $f_n(q)$ as the minimum present cost of providing a capacity of exactly q to meet demand with exactly n projects. Then invoking the principle of optimality, we obtain the following much simpler functional equation for $n = 1, 2, \ldots, N$:

$$f_n(q) = \min_{i \notin k_{n-1}^*} [C_i(1+r)^{-\psi(q-Q_i)} + f_{n-1}(q-Q_i)]. \tag{5.18}$$

Once again, our boundary condition is

$$f_0(q) = 0, \quad q \le 0 \tag{5.13}$$

$$f_0(q) = \infty, \quad \text{otherwise}$$

Also, since it is not necessary to calculate $f_n(q)$ for $q \notin \Omega_n$, we can set

$$f_n(q) = 0, \quad q \le 0 \tag{5.14}$$

$$f_n(q) = \infty, \quad \text{for all positive } q \notin \Omega_n$$

for all $q \notin \Omega_n$.

The computational superiority of DP2 over DP1 for the sequencing problem will now be illustrated by solving the following example.

5.8. An Illustrative Example

We will show the power of Morin and Esogbue's imbedded-state space technique by solving a problem posed originally by Butcher *et al.* (1969). Consider the problem of planning for the capacity expansion of a water-resources facility in which

$$\sum_{i=1}^{4} Q_i = D(T).$$

Let $r = 0.05$ and $T = 30$ years. Furthermore, let

Project i	1	2	3	4
Cost, C_i	30	50	65	75
Capacity, Q_i	2	4	4	7

and the demand function $D(T)$ given by Fig. 5.3.

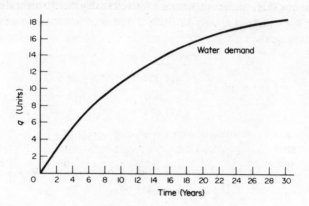

FIG. 5.3. General water demand versus time curve.

With the problem as posed,

$$\sum_{i=1}^{N} Q_i = 17 - D(T).$$

Using the state space reduction technique presented above, we first calculate $f_1(q)$ for $q = 2, 4, 7$, then $f_2(q)$ for $q = 6, 8, 9, 11$, then $f_3(q)$ for $q = 10, 13, 15$, and finally $f_4(q)$ for $q = 17$, rather than calculate $f_n(q)$ for $q = 0, 1, 2, \ldots, 17$ for all $n = 1, 2, 3, 4$. This technique represents a reduction from 64 calculations

TABLE 5.1. *Summary of Calculation for DP2*

n	q	$f_n(q)$	$k_n{}^*$
1	2	30	(1)
	4	50	(2)
	7	75	(4)
2	6	75.91	(2,1)
	8	106.15	(2,3)
	9	97.39	(4,1)
	11	112.31	(4,2)
3	10	126.45	(2,3,1)
	13	129.01	(4,2,1)
	15	148.50	(4,2,3)
4	17	159.81	(4,2,3,1)

with a minimization over q_n at each step to 11 calculations with no minimizations over q_n at each step. Since each calculation referred to involves comparisons to determine the optimal solution, the reduction effected by this approach becomes more appreciable.

We will show the computational process of DP2 by computing $f_2(8)$. The rest of the calculations is shown in Table 5.1.

Note that $q = 8$ is a permutation point with exactly two projects for only $k_2 = (2, 3)$ or $k_2 = (3, 2)$, i.e. only projects 2 and 3 together have a cumulative capacity that equals 8.

$$f_2(8) = {}_i\min^*_{kl} \left\{ \begin{array}{l} C_1(1.05)^{-\psi(8-Q_1)} + f_1(8-Q_1) \\ C_2(1.05)^{-\psi(8-Q_2)} + f_1(8-Q_2) \\ C_3(1.05)^{-\psi(8-Q_3)} + f_1(8-Q_3) \\ C_4(1.05)^{-\psi(8-Q_4)} + f_1(8-Q_4) \end{array} \right\}$$

$$= \min \left\{ \begin{array}{l} 30(1.05)^{-\psi(6)} + f_1(6) = 27.21 + \infty = \infty \\ 50(1.05)^{-\psi(4)} + f_1(4) = \infty \\ 65(1.05)^{-\psi(4)} + f_1(4) = 56.15 + 50 - 106.15 \\ 75(1.05)^{-\psi(1)} + f_1(1) = 75 + \infty = \infty \end{array} \right\}$$

$$= 106.15$$

Note that ${}_i\min^*_{k_i} \{C_2(1.05)^{-\psi(8-Q_1)} + f_1(8-Q_2)\}$

$$= \min\{50(1.05)^{-\psi(4)} + f_1(4) = \infty, \text{ since } k_1^* = \{2\}\}.$$

5.9. Reducing M&E Imbedded State Space for Large-capacity Expansion Problems

For large size capacity expansion problems such as those occurring in real life instead of calculating $f_n(q)$ for all the $N!/(N-n)!\, n!$ states of the imbedded state space Ω_n, it is possible by recourse to the following results to effect a further reduction of the state space that should be searched in the computational process.

THEOREM 2. *If in the one-dimensional sequencing problem there exist m, $1 \le m < N$, distinct subsets of projects $\Phi_1, \Phi_2, \ldots, \Phi_m$, all of whose respective members have either (1) the same capacity $Q^{(j)}$ for $j \in \{1, 2, \ldots, m\}$ or (2) the same capital cost $C^{(j)}$, then in any optimal sequence these projects will appear in nondecreasing order of the ratio of their respective costs to their respective capacities $(C_i/Q_i \, \forall\, i \in \Phi_j)$.*

Proof. The theorem will be proved for the equal capacity case. Since the proof for the equal cost case parallels the proof for the equal capacity case, *mutatis mutandis* we demonstrate only that for the equal capacity case.

Let the subsets of projects that have equal capacity be denoted by $\Phi_1, \Phi_2, \ldots, \Phi_m$, where $m \leq N$, N being the number of feasible projects; i.e. for each $j = 1, 2, \ldots, m$

$$\exists Q^{(j)} > 0 \ni,$$

$$Q_i = Q^{(j)} \ \forall i \in \Phi_j. \tag{5.22}$$

Morin and Esogbue (1971) showed that all permutation schedules are feasible for the one-dimensional sequencing problem and furthermore that at least one permutation schedule is optimal. We assume to the contrary that there is some permutation schedule S_N that is optimal but that does not satisfy the conditions of the theorem. Therefore, there exists at least one pair of projects in S_N such that

$$t_{[l]} > t_{[K]} \quad C_{[l]}/Q_{[l]} < C_{[K]}/Q_{[K]} \tag{5.23}$$

where $[l]$, $[K]$, $\in \Phi_j$.

Without loss of generality, let $n = [l]$, $p = [K]$, and $Q_n = Q_p = Q^{(j)}$. Consider another permutation schedule that is identical to S_N except that project n is in the Kth position and project p is in the lth position of the sequence. Notice that because of the equal capacities the completion times remain the same.

Then the present cost $PV(S_N)$ of S_N is

$$PV(S_N) = \sum_{\substack{i=1 \\ i \neq n, p}}^{N} C_i(1+r)^{-\langle t_i \rangle}$$

$$+ C_n(1+r)^{-\langle t_{[l]} \rangle} + C_p(1+r)^{-\langle t_{[K]} \rangle}. \tag{5.24}$$

The present cost of S'_N is

$$PV(S'_N) = \sum_{\substack{i=1 \\ i \neq n, p}}^{N} C_i(1+r)^{-\langle t_i \rangle}$$

$$+ C_p(1+r)^{-\langle t_{[l]} \rangle} + C_n(1+r)^{-\langle t_{[K]} \rangle}. \tag{5.25}$$

Subtracting $PV(S'_N)$ from $PV(S_N)$ and simplifying, we obtain

$$PV(S_N) - PV(S'_N)$$

$$= (C_p - C_n)[(1+r)^{-\langle t_{[K]} \rangle} - (1+r)^{-\langle t_{[l]} \rangle}]. \tag{5.26}$$

But we assumed that $C_{[l]}/Q_{[l]} < C_{[K]}/Q_{[K]}$ and $t_{[l]} > t_{[K]}$. Therefore we have that $C_p > C_n$, since $Q_p = Q_l = Q^{(j)}$. Furthermore, from the definition of the $\langle \ \rangle$ operator we have

$$\langle t_{[l]} \rangle \geq \langle t_{[K]} \rangle \tag{5.27}$$

and it follows that

$$(1+r)^{-\langle t_{[K]} \rangle} \geq (1+r)^{-\langle t_{[l]} \rangle} \tag{5.28}$$

Hence

$$PV(S_N) \geq PV(S'_N) \tag{5.29}$$

which is a contradiction, since S_N was assumed to be optimal. Thus any permutation schedule that is composed of subsets of projects having equal capacities and whose corresponding projects are not in nondecreasing order of the ratio C_i/Q_i for any $i \in \Phi_j$ and $j = 1, 2, \ldots, m$ may be improved by interchanging the corresponding pairs of projects into nondecreasing order of the respective ratios C_i/Q_i. There exists only a finite number of such interchanges, and their end result is a schedule all of whose projects having equal capacity are sequenced in nondecreasing order of the respective ratios of their costs to their capacities. Q.E.D.

5.10. Discussion

As a result of this theorem, since projects 2 and 3 of the example discussed in Section 5.7 have the same capacities (4 units), we know that project 2 must always precede project 3 in an optimal sequence, since project 2 has a lower cost than project 3, i.e. 50 units versus 65 units. Therefore instead of calculating $f_1(q)$ for $q = 2, 4^{(2)}, 4^{(3)}, 7$; then $f_2(q)$ for $q = 6^{(2)}, 6^{(3)}, 8, 9, 11^{(2)}, 11^{(3)}$; then $f_2(q)$ for $q = 10, 13^{(2)}, 13^{(3)}, 15$; and finally $f_4(q)$ for $q = 17$, where the superscripts designate projects 2 and 3; it is sufficient to consider only those members of the imbedded state space in which project 2 can precede project 3. That is, it suffices to calculate $f_1(q)$ for $q = 2, 4^{(2)}, 7$; then $f_2(q)$ for $q = 6^{(2)}, 8, 9, 11^{(2)}$; then $f_2(q)$ for $q = 10, 13^{(2)}, 15$; and finally $f_4(q)$ for $q = 17$.

Notice that this further reduction of dimensionality was possible only because the particular example considered here satisfied the conditions of the theorem. Indeed, if there were two or more distinct combinations of projects that had the same cumulative capacity but that did not satisfy the conditions of the theorem, then it would be necessary to consider each of the corresponding capacities. For example, if the project capacities were $Q_1 = 1, Q_2 = 2, Q_3 = 4$, and $Q_4 = 5$, then at the second stage of the recursion we would have to calculate $f_2(q)$ for $q = 3, 5, 6^{(1,4)}, 6^{(2,3)}, 7, 9$, where the superscripts indicate the component projects. In general, the failure to calculate $f_n(q)$ for all the $N!/(N-n)! \, n!$ states $q \in \Omega_n$ may result in a nonoptimal schedule.

Finally, we note that a similar result can be proved for scheduling problems and that these results hold regardless of both the value of the interest rate r (as long as it is a nonnegative constant) and the form of the water supply demand requirement $D(t)$. This theorem can also be used to derive a "myopic" scheduling rule. That is, in both the one-dimensional sequencing and the one-dimensional scheduling problems, if all projects have either equal costs or equal capacities (or both), then the optimal permutation schedule is one whose component projects are selected and sequenced by ranking the N projects in nondecreasing order of their respective ratios of cost to capacity and then selecting as many projects as are necessary to meet the water-supply demand requirement at the end of the planning horizon. This is simply a special case of the theorem for which we have $m = 1$, and $\Phi_1 = \{1, 2, \ldots, N\}$. In such cases it is not even necessary to use dynamic programming in order to solve the corresponding problem, since the myopic rule yields the optimal solution.

5.11. Multi-dimensional Sequencing Problem—Theory

Prior to formulating the problem, some additional notation must first be introduced. Let the set of capacity expansion projects be denoted by $\psi = \{1, 2, \ldots, N\}$. A sequence, S_N, consists of an ordering or concatenation of the N projects from ψ. As before, let $[j] = i$, denote project number $i \in \psi$ is in the jth position of sequence S_N. A schedule, S_N, consists of a sequence, S_N, together with the associated completion times of the projects in that sequence, i.e.

$$S_N = \{(p_{[1]}, t_{[1]}), (p_{[2]}, t_{[2]}), \ldots, (p_{[N]}, t_{[N]})\} \tag{5.30}$$

in which $(p_{[1]}, p_{[2]}, \ldots, p_{[N]}) = S_N$.

The mutidimensional sequencing problem can be stated as: find a schedule, S_N, so as to

$$\min_{S_N \in S,\ i \in \Psi} \sum C_i\, e^{-rt_i} \tag{5.31}$$

in which C_i denotes the capital cost of construction for the ith multipurpose project at its completion time; r denotes the continuous interest rate; t_i denotes the construction completion time of the ith project (it is tacitly assumed that any project can be completed by the beginning of the planning horizon, i.e. by time zero); and S denotes the space of all schedules satisfying the demand requirements

$$S = \left\{ S_N \,\Big|\, \sum_{i \in \Psi} Q_{ij}(t) \geqq D_j(t)\ \forall\, t \in [0, T],\ j = 1, 2, \ldots, M \right\} \tag{5.32}$$

in which T = the length of the planning horizon; Q_{ij} denotes the capacity of the ith multipurpose project to meet the jth demand; $Q_{ij}(t) = Q_{ij}$ if $t_i \leqq t$ and 0 otherwise; and $D_j(t)$ denotes the level of the jth demand at time t.

Simply stated, the optimal schedule is the schedule which satisfies the M demand requirements at each point in the planning horizon at the minimum total discounted cost. Because of the fact that S contains an infinite number of points, initial attempts at solution of even one-dimensional ($M = 1$) sequencing problems via dynamic programming were plagued by what Bellman has termed the "curse of dimensionality". However, by adroitly exploiting the mathematical structure of the multidimensional sequencing problem, it is possible to mitigate the effects of dimensionality, thereby making the solution of problems which were previously "unsolvable" possible. We have also shown that the optimal schedule must belong to a finite set of "permutation schedules", a result analogous to the well-known Wagner–Whitin theorem.

The optimal project timing function, for multiple-purpose projects, as a function of the current capacity, q, to satisfy demand is

$$\tau(\mathbf{q}) = \min_{j=1,2,\ldots M} \left\{ \sup_{t_j \leqq T} \left(t_j | q_j \geqq \max_{t^l \leq t_j} \{D_j(t^l)\} \right) \right\} \tag{5.33}$$

in which $\mathbf{q} = (q_1, q_2, \ldots, q_M)$ denotes the current capacity vector, where q_j = the total current capacity available to satisfy the jth demand. In other words, it is optimal to construct a new project as late as is feasibly possible with respect to the demand requirements. That is, from a capacity vector of $\mathbf{q}$ it is optimal to construct a new project just before the first time that any one of the M demands. $D_j(t)$ would exceed the corresponding current capacity, q_j. Note that: (1) If all the $D_j(t)$ functions were nondecreasing, then equation (5.33) would reduce to $\tau(\mathbf{q}) - \min_j\{\sup_{t_j \leq \tau}[t_j | q_j \geqq D_j(t_j)]\}$; and (2) if all the $D_j(t)$ functions were continuous as well as being nondecreasing, then their inverses $D_j^{-1}(q_j) = t_j$ would exist and would be unique and, thus equation (5.33) would reduce to $\tau(\mathbf{q}) = \min_j[D_j^{-1}(q_j)]$.

We know that if an optimal solution exists, then all permutation schedules are feasible and at least one permutation schedule is optimal. An n-project permutation schedule, P_n, is a schedule, S_n, in which the completion times of the n-component projects in the sequence, S_n, are specified as follows:

$$\tau_{[i]} = \tau\left(\sum_{j=1}^{i-1} Q_{[j]^1}, \sum_{j=1}^{i-1} Q_{[j]^2}, \ldots, \sum_{j=1}^{i-1} Q_{[j]^m} \right); \quad i = 1, 2, \ldots, n,$$
$$\tag{5.34}$$

i.e. in a permutation schedule the ith project in sequence is constructed as late as is feasibly possible from a capacity vector composed of the sum of capacity vectors of all permutation schedules composed of n projects.

The imbedded state space Ω_n, is the set of the $\binom{N}{n}$ possible cumulative capacity vectors of all permutation schedules composed of n projects. For each of the $\binom{N}{n}$ state vectors, $q^1, q^2, \ldots, q^{\binom{N}{n}}$ in Ω_n, let $\omega_n(\mathbf{q}^l) \subset \psi$ denote the set of the n component capacity expansion projects which uniquely generate (and, thus, have a cumulative capacity vector equal to) the state vector, $\mathbf{q}^l$. Let ψ_n denote the set of all $\binom{N}{n}$ possible distinct n-project sets. Then the state vectors, $\mathbf{q}^l \in \Omega_n$, are in one-to-one correspondence with the n-project sets, $\omega_n(\mathbf{q}^l) \in \psi_n$.

For each state vector, $\mathbf{q}^l$, in the imbedded state space, Ω_n, let $f_n(q_1^l, \ldots, q_M^l)$ denote the minimum discounted cost of providing a capacity vector of exactly $(q_1^l, \ldots, q_M^l)$ with the n projects that generate the state vector, $\mathbf{q}^l$. Then $f_n(q_1^l, \ldots, q_M^l)$ is the discounted cost of the permutation schedule, $P_n^*(\mathbf{q}^l)$, having the lowest discounted cost of the $n!$ possible n-project permutation schedules, $P_n(\mathbf{q}^l)$, which can be formed by permuting the n-projects in $\omega_n(\mathbf{q}^l)$.

The $f_n(q_1^l, \ldots, q_M^l)$ can be calculated recursively from the following functional equation of the imbedded state space DP algorithm.

$$f_n(q_1^l, \ldots, q_M^l) = \min_{i \in I} \{ C_i \exp [-r\tau(q_1^l - Q_{i1}, \ldots, q_M^l - Q_{iM})] + f_{n-1}(q_1^l$$

$$- Q_{i1}, \ldots, q_M^l - Q_{iM}) \}; \quad n = 1, 2, \ldots, N \text{ and } l = 1, 2, \ldots, \binom{N}{n} \quad (5.35)$$

in which $I = \{ s_n(\mathbf{q}^l) - s_{n-1}(\mathbf{q}^l - Q_i) \}$, i.e. $i \in \omega_n(\mathbf{q}^l)$ and $\omega_{n-1}(\mathbf{q}^l - Q_i)$ $= (\omega_n(\mathbf{q}^l) - i)$; i.e. for $i \subset \omega_n(\mathbf{q}^l)$, $f_{n-1}(\mathbf{q}^l - Q_i)$ is the minimum discounted cost of providing a capacity vector of exactly $(\mathbf{q}_1^l - Q_{i1}, \ldots, q_M^l - Q_{iM})$ with an $(n-1)$-project permutation schedule, $P_{n-1}(\mathbf{q}^l - Q_i)$, which is composed of the $(n-1)$ projects, $(\omega_n(\mathbf{q}^l) - i) \in \psi_{n-1}$, that uniquely generate the state vector $(\mathbf{q}^l - Q_i) \in \Omega_{n-1}$.

Since $\Omega_0 = \{ (0, \ldots, 0) \}$ and $\omega_0(0, \ldots, 0) = \phi$, in which $(0, \ldots, 0)$ denotes the zero vector and ϕ denotes the empty set, the recursive solution is initiated with the following boundary condition:

$$f_0(0, \ldots, 0) = 0. \quad (5.36)$$

The computation process involved in the solution of the functional equations is similar to that employed in the illustrative example of Section 5.7. Note that the usual M-dimensional search over all possible values of the state vector $(q_1, \ldots, q_M)$ has been reduced to a one-dimensional search over the state vectors, $\mathbf{q}^l$, in the imbedded state spaces. Therefore, the high-speed computer storage requirement does not increase with increasing M, and the computational time only increases by a small additive factor with increasing M. This reduction of dimensionality is significant when contrasted to the exponential increases in both high-speed computer storage requirements and computational time which are normally encountered in conventional dynamic programming algorithms.

5.12. A Graphical Illustration

The relationship between the imbedded-state space approach and the deletion of the vector minimization operation over q^n in the evaluation of $f_n(\mathbf{q})$ can be interpreted graphically as shown in Fig. 5.4. In this figure the solid circles and the solid triangles represent components of the cumulative capacity vectors of permutation schedules composed of $(n-1)$ and n projects, respectively. The cumulative capacity vector, $\mathbf{q}$, of a permutation schedule composed of n projects is equal to the cumulative capacity vector, $(\mathbf{q} - Q_i)$, of some permutation schedule composed of $n-1$ projects plus the capacity vector corresponding to some project i which has not already been used. Therefore, starting with the cumulative capacity vector of a permutation schedule S_n^p composed of n projects, we can generate all of the possible cumulative capacity vectors corresponding to the $(n-1)$ permutation

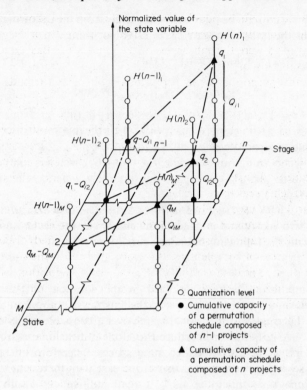

FIG. 5.4. Construction of neighbouring permutation schedules in the imbedded-state space approach.

schedules composed of $n - 1$ projects by simply subtracting the capacity vector of each project in S_n^p. If we start with all of the possible cumulative capacity vectors $\mathbf{q} \in \mathbf{\Omega}_n$ then the cumulative capacity vector of every possible permutation schedule composed of $(n - 1)$ projects will be generated at least once. Hence, if we utilize the imbedded-state approach an optimal schedule cannot be missed.

The reduction of dimensionality effected by the introduction of the concept of the imbedded state space is especially significant in problems in which there are a large number of state variables. This is a result of the fact that the functional equation is only evaluated at $\binom{N}{n}$ states of the M-dimensional state space at each stage n, regardless of the size of M.

5.13. Computational Experience on Real-world Problems

The DP2 algorithm was coded in FORTRAN V and implemented both on an UNIVAC 1108 and a CDC 6400. In order to make the computational analysis as meaningful as possible, in terms of real-world problems, the input data to the computer program were based upon real-world systems. The systems involved were the sub-basins of the Ohio River Basin and six of the major river basins of Texas. Both of these major water-resource systems involved multi-purpose projects displaying the one-shot attributes. We define a one-shot project as one with a high capital cost which is largely incurred at the time of construction, a small salvage value at the end of an extremely long ($\geq$ 50 years) economic life, and a set of fixed finite capacities to meet demands. Taken together, their attributes add an almost irreversible dimension to capital investment decisions. Real life examples occurring in diverse systems include: water resources (dams), transportation (highways), waste treatment (disposal plants), petrochemical (pipelines), etc.

In the problems used to illustrate the feasibility of the DP2 algorithm, the future demand requirements, potential expansion projects, and both the capacities and the capital costs of the projects were estimated for both systems in varying degrees of completeness. Specific details as to the sources, nature, and use of these basic data as input to the sequencing algorithm, as well as the results of a sensitivity analysis, are discussed elsewhere. The resulting computational times are presented in condensed form in Table 5.2 for illustrative purposes. The reported times are the execution times on a UNIVAC 1108. These times do not include the compilation time. It should be emphasized that a primary objective of writing these programs was ease of programming and modification for experimental purpose and not the attainment of the most rapid execution times. Because of this, a compiler language was used, and the problems were solved in core. Even with these facts in mind, the computational times are reasonable for problems of the dimension encountered in real-world

TABLE 5.2. *Computational Experience*

No. of stages N	Dimensionality of the State Vector M	Number of different problems run	Mean execution time (sec) per problem
2	2	2	0.106
4	2	2	0.280
6	2	1	0.944
2	3	1	0.144
3	3	1	0.175
4	3	3	0.311
5	3	1	0.484
6	3	2	1.004
7	3	1	2.302
8	3	1	6.583
9	3	1	11.503
10	3	3	27.835
11	3	1	112.085

systems. We note from the table that a faster growth in computation time occurs for the stage variable than for the state vector. That is, the computational requirements (and in particular the time) are in the order of $MN2^{N-1}$. The high-speed (core) computer requirement is in the order of $\max_{n} \binom{N}{n}$. Therefore the number of calculations only increase linearly with the dimensionality of the state vector!

5.14. Variations and Extensions

Variations of the simple capacity expansion sequencing problem lead to more complicated problem situations. Some of these extensions include:

1. Projects in which the operating costs are no longer negligible or related to the production, but vary with project characteristics such as location, etc. For example, the problem of minimizing total discounted capital and operating costs subject to meeting demand requirements at all times has been investigated under different assumptions on production and operating costs by Lucke (1976).

2. Projects in which the accumulation of inventories from current production to meet subsequent demand with a holding cost $h > 0$ per unit of inventory per unit of time is tolerated. Minimization of the discounted costs for capacity expansion, production, inventories and imports subject to meeting demand projection over an infinite planning horizon has been studied by Erlenkotter (1974) under the following assumptions: (a) no-import, no-inventory; (b) import, no-inventory; (c) inventories, no-import; and (d) inventories and imports.

5.15. Miscellaneous Exercises

1. Compare the computational effort requirements of DP1 with that of DP2, i.e. how many additions and minimizations are involved in each for the example solved in Section 5.8. Show that the differences become more impressive with increase in size and complexity of a given problem. (See, for example, T. L. Morin and A. O. Esogbue, "Some efficient dynamic algorithms for the optimal sequencing and scheduling of water supply projects", *Water Resources Research*, Vol. 7 (1971), pp. 479–484.)

2. Discuss situations, both pathological and otherwise, in which the conventional dynamic program DP1 version of the capacity expansion sequencing problem may yield nonoptimal solutions. A useful insight to this problem will be obtained by consulting: (a) T. L. Morin and A. O. Esogbue, *op. cit.*, (b) T. L. Morin, "Pathology of a dynamic programming sequencing algorithm", *Water Resources Research*, Vol. 9, No. 5, 1973, pp. 1178–1185.

3. Consider the following capacity expansion problem involving four projects and an artificial project. Let $r = .05$ and $T = 10$ years. Let C_i and Q_i be as given in Table 5.3.

Let the project timing function be as given below:

$$\psi \langle g \rangle = 0 \begin{cases} 0, & 0 \leq q \leq 40, \\ 5, & q = 50, \\ 10, & 60 \leq q \leq 100 \end{cases}$$

TABLE 5.3. *Costs and Capacities of Four Projects and an Artificial Project*

	i	Project 1	Project 2	Project 3	Project 4	Artificial Project 0
Cost	C_i	20	35	40	50	0
Capacity	Q_i	10	20	30	40	0

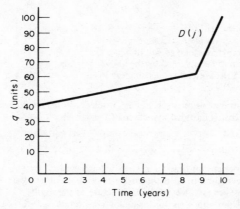

FIG. 5.5

Further, let the demand requirement $D(j)$ be the strictly increasing function given in Fig. 5.5. Solve the sequencing problem using DP1. Is this optimal? Why or why not?

4. Using the imbedded state space approach (DP2) obtain the solution to the capacity expansion-sequencing problem posed in problem 3.

5. Show that for the sequencing problem, when $f_n^{k_n}(q)$ of equation (5.33) is composed of exactly n projects then the $f^{k_n}(q)$ of DP1 can be obtained from the $f_n(q)$ of DP2. See, for example, T. L. Morin and A. O. Esogbue, *op. cit.*

6. Consider a one-dimensional capacity expansion scheduling problem in which the Q_i are arranged in a nonincreasing order. Show that DP2 can be used to calculate $f_n^{k_n}(q)$ of DP1, for $n = 1, 2, \ldots, M$ where $M + 1$ is the smallest integer such that

$$\sum_{i=1}^{M+1} Q_i > D(T).$$

(T. L. Morin and A. O. Esogbue, *op. cit.*)

7. Consider the following four project sequencing problems with the data given below:

i	1	2	3	4
Q_i	1	2	3	4
C_i	150	280	350	400

$$D(t) = \begin{cases} 0, & t = 0 \\ 2, & 0 < t \le 10 \\ 5 & 10 < t \le 20 \\ 10, & 20 < t \le \infty \end{cases} \quad ; \quad \exp(-rt) = \begin{cases} 1.000, & t = 0 \\ 0.6065, & t = 10 \\ 0.3678, & t = 20 \end{cases}$$

Let $\psi(q) \stackrel{\Delta}{=} \psi \left[\sum_{i=1}^{N} Q_i + D(0) \right]$ be given by

$$\psi(q) = \begin{cases} 0, & 0 \le \sum_i Q_i < 2, \\ 10, & 2 \le \sum_i Q_i < 5, \\ 20, & 5 \le \sum_i Q_i < 10, \\ \infty, & 10 \le \sum_i Q_i < 20. \end{cases}$$

(a) Solve the problem via DP1.
(b) Solve the problem via DP2.
(c) Provide an alternate method of solution.
(d) Compare the solutions obtained by the above methods.
(See, for example, D. Erlenkotter, "Sequencing expansion projects", *Operations Research*, Vol. 2 (1973), pp. 543–553.)

8. Consider a multi-dimensional scheduling problem treated in Section 5.11 in which the project maintenance cost is included by defining $\hat{C}_i$ as

$$\hat{C}_i = C_i + \int_{t_i}^{T} \xi(t) e^{-r(t - t_i)} dt$$

with $\xi(t) = $ maintenance cost at time t and C_i as defined earlier.

(a) Show that the inclusion of these costs, as well as other costs such as social and environmental, does not alter the basic structure of the results.
(b) What effect, if any, does the inclusion of constraints such as cumulative budgetary restrictions at time t have on the structure of the results?

9. Formulate problem 3 as an integer programming problem and then solve via branch and bound algorithm.

10. Compare and contrast the branch and bound method and the imbedded state dynamic programming algorithm for the multi-dimensional sequencing problem particularly with regards to numerical computation via the digital computer.

Bibliography and Comments

Section 5.1
Various applications of capacity expansion sequencing and scheduling abound. For applications to:

Water Resources, see
BUTCHER, W. S., HAMES, Y. Y. and HALL, W. A., "Dynamic programming algorithm for the optimal sequencing of water supply projects", *Water Resources Research*, 5, No. 6 (1969), 1196–1204.
This appears to be the first account of an application to water-supply systems. The model presented is not only inefficient from a computational standpoint but has been found to yield nonoptimal solutions at times.

Developing Countries, see
MANE, A. S., *Investments for Capacity Expansion: Size, Location and Time-Phasing*, MIT Press, Cambridge, Mass., 1967.
The use of recurrent of regenerative expansion sequences is discussed here.
For the use of differential calculus in these analyses see
McDOWELL, I., "The economical planning for engineering works", *Operations Research*, 8, (1960), 533–542.
For an application of Integer Programming methods to investment sequencing decisions in industry see

KENDRICK, D., *Programming Investment in the Process Industries*, MIT Press, Cambridge, Mass., 1967.

The use of search techniques to scan or screen off rapidly all but the most promising projects out of a large set is discussed in

TSOU, C. A. *et al.*, "Search techniques for project sequencing", *ASCE, Journal of the Hydraulics Division*, Vol. HY 5 (1973), 833–839.

Section 5.2

An improvement of the algorithm presented by Butcher *et al.* and the first application of the highly efficient imbedded state space dynamic programming method was presented by:

MORIN, T. L. and A. O. ESOGBUE, "Some efficient dynamic programming algorithms for the optimal sequencing and scheduling of water supply projects", *Water Resources Research*, 7, No. (1971), 479–484.

Section 5.3

A branch and bound procedure for the treatment of this problem may be found in:

ESOGBUE, A. O. and T. L. MORIN, "A branch and bound algorithm for the optimal sequencing of water resources projects", 18th Int. Meeting of the Institute of Management Sciences, Washington, D. C., 1971.

Also, see:

MORIN, T. L., "Optimal scheduling of one shot projects", Ph.D. Dissertation Dept. of Operations Research, Case Western Reserve University, Cleveland, Ohio, 1971.

Section 5.4

For a detailed discussion see

MORIN, T. L. and A. O. ESOGBUE (1971), *op. cit.*

Section 5.5

The substance of this presentation was developed in the work cited above.

Sections 5.5 and 5.6

For a mathematical exposition of this technique see

MORIN, T. L. and A. O. ESOGBUE, "Imbedded state space approach to reduction of dimensionality in dynamic programming of higher dimension", *Journal of Mathematical Analysis and Applications*, 4, No. 3 (1974).

Sections 5.7 and 5.8

The superiority of DP2 over DP1 was demonstrated in:

MORIN, T. L. and A. O. ESOGBUE (1971), *op. cit.*

Further clarifications and discussion may be found in

MORIN, T. L., "Optimal sequencing of capacity expansion projects", *ASCE, Journal of the Hydraulics Division*, Vol. NY 9 (1973), 1605–1622.

Section 5.9

This theorem was first proposed by:

MORIN, T. L. and A. O. ESOGBUE, "A useful theorem in the dynamic programming solution of sequencing and scheduling problems occurring in capital expenditure planning", *Water Resources Research*, 10, No. 1 (1974).

Section 5.11

For additional treatment see the following:

MORIN, T. L. and A. O. ESOGBUE, "A class of multi-dimensional scheduling problems in capacity expansion", presented at the 41st National Meeting of the Operations Research Society of America, New Orleans (1972).

ERLENKOTTER, D. (1973), *op. cit.*

Section 5.12

Interesting variations and extensions appear in the following:

ERLENKOTTER, D. (1973), *op. cit.*

ERLENKOTTER, D., "Capacity expansion with imports and inventories", working Paper No. 223, Western Management Science Institute, UCLA (1974).
This formulation is essentially continuous. Application to capacity expansion of India's aluminium industry is discussed.

LUCKE, J. B., "Minimizing the operating and capital costs of water supply projects", *Water Resources Research*, **12** (1976), p. 101. The model considered is patterned after Erlenkotter (1973). However, the solution technique employed is based on network theory.

CHAPTER 6

Sequencing Problems with Nonserial Structures

6.1. Introduction

The literature in sequencing theory and applications deals mostly with serial systems. While such systems are common and important, it is instructive to recognize the existence of another important class of sequencing problems – namely, those involving nonserial structures. In this chapter, therefore, we wish to introduce the reader to nonserial systems and how techniques developed for serial systems can be modified for use in nonserial systems analysis. We will also consider new techniques developed especially for nonserial systems. We will use as our basic model PERT-Cost or CPM-Cost scheduling problems with nonserial precedence relations. These problems constitute an important class of problems encountered in diverse systems including the planning, management and associated scheduling problems faced by Research and Development (R&D) organizations.

In the literature, these problems, particularly those of the CPM-Cost problem variety, have received many different formulations depending upon the nature of the cost-duration relationships for each phase of the project. Various mathematical programming models, but primarily linear programming, integer programming, and separable convex programming are quite common. Heuristic methods, of course, abound. This class is, by far, the favourite among practitioners who tend to devise their own algorithms. We are not interested in such methods here, however. Dynamic programming models, on the other hand, exist only in a limited sense. Despite the many attractions for using dynamic programming, its limited use is often attributed to the curse of dimensionality. Because of this difficulty, many authors tend to dismiss the use of dynamic programming as a feasible approach to this class of problems. We will therefore concern ourselves with the development of *efficient* dynamic programming formulations for these novel areas of application. Although we are primarily interested in the less common nonserial systems, we will motivate our treatment with a brief introduction to serial multistage sequencing decisions.

6.2. Serial Multistage Sequencing Processes

The cornerstone of dynamic programming is the almost intuitive principle of optimality on which most applications of dynamic programming are based. It is, however, well known that while in a majority of cases the application of this principle is routine and its validity immediate in some major problem situations, care must be taken in choosing the state and decision variables. It is also necessary to validate such assumptions in the theory as the independence of the future from the past. The principle of optimality can then be applied directly to serial multistage decision processes (Fig. 6.1) if the sufficiency conditions are satisfied.

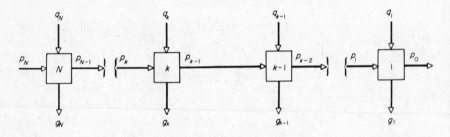

FIG. 6.1. A serial multistage decision process.

For example, consider the serial multistage decision process illustrated in Fig. 6.1 with a return function:

$$G = \sum_{k=1}^{N} g_k(p_k, q_k) \tag{6.1}$$

and transition function

$$p_{k-1} = T(p_k, q_k) \tag{6.2}$$

where p_k and q_k are the state and decision variables for stage k, respectively. Developing the functional equation for this process depends, among other things, upon whether or not the initial state, the final state or both states are fixed. Various perturbations of these parameters lead to various forms of functional equations of dynamic programming. A correct system of equations when the initial state is fixed and the final state is free results in

$$f_k(p_k) = \underset{q_k}{\text{opt.}} \{g_k(p_k, q_k) + f_{k-1}[T(p_k, q_k)]\} \quad \text{for } k = 2, \dots, N \tag{6.3}$$

with:

$$f_1(p_1) = \underset{q_1}{\text{opt.}} \{g_1(p_1, q_1)\} \quad \text{for } k = 1. \tag{6.4}$$

If, however, the final state is fixed and the initial state is free, state inversion is required. Such an inversion generates the transition function:

$$p_k = \hat{T}(p_{k-1}, q_k) \tag{6.5}$$

and the resultant reward function, $\hat{g}_k(p_{k-1}, q_k)$. The corresponding functional equations for this system become:

$$f_k(p_{k-1}) = \operatorname*{opt}_{q_k} \{\hat{g}_k(p_{k-1}, q_k) + f_{k+1}[\hat{T}(p_{k-1}, q_k)]\}$$
$$k = 1, 2, \ldots, N-1 \tag{6.6}$$

with:

$$f_N(p_{N-1}) = \operatorname*{opt}_{q_N} \{\hat{g}_N(p_{N-1}, q_N)\} \quad for \ k = N. \tag{6.7}$$

If both the initial state and the final state are fixed, decision inversion is needed on the first stage. The new transition function is:

$$q_k = \tilde{T}(p_{k-1}, p_k) \tag{6.8}$$

and the corresponding functional equations are:

$$f_k(p_k, p_1) = \operatorname*{opt}_{q_k} \{g_k(p_k, q_k) + f_{k-1}[T(p_k, q_k), p_1]\} \quad k = 2, \ldots, N \tag{6.9}$$

with:

$$f_1(p_0, p_1) = g_1[p_1, \tilde{T}(p_0, p_1)] \quad for \ k = 1. \tag{6.10}$$

While considerable attention has been devoted in the literature to the analysis of serial systems, a natural extension is the study of nonserial systems. These are usually treated via the tools developed for serial systems.

6.3. Nonserial Multistage Sequencing Processes

Define a nonserial structure as a structure where at least one stage in the system receives inputs from more than one stage or sends outputs to more than one stage. This situation exists whenever a system is a combination of serial and parallel processes. Such systems are found in the study of chemical-processing systems, natural gas transmission pipelines, water-resource systems and various other processes.

The four basic non-serial systems usually discussed in the literature are:

(a) A diverging branch system (Fig. 6.2(a)). A simple example of this is a linear allocation problem occurring when several small firms are attached to a parent organization. Another example is found in water-resource management systems when a river basin may consist of a main stream branching off into tributaries.

(b) A converging branch system (Fig. 6.2(b)). This system is illustrated by a linear allocation problem that arises when a number of companies

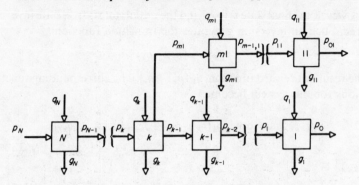

FIG. 6.2(a) A non-serial system with a diverging branch structure.

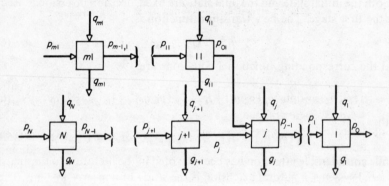

FIG. 6.2(b) A non-serial system with a converging branch structure.

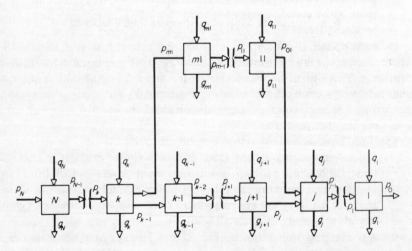

FIG. 6.2(c) A nonserial system with a feedforward loop structure.

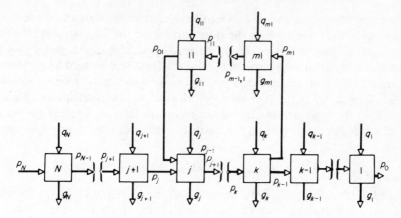

Fig. 6.2(d) A nonserial system with a feedback loop structure.

merge into one. Another example from water-resources systems analysis involves the analysis of reservoir or treatment plants located in various separate streams flowing into a main one in a delta.

(c) A feedforward loop system (Fig. 6.2(c)). Such a system may arise in gas transmission pipelines and networks where some nodes in adjoining areas are fed by a "bypass" line which later on joins the parent transmission line.

(d) A feedback loop system (Fig. 6.2(d)). For example, in chemical engineering processes with product recycle characteristics, fresh feed entering a stage with a certain quality level and flow rate is mixed with part of the product stream leaving another stage at different quality level and recycle rate.

More complex nonserial processes can always be constructed by various combinations of these four basic nonserial systems. Unlike serial systems, the literature is devoid of any set of sufficiency or other similar conditions which are developed primarily for nonserial systems. Employing the concept of state and decision inversion one can extend the principle of optimality to the analysis of nonserial systems. For diverging branch systems, however, the principle of optimality can be directly applied without the use of state or decision inversion. Converging branches which have their initial states free can be optimized using state inversion. The mechanics of inversion is an approach employed to transform a system output variable into the inverse of the input variable, and vice versa. This would normally lead to equations of the form given in (6.1) to (6.7). In the converging branch system of Fig. 6.2(b), if the state variable p_{m1} is free, then state inversion is performed on stages $m1$ to 11.

However, converging branches which have their initial states fixed must use decision inversion instead on the stage just before the junction stage. In our example, decision inversion would be performed at stage 11, giving rise to equations of the form given in (6.8) to (6.10). Both feedforward loop systems and feedback loop systems require decision inversion. Such an inversion can take place at either the stage just before the junction with the main serial system or the stage just after leaving the main serial system. These stages are 11 and $m1$, respectively, both in the feedback and feedforward loop systems.

6.4. CPM-Cost Problem: the Basic Model

PERT, PERT-Cost, CPM-Cost and their variations are perhaps the best known applications of activity network scheduling methodology. We will concern ourselves in this chapter with CPM-Cost problems. The information required in the CPM-Cost problem is a set of cost-duration functions for each of the phases of a project and the precedence relations between each of the phases of the project. The CPM-Cost problem then seeks answers to the following classic questions:

1. What is the optimal cost–duration curve for the entire project?
2. Given a budget for the project, what is the sequence of decisions which will minimize the completion time of the project?
3. Given a completion time for the project, what is the sequence of decisions which will minimize the cost of completing the project?

Throughout the literature the approach to answering these three questions has been basically the same. The favourite procedure is to minimize the cost of completing the project in a given time interval, and then to parametrically vary the time interval of completion until an optimal solution is obtained. One can also employ this approach to minimize the cost of completing the project for various completion times. This method, however, will lead to complex dynamic programming formulations for projects with nonserial precedence relations. We seek to avoid this quagmire.

An alternative approach is to minimize the completion date subject to all possible completion costs for the project. This method leads to simpler and more efficient dynamic programming formulations especially for those with certain nonserial precedence relationships. The duality (in dynamic programming sense) between policy and the optimal value functions allows us to still generate the same solutions to the basic problem in spite of proceeding on a different tack.

For both the project cost and completion time minimization approaches, the problem can usually be converted to simple resource allocation problems for which one can readily develop dynamic programming formulations. If the precedence relations possess a serial structure, the resultant dynamic programs possess identical structures, and either approach may be employed.

6.5. CPM-Cost Problems with Serial Structures

In the previous section we emphasized the fact that a cost minimization approach will not give a feasible dynamic programming formulation for projects whose phases are not in a serial order. By serial order, we mean that at most only one phase can immediately precede or immediately succeed a given project phase. An example of a project with five phases can be found in Fig. 6.3. Whenever any phase in a project has more than one phase immediately preceding or immediately succeeding it, then the project has a nonserial structure. These definitions are similar to those we used for defining serial and nonserial dynamic programming in Sections 6.2 and 6.3 respectively.

FIG. 6.3. A project with five serial precedence phases.

As we mentioned earlier, the conventional approach is to minimize the cost of completing the project within a given completion time. Once we give the mathematical programming formulation for the serial project given in Fig. 6.3, the dynamic programming formulation will be apparent. For both formulations we introduce the following definitions: Let

d_j = the completion time of phase j,
$g_j(d_j)$ = the cost for completing phase j in a duration d_j,
A^+ = the latest allowable completion time for the project,
d_j^- = the minimum length of time in which phase j can be completed,
d_j^+ = the maximum amount of time in which phase j will be completed.

Thus, the mathematical programming formulation of the project cost minimization model is the following:

$$\text{minimize} \sum_{j=1}^{5} g_j(d_j)$$

$$\text{subject to} \sum_{j=1}^{5} d_j \leq A^+$$

$$d_j^- \leq d_j \leq d_j^+ \quad j = 1, 2, \ldots, 5$$

This mathematical programming problem is a simple one-constraint resource allocation model. The dynamic programming formulation for a resource allocation is very easily developed. Define $f_n(A)$ as the minimum cost of completing the last nth phase of the project given A time units are still remaining until the project must be completed. The project cost minimization dynamic programming formulation is therefore the following:

$$f_5(A) = \min\,(g_5(d_5))$$
$$d_5^- \le d_5 \le \min\,(A, d_5^+),$$
$$f_n(A) = \min\,\{g_n(d_n) + f_{n-1}(A - d_n)\}, \quad n = 1, 2, 3, 4$$
$$d_n^- \le d_n \le \min\,(A, d_n^+).$$

We suggest the minimization of the completion time of the project for a given budget. Again, we will assume that the precedence relations have a serial form. The constraints upon the minimum and maximum completion time of a phase will be replaced by the minimum and maximum cost of completing that phase. The following additional definitions are used in this model. Let

k_j = the cost of completing phase j,
$h_j(k_j)$ = the completion time of phase j given k_j dollars are spent on it,
L^+ = the maximum cost for the entire project,
k_j^- = the minimum expenditure allowed for phase j,
k_j^+ = the maximum expenditure allowed for phase j,
N = the number of phases in the project.

The mathematical programming formulation for this model is then the following:

$$\min\ \sum_{j=1}^{5} h_j(k_j)$$

$$\text{s.t.}\ \sum_{j=1}^{5} k_j \le L^+$$

$$k_j^- \le k_j \le k_j^+ \quad j = 1, 2, \ldots, 5$$

We note that this mathematical programming formulation also has the structure of a one-constraint resource allocation model. Define $f_n(L)$ as the minimum time to complete the last nth phase of the project given L dollars are left to spend on it. The resultant dynamic programming formulation is

$$f_5(L) = \min\,\{h_5(k_5)\}$$
$$k_5^- \le k_5 \le \min\,(k_5, L),$$
$$f_n(L) = \min\,\{h_n(k_n) + f_{n-1}(L - k)\} \quad n = 1, 2, 3, 4$$
$$k_n^- \le k_n \le \min\,(k_n^+, L).$$

We must emphasize that either approach is a feasible method for finding the time–cost completion curve for a project, if its phases have a serial structure. However, the project cost minimization method leads to complex dynamic programming formulation when the precedence relations have a nonserial structure.

The reason why the approach of minimizing the cost of the project given a completion time for the project does not lead to easily soluble dynamic programming formulations becomes obvious once the mathematical programming formulation of a project with a nonserial structure is constructed. Therefore, we will develop the mathematical programming formulation for the nonserial project in Fig. 6.4.

6.6. CPM-Cost Problems with Nonserial Phase Structure

Our principal concern is with sequencing for nonserial CPM-Cost problems. There exists a large body of such problems in which the phases of the project are strung together in a nonserial fashion. Such situations arise whenever there exists a project task that either depends on the completion of more than one separate and parallel activity or generates more than one parallel phase for other project tasks. For this class of problems, the cost minimization approach usually leads to a highly complex dynamic program which is expensive to solve. Consider, for example, a project such as the one depicted in Fig. 6.4. We proceed to treat this problem in the following section.

6.7. Nonserial Networks: Project Cost Minimization Approach [PCM]

Define the additional variable t_n as the completion time of phase n. We also assume that phases 1 and 4 start at the same time, although this restriction is not necessary. The mathematical programming formulation using the minimization of cost strategy is thus the following:

$$\min \sum_{j=1}^{7} g_j(d_j),$$

$$\text{s.t. } -t_1 + d_1 \leq 0,$$
$$t_1 - t_2 + d_2 \leq 0,$$
$$t_2 - t_3 + d_3 \leq 0,$$
$$-t_4 + d_4 \leq 0,$$
$$t_4 - t_5 + d_5 \leq 0,$$
$$t_5 - t_6 + d_6 \leq 0,$$
$$t_3 - t_7 + d_7 \leq 0,$$
$$t_6 - t_7 + d_7 \leq 0,$$
$$t_7 \leq A^+,$$
$$d_j^- \leq d_j \leq d_j^+ \quad j = 1, 2, \ldots, 7.$$

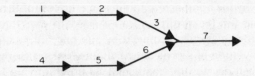

FIG. 6.4. Project with nonserial precedence phases.

We note that the simple form of the one constraint resource allocation model of Section 6.5 has vanished. However, if we attempt to minimize the completion time instead of the cost, this basic structure still reappears. The mathematical formulation using the minimization of time approach then becomes

$$\min \left\{ \left[\max \left(h_1(k_1) + h_2(k_2) + h_3(k_3),\ h_4(k_4) + h_5(k_5) + h_6(k_6) \right) \right] + h_7(k_7) \right\},$$

$$\text{s.t.} \sum_{j=1}^{7} k_j \leq L^+,$$

$$k_j^- \leq k_j \leq k_j^+ \quad j = 1, 2, \ldots, 7.$$

The difference between the mathematical programming formulation of the serial and nonserial projects is the fact that the nonserial model has a more complex objective function. One property that both objective functions do have in common, however, is that their variables are separable. The property of monotonicity also exists. Therefore, if the objective function can be decomposed, the mathematical program satisfies the sufficiency conditions of Mitten. Thus, the program can be solved via dynamic programming. The ease with which this decomposition can be accomplished determines whether or not the program should be optimized via dynamic programming.

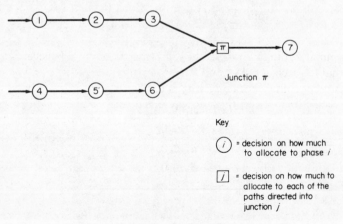

FIG. 6.5. A converging branch structure.

The decomposition for the project in Fig. 6.4 is rather straightforward. Define $f_n(L)$ as the minimum time to complete all the preceding phases up to phase n of the project given L dollars were allocated to these phases. Define $\Phi_n(L)$ as the minimum time to complete all the paths leading into junction n given that L dollars were allocated to all these paths. A series of phases is referred to as a path. In Fig. 6.4 phases 1, 2, and 3 correspond to a path. The junction between the two paths occurs before the start of phase 7. Decisions of the first type are the circled stages in Fig. 6.5 while decisions of the second type are in the square stages. We are thus led to the following dynamic programming formulation for the network:

$$f_1(L) = \min\{h_1(k_1)\}$$
$$k_1^- \leq k_1 \leq \min(k_1^+, L),$$

$$f_n(L) = \min\{h_n(k_n) + f_{n-1}(L - k_n)\} \quad n = 2, 3$$
$$k_n^- \leq k_n \leq \min(k_n^+, L),$$

$$f_4(L) = \min\{h_4(k_4)\}$$
$$k_4^- \leq k_4 \leq \min(k_4^+, L),$$

$$f_n(L) = \min\{h_n(k_n) + f_{n-1}(L - k_n)\} \quad n = 5, 6,$$
$$k_n^- \leq k_n \leq \min(k_n^+, L),$$

$$\Phi_1(L) = \min[\max\{f_3(c), f_6(L - c)\}]$$
$$0 \leq c \leq L$$

and finally,

$$f_7(L) = \min\{h_7(k_7) + \Phi_1(L - k_7)\}$$
$$k_7^- \leq k_7 \leq \min(k_7^+, L).$$

In this section we have demonstrated how the minimization of time approach can be applied to the CPM-Cost problem so that the CPM-Cost problem can be solved via dynamic programming.

We summarize our analysis via the following assertion. Whenever a network is such that for each activity i and j, with activity i preceding j $(i < j)$ the set of paths p_i and p_j containing activities i and j, respectively, is given by $p_i \subseteq p_j$ or $p_j \subseteq p_i$, then we can assert that the functional equation for $f_n(L)$ decomposes into a sequence of one-dimensional dynamic programming problems. This is a sufficient condition. The proof of this theorem is left to the reader in the form of an exercise.

The major difficulty with using the above strategy is that the objective function may not be easily decomposed. We can easily construct examples of networks in which this condition is violated. Since the objective function is derived from the precedence relationships, a *study of the various forms of the precedence relationships will indicate when dynamic programming is a feasible optimization method for CPM-Cost problems.* Also, the application of the latest computational advances in dynamic programming will influence the decision of whether or not the CPM-Cost problem should be optimized via dynamic programming. These two topics will be investigated in the next section.

6.8. Project Time Minimization Approach [PTM]

The simple resource allocation structure, which as we observed characterizes both the cost and time minimization problems in serial systems, can be regained by attempting to minimize the completion time of the project for any project cost. We need the notations introduced in Section 6.5 for the discussions that follow. Consider the network diagrammed in Fig. 6.5. The mathematical program for the problem is

$$[PTM] \quad \min\left\{\max\left[\sum_{j=1}^{3} h_j(k_j), \sum_{j=4}^{6} h_j(k_j)\right] + h_7(k_7)\right\}, \quad (6.11)$$

$$\text{s.t.} \sum_{j=1}^{N} k_j \leq L^+, \quad (6.12)$$

$$k_j^- \leq k_j \leq k_j^+, \quad \forall j.$$

We note that the time minimization approach generates problems of similar structures for both the serial and nonserial cases except for the form of the objective function. On the other hand, the main difference, using the cost-minimization approach, between the serial and nonserial cases is the introduction of a set of new constraints in the nonserial cases. However, Mitten's sufficiency condition is still satisfied, and thus a dynamic program can be developed.

6.9. A Dynamic Programming Model of the PTM Problem

If we define $f_n(L)$ as the minimum time to complete all phases in a project which precede and include phase n, given L dollars are available for spending on these phases, and m as the phase following junction node π, equations can then be developed for each branch as follows:

$$f_1(L) = \min[h_1(k_1)], \qquad k_1^- \leq k_1 \leq \min(k_1^+, L), \text{ with } (6.13)$$
$$f_i(L) = \min[h_i(k_i) + f_{i-1}(L - k_i)] \quad k_i^- \leq k_i \leq \min(k_i^+, L),$$
$$i = 2, 3, \ldots, b. \quad (6.14)$$

Similarly,

$$f_{b+1}(L) = \min[h_{b+1}(k_{b+1})], \text{ with } \quad (6.15)$$
$$f_j(L) = \min[h_j(k_j) + f_{j-1}(L - k_j)], \quad (6.16)$$
$$k_j^- \leq k_j \leq \min(k_j^+, L), \quad j = b+2, b+3, \ldots, m-1.$$

Thus

$$f_m(L) = \min_{k_m} \{\max[f_b(k_m), f_{m-1}(L - k_m)]\}, \text{ with} \qquad (6.17)$$

$$f_{m+1}(L) = f_n(L) = \min_{k_{m+1}} [h_{m+1}(k_{m+1}) + f_m(L - k_{m+1})]. \qquad (6.18)$$

For an example, in a two-branch (Fig. 6.5) system, branch 1 consists of phases 1 through b and branch 2, phases $b + 1$, $b + 2$, ..., through $m - 1$. For this problem we have

$$f_1(L) = \min[h_1(k_1)], \qquad k_1^- \le k_1 \le \min(k_1^+, L), \quad (6.19)$$

$$f_2(L) = \min[h_2(k_2) + f_1(L - k_2)], \qquad k_2^- \le k_2 \le \min(k_2, L), \quad (6.20)$$

$$f_3(L) = \min[h_3(k_3) + f_2(L - k_3)], \qquad k_3^- \le k_3 \le \min(k_3, L), \quad (6.21)$$

$$f_4(L) = \min[h_4(k_4)], \qquad k_4^- \le k_4 \le \min(k_4^+, L), \quad (6.22)$$

$$f_7(L) = \min_{0 \le k_7 \le L} \{\max[f_3(k_7), f_6(L - k_7)]\}, \qquad (6.23)$$

with

$$\max\left[\sum_{i=1}^{3} k_i^-, \sum_{j=4}^{6} k_j^-\right] \le k_7 \le \min\left[\sum_{i=1}^{3} k_i^+, \sum_{j=4}^{6} k_j^+, L\right]$$

and

$$f_8(L) = \min(h_8(k_8) + f_7(L - k_8)], \qquad k_8^- \le k_8 \le \min(k_8^+, L), \quad (6.24)$$

where $f_5(\cdot)$ and $f_6(\cdot)$ are derived in a manner akin to $f_2(\cdot), f_3(\cdot)$, of the foregoing.

We note that the dynamic programming formulation can be divided into two groups as follows:

Group 1: Stages with decisions on how much to invest on phases of the project (i.e. stages 1 through 6 and stage 8).

Group 2: Stages with decisions on how much to allocate between different paths on the project (i.e. stage 7).

In general, the level of difficulty of conversion to a dynamic program is highly precedence-structure dependent. This, however, does not create insurmountable problems, as we shall soon demonstrate. In the sequel, we proceed to invoke some recent methods for ameliorating the dimensionality problem which is usually encountered in nonserial dynamic programs.

6.10. EXAMPLE 1. The Pseudo-stage Concept and CPM-Cost Problem

Consider a project network with nonserial phases as diagrammed in Fig. 6.6 below. Again, we can develop standard DP formulations for the problem which may be employed in calculating $f_n(L)$, $n = 1, 2, \ldots, 6$, where $f_n(L)$ is defined as the minimum time to complete all phases up to phase n, given that L dollars are left and employing an optimal policy. A function, $\Phi_\pi(L)$, is next

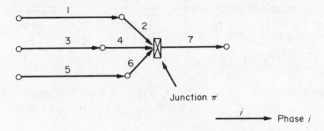

Junction π

$\xrightarrow{\hspace{1cm}i}$ Phase i

FIG. 6.6. A three-branch converging system.

defined for the minimum time to complete all phases in each path preceding junction node π. By the principle of optimality we have:

$$\Phi_\pi(L) = \min_{c_1, c_2} \{\max[f_2(c_1), f_4(c_2), f_6(L - c_1 - c_2)]\} \qquad (6.25)$$

with the constraints on c_1 and c_2 given as:

$$\max\{(k_1^- + k_2^-), 0\} \le c_1 \le \min\{(k_1^+ + k_2^+), L\},$$
$$\max\{(k_3^- + k_4^-), 0\} \le c_2 \le \min\{(k_3^+ + k_4^+), L\},$$
$$\max\{(k_5^- + k_6^-), 0\} \le c_1 + c_2 \le \min\{(k_5^+ + k_6^+), L\}.$$

We then compute $f_7(L)$ using

$$f_7(L) = \min[h_7(k_7) + \Phi_\pi(L - k_7)], \quad k_7^- \le k_7 \le \min(k_7^+, L). \quad (6.26)$$

We make the following observations relative to the foregoing functional equations:

(1) $f_n(\cdot)$ is a single-state variable problem with one decision variable.

(2) $\Phi_\pi(\cdot)$ is a single-state variable problem with two decision variables.

(3) $\Phi_\pi(L)$ is separable and monotone increasing.

A more demanding computational problem than the preceding will result with this formulation. Thus, with increasing number of branches, the level of computational difficulty increases. What is responsible for this unpalatable increase? What can be done about it at this juncture?

To reduce dimensionality, we can ask a number of questions. We basically do not wish to deal with a formulation consisting of more than one state variable and one decision variable. So how can we attain this more pleasant state of affairs? We can do so by introducing a "pseudo-stage" generally at the junction node between two converging branches. This means that the dynamic programming process at the junction stage is decomposed into a series of simpler dynamic programming processes each imbedded within another. Thus instead of optimizing over two decision variables at the junction node, two one-decision variable optimizations are performed, one at the junction node and the other at the pseudo-stage. Let us apply this concept to our problem.

To use the pseudo-stage concept, we begin by decomposing $\Phi_\pi(L)$ into two stages. Let the corresponding functional equations $\Phi_\pi^1(L)$ and $\Phi_\pi^2(L)$ for the first and second pseudo-stages. The first functional equations in the new dynamic programming formulation remain the same as in the standard formulation. The last equations are, however, replaced by

$$\Phi_\pi^1(L) = \min_{c_1} \{\max[f_2(c_1), f_4(L - c_1)]\} \text{ with} \tag{6.27}$$

$$\max\{(k_1^- + k_2^-), 0\} \le c_1 \le \min\{k_1^+ + k_2^+), L\},$$

$$\Phi_\pi^2(L) = \min_{c_2} \{\max[f_6(c_2), \Phi_\pi^1(L - c_2)]\} \text{ with} \tag{6.28}$$

$$\max\{(k_5^- + k_6^-), 0\} \le c_2 \le \min\{(k_5^+ + k_6^+), L\}, \text{ and}$$

$$f_7(L) = \min_{k_7} [h_7(k_7) + \Phi_\pi^2(L - k_7)] \text{ with } k_7^- \le k_7 \le \min(k_7^+, L) \tag{6.29}$$

As can be seen, this problem has now been completely formulated as a DP problem with one state variable and one decision variable – a reduction in dimensionality of significant importance in the computational solution of DP problems.

6.11. EXAMPLE 2. A CPM-Cost Problem with Many Paths Departing from Junction

The next example employed to illustrate the utility of our approach (Fig. 6.7) concerns a project network where more than one path leaves a junction node. A conventional approach would produce a much more complex dynamic programming formulation than in the previous examples. However, by a judicious selection of the order of optimization of the phases, a computationally tractable dynamic programming formulation is feasible. The key to the approach is the introduction of "pseudo-tasks" in an appropriate manner and a determination of an optimal order of optimization. Let us begin by defining two key terms to this approach.

DEFINITION 1. *A pseudo-task is a combination of phases for which a time-cost function is available.*

DEFINITION 2. $\xi_n(L) = $ *minimum time to perform pseudo-task n given L dollars have been allocated to it and optimal policy is followed throughout.*

OBSERVATION. *The first pseudo-task determines whether phase 3 or phase 4 in the project belongs to a critical path.*

The DP version for this pseudo-task is

$$\xi_1(L) = \min_{c_1} \{\max[h_3(c_1), h_4(L - c_1)]\}, \tag{6.30}$$

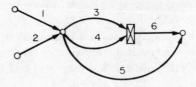

with the constraints on c_1 given by:

$$\max\{(k_1^- + k_3^-), (k_2^- + k_4^-), 0\} \le c_1 \le \min\{(k_1^+ + k_3^+), (k_2^+ + k_4^+), L\}.$$

In Fig. 6.8 the precedence relations are redrawn with pseudo-task 1 replacing phases 3 and 4. Since two paths still leave from junction node π', it is necessary to introduce a second pseudo-task. This leads to the following:

$$f_1(L) = \min_{0 \le d_1 \le L} \{\xi_1(d_1)\}, \tag{6.31}$$

$$f_2(L) = \min [h_6(k_6) + f_1(L - k_6)], \ k_6^- \le k_6 \le \min(k_6^+, L), \tag{6.32}$$

$$f_3(L) = \min [h_5(k_5)], \ k_5^- \le k_5 \le \min(k_5^+, L), \text{ and} \tag{6.33}$$

$$\xi_2(L) = \min_{c_2}\{\max [f_2(c_2), f_3(L - c_2)]\}, \tag{6.34}$$

$$\max\{(k_1^- + k_6^-), (k_2^- + k_5^-), 0\} \le c_2 \le \min\{(k_1^+ + k_6^+), (k_2^+ + k_5^+), L\}.$$

Junction π'

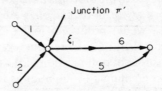

FIG. 6.8. Using pseudo-task 1 to replace phases 3 and 4.

Figure 6.9 is in the final reduced form with pseudo-task 2 introduced to replace pseudo-task 1 and phases 6 and 5. The functional equations are now

$$f_4(L) = \min_{k_1} [h_1(k_1)], \tag{6.30}$$

$$f_5(L) = \min_{k_2} [h_2(k_2)], \tag{6.31}$$

$$\Phi_{\pi'}(L) = \min_{c_3}\{\max [f_4(c_3), f_5(L - c_3)]\}, \tag{6.32}$$

$$f_6(L) = \min_{d_2} [\xi_2(d_2) + \Phi_{\pi'}(L - d_2)] \tag{6.33}$$

where k_1, k_2, c_3 and d_2 are chosen over their appropriate ranges. Problems with more than one path leaving a junction are thus tractable via DP by introducing the concept and operation of "pseudo-task".

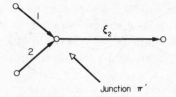

FIG. 6.9. Using pseudo-task 2 to replace pseudo-task 1 and phases 3 and 4.

6.12. EXAMPLE 3. A Complex Nonserial System as in Fig. 6.10

Remark 1. The structure of this project network is such that it is virtually impossible to reduce the problem to one involving only one state variable and one decision variable via the standard approach.

2. The method of Nemhauser and Ullman (1969) for problems of this general form can be invoked only after the problem has been reduced as in Fig. 6.11 by introducing pseudo-tasks ψ_1 and ψ_2.

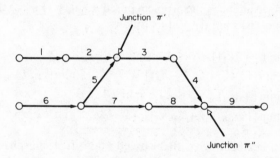

FIG. 6.10. Complex converging–diverging–converging system.

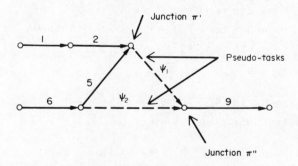

FIG. 6.11. Compression of Fig. 6.4 via pseudo-tasks.

Analysis 1. Using Nemhauser and Ullman's method directly leads to a system of eleven functional equations in which (a) six nonrecursive functional equations have two state variables and one decision variable; (b) one functional equation has one state variable and two decision variables.

2. Using a judicious combination of pseudo-task and the Nemhauser–Ullman method, the six nonrecursive functional equations can be reduced to only four.

3. Even if phases 5, 4 and 8 were replaced by an arbitrarily large number, say twenty different phases, our method still produces a system with only four equations – a substantial saving in computational requirements for large-scale CPM-Cost systems.

The technique is to consolidate all the phases between junction points into pseudo-tasks prior to applying the technique of formulation for nonserial systems proposed by Nemhauser and Ullman. This technique is invariant in the sense that irrespective of the number of phases involved in the converging branches (junction points), the number of the resultant functional equations remains the same. On the other hand, a brute-force application of the method of Nemhauser and Ullman produces a system of equations whose number is dependent on the number of phases in the branches. We proceed to illustrate the use of this technique in the problem posed in Fig. 6.10a. For this problem, the two pseudo-tasks are derived as follows:

$$f_1(L) = \min[h_3(k_3)], \ k_3^- \leq k_3 \leq \min(k_3^+, L), \tag{6.35}$$

$$\psi_1(L) = \min[h_4(k_4) + f_1(L - k_4)], \ k_4^- \leq k_4 \leq \min(k_4^+, L), \tag{6.36}$$

$$f_2(L) = \min[h_7(k_7)], \ k_7^- \leq k_7 \leq \min(k_7^+, L), \tag{6.37}$$

$$\psi_2(L) = \min[h_8(k_8) + f_2(L - k_8)], \ k_8^- \leq k_8 \leq \min(k_8^+, L). \tag{6.38}$$

The problem is next redrawn with the pseudo-tasks replacing phases 3, 4, 7 and 8, as in Fig. 6.9. The resultant nonserial dynamic programming formulation is

$$f_3(L) = \min[h_1(k_1)], \ k_1^- \leq k_1 \leq \mathrm{in}(k_1^+, L), \tag{6.39}$$

$$f_4(L) = \min[h_2(k_2) + f_3(L - k_2)], \ k_2^- \leq k_2 \leq \min(k_2^+, L), \tag{6.40}$$

$$f_5(L) = \min[h_6(k_6)], \ k_6^- \leq k_6 \leq \min(k_6^+, L), \tag{6.41}$$

$$f_6(L, k_6) = \min_{d_2} [\psi_2(d_2) + f_5(k_6)], \tag{6.42}$$

$$f_7(L, k_6) = \min[h_5(k_5) + f_5(k_6)], \ k_5^- \leq k_5 \leq \min(k_5^+, L), \tag{6.43}$$

$$\Phi_{\pi'}(L, k_6) = \min_{c_1} \{\max[f_4(c_1), f_7(L - c_1, k_6)]\},$$

$$f_8(L, k_6) = \min[\psi_1(d_1) + \Phi_{\pi'}(L - d_1, k_6)],$$

$$\Phi_{\pi''}(L) = \min\{\max[f_6(c_2, c_3), f_8(L - c_2, c_3)]\}$$

with the constraints on c_2, c_3 given by

$$0 \leq c_2 + c_3 \leq L, 0 \leq c_2 \leq c_3$$

and finally,

$$f_9(L) = \min_{k_9} [f_9(k_9) + \Phi_{\pi''}(L - k_9)], \; k_9^- \leq k_9 \leq \min(k_9^+, L).$$

In the foregoing, the decision variables c_1, c_2, c_3 and d_1, d_2 are constrained appropriately, as in the Example 2.

Thus, the number of functional equations with two state variables and one decision variable has been reduced from six equations to four equations. As noted previously, if, for example, phases 5, 4 and 8 were each replaced with twenty different phases, then the number of functional equations with two state variables and one decision variable would still remain at four. This is so because the number of such functional equations is strictly a function of the cardinality of the pseudo-stages and the pseudo-tasks. Thus, this technique can lead to substantial savings in computations for large CPM-Cost problems.

6.13. Discussion

In the preceding models no structure was nor need be imposed on the functions $h_i(k_i)$. If the function $h_i(k_i)$ is discontinuous and in particular transformable to step functions, a special computational technique called the imbedded-state-space approach can be introduced into the solution of the dynamic programming problem. Morin and Esogbue (1971) introduced this procedure for the optimal sequencing and scheduling of water-supply projects and subsequently generalized it to other systems. This technique, capable of producing extremely efficient and sometimes myopic decision rules, should ease the computational burden for CPM-Cost problems whose dynamic programming formulation contains functional equations with more than one state variable. Recall that we discussed this technique in detail in Chapter 5.

Other methods for reducing the computational burden exist. For example, in certain CPM-Cost problems, the objective functions can be decomposed into sequences of one-dimensional dynamic programs. Even in some complex network situations such as those of the "Wheatstone Bridge" variety in which the conditions necessary for decomposition are not satisfied, the problem structure can be exploited to generate subproblems in which the dimensions of the fractions are considerably less than the number of activities involved. This generally leads to simpler dynamic programming formulations. Problems based on these notions are included in the exercises.

There are at least three incentives for solving the CPM-Cost problem via dynamic programming. First, the technique is insensitive to the nature of the time–cost function for each phase in the project. The method can handle linear functions as well as nonlinear functions. The functions can be discrete or continuous. Second, the objective of the CPM-Cost problem is to find the time–cost function for the entire project. All the information which is required to find the time–cost function for the project is usually readily available at the last stage of dynamic programming procedure. Of the other mathematical programming algorithms, only linear programming has an extremely efficient parametrization routine, but its limitations are obvious. The last advantage is the fact that the complexity of the dynamic programming problem does not increase with the number of tasks, but only with the degree in which the additional tasks change the structure of the precedence relations. With other mathematical programming techniques the difficulty of solving problems is usually dependent upon the number of phases in the project. Unless all the time–cost functions for each stage are linear, dynamic programming should be considered as a very useful optimization method for the CPM-Cost problem.

Whether or not dynamic programming is a computationally feasible method for solving the CPM-Cost problem is dependent upon the structure of the precedence relations for the project. Several examples on how to efficiently formulate nonserial projects were presented here. Perhaps dynamic programming could also be implemented in complex nonserial projects with linear and nonlinear time–cost functions. If the linear and nonlinear time–cost functions could be separated in some manner so that each group of phases could be optimized separately, then dynamic programming could be used to combine the separate time–cost function from each group. In other words, dynamic programming could also be used as a decomposition procedure.

Bibliography and Comments

Section 6.1
    A good review of Critical Path Method as well as CPM-Cost problems and their applications in scheduling including R&D systems may be found in:
FRIEDEL, D., "Deterministic and stochastic R&D resource allocation models", Tech Memo No. 195, Department of Operations Research, Case Western Reserve University, Cleveland, Ohio (1970).
    The use of techniques other than dynamic programming to treat these problems is provided by:
KELLEY, J. E., Jr., "Critical-path planning and scheduling: mathematical basis", *Operations Research*, **9**, No. 3 (1961), 296–320.
and
KELLEY, J. E., Jr., "The Critical Path Method: resources planning and scheduling", *Industrial Scheduling*, MUTH and THOMPSON (eds.) (1963), pp. 347–365.
    The CPM-Pert Cost Problem is essentially a network scheduling problem. This viewpoint is elaborated on by
ELMAGHRABY, S. E., *Activity Networks*, John Wiley & Sons, New York, 1977.

Section 6.2
    A full review of these various structures may be found in:
ESOGBUE, A. O. and B. R. MARKS, "Nonserial dynamic programming: a survey", *Operational Research Quarterly*, **25**, No. 2 (1974), 253–265.
NEMHAUSER, G. L., *Introduction to Dynamic Programming*, John Wiley & Sons, New York, 1967.
    Sufficiency conditions to be satisfied justifying the correct application of Bellman's Principle of Optimality were formally introduced in:
MITTEN, L. G., "Composition principles for synthesis of optimal multistage process", *Operations Research*, **12** (1964), 610–619.
    For an application to water resources see:

MEIER, W. and C. S. BEIGHTLER, "An optimization method for branching multistage water resources systems", *Water Resources Research*, **3** (1967), 645–652.

Sections 6.3, 6.4 and 6.5
This account is given in:
ESOGBUE, A. O. and B. R. MARKS, "Dynamic programming models of nonserial critical path-cost problem", *Management Science*, **24**, No. 2 (1977), 200–209.
A formal definition of a nonserial system was provided in:
BEIGHTLER, C. S. and W. MEIER, "Design of optimum branched allocation problems", *Industrial and Engineering Chemistry*, **60**, No. 2 (1968), 45–49.
MEIER, W. L., Jr., "Optimal planning of nonserial multistage water resource systems," Unpublished doctoral dissertation, The University of Texas, Austin, 1967.

Sections 6.6 and 6.7
Aspects of these models were presented in:
ESOGBUE, A. O. and B. R. MARKS (1977), *op. cit.*
For a discussion of the curse of dimensionality see:
BELLMAN, R. E. and S. E. DREYFUS, *Applied Dynamic Programming*, Princeton University Press, 1962.
ESOGBUE, A. O., "Fundamentals of modern dynamic programming", mimeographed Lecture Notes, Department of Operations Research, Case Western Reserve University, Cleveland, Ohio, 1969.

Sections 6.8 and 6.9
The project time minimization approach [PTM] was introduced in
ESOGBUE, A. O. and B. R. MARKS (1977), *op. cit.*

Section 6.10
The pseudo-stage concept, the concept of a "cut state" and related concepts have important and interesting ramifications which aid in problem compression strategies. The concept of a cut state was employed in:
ARIS, R. *et al.* (1964), *op cit.*
This approach was improved upon considerably in a work reported by BEIGHTLER, C. S. and W. MEIER (1967, 1968), *op. cit.* They used a suitable decomposition of the optimization procedure at the branch junction point and a version of the compression principle introduced by:
BEIGHTLER, C. S., D. B. JOHNSON and D. J. WILDE, "Superposition in branching allocation problems", *Journal of Mathematical Analysis and Applications*, **12** (1965), 65–70.
The underlying mathematical structure can be gleaned from the subsequent work of
ROSE, C. J., "Dynamic programming processes within dynamic programming processes", *Journal of Mathematical Analysis and Applications*, **26** (1969), 669–683.

Sections 6.11 and 6.12
The invocation of recent computational techniques for reducing dimensionality in DP problems of high dimensions in treating complex nonserial problems was advocated in:
ESOGBUE, A. O. and B. MARKS, "The status of nonserial dynamic programming", *Management Science Theory* (1972), pp. 350–352.
These examples and analysis were first presented by ESOGBUE, A. O. and B. R. MARKS (1977), *op. cit.*, pp. 207–209. The concept of pseudo-task introduced here is similar to, but different from those expressed in:
BERTELE, U. and F. BRIOSCHI, *Nonserial Dynamic Programming*, Academic Press, New York, 1973.
For some techniques of formulation of complex nonserial systems as well as an interesting application to capital budgeting problems, see:
NEMHAUSER, G. L. and Z. ULLMAN, "Discrete dynamic programming and capital allocation", *Management Science*, **15**, No. 9 (1969), 494–505.
A comprehensive and advanced treatment of nonserial dynamic programming is given by:
BERTELE, U. and F. BRIOSCHI (1973), *Nonserial Dynamic Programming*.

Section 6.13

The techniques and methodology introduced in this chapter are particularly of great appeal when dealing with nonlinear return or transition functions.

An example of the decomposition of a complex network objective function into series of one-dimensional optimizations as well as other variations may be found in

ROBINSON, Don R., "A dynamic programming solution to cost–time tradeoff for CPM", *Management Science*, **22**, No. 2 (1975), 158–166.

When dealing with complex problems one can usually reduce the dimension of the resultant networks by recourse to theories and techniques developed elsewhere. Related concepts and approaches are found in graph theory, particularly signed flow graphs. For such treatment see:

HENLEY, E. and R. A. WILLIAMS, *Graph Theory in Modern Engineering*, Academic Press, New York, 1973.

LORENS, C. S., *Signal Flow Graphs*, McGraw-Hill Book Co., New York, 1964.

Miscellaneous Exercises

1. Examples of multistate allocation (sequencing) problems which show how the four basic structures of the nonserial system variety may occur in diverse systems were provided in Section 6.3. Consider one specific field such as an industrial R&D organization. For a realistic problem occurring within this organization, draw systems diagrams illustrating the following:

    (a) A serial system.
    (b) A converging system with four branches.
    (c) A diverging system with three branches.
    (d) A system with two feedback loops,
    (e) A system consisting of (a), (b), (c) and (d).

2. Consider a CPM-Cost problem. For each of the two possible objective functions, i.e. minimization of total project cost and minimization of project-completion data, develop a dynamic programming model of the resultant resource-allocation problem under the assumption that projects possess a serial phase structure.

3. Suppose that in problem 1 the phases of the project are strung together in a nonserial manner and in particular, are of the diverging type as in Fig. 6.2(a). If the object is to minimize the total project cost subject to various project time completion constraints, develop a dynamic programming model which can provide management with the requisite answers. Is your model "efficient"? Why or why not?

4. Consider the following CPM-Cost network in which nodes 1 and 6 are connected by every path p_i with nodes 2 < 5, and 3 < 5. The path p_2 containing node 2 contains node 5 with path p_3 also containing node 5. Let $h_j(k_j)$ = completion time of phase j given k_j dollars spent on it. Use the decomposition procedure suggested by the assertion in Section 6.13 to develop explicit dynamic programming equations for $f_n(L) \lor n$.

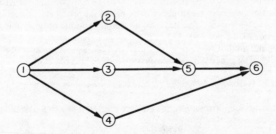

5. The Wheatstone bridge network depicted below does not satisfy the necessary condition embodied in the assertion referred to in Section 6.13. Why? Exploit the special structure of this network to generate the recursive procedures for computing $f_n(L) \lor n$. How many stages are involved in the DP formulation and why? Comment on the dimensionality problem apparent in your formulation.

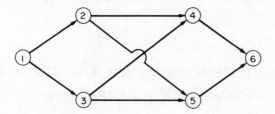

6. Consider the following nonserial CPM-Cost Problem similar to but more complex than Fig. 6.7.

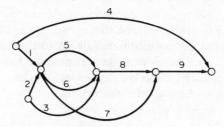

Using the pseudo-task concept, develop an efficient dynamic programming formulation of the problem.

7. The network of problem 6 is also similar to that of Fig. 6.10a. Using a combination of the pseudo-task concept and the techniques of Nemhauser and Ullman, develop an efficient dynamic program for this problem.

8. There are several techniques of branch compression and elimination which are in use in different fields of systems theory. One should invoke any and all possible tools that work well in a given problem situation. Usually an adroit combination of techniques is instructive. Consider the following problem.

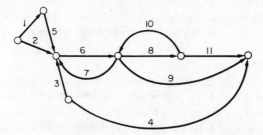

Using techniques of signal-flow graphs, pseudo-task concepts and Nemhauser and Ullman approaches, develop an efficient dynamic program for this complex network.

CHAPTER 7

Analytical Results for the Flow-shop Scheduling Problem

7.1. Introduction

Many analytical results for the sequencing problem are concerned with the minimization of the total elapsed time, that is, makespan, in a flow shop. Since the determination of an optimal schedule by the sequence-determining criterion for the two-machines case, described in the following, is the first efficient analytical result for the scheduling problem, related problems for this will be investigated in detail in this chapter.

7.2. Characteristics of Schedules

Let each of n jobs be processed by m machines $M_1, M_2, \ldots, M_m$ in this machine order. In this case, if we assume no passing of jobs, that is, the identity of the job sequence on each machine, the active schedules correspond to the permutations of n jobs and so their number amounts to $n!$. Each active schedule in this case is called a permutation schedule or a sequence.

Even in the case where passing is allowed in a flow shop, it is sufficient to consider that the job sequences on the first two machines M_1, M_2 are the same for any normal objective function (Section 4.3 in Chapter 4) and, moreover, the job sequences on the last two machines M_{m-1}, M_m are the same only when the objective function is the makespan. These facts are stated in the following theorem.

THEOREM 1. *For the flow-shop scheduling problem with any normal objective function to be minimized, it is sufficient to consider that the job sequences on the first two machines are the same and, moreover, the job sequences on the last two machines are the same only when the objective function is the makespan.*

Proof. If we assume that the job sequences on the first two machines M_1, M_2 are not the same, then there must exist at least one pair of jobs (i, j) such that the job j precedes the job i on M_2 while the latter precedes directly the former on M_1 (cf. Fig. 7.1). However, a schedule with inverted order of two

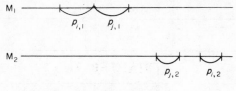

FIG. 7.1

jobs i, j on M_1 has no influence on the processing of i and j on M_2 in the assumed schedule and so this also holds for the succeeding sequences of jobs and then completion time of every job is the same as before. By repeating the above procedure we have a schedule with the same job sequences on M_1 and M_2 and the same completion times of all jobs as in the assumed schedule.

Next if we assume that the job sequences on the last two machines M_{m-1}, M_m are not the same, then there must exist at least one pair of jobs (i, j) such that the job j precedes the job i on M_{m-1} while the latter precedes directly the former on M_m (cf. Fig. 7.2). However, in this case a schedule with inverted order of two jobs i, j on M_m does not change the completion time of this pair in the assumed schedule and then makespan is the same as in the assumed schedule. By repeating the above procedure we have a schedule with the same job sequences on M_{m-1} and M_m and the same makespan as in the assumed schedule.

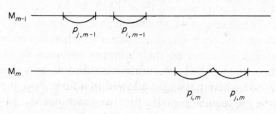

FIG. 7.2

Therefore, in the min-makespan problem, we can assume without loss of generality that no passing is allowed for the cases where $m = 2$ and 3. For the cases where $m \geq 4$ we must allow the passing of jobs except for the first two machines and the last two machines. However, since the analysis in the case where passing is allowed is difficult, analytical results are concerned with the case where no passing is allowed, that is, the permutation schedules.

7.3. Calculation of Makespan

For any sequence $\omega = i_1 i_2 \ldots i_n$, let $C_k(i_q)$ be the completion time of job i_q on machine M_k, $q = 1, 2, \ldots, n$; $k = 1, 2, \ldots, m$. Then since the start time of the processing of job i_q on M_1 is the same as the completion time of job i_{q-1}

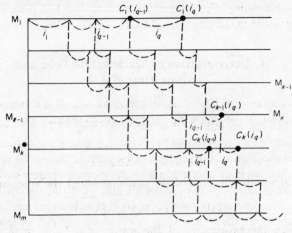

FIG. 7.3

on M_1 $(q = 2, 3, \ldots, n)$ and the job i_q can be processed on M_k as soon as possible after both are completed on M_{k-1} and the job i_{q-1} completes on M_k $(q = 2, 3, \ldots, n; k = 2, 3, \ldots, m)$, we have the next relations (cf. Fig. 7.3):

$$C_1(i_q) = C_1(i_{q-1}) + p_{i_q, 1}$$
$$C_k(i_q) = \max \left[C_{k-1}(i_q), C_k(i_{q-1}) \right] + p_{i_q, k} \qquad (7.1)$$
$$(q = 1, 2, \ldots, n; k = 2, 3, \ldots, m)$$

where

$$C_k(i_0) = 0 \quad (k = 1, 2, \ldots, m).$$

Hence the makespan of the sequence ω is equal to $C_m(i_n)$ and is calculated by using (7.1) successively for $k = 1, 2, \ldots, m$ for each $q(q = 1, 2, \ldots, n)$ in increasing order.

EXAMPLE 1. In the case of six jobs four machines, that is, the 6×4 permutation scheduling problem with processing times shown in Table 7.1, makespan of a sequence $\omega = 615243$ is calculated as in Table 7.2 by

TABLE 7.1

i	$p_{i,1}$	$p_{i,2}$	$p_{i,3}$	$p_{i,4}$
1	4	4	5	4
2	2	5	8	2
3	3	6	7	4
4	1	7	5	3
5	4	4	5	3
6	2	5	5	1

TABLE 7.2

i	6	1	5	2	4	3
$C_1(i)$	2	6	10	12	13	16
$C_2(i)$	7	11	15	20	27	33
$C_3(i)$	12	17	22	30	35	42
$C_4(i)$	13	21	25	32	38	$46 = M(\omega)$

successively calculating $C_k(i_q)$ $(q = 1, 2, \ldots, 6; k = 1, 2, 3, 4)$ by (7.1) and finally we have the makespan of ω, $M(\omega) = C_4(3) = 46$.

7.4. Determination of Machine Idle Time and Waiting Time of Job

For the sequence $\omega = i_1 i_2 \ldots i_n$, in the right side of the second equation in (7.1) we consider the following three cases (a), (b) and (c).

(a) When

$$C_{k-1}(i_q) > C_k(i_{q-1})$$

holds there arises an idle time of the machine M_k of the amount

$$I_k(i_q) \equiv C_{k-1}(i_q) - C_k(i_{q-1})$$

directly before the processing of the job i_q, $q = 2, \ldots, n; k = 2, \ldots, m$ (cf. Fig. 7.4(a)). Also since

$$C_k(i_0) = 0$$

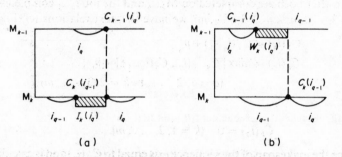

FIG. 7.4. Examples of $I_k(i_q)$, $W_k(i_q)$.

there arises always an idle time of M_k of the amount

$$I_k(i_1) \equiv C_{k-1}(i_1) = \sum_{r=1}^{k-1} p_{i_1,r}$$

directly before the processing of the job i_1, $k = 2, \ldots, m$

(b) When

$$C_{k-1}(i_q) < C_k(i_{q-1})$$

holds there arises a waiting time for processing on M_k of the job i_q of the amount

$$W_k(i_q) \equiv C_k(i_{q-1}) - C_{k-1}(i_q)$$

$q = 2, \ldots, n; k = 2, \ldots, m$. (cf. Fig. 7.4(b).)

(c) When

$$C_{k-1}(i_q) = C_k(i_{q-1})$$

holds they become

$$I_k(i_q) = 0, \ W_k(i_q) = 0 \quad (q = 2, \ldots, n; \ k = 2, \ldots, m).$$

Calculations of the idle times $I_k(i_q)$ $(q = 1, \ldots, n; \ k = 2, \ldots, m)$, waiting times $W_k(i_q)$ $(q = 2, \ldots, n; \ k = 2, \ldots, m)$ are made along with the process of the calculation of the makespan $M(\omega)$ as shown in the Table 7.3.

TABLE 7.3

i	$i_1 \ldots \ldots \ldots i_{q-1}$	i_q
$\vdots$	$\vdots$	$\vdots$
$\vdots$	$\vdots$	$\vdots$
$C_{k-1}(i)$	$\ldots\ldots\ldots\ldots\ldots$	$C_{k-1}(i_q)$
$C_k(i)$	$\overline{I_k(i_1)} C_k(i_1) \ldots C_k(i_{q-1}) \overline{I_k(i_q)} C_k(i_q)$	$\mid W_k(i_q)$
$\vdots$		

Exercises

1. Verify the following definitions of $I_k(i_q)$ and $W_k(i_q)$:

$$I_k(i_q) \equiv \max[C_{k-1}(i_q) - C_k(i_{q-1}), 0]$$
$$W_k(i_q) \equiv \max[C_k(i_{q-1}) - C_{k-1}(i_q), 0]$$

$q = 2, \ldots, n; \ k = 2, \ldots, m.$

2. Show that $I_k(i_q) > 0$ is equivalent with $W_k(i_q) = 0$ in Exercise 1.

3. Verify the relation:

$$C_k(i_q) = \sum_{t=1}^{q} p_{i_t, k} + \sum_{i=1}^{q} I_k(i_i) \quad (q = 1, \ldots, n; \ k = 2, \ldots, m).$$

7.5. Flow Time $T_k(i_q)$

For any sequence $\omega = i_1 i_2 \ldots i_n$ let $T_k(i_q)$ be the flow time of the job i_q from the completion on M_1 to the completion on $M_k (k \geq 2)$, then $T_k(i_q)$ can be expressed by

$$T_k(i_q) = C_k(i_q) - C_1(i_q), \left(C_1(i_q) = \sum_{t=1}^{q} p_{i_t, 1} \right).$$

$$(q = 1, 2, \ldots, n; \ k = 2, 3, \ldots, m)$$

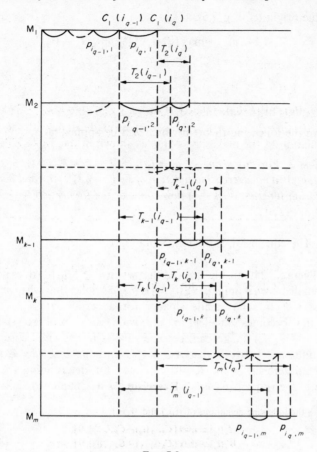

FIG. 7.5

$T_k(i_q)$ is a flow time on $(k-1)$ machines $M_2, M_3, \ldots, M_k$ (cf. Fig. 7.5). Also from the relations in Exercise 3 of Section 7.4, the next relation holds:

$$T_k(i_q) = \sum_{t=1}^{q} I_k(i_t) + \sum_{t=1}^{q} (p_{i_t,k} - p_{i_t,1}).$$
$$(q = 1, \ldots, n; \ k = 2, \ldots, m)$$

7.6. Recurrence Relation for Flow Time $T_k(i_q)$

Since the start of the processing of job i_q on M_k follows both the completion of i_q on M_{k-1} and the completion of i_{q-1} on M_k, the following recurrence relation holds for every $T_k(i_q)$ by taking the completion time $C_1(i_q)$ of i_q on M_1

as the time origin (cf. Fig. 7.5):

$$T_k(i_q) = p_{i_q,k} + \max\,[T_k(i_{q-1}) - p_{i_q,1}, T_{k-1}(i_q)],$$
$$(q = 1, 2, \ldots, n; \; k = 2, 3, \ldots, m) \tag{7.2}$$

where

$$T_k(i_0) = 0, T_1(i_q) = 0, \quad (k = 2, 3, \ldots, m; \; q = 1, 2, \ldots, n).$$

We give the following theorem which will be applied later.

THEOREM 2. *For any sequence $\omega = i_1 i_2 \ldots i_n$, each $T_k(i_q)$ $(q = 2, \ldots, n; k = 2, \ldots, m)$ is a nondecreasing function of $T_k(i_{q-1}), T_{k-1}(i_q)$ and hence it is a nondecreasing function of $(k-1)$ flow times of the former job i_{q-1}: $T_2(i_{q-1}), T_3(i_{q-1}), \ldots, T_k(i_{q-1})$.*

Proof. The conclusion is obvious from (7.2).

From Theorem 2 it must be noticed that when $m \geqq 3$ $T_m(i_q)$ does not always become smaller even if only the $T_m(i_{q-1})$ is made smaller, but when $m = 2$ (two machines) if $T_2(i_{q-1})$ is made smaller for a certain $q (q = 2, \ldots, n-1)$ then $T_2(i_q)$ becomes smaller in the wide sense and so successively $T_2(i_{q+1}), \ldots, T_2(i_n)$ (makespan) become smaller in the wide sense.

This difference between the case $m \geqq 3$ and the case $m = 2$ yields an important difference in the results obtained for determining the optimal sequence in the respective cases (cf. Section 8.7 in Chapter 8).

Exercises

1. Derive the recurrent relation (7.2) from the definition of $T_k(i_q)$ and the relations (7.1) on $C_k(i_q)$'s at Section 7.3.

2. Prove the following equation by induction by successively using (7.2) for the sequence $i_1 i_2 \ldots i_n$:

$$T_k(i_q) = \max_{1 \leqq r_1 \leqq \ldots \leqq r_{k-1} \leqq q} \left[\sum_{w=1}^{k-1} \left(\sum_{t=1}^{r_w} p_{i_t, w} - \sum_{t=1}^{r_w - 1} p_{i_t, w+1} \right) \right] + \sum_{t=1}^{q} (p_{i_t, k} - p_{i_t, 1}).$$
$$(q = 1, \ldots, n; \; k = 2, \ldots, m).$$

7.7. Expressions of Makespan

In this section two simple types of expression of the makespan $M(\omega)$ of any sequence $\omega = i_1 i_2 \ldots i_n$ are described as below (cf. Fig. 7.6).

1. *An expression which uses the idle times on the last machine,*

$$M(\omega) = \sum_{t=1}^{n} p_{i_t, m} + \sum_{t=1}^{n} I_m(i_t). \tag{7.3}$$

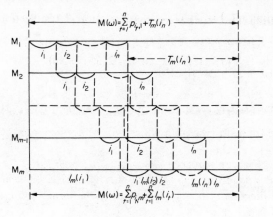

FIG. 7.6

Since the first term of the right side is constant it is sufficient to determine a sequence which minimizes the second term, that is, the sum of the idle times on the last machine, in order to minimize the makespan.

2. *An expression which uses the flow time* $T_m(i_n)$,

$$\mathbf{M}(\omega) = \sum_{t=1}^{n} p_{i_t,1} + T_m(i_n). \qquad (7.4)$$

Since the first term of the right side is constant it is sufficient to determine a sequence which minimizes the second term, that is, $T_m(i_n)$, in order to minimize the makespan. For the other expressions, see Section 7.10 and its Exercise 2.

7.8. Calculation of Machine Idle Time

By putting

$$I_k(i_1 i_2 \ldots i_q) = \sum_{t=1}^{q} I_k(i_t)$$

in the last relation, at Section 7.5, that is,

$$T_k(i_q) = \sum_{t=1}^{q} I_k(i_t) + \sum_{t=1}^{q} (p_{i_t,k} - p_{i_t,1}) \qquad (7.5)$$

we have

$$T_k(i_q) = I_k(i_1 i_2 \ldots i_q) + \sum_{t=1}^{q} (p_{i_t,k} - p_{i_t,1}). \qquad (7.6)$$

By substituting (7.6) into the recurrence relation (7.2) at Section 7.6 on $T_k(i_q)$, we obtain

$$I_k(i_1 i_2 \ldots i_q) + \sum_{t=1}^{q} (p_{i_t, k} - p_{i_t, 1})$$

$$= p_{i_q, k} + \max \left[I_k(i_1 i_2 \ldots i_{q-1}) + \sum_{t=1}^{q-1} (p_{i_t, k} - p_{i_t, 1}) - p_{i_q, 1}, I_{k-1}(i_1 i_2 \ldots i_q) \right.$$

$$\left. + \sum_{t=1}^{q} (p_{i_t, k-1} - p_{i_t, 1}) \right],$$

By subtracting the quantity

$$\sum_{t=1}^{q} (p_{i_t, k} - p_{i_t, 1})$$

from both sides of the above equation, we obtain the recurrence relation for $I_k(i_1 i_2 \ldots i_q)$ $(q = 1, 2, \ldots, n; \ k = 2, 3, \ldots, m)$:

$$I_t(i_1 i_2 \ldots i_q) = \max \left[I_k(i_1 i_2 \ldots i_{q-1}), \right.$$

$$\left. I_{k-1}(i_1 i_2 \ldots i_q) + \left(\sum_{t=1}^{q} p_{i_t, k-1} - \sum_{t=1}^{q-1} p_{i_t, k} \right) \right] \qquad (7.7)$$

$$(q = 1, 2, \ldots, n; \ k = 2, 3, \ldots, m)$$

where

$$I_k(i_1 i_2 \ldots i_0) = 0 \ (q = 1), \ \sum_{t=1}^{0} p_{i_t, k} = 0 \ (q = 1), \ I_1(i_1 i_2 \ldots i_q) = 0.$$

Now for simplicity, let us put in the right side of (7.7)

$$D_k^{k-1}(q) = \sum_{t=1}^{q} p_{i_t, k-1} - \sum_{t=1}^{q-1} p_{i_t, k} \qquad (7.8)$$

then recurrence relations (7.8) become as shown below:

$$\left. \begin{aligned} I_2(i_1) &= D_2^1(1) = p_{i_1, 1}, I_2(i_1 i_2 \ldots i_q) = \max [I_2(i_1 i_2 \ldots i_{q-1}), \\ &\qquad\qquad\qquad\qquad D_2^1(q)], \quad (q = 2, 3, \ldots, n), \\ I_k(i_1) &= I_{k-1}(i_1) + D_k^{k-1}(1) = I_{k-1}(i_1) + p_{i_1, k-1}, \\ &\qquad\qquad\qquad\qquad (k = 3, 4, \ldots, m), \\ I_k(i_1 i_2 \ldots i_q) &= \max [I_k(i_1 i_2 \ldots i_{q-1}), I_{k-1}(i_1 i_2 \ldots i_q) \\ &\qquad + D_k^{k-1}(q)] \ (q = 2, 3, \ldots, n; k = 3, 4, \ldots, m) \end{aligned} \right\} \qquad (7.9)$$

Since we have

$$I_2(i_1 i_2 \ldots i_q) = \max_{1 \le u \le q} D_2^1(u) \tag{7.10}$$

$$I_3(i_1 i_2 \ldots i_q) = \max_{1 \le v \le q} \left[D_3^2(v) + \max_{1 \le u \le v} D_2^1(u) \right]$$

$$= \max_{1 \le u \le v \le q} \left[D_2^1(u) + D_3^2(v) \right] (q = 1, 2, \ldots, n) \tag{7.11}$$

by successively calculating by using (7.9), generally the following expression holds from (7.9) by induction:

$$I_k(i_1 i_2 \ldots i_q) = \max_{1 \le u_1 \le u_2 \le \ldots \le u_{k-1} \le q} \sum_{r=1}^{k-1} D_{r+1}^r(u_r), \tag{7.12}$$

$$(q = 1, 2, \ldots, n; k = 2, 3, \ldots, m)$$

where $D_{r+1}^r(u_r)$ is defined by (7.8).

Exercises

1. Derive the relation (7.7) from (7.1) in Section 7.3 and

$$C_k(i_q) = \sum_{i=1}^q p_{t_1,k} + I_k(i_1 i_2 \ldots i_q), \quad (q = 1, 2, \ldots, n; k = 2, 3, \ldots, m)$$

2. Prove the expression (7.12) by induction.

3. Obtain the expressions of every normal objective function other than makespan (cf. Section 10.4 in Chapter 10).

7.9. Flow Network Expression in Critical Path Method

For any definite sequence $\omega = i_1 i_2 \ldots i_n$ we can construct a flow network $G = (N, A)$ where N is the set of nodes, each of them corresponds to each

FIG. 7.7. $G = (N, A)$.

operation $i_{q,k}$ of job i_q on machine M_k $(q = 1, \ldots, n; k = 1, \ldots, m)$ and is denoted by a node (q, k) on which related job i_q is supposed to spend p_{i_q} times, and A is the set of directed arcs, each of them leads from a node (q, k) to a node $(q+1, k) q = 1, \ldots, n-1; k = 1, \ldots, m$, or leads from a node (q, k) to a node $(q, k+1)$, $q = 1, \ldots, n; k = 1, \ldots, m-1$ (cf. Fig. 7.7).

7.10. Critical Path Length between Two Nodes and Makespan

Let $C(r \sim s, u \sim v)$ be the critical path length from a node (r, u) (an operation $i_{r,u}$) to a node (s, v) (an operation $i_{s,v}$), that is, total elapsed time of a sequence $i_r i_{r+1} \ldots i_s$ on machines $M_u, M_{u+1}, \ldots, M_v, 1 \leq r \leq s \leq n, 1 \leq u \leq v \leq m$, then the following expressions of $C(r \sim s, u \sim v)$ and the makespan $M(\omega)$ for any sequence $\omega = i_1 i_2 \ldots i_n$ hold:

$$C(r \sim v, u \sim v) = \max_{u \leq w_r \leq w_{r+1} \leq \ldots \leq w_{s-1} \leq v} \left[\sum_{k=u}^{w_r} p_{i_r,k} + \sum_{k=w_r}^{w_{r+1}} p_{i_{r+1},k} + \cdots \right.$$

$$\left. + \sum_{k=w_{s-2}}^{w_{s-1}} p_{i_{s-1},k} + \sum_{k=w_{s-1}}^{v} p_{i_s,k} \right] \tag{7.13}$$

$$= \max_{r \leq x_u \leq x_{u+1} \leq \ldots \leq x_{v-1} \leq s} \left[\sum_{l=r}^{x_u} p_{i_l,u} + \sum_{l=x_u}^{x_{u+1}} p_{i_l,u+1} + \cdots \right.$$

$$\left. + \sum_{l=x_{v-2}}^{x_{v-1}} p_{i_l,v-1} + \sum_{l=x_{v-1}}^{S} p_{i_l,v} \right]. \tag{7.14}$$

$$M(\omega) = \max_{1 \leq w_1 \leq w_2 \leq \ldots \leq w_{n-1} \leq m} \left[\sum_{k=1}^{w_1} p_{i_1,k} + \sum_{k=w_1}^{w_2} p_{i_2,k} + \cdots \right.$$

$$\left. + \sum_{k=w_{n-2}}^{w_{n-1}} p_{i_{n-1},k} + \sum_{k=w_{n-1}}^{m} p_{i_n,k} \right] \tag{7.15}$$

$$= \max_{1 \leq x_1 \leq x_2 \leq \ldots \leq x_{m-1} \leq n} \left[\sum_{l=1}^{x_1} p_{i_l,1} + \sum_{l=x_1}^{x_2} p_{i_l,2} + \cdots \right.$$

$$\left. + \sum_{l=x_{m-2}}^{x_{m-1}} p_{i_l,m-1} + \sum_{l=x_{m-1}}^{n} p_{i_l,m} \right]. \tag{7.16}$$

Let us consider a subnetwork $G_1 = (N_1, A_1)$ of $G = (N, A)$, where N_1 is a set of nodes $(q, k), r \leq q \leq s, u \leq k \leq v$, and A_1 is a subset of A associated with N_1 (cf. Fig. 7.8) and let $t_{q,k}$ be the earliest start time of the node $(q, k), r \leq q \leq S, u \leq k \leq v$, under $t_{r,u} = 0$.

Then we have

$$C(r \sim S, u \sim v) = t_{s,v} + p_{i_s,v}.$$

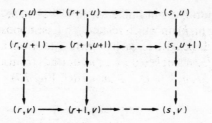

FIG. 7.8

Hence, in order to prove (7.13), it is sufficient to prove

$$t_{s,v} = \max_{u \leq w_r \leq w_{r+1} \leq \ldots \leq w_{s-1} \leq v} \left[\sum_{k=u}^{w_r} p_{i_r,k} + \sum_{k=w_r}^{w_{r+1}} p_{i_{r+1},k} + \cdots \right.$$

$$\left. + \sum_{k=w_{s-2}}^{w_{s-1}} p_{i_{s-1},k} + \sum_{k=w_{s-1}}^{v} p_{i_s,k} \right] - p_{i_s,v}. \tag{7.17}$$

The proof of (7.17) proceeds by induction as follows:
1. We have $t_{r+1,u} = t_{r,u} + p_{i_r,u} = p_{i_r,u}$. On the other hand, (7.17) becomes

$$t_{r+1,u} = \max_{u=w_r=u} [p_{i_r,u} + p_{i_{r+1},u}] - p_{i_{r+1},u} = p_{i_r,u}.$$

Hence, (7.12) holds for $t_{r+1,u}$. Next, if we assume that (7.12) holds for a certain $t_{q,u}(r < q < s)$, that is, we have

$$t_{q,u} = \max_{u=w_r=w_{r+1}=\ldots=w_{q-1}=u} [p_{i_r,u} + p_{i_{r+1},u} + \ldots + p_{i_q,u}] - p_{i_q,u}$$

$$= \sum_{l=r}^{q-1} p_{i_l,u}, \quad (v=u)$$

then since we have

$$t_{q+1,u} = t_{q,u} + p_{i_q,u} = \sum_{l=r}^{q} p_{i_l,u}$$

and (7.17) becomes

$$t_{q+1,u} = \sum_{l=r}^{q} p_{i_l,u},$$

(7.17) holds also for $t_{q+1,u}$. Thus (7.17) holds for every $t_{q,r}$ where $r < q \leq s$ by induction.
2. We have $t_{r,u+1} = t_{r,u} + p_{i_r,u} = p_{i_r,u}$. On the other hand, (7.17) becomes

$$t_{r,u+1} = \max_{u=w_r=u} [p_{i_r,u}] = p_{i_r,u}.$$ Hence (7.17) holds for $t_{r,u+1}$. Next if we assume

that (7.17) holds for a certain $t_{r,j}(u < j < v)$, that is, we have

$$t_{r,j} = \max_{u \,\leqq\, w_r = j} \left[\sum_{k=u}^{j} p_{i,k} \right] - p_{i,j} = \sum_{k=u}^{j-1} p_{i,k}, \; (s-1 = r-1 < r, v = j)$$

then since we have

$$t_{r,j+1} = t_{r,j} + p_{i_r,j} = \sum_{k=u}^{j} p_{i_r,k}$$

and (7.17) becomes

$$t_{r,j+1} = \sum_{k=u}^{j} p_{i_r,k},$$

(7.17) holds also for $t_{r,j+1}$. Therefore, (7.17) holds for every $t_{r,j}$ where $u < j \leqq v$ by induction.

3. Now let us assume that (7.17) holds for both $t_{q+1,j}$ and $t_{q,j+1}$, that is, they hold

$$t_{q+1,j} = \max_{u \,\leqq\, w_r \,\leqq\, \ldots \,\leqq\, w_q \,\leqq\, j} \left[\sum_{k=u}^{w_r} p_{i_r,k} + \sum_{k=w_r}^{w_{r+1}} p_{i_{r+1},k} + \ldots \right.$$

$$\left. + \sum_{k=w_{q-1}}^{w_q} p_{i_q,k} + \sum_{k=w_q}^{j} p_{i_{q+1},k} \right] - p_{i_{q+1},j},$$

$$t_{q,j+1} = \max_{u \,\leqq\, w_r \,\leqq\, \ldots \,\leqq\, w_{q-1} \,\leqq\, j+1} \left[\sum_{k=u}^{w_r} p_{i_r,k} + \sum_{k=w_r}^{w_{r+1}} p_{i_{r+1},k} + \ldots \right.$$

$$\left. + \sum_{k=w_{q-2}}^{w_{q-1}} p_{i_{q-1},k} + \sum_{k=w_{q-1}}^{j+1} p_{i_q,k} \right] - p_{i_q,j+1},$$

then since we have, by substituting these equations,

$$t_{q+1,j+1} = \max \left[t_{q+1,j} + p_{i_{q+1},j}, t_{q,j+1} + p_{i_q,j+1} \right]$$

$$= \max \left[\max_{u \,\leqq\, w_r \,\leqq\, \ldots \,\leqq\, w_q \,\leqq\, j} \left\{ \sum_{k=u}^{w_r} p_{i_r,k} + \ldots + \sum_{k=w_q}^{j+1} p_{i_{q+1},k} \right\} - p_{i_{q+1},j+1}, \right.$$

$$\max_{u \,\leqq\, w_r \,\leqq\, \ldots \,\leqq\, w_{q-1} \,\leqq\, j+1} \left\{ \sum_{k=u}^{w_r} p_{i_r,k} + \ldots \right.$$

$$\left. \left. + \sum_{k=w_{q-1}}^{j+1} p_{i_q,k} + p_{i_{q+1},j+1} \right\} - p_{i_{q+1},j+1} \right]$$

where the first term in brackets is a case $w_q \leqq j < j+1$ and the second term is a case $w_{q-1} \leqq w_q = j+1$ in the range $u \leqq w_r \leqq \ldots \leqq w_q$ of (7.17) for $t_{q+1,j+1}$, hence (7.17) holds also for $t_{q+1,j+1}$ (cf. Fig. 7.9).

$$(q+1,j)$$
$$\downarrow$$
$$(q,j+1) \longrightarrow (q+1,j+1)$$

FIG. 7.9

4. From proofs 1 and 2, if we put $j = u$ and successively $q = r, r+1, \ldots,$ $s-1$ in proof 3, (7.17) holds for all $t_{q,u+1}$ $(r \leq q \leq s)$. Hence, if we put $j = u+1$ and successively $q = r, r+1, \ldots, s-1$ in proof 3, (7.17) holds for all $t_{q,u+2}$ $(r \leq q \leq s)$. In the same way, we can conclude that (7.17) holds for all $t_{q,j}$ $(r \leq q \leq s, u \leq j \leq v)$ where $t_{r,u} = 0$ holds obviously in (7.17). Therefore (7.17) holds for $t_{s,v}$ and then (7.17) holds.

Exercises

1. Prove the expression (7.14).

2. Derive the expressions (7.15), (7.16) of the makespan.

3. Transform (7.13) and (7.14) to the following expressions:

$$C(r \sim s, u \sim v) = \max_{u \leq w_r \leq w_{r+1} \leq \ldots \leq w_{s-1} \leq v} \left[\sum_{l=r}^{s-1} \left(\sum_{k=1}^{w_l} p_{i_l,k} - \sum_{k=1}^{w_l-1} p_{i_{l+1},k} \right) \right] - \sum_{k=1}^{u-1} p_{i_r,k} + \sum_{k=1}^{v} p_{i_s,k}$$

$$= \max_{r \leq x_u \leq x_{u+1} \leq \ldots \leq x_{v-1} \leq s} \left[\left(\sum_{k=u}^{v-1} \left(\sum_{l=1}^{x_k} p_{i_l,k} - \sum_{l=1}^{x_k-1} p_{i_l,k+1} \right) \right) \right]$$
$$- \sum_{l=1}^{r-1} p_{i_l,u} + \sum_{l=1}^{s} p_{i_l,v}.$$

4. Using the definition of $D_k^{k-1}(q)$ in (7.8) in Section 7.8, derive the expression

$$\mathbf{M}(\omega) = \max_{1 \leq x_1 \leq x_2 \leq \ldots \leq x_{m-1} \leq n} \left[\sum_{k=1}^{m-1} D_{k+1}^k (x_k) \right] + \sum_{l=1}^{n} p_{i_l,m}$$

which is equivalent with (7.3) by (7.12).

5. Derive the following expression for a sequence ij of two jobs i, j:

$$C(ij, u \sim v) = \max_{u \leq w \leq v} \left[\sum_{k=u}^{w} p_{i,k} + \sum_{k=w}^{v} p_{j,k} \right].$$

6. Derive the following expressions of $T_k(i_q)$:

$$T_k(i_q) = C(1 \sim q, 1 \sim k) - \sum_{l=1}^{q} p_{i_l,1}$$

$$= \max_{1 \leq r_1 \leq r_2 \leq \ldots \leq r_{k-1} \leq q} \left[\sum_{w=1}^{k-1} \left(\sum_{l=1}^{r_w} p_{i_l,w} - \sum_{l=1}^{r_w-1} p_{i_l,w+1} \right) \right]$$
$$+ \sum_{l=1}^{q} (p_{i_l,k} - p_{i_l,1}).$$

7.11. Two-Machine Min-Makespan Problem

An optimal sequence is determined by the following theorems, where the ordering is the order M_1, M_2.

THEOREM 3. *An optimal sequence is determined by the next rule: If a criterion*

$$\min (p_{i,1}, p_{j,2}) \leq \min (p_{j,1}, p_{i,2}) \qquad (7.18)$$

holds with an inequality, then job i precedes job j. If equality holds in (7.18) *either ordering is optimal.*

The proof of this theorem will be described in detail in later Sections 7.12–7.14.

Theorem 3 can be stated in different forms as shown in the following two theorems:

THEOREM 4. *Let the set of n jobs be decomposed into its two subsets* $J_1 = \{i | p_{i,1} \leq p_{i,2}\}$, $J_2 = \{i | p_{i,1} > p_{i,2}\}$, *then an optimal sequence is determined by the next rule:*
1. *After the jobs in* J_1 *arrange the jobs in* J_2.
2. *In* J_1 *arrange the jobs in increasing order of* $p_{i,1}$. *If a tie occurs either ordering is optimal.*
3. *In* J_2 *arrange the jobs in decreasing order of* $p_{i,2}$. *If a tie occurs either ordering is optimal.*

Proof. (1) Let $i \in J_1, j \in J_2$, then (7.18) holds since $p_{i,1} \leq p_{i,2}$ and $p_{j,1} > p_{j,2}$ hold by definition. Hence job i precedes job j. (2) Let $i \in J_1, j \in J_1$, then (7.18) holds when $p_{i,1} \leq p_{j,1}$ holds since $p_{i,1} \leq p_{i,2}$ and $p_{j,1} \leq p_{j,2}$ hold by definition. Hence, job i precedes job j when $p_{i,1} \leq p_{j,1}$ holds. (3) Let $i \in J_2$, $j \in J_2$, then (7.18) holds when $p_{i,2} \geq p_{j,2}$ holds since $p_{i,1} > p_{i,2}$ and $p_{j,1} > p_{j,2}$ hold by definition. Hence job i precedes job j when $p_{i,2} \geq p_{j,2}$ holds.

THEOREM 5. *Let us put*

$$(\text{Sign of } p_{i,1} - p_{i,2}) = \begin{cases} +1 \text{ in case } p_{i,1} > p_{i,2}, \\ -1 \text{ in case } p_{i,1} \leq p_{i,2}, \end{cases}$$

then an optimal sequence is determined by arranging the jobs in increasing order of

$$Z_i = (\text{sign of } p_{i,1} - p_{i,2})/\min (p_{i,1}, p_{i,2}).$$

Proof. The conclusion follows from Theorem 4, since $Z_1 = -1/p_{i,1}$ holds for the job i in J_1 and $Z_i = 1/p_{i,2}$ holds for the job i in J_2.

In the following, as the proof of the Theorem 3, we show three solution techniques, each of them uses idle time of the last machine, dynamic programming, and flow time $T_2(i)$ respectively.

7.12. Solution by Using Machine Idle Time

For simplicity let the sequence be $\omega = 1 \cdot 2 \cdot 3 \ldots n$, then the sum of idle times of M_2 is

$$I_2(1 \cdot 2 \cdot 3 \ldots n) = \max_{1 \leq u \leq n} D_2^1(u), \quad D_2^1(u) = \sum_{i=1}^{u} p_{i,1} - \sum_{i=1}^{u-1} p_{i,2}$$

from (7.10) in Section 7.8 and the makespan is

$$M(\omega) = \sum_{i=1}^{n} p_{i,2} + I_2(1 \cdot 2 \cdot 3 \ldots n).$$

Here since the first term is constant it is sufficient to determine a sequence ω_0 which satisfies

$$I_2(\omega_0) \leq I_2(\omega)$$

where

$$I_2(\omega) \equiv I_2(1 \cdot 2 \cdot 3 \ldots n) = \max_{1 \leq u \leq n} D_2^1(u)$$

for any sequence ω.

Let a sequence ω' be the sequence obtained by exchanging the job j and job $j+1$ in the sequence ω and let us put

$$I_2(\omega') \equiv \max_{1 \leq u \leq n} D_2^{1\prime}(u), \quad D_2^{1\prime}(u) = \sum_{i=1}^{u} p'_{i,1} - \sum_{i=1}^{u-1} p'_{i,2}.$$

Then, when $i \neq j, j+1$, we have $p'_{i,1} = p_{i,1}, p'_{i,2} = p_{i,2}$ and $p'_{j,1} = p_{j+1,1}, p'_{j,2} = p_{j+1,2}; p'_{j+1,1} = p_{j,1}, p'_{j+1,2} = p_{j,2}$. Hence $D_2^{1\prime}(u) = D_2^{1\prime}(u)$ holds for $u \neq j$, $j+1$. Therefore in order to have $I_2(\omega) \leq I_2(\omega')$ it is sufficient to have

$$\max[D_2^1(j), D_2^1(j+1)] \leq \max[D_2^{1\prime}(j), D_2^{1\prime}(j+1)], \tag{7.19}$$

(7.19) is equivalent with

$$\max\left[\sum_{i=1}^{j} p_{i,1} - \sum_{i=1}^{j-1} p_{i,2}, \sum_{i=1}^{j+1} p_{i,1} - \sum_{i=1}^{j} p_{i,2}\right]$$

$$\leq \max\left[\sum_{i=1}^{j-1} p_{i,1} + p_{j+1,1} - \sum_{i=1}^{j-1} p_{i,2}, \sum_{i=1}^{j+1} p_{i,1} - \sum_{i=1}^{j-1} p_{i,2} - p_{j+1,2}\right]$$

and therefore by subtracting

$$\sum_{i=1}^{j+1} p_{i,1} - \sum_{i=1}^{j-1} p_{i,2}$$

from both sides of the above inequality we have an equivalent inequality

$$\max(-p_{j+1,1}, -p_{j,2}) \leq \max(-p_{j,1}, -p_{j+1,2}). \tag{7.20}$$

By an identical equation

$$\max(A, B) = -\min(-A, -B)$$

(7.20) is equivalent with

$$-\min(p_{j+1,1}, p_{j,2}) \leqq -\min(p_{j,1}, p_{j+1,2}).$$

Therefore, we obtain

$$\min(p_{j,1}, p_{j+1,2}) \leqq \min(p_{j+1,1}, p_{j,2}). \tag{7.21}$$

Therefore, if (7.21) holds then $I_2(\omega) \leqq I_2(\omega')$ holds.

When this inequality holds without equality the order of two adjacent jobs $j, j+1$ must be the order $j, j+1$. On the contrary when (7.21) holds with equality we have $I_2(\omega) = I_2(\omega')$ and so either ordering of j and $j+1$ is optimal. When (7.21) holds without equality, generally we have $I_2(\omega) \leqq I_2(\omega')$, but in this case we make a practice of putting the job j before the job $j+1$. Since the ordering of two adjacent jobs by (7.21) satisfies the transitive property as shown in Theorem 6, we can determine the optimal sequence ω_0 by successively exchanging the jobs of any sequence ω by (7.21) and then $I_2(\omega_0) \leqq I_2(\omega)$ holds.

THEOREM 6. *Ordering of two adjacent jobs by* (7.21) *satisfies the transitive property, that is to say, if job 1 precedes directly job 2, where* $\min(p_{1,1}, p_{2,2}) < \min(p_{2,1}, p_{1,2})$ *holds, and job 2 precedes directly job 3, where* $\min(p_{2,1}, p_{3,2}) < \min(p_{3,1}, p_{2,2})$ *holds, then an inequality* $\min(p_{1,1}, p_{3,2}) < \min(p_{3,1}, p_{1,2})$ *holds, which shows that job 1 precedes job 3.*

Proof. We divide the cases by the values of $A = \min(p_{1,1}, p_{2,2})$, $B = \min(p_{2,1}, p_{3,2})$.

1. The case where $A = p_{1,1}, B = p_{2,1}$ hold. Since $p_{1,1} < p_{2,1}, p_{1,2}; p_{2,1} < p_{3,1}, p_{2,2}$ hold from the assumed inequalities they become $p_{1,1} < p_{2,1} < p_{3,1}, p_{1,1} < p_{1,2}$ and then $\min(p_{1,1}, p_{3,2}) \leqq p_{1,1} < \min(p_{3,1}, p_{1,2})$ holds.
2. The case where $A = p_{1,1}, B = p_{3,2}$ hold. Since $p_{1,1} < p_{2,1}, p_{1,2}; p_{3,2} < p_{3,1}, p_{2,2}$ hold they become $p_{1,1} < p_{1,2}, p_{3,2} < p_{3,1}$ and then $\min(p_{1,1}, p_{3,2}) < \min(p_{3,1}, p_{1,2})$ holds.
3. The case where $A = p_{2,2}, B = p_{3,2}$ hold. Since $p_{2,2} < p_{2,1}, p_{1,2}; p_{3,2} < p_{3,1}, p_{2,2}$ hold they become $p_{3,2} < p_{3,1}, p_{3,2} < p_{2,2} < p_{1,2}$ and then $\min(p_{1,1} p_{3,2}) \leqq p_{3,2} < \min(p_{3,1}, p_{1,2})$ holds.
4. The case where $A = p_{2,2}, B = p_{2,1}$ hold. Since $p_{2,2} < p_{2,1}, p_{1,2}; p_{2,1} < p_{3,1}, p_{2,2}$ hold they become $p_{2,2} < p_{2,1}$ and $p_{2,1} < p_{2,2}$, which is a contradiction. Hence this case does not occur.

The case 4 in the above proof occurs only when the assumed inequalities are both equalities and $p_{2,1} = p_{2,2}$ holds. And in this case the orders of two jobs 1,

2 and two jobs 2, 3 are arbitrary respectively. We may regard that job 1 precedes job 3. The cases 1 to 3 hold also when three inequalities in the theorem contain equalities.

From this theorem, for any job i which precedes (follows) a job j in an optimal sequence ω_0 we must have

$$\min{(p_{i,1}, p_{j,2})} \leqq (\geqq) \min{(p_{j,1}, p_{i,2})}$$

where equality corresponds to the job i taking arbitrary order with the job j. Therefore, for any two jobs i, j, if

$$\min{(p_{i,1}, p_{j,2})} \leqq \min{(p_{j,1}, p_{i,2})} \tag{7.22}$$

holds without equality we must process job i before job j, but if (7.22) holds with equality we can process the two jobs i, j in any order.

Exercises

1. Prove an identical equation

$$\max{(A, B)} = -\min{(-A, -B)}.$$

2. Consider the reason why $I_2(\omega) = I_2(\omega')$ can hold even when (7.21) holds without equality.

7.13. Solution by Dynamic Programming

This solution method also considers the exchange of any two adjacent jobs i, j.

Let

$$f(p_{1,1}, p_{2,2}; \ldots; p_{N,1}, p_{N,2}; t), \quad N = n, n-1, \ldots, 2$$

be the total elapsed time of the processing of N jobs in the case when there remains the processing of N jobs $1, 2, \ldots, N$ and machine M_2 is committed t time units ahead of machine M_1 and an optimal scheduling policy is employed, where $t = 0$ when $N = n$.

If job i is processed first then the committed time t_i, which corresponds to the previous time t, after the processing of job i on M_1 and M_2 becomes as below (cf. Fig. 7.10): (a) when $t \geq p_{i,1}$ holds we have $t_i = p_{i,2} + (t - p_{i,1})$, (b) when $t \leq p_{i,1}$ holds since $t_i = p_{i,2}$ we have $t_i = p_{i,2} + \max{(t - p_{i,1}, 0)}$.

When there remains $N - 1$ jobs after the processing of job i by an optimal scheduling policy, total elapsed time of the processing of these $N - 1$ jobs is equal to

$$f(p_{1,1}, p_{1,2}; \ldots; 0, {}^{i}0; \ldots; p_{N,1}, p_{N,2}; t_i)$$

by taking the time origin at the completion time $C_1(i)$ of job i on M_1. Hence total elapsed time in the case when job i is processed first and an optimal scheduling policy is employed afterward is equal to

$$p_{i,1} + f(p_{1,1}, p_{1,2}; \ldots; 0, {}^{i}0; \ldots; p_{N,1}, p_{N,2}; t_i)$$

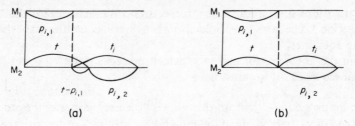

FIG. 7.10

By selecting the job i which minimizes this total elapsed time we obtain a functional equation

$$f(p_{1,1}, p_{1,2}; \ldots; p_{N,1}, p_{N,2}; t)$$
$$= \min_{i=1,\ldots,N} [p_{i,1} + f(p_{1,1}, p_{1,2}; \ldots; 0, {}^i0; \ldots; p_{N,1}, p_{N,2}; t_i)] \quad (7.23)$$

where

$$t_i = p_{i,2} + \max(t - p_{i,1}, 0). \quad (7.24)$$

In (7.23), the notation 0^i0 shows that the job i is not contained.

Then, if job j is processed second under the time t_i after the processing of the first job i, since this is the same situation as the case when the first job i is processed under the time t, the equation which expresses the time t_{ij}, during which M_2 is committed ahead of M_1 after the processing of two jobs i, j in this order, as a function of t_i becomes

$$t_{ij} = p_{j,2} + \max(t_i - p_{j,1}, 0)$$

or equivalently, by substituting (7.24),

$$t_{ij} = p_{j,2} + \max[p_{i,2} + \max(t - p_{i,1}, 0) - p_{j,1}, 0].$$

Then by adding $p_{i,2} - p_{j,1}$ to the first term of the right side and subtracting $p_{i,2} - p_{j,1}$ from each term in the bracket we have

$$t_{ij} = p_{i,2} + p_{j,2} - p_{j,1} + \max[\max(t - p_{i,1}, 0), p_{j,1} - p_{i,2}]$$

and by

$$\max[\max(A, B), C] = \max[A, B, C]$$

we have

$$t_{ij} = p_{i,2} + p_{j,2} - p_{j,1} + \max[t - p_{i,1}, 0, p_{j,1} - p_{i,2}]$$

which ultimately reduces to

$$t_{ij} = p_{i,2} + p_{j,2} - p_{i,1} - p_{j,1} + \max[t, p_{i,1}, p_{i,1} + p_{j,1} - p_{i,2}]. \quad (7.25)$$

By the same reasoning as for the functional equation (7.23) we obtain the following functional equation when an optimal scheduling policy is employed after the processing of jobs i, j:

$$f(p_{1,1}, p_{1,2}; \ldots; 0, {}^i0; \ldots; p_{N,1}, p_{N,2}; t_i)$$
$$= \min_{i < j} [p_{j,1} + f(p_{1,1}, p_{1,2}; \ldots; 0, {}^i0; \ldots; 0, {}^j0; \ldots; \qquad (7.26)$$
$$p_{N,1}, p_{N,2}; t_{ij})]$$

where the notation $i < j$ means that job j is processed just after the processing of job i. By substituting (7.26) into (7.23) we obtain

$$f(p_{1,1}, p_{1,2}; \ldots; p_{N,1}, p_{N,2}; t)$$
$$= \min_{i=1,\ldots,N} [p_{i,1} + \min_{i \lessdot j} \{p_{j,1} + f(p_{1,1}, p_{1,2};$$
$$\ldots; 0, {}^i0; \ldots; 0, {}^j0; \ldots; p_{N,1}, p_{N,2}; t_{ij})\}]. \qquad (7.27)$$
$$= \min_{\substack{i \lessdot j \\ i,j = 1,\ldots,N}} [p_{i,1} + p_{j,1} + f(p_{1,1}, p_{1,2};$$
$$\ldots; 0, {}^i0; \ldots; 0, {}^j0; \ldots; p_{N,1}, p_{N,2}; t_{ij})].$$

Next we exchange the order of the processing of two jobs i, j, that is, if job j is processed first and then job i is processed second when N jobs remain, the time t_{ji} which corresponds to the time t_{ij} for the order ij is expressed by an equation obtained by exchanging i, j in (7.25), that is

$$t_{ji} = p_{j,2} + p_{i,2} - p_{j,1} - p_{i,1} + \max[t, p_{j,1}, p_{j,1} + p_{i,1} - p_{j,2}]. \qquad (7.28)$$

Also an equation which corresponds to (7.27) becomes similarly

$$f(p_{1,1}, p_{1,2}; \ldots; p_{N,1}, p_{N,2}; t)$$
$$= \min_{\substack{j \lessdot i \\ j,i = 1\ldots,N}} [p_{j,1} + p_{i,1} + f(p_{1,1}, p_{1,2}; \ldots; 0, {}^i0; \ldots;$$
$$0, {}^j0; \ldots; p_{N,1}, p_{N,2}; t_{ji})]. \qquad (7.29)$$

When any one pair $\{i, j\}$ among $({}_NC_2)$ pairs $\{i, j\}$ of any two jobs i, j is processed first and then the remaining $N - 2$ jobs are processed on M_1, M_2 optimally, the processing of these $N - 2$ jobs begins at $p_{i,1} + p_{j,1}$ on M_1 regardless of the order of i and j and so if committed time t_{ij} by M_2 ahead of M_1 for the order of ij is less than or equal to the time t_{ji} for the order ji, that is, if we have $t_{ij} \leq t_{ji}$, or the following inequality obtained by eliminating $p_{i,2} + p_{j,2} - p_{i,1} - p_{j,1}$ from (7.25) and (7.28):

$$\max[t, p_{i,1}, p_{i,1} + p_{j,1} - p_{i,2}] \leq \max[t, p_{j,1}, p_{j,1} + p_{i,1} - p_{j,2}] \qquad (7.30)$$

the order ij does not make longer the total elapsed time of N jobs than the order ji for the first pair $\{i, j\}$ (when (7.30) holds with equality the total elapsed times for the order ij and the order ji are the same). Since (7.30) is equivalent with

$$\max[t, \max(p_{i,1}, p_{i,1} + p_{j,1} - p_{i,2})] \leq \max[t, \max(p_{j,1}, p_{j,1} + p_{i,1} - p_{j,2})]$$

if

$$\max (p_{i,1}, p_{i,1} + p_{j,1} - p_{i,2}) \leqq \max (p_{j,1}, p_{j,i} + p_{i,1} - p_{j,2}) \qquad (7.31)$$

holds then (7.30) follows.

When we have $t > \max (p_{j,1}, p_{j,1} + p_{i,i} - p_{j,2})$, (7.30) holds with equality even if case (7.31) holds without equality and then the same total elapsed times occur for any order. But since (7.31) holds without equality we regard that the processing proceeds in the order ij. Also when (7.31) holds with equality either ordering of two jobs i, j is optimal regardless of the value of t.

By subtracting $p_{i,1} + p_{j,1}$ from every term in the brackets of both sides of (7.31) we obtain an equivalent inequality:

$$\max (- p_{j,1}, - p_{i,2}) \leqq \max (- p_{i,1}, - p_{j,2}).$$

By applying $\max (A, B) = - \min (- A, - B)$, finally we obtain an equivalent inequality:

$$- \min (p_{j,1}, p_{i,2}) \leqq - \min (p_{i,1}, p_{j,2}),$$

that is

$$\min (p_{i,1}, p_{j,2}) \leqq \min (p_{j,1}, p_{i,2}). \qquad (7.32)$$

If (7.32) holds without equality for the case when there remains the processing of N jobs ($N = n, n - 1, \ldots, 2$) and a pair $\{i, j\}$ of any two jobs i, j among them is processed as the first two jobs, we must process this pair in the order ij. If (7.32) holds with equality either ordering is optimal.

Since (7.32) is a criterion (7.18) in Theorem 3, the conclusion of Theorem 3 follows as in the former section.

Exercise

1. Show that the inequality (7.31) is a sufficient condition and not a necessary condition for the inequality (7.30) to hold.

7.14. Solution by Using Flow Time $T_2(i)$

Committed times t, t_i, t_{ij} represent the flow times on the second machine defined in Section 7.5. Since we can obtain a criterion (7.18) in Theorem 3 by comparing the value of t_{ij} under the order ij with the value of t_{ji}, in this section we give the demonstration of Theorem 3 by using the flow time $T_2(i)$. As shown in Section 7.7, the total elapsed time (makespan) $M(\omega)$ of any sequence $\omega = i_1 i_2 \ldots i_n$ is expressed by

$$M(\omega) = \sum_{t=1}^{n} p_{i,1} + T_2(i_n),$$

where the first term in the right side is constant regardless of the sequence. Hence it is sufficient to determine a sequence ω which minimizes $T_2(i_n)$.

Between $T_2(i_q)$ for $q = 1, 2, \ldots, n$ the following recurrence relation holds. This relation is a case $k = 2$ in (7.2) in Section 7.6.

$$T_2(i_1) = p_{i_1,2}, T_2(i_q) = p_{i_q,2} + \max[T_2(i_{q-1}) - p_{i_q,1}, 0]. \qquad (7.33)$$

Hence every $T_2(i_q)$ is a nondecreasing function of $T_2(i_{q-1})$ (Theorem 2) and therefore $T_2(i_n)$ is a nondecreasing function of $T_2(i_q)$ $(q = 2, 3, \ldots, n)$.

Then, when an optimal scheduling policy is employed let two jobs i, j be processed after the processing of a certain subsequence S with last job l, where if i, j are the first two jobs to be processed then S does not exist and $T_2(l) = 0$. If these two jobs are processed in the order ij after S, we have from (7.33) (cf. Fig. 7.11),

$$T_2(i) = p_{i,2} + \max[T_2(l) - p_{i,1}, 0],$$
$$T_2(ij) \equiv T_2(j) = p_{j,2} + \max[T_2(i) - p_{j,1}, 0],$$

where $T_2(ij)$ shows $T_2(j)$ under the order ij. $T_2(i), T_2(ij)$ are t_i, t_{ij} respectively in the former section.

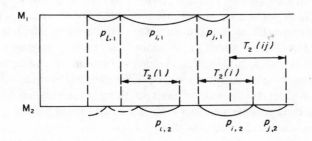

FIG. 7.11

By substituting the above expression of $T_2(i)$ into that of $T_2(ij)$ and rearranging, we have

$$T_2(ij) = p_{j,2} + \max[p_{i,2} + \max\{T_2(l) - p_{i,1}, 0\} - p_{j,1}, 0]$$
$$= p_{i,2} + p_{j,2} - p_{i,1} - p_{j,1} + \max[T_2(l), p_{i,1}, p_{i,1} + p_{j,1} - p_{i,2}],$$

which corresponds to (7.25) at the former Section 7.13.

On the other hand, if two jobs i, j are processed in the order ji after S, we obtain in the same way

$$T_2(ji) = p_{j,2} + p_{i,2} - p_{j,1} - p_{i,1} + \max[T_2(l), p_{j,1}, p_{j,1} + p_{i,1} - p_{j,2}].$$

Hence, since $T_2(i_n)$ is a nondecreasing function of $T_2(i_q)$ $(q = 2, 3, \ldots, n-1)$, if an inequality

$$T_2(ij) \leqq T_2(ji) \qquad (7.34)$$

holds without equality two jobs i, j must be processed in order ij after S in order to obtain an optimal sequence. If (7.34) holds with equality either ordering of two jobs i, j is optimal.

By substituting the expressions of $T_2(ij)$ and $T_2(ji)$ into (7.34) the conclusion of Theorem 3 follows as in Section 7.13.

Exercises

1. In the $n \times 2$ flow-shop min-makespan problem, where n jobs are $1, 2, \ldots, n$, when an inequality $p_{i,2} \geqq p_{j,2}$ holds for any two jobs i, j where $i < j$ and an inequality $p_{i,1} \geqq p_{i,2}$ holds for every job i, prove that a sequence $1 \cdot 2 \ldots n$ is an optimal sequence.

2. Derive the criterion (7.18) in Theorem 3 by the critical path approach. Use the formula in exercise 5 in Section 7.10.

7.15. Working Rules

Restricted working rule given by Johnson as a working rule for generating the optimal sequence by using a criterion (7.18) in Theorem 3 is a rule for determining only one optimal sequence. On the other hand, if equality holds in a criterion (7.18) either ordering of two jobs i, j is optimal, hence a working rule which generates all possible optimal sequences obtained from a criterion (7.18) including the above equality case, will be called a general working rule. Usually a general working rule is used without anything being denoted. However, it must be noticed that even a general working rule cannot always generate all optimal sequences (cf. later remarks).

These working rules have a common nature which first arranges $np_{i,1}$'s and $np_{i,2}$'s $(i = 1, 2, \ldots, n)$, selects the smallest among these $2n$ processing times and decides the position of the associated job and successively repeats the above procedures for the set of remaining processing times. It excludes the processing times of jobs already decided.

Remark. There exists another method which arranges all jobs in increasing order of Z_i as in Theorem 5.

7.16. General Working Rule

When N jobs $1, 2, \ldots, N$ $(N = n, n - 1, \ldots, 2)$ remain to be processed, let job i_0 be the job with the smallest among the $2N$ processing times, that is,

$$\min(p_{i_0, 1}, p_{i_0, 2}) = \min_{i = 1, \ldots, N} \min(p_{i, 1}, p_{i, 2})$$

holds.

Then we consider the following two cases:

1. The case where only one such job i_0 exists.

(a) If $p_{i_0,1} < p_{i_0,2}$ holds, since $p_{i_0,1} < p_{i_0,2}, p_{i,1}, p_{i,2}$ holds for every job $i \neq i_0$, we have

$$\min(p_{i_0,1}, p_{i,2}) = p_{i_0,1} < \min(p_{i,1}, p_{i_0,2})$$

for every job $i \neq i_0$ and therefore i_0 precedes all other jobs i. Consequently, job i_0 must be processed first among N jobs for each $N = n, n-1, \ldots, 2$.

(b) If $p_{i_0,1} > p_{i_0,2}$ holds, since $p_{i_0,2} < p_{i_0,1}, p_{i,1}, p_{i,2}$ holds for every $i \neq i_0$, we have

$$\min(p_{i_0,1}, p_{i,2}) > p_{i_0,2} = \min(p_{i,1}, p_{i_0,2})$$

for every $i \neq i_0$ and therefore job i_0 follows behind all other jobs i. Hence, job i_0 must be processed last among N jobs for each $N = n$, $n-1, \ldots, 2$.

(c) If $p_{i_0,1} = p_{i_0,2}$ holds, since $p_{i_0,1} = p_{i_0,2} < p_{i,1}, p_{i,2}$ holds for every $i \neq i_0$, we have

$$\min(p_{i_0,1}, p_{i,2}) = p_{i_0,1} = p_{i_0,2} = \min(p_{i,1}, p_{i_0,2})$$

for every $i \neq i_0$ and therefore the order of two jobs i_0, i is arbitrary. Hence, the position of job i_0 is any place among N jobs for each $N = n$, $n-1, \ldots, 2$.

2. The case where more than one such jobs exist.

Let us put

$$J_0 = \{i_0\}, J_1 = \{i_0 | p_{i_0,1} < p_{i_0,2}\}, \quad J_2 = \{i_0 | p_{i_0,1} > p_{i_0,2}\},$$
$$J_3 = \{i_0 | p_{i_0,1} = p_{i_0,2}\}.$$
$$(J_0 = J_1 + J_2 + J_3).$$

(a) When $i_0 \in J_1$, job i_0 precedes all jobs i, where $i \neq J_0$, by the same argument as in 1(a). Also, since

$$\min(p'_{i_0,1}, p''_{i_0,2}) = p'_{i_0,1} = p''_{i_0,1} = \min(p''_{i_0,1}, p'_{i_0,2})$$

holds for $i'_0 \in J_1, i''_0 \in J_1$, the position of the job i_0 in J_1 is arbitrary.

(b) When $i_0 \in J_2$, job i_0 follows behind all jobs i, where $i \neq J_0$, by the same argument as in 1(b). Also, since

$$\min(p'_{i_0,1}, p''_{i_0,2}) = p''_{i_0,2} = p'_{i_0,2} = \min(p''_{i_0,1}, p'_{i_0,2})$$

holds for $i'_0 \in J_2, i''_0 \in J_2$, the position of the job i_0 in J_2 is arbitrary.

(c) When $i_0 \in J_3$, the order of job i_0 and job i is arbitrary for all jobs $i \neq i_0$ by the same argument as in 1(c), that is, the position of the job $i_0 \in J_3$ is any place in N jobs ($N = n, n-1, \ldots, 2$). A rough figure of the optimum sequence is shown in Fig. 7.12, where orderings in J_1 and J_2 are arbitrary respectively, and any job in J_3 can be placed anywhere in the sequence.

J_1	$i \neq J_0$	J_2

FIG. 7.12

From the foregoing, generation of the optimal sequence of n jobs by a general working rule proceeds along the following lines:

1. Arrange $np_{i,1}$'s and $np_{i,2}$'s in a table like Table 7.4.
2. Select the smallest among these $2n$ processing times $(N = n)$.
3. In the case when the number of the smallest is one, if it is $p_{i,1}$ then place job i at the top of jobs in the table: if it is $p_{j,2}$ then place job j at the end of jobs in the table.

TABLE 7.4

i	$p_{1,1}$	$p_{i,2}$
1	$p_{1,1}$	$p_{1,2}$
2	$p_{2,2}$	$p_{2,2}$
$\vdots$	$\vdots$	$\vdots$
n	$p_{n,1}$	$p_{n,2}$

In the case when the number of the smallest is more than one, place the jobs in J_1 (only $p_{i,1}$ is the smallest) at the top of the jobs in the table, where the order of jobs in J_1 is arbitrary, and place the jobs in J_2 (only $p_{i,2}$ is the smallest) at the end of the jobs in the table, where the order of jobs in J_2 is arbitrary. Also, the positions of jobs in J_3 (both $p_{i,1}$ and $p_{i,2}$ are the smallest) are arbitrary within the jobs in the table.

4. Exclude all jobs with the above smallest processing times from the current table and repeat the above steps for the remaining $N - |J_0|$ jobs in order to fill up a list of jobs already placed in optimal sequences.

EXAMPLE 1. For the 6×2 flow-shop min-makespan problem with processing times given by Table 7.5, determine the optimal sequences by the general working rule.

Solution. First, since a smallest processing time is 1 of job 3 with $p_{3,1} = 1$ and job 5 with $p_{5,2} = 1$, job 3 becomes the top and job 5 becomes the end of the

TABLE 7.5

i	1	2	3	4	5	6
$p_{i,1}$	2	5	1	3	2	6
$p_{i,2}$	2	3	4	4	1	2

optimal sequence. Excluding the jobs 3, 5, the smallest is 2 of jobs 1, 6 and then the position of job 1 is arbitrary within four jobs 1, 2, 4 and 6 and job 6 is made the second, except job 1, from the end of the optimal sequence. Excluding jobs 1, 6, the smallest is 3 of jobs 2; 4 and then we have the order 42. Hence, we obtain optimal sequences 314265, 341265, 342165, and 342615. Here the makespan is 20, idle time I_2 on M_2 is 4 and $T_2(5) = 1$.

EXAMPLE 2. For the 6×2 flow-shop min-makespan problem with processing times given by Table 7.6, determine the optimal sequences by the general working rule.

TABLE 7.6

i	1	2	3	4	5	6
$p_{i,1}$	3	4	4	1	5	4
$p_{i,2}$	5	3	10	3	2	4

Solution. In the same way as in the above example we obtain optimal sequences 413625 and 416325. Here makespan is 28, $I_2 = 1$; $T_2(5) = 7$.

Remark. The set of optimal sequences determined by the general working rule does not always coincide with the set of all optimal sequences in case no passing is allowed.

The reason for this proposition will be explained by Example 2 as shown below:

In Example 2 there exists another optimal sequence 413265 which cannot be obtained by the general working rule, because for $i = 2$, $j = 6$ in the criterion (7.18) in Theorem 3, it becomes

$$\min(4, 4) > \min(4, 3)$$

Job 6 must precede job 2, that is, the order 26 cannot be obtained from the criterion. The reason why the sequence 413265 including the order 26 becomes optimal is as follows.

For example, as seen in the proof of Theorem 3, in Section 7.13 the criterion is equivalent with (7.31) in Section 7.13, that is

$$\max(p_{i,1}, p_{i,1} + p_{j,1} - p_{i,2}) \leqq \max(p_{j,1}, p_{j,1} + p_{i,1} - p_{j,2}). \quad (7.35)$$

Also an inequality $t_{ij} \leq t_{ji}$ is equivalent with (7.30) in Section 7.13, that is

$$\max[t, p_{i,1}, p_{i,1} + p_{j,1} - p_{i,2}] \leqq \max[t, p_{j,1}, p_{j,1} + p_{i,1} - p_{j,2}]. \quad (7.36)$$

Then even in the case where job j precedes job i by the criterion because of the existence of an inequality

$$\max(p_{i,1}, p_{i,1} + p_{j,1} - p_{i,2}) > \max(p_{j,1}, p_{j,1} + p_{i,1} - p_{j,2}),$$

if we have

$$t \geqq \max(p_{i,1}, p_{i,1} + p_{j,1} - p_{i,2}),\qquad(7.37)$$

(7.36) holds with equality, which leads to $t_{ij} = t_{ji}$.

Hence, after a job l being just prior to a pair $\{i, j\}$ the order of two jobs i, j becomes arbitrary.

Concerning Example 2, when we consider the case $l = 3$, $i = 2$, $j = 6$ $t = 19 - 8 = 11$ holds and (7.32) does not hold. However, it becomes

$$t = 11 > \max[4, 4+4-3) > \max (4, 4+4-4)$$

and (7.36) holds with equality;

$$\max[11, 4, 4+4-3] = \max[11, 4, 4+4-4].$$

Hence, after $l = 3$ either ordering of $i = 2$ and $j = 6$ becomes optimal and then we have an optimal sequence with the order 26 after job 3.

The order of two jobs i, j by a criterion (7.18) in Theorem 3 is fixed whatever job l may be just prior to two jobs $\{i, j\}$. But the order 26 in the above example depends on a job l being just prior to these two jobs 2, 6. For example, (7.37) does not hold in case $l = 4$, because $t = 4 - 1 = 3$ holds, and then only the order 462 is possible by the criterion. Since the determination of the optimal sequence by using a criterion which includes the value of t becomes somewhat complex, we are forced to look for an inequality such as the criterion (7.18) in Theorem 3 which does not include $t \equiv T_2(l)$, that is, does not depend on the job l being just prior to two jobs i, j, and moreover satisfies transitive property, as an order determining criterion of any two adjacent jobs. Determination of the optimal sequence by a certain criterion of the type of the criterion (7.18) in Theorem 3 is effective even for somewhat large n. That is, its computational complexity is of order $O(n \log n)$.

Also, usually we are used to looking for at least one optimal schedule for general scheduling problems (cf. Section 7.17).

7.17. Restricted Working Rule

A working rule which was defined in order to obtain only one optimal sequence when S. M. Johnson presented Theorem 3 lays down a rule with which to select a preferred processing time in situations when there exist more than one smallest processing times in the Table under general working rule.

That is to say, this restricted working rule follows the next steps:

1. Arrange $np_{i,1}$'s and $np_{i,2}$'s in a table like Table 7.4.
2. Select the smallest among these $2n$ processing times.
3. In the case when the number of the smallest is one, if it is $p_{i,1}$ then place job i at the top of jobs in the table; if it is $p_{j,2}$ then place job j at the end of jobs in the table. But in the case when the number of the smallest is more than one,

select the one with the smallest job number and place a related job by the above rule, where if both $p_{i,1}$ and $p_{i,2}$ of the above job are the smallest processing times then place this job i at the top by preferring the processing time on M_1 to that on M_2.

4. Exclude two processing times of a job thus selected from the table, repeat the above steps for the remaining processing times and fill up a list of jobs already placed in optimal sequence.

EXAMPLE 3. Decide an optimal sequence by restricted working rule in Example 1 and Example 2 respectively.

Solution. They are 314265 in Example 1 and 413625 in Example 2.

Exercises

1. Verify that the following working rule deciding only one optimal sequence which is obtained from Theorem 4 is equivalent with the restricted working rule.
   (a) Divide the set of n jobs into two subsets

$$J_1 = \{i | p_{i,1} \leqq p_{i,2}\}. \quad J_2 = \{i | p_{i,1} > p_{i,2}\}.$$

   (b) First arrange the jobs in J_1 in increasing order of $p_{i,1}$ where if a tie occurs place first the job with the smaller job number. After the jobs in J_1 arrange the jobs in J_2 in decreasing order of $p_{i,2}$, where if a tie occurs place first the job with the larger job number.

2. Decide one optimal sequence in Example 1 and Example 2 respectively by using a working rule in exercise 1.

3. Verify that the following working rule which is applied to a criterion in Theorem 3:

$$\min[p_{i,1}, p_{j,2}] \leqq \min[p_{j,1}, p_{i,2}]$$

is equivalent with the restricted working rule.
   (a) When the criterion holds without equality, put job i before job j.
   (b) When the criterion holds with equality, if the smallest terms are $p_{i,1}$ and $p_{j,1}$, then put first the job with the smallest job number among i and j; if the smallest terms are $p_{j,2}$ and $p_{i,2}$, then put first the job with larger job number among i and j; if the smallest terms contain the processing times both on M_1 and on M_2, put first the job with processing time on M_1, where if there exist two such jobs take the job with smaller job number.
   For a practical procedure by this rule, see the next exercise 4.

4. The directed graph is $G = (X, Z)$, where X is a set of n nodes that correspond to n jobs and Z is a set of every directed arc (i, j). This shows that job i precedes job j by the rule applied to the criterion in exercise 3, for the pair $\{i, j\}$ of any two jobs i, j. This becomes as shown in Fig. 7.13 for Example 1.

An optimal sequence by the restricted working rule corresponds to a Hamiltonian path, that is, a path which passes through all nodes once, in this directed graph. One way of determining a Hamiltonian path is the following successive latin product method:

First let us define a latin matrix L^0 as an n order square matrix with the (i, j) element which is equal to j or 0 according to whether arc (i, j) exists or not and another latin matrix L^1 be an n order square matrix with the (i, j) element which is equal to ij or 0 according to whether arc (i, j) exists or not. Then we proceed as follows:
   (1) Successive products of two latin matrices:

$$L^2 = L^1 L^0, \ L^3 = L^2 L^0, \ldots, \ L^{k+1} = L^k L^0, \ldots, \ L^{n-1} = L^{n-2} L^0.$$

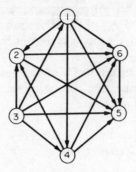

FIG. 7.13

are calculated by the next rules (a) and (b), where (i, r) element of L^{k+1} is denoted by l_{ir}^{k+1}, $k = 1, 2, \ldots, n-2$.
  (a) For each $j(j = 1, 2, \ldots, n)$, if (i, j) element of L^k is zero, or equal to $i_1 i_2 \ldots i_{k+1}$ and (j, r) element of L^0 is zero or equal to a certain i_q $(q = 1, 2, \ldots, k+1)$, then $1_{ir}^{k+1} = 0$ holds.
  (b) For each $j(j = 1, 2, \ldots, n)$, if (i, j) element of L^k is equal to $i_1 i_2 \ldots i_{k+1}$ and (j, r) element of L^0 is equal to $i_q (q \neq 1, 2, \ldots, k+1)$, then $1_{ir}^{k+1} = i_1 i_2, \ldots, i_{k+1} i_q$ holds.
Hence the number of each (i, r) element of L^{k+1} is not necessarily one.
  (2) Finally a nonzero element of L^{n-1} gives an optimal sequence.

5. Derive an optimal sequence by the restricted working rule in Example 1 and Example 2 respectively by using the above successive latin product method.

Bibliography and Comments

Section 7.2
  Theorem 1 for the min-makespan problem has been developed by
S. M. JOHNSON, "Optimal two and three-stage production schedule with setup times included", *Nav. Res. Log. Quart.* **1**, No. 1 (1954), 61–68; Chapter 2, *Industrial Scheduling*, J. F. MUTH and G. L. THOMPSON (eds.), Prentice-Hall, 1963.
  For the normal objective function see, for example,
R. W. CONWAY, W. L. MAXWELL and L. W. MILLER, *Theory of Scheduling*, Addison-Wesley, 1967, Chapter 5, pp. 80–81.
Section 7.7
  The flow time $T_k(i_q)$ and an expression of makespan by using the flow time is found in
I. NABESHIMA, "The order of n items processed on m machines. [III]", *J. Oper. Res. Soc. Japan*, **16**, No. 3 (1973), 163–185.

Section 7.10
  Expressions of makespan and/or the other equations are found in
M. L. SMITH, S. S. PANWALKAR and R. A. DUDEK, "Flowshop sequencing problem with ordered processing time matrices", *Manag. Science*, **21**, No. 5 (1975), 544–549.
W. SZWARC, "Precedence relation of the flow-shop problem", *Working Paper, School of Business Administration*, University of Wisconsin-Milwaukee, April 1977.
I. NABESHIMA, "Notes on the analytical results in flow shop scheduling: Part 5", *Rep. Univ. of Electro-Comm.* **28**, No. 1 (1977), 57–65.

Section 7.12
S. M. JOHNSON, *op. cit.*

Section 7.13
R. BELLMAN, *Dynamic Programming of Continuous Process*, Rand Paper R-271, The RAND Corp., 1954, pp. 126–133.
R. BELLMAN and S. DREYFUS, *Applied Dynamic Programming*, Princeton University Press, 1962, pp. 142–145.

Section 7.14
I. NABESHIMA, *Scheduling Theory* (in Japanese), Morikita Shuppan, 1974, pp. 56–57.
Exercise 2: W. SZWARC, *op. cit.*, p. 4.

Section 7.15
S. M. JOHNSON, *op. cit.*
I. NABESHIMA, *op. cit.*, pp. 58–63.

Section 7.16
I. NABESHIMA, *op. cit.*, pp. 58–61.
For the computational complexity see, for example,
E. G. COFFMAN, Jr. (ed.), *Computer and Job-shop Scheduling Theory*, John-Wiley, 1976, p. 20.
A. H. G. RINNOOY KAN, *Machine Scheduling Problems*, Martinus Nijhoff, 1976, p. 90.

Section 7.17
S. M. JOHNSON, *op. cit.*
Exercise 4: A. KAUFMAN, *Graphs, Dynamic Programming, and Finite Games*, Academic Press, Inc., 1967, pp. 271–280.

CHAPTER 8

Flow-shop Scheduling Problems: Analytical Results II and Extensions

8.1. Introduction

In this chapter we continue our investigation of analytical results for the sequencing problem under different conditions. This is a continuation of our objectives and spirit of study utilized extensively in Chapter 7. We begin with the three-machine min-makespan problem and develop results in the form of theorems for this problem under certain assumptions on processing times and idle times. We then formulate dynamic programming-type models for each problem and investigate their properties. We then return to the two-machine problem but this time considering situations with time lags. We conclude the chapter by generalizing our results to the m-machine problem.

8.2. Three-machine Min-Makespan Problem

For the three-machine flow-shop min-makespan problem it is sufficient to consider the problem in the case where no passing is allowed, as shown in Section 7.2 of Chapter 7. Let the ordering be the order $M_1 M_2, M_3$ then, as described in the following, since we cannot decide the optimal sequence without taking into account the idle time or flow time on the second machine M_2, in addition to either of them on the last machine M_3, we cannot obtain an efficient criterion as in the two-machines case.

Then we look for a criterion or a procedure which decides the optimal sequence under some restraints on the processing times, which means that a limited solution is derived under a certain restraint.

Further, we look for the sufficient conditions for any two adjacent jobs in optimal sequence to be a definite order regardless of the position of these two jobs.

These criteria and sufficient conditions are inequalities of the type of a criterion (7.18) in Theorem 3 of Chapter 7 possessing transitive property. In the latter case we examine in detail the difference between the general working rule and the restricted working rule.

162

8.3. Limited Solution under Special Processing Times

We can obtain a criterion by which an optimal sequence, that is, limited solution can be determined under the restraint that no processing time on the first machine M_1 is smaller than that on the second machine M_2, or no processing time on the third (last) machine M_3 is smaller than that on the second machine M_2. This fact is stated in the next theorem.

THEOREM 1. *In the three-machine flow-shop min-makespan problem, let the ordering be M_1, M_2, M_3, then if (a)*

$$\min_i p_{i,1} \geqq \max_i p_{i,2},$$

or (b)

$$\min_i p_{i,3} \geqq \max_i p_{i,2}.$$

holds, the optimal sequence can be determined by the next rule: if

$$\min[p_{i,1} + p_{i,2},\ p_{j,2} + p_{j,3}] \leqq \min[p_{j,1} + p_{j,2},\ p_{i,2} + p_{i,3}] \quad (8.1)$$

holds without equality, job i precedes job j. Otherwise either ordering is optimal.

Remark. For a weaker condition than (a) or (b), see Miscellaneous Exercises 6 and 7 ($m = 3$) at the end of this chapter.

Any working rule by this theorem is the same as that by a criterion in Theorem 3 of chapter 7 for the two-machines case, by taking $p_{i,1} + p_{i,2}$, $p_{i,2} + p_{i,3}$ for $p_{i,1}$, $p_{i,2}$, respectively.

In the following Sections 8.4 and 8.5–8.12 we give the proof of this theorem by using idle time on the last machine and flow times respectively.

8.4. Solution by Using Machine Idle Time

For simplicity let any sequence be $\omega = 1 \cdot 2 \cdot 3 \cdot \ldots \cdot n$, then the sum of idle times on the last machine M_3 is, from (7.11) ($m = 3$) in Section 7.8 of chapter 7,

$$I_3(1 \cdot 2 \cdot 3 \cdot \ldots \cdot n) = \max_{1 \leq u \leq v \leq n} [D_2^1(u) + D_3^2(v)],$$

where

$$D_2^1(u) = \sum_{i=1}^{u} p_{i,1} - \sum_{i=1}^{u-1} p_{i,2}, \quad D_3^2(v) = \sum_{i=1}^{v} p_{i,2} - \sum_{i=1}^{v-1} p_{i,3},$$

and makespan is, from (7.3) at Section 7.7 of Chapter 7

$$M(\omega) = \sum_{i-1}^{n} p_{i,3} + I_3(1 \cdot 2 \cdot 3 \cdot \ldots \cdot n)$$

and its first term is constant. Hence by

$$I_3(\omega) \equiv I_3(1 \cdot 2 \cdot 3 \cdot \ldots \cdot n)$$

it is sufficient to decide a sequence ω_0 such that we have

$$I_3(\omega_0) \leqq I_3(\omega)$$

for any sequence ω.

Next let ω' be a sequence constructed by the exchange of two jobs j and $j+1$ in a sequence ω and put

$$I_3(\omega') = \max_{1 \leq u \leq v \leq n} [D_2^{1'}(u) + D_3^{2'}(v)],$$

$$D_2^{1'}(u) = \sum_{i=1}^{u} p'_{i,1} - \sum_{i=1}^{u-1} p'_{i,2}, \quad D_3^{2'}(v) = \sum_{i=1}^{v} p'_{i,2} - \sum_{i=1}^{v-1} p'_{i,3},$$

then, for $i \neq j, j+1$, $p'_{1,k} = p_{i,k} (k = 1, 2, 3)$ holds and also $p'_{j,k} = p'_{j+1,k}, p'_{j+1,k} = p_{j,k} (k = 1, 2, 3)$ hold, so we have $D_2^{1'}(u) = D_2^1(u)$ for $u \neq j, j+1$, $D_3^{2'}(v) = D_3^2(v)$ for $v \neq j, j+1$. Also, since we can express as below:

$$I_3(\omega) = \max_{1 \leq v \leq n} [\max_{1 \leq u \leq v} D_2^1(u) + D_3^2(v)],$$

$$I_3(\omega') = \max_{1 \leq v \leq n} [\max_{1 \leq u \leq v} D_2^{1'}(u) + D_3^{2'}(v)],$$

in order to have $I_3(\omega) \leq I_3(\omega')$ it is sufficient to have

$$\max[\max_{1 \leq u \leq j} D_2^1(u) + D_3^2(j), \quad \max_{1 \leq u \leq j+1} D_2^1(u) + D_3^2(j+1)]$$

(8.2)

$$\leq \max[\max_{1 \leq u \leq j} D_2^{1'}(u) + D_3^{2'}(j), \quad \max_{1 \leq u \leq j+1} D_2^{1'}(u) + D_3^{2'}(j+1)]$$

(8.2) is a sufficient condition to be $I_3(\omega) \leq I_3(\omega')$.

Since (8.2) includes u such as $1 \leq u \leq j-1$, which differs from (7.19) of Section 7.12 (in Chapter 7) for the two-machine case, we cannot decide (8.2) independently of every job u $(1 \leq u \leq j-1)$. which precedes two jobs $j, j+1$, that is to say, we cannot obtain an efficient criterion, which determines an optimal sequence from (8.2). However, in case condition (a) holds on the one hand, since we have

$$D_2^1(j) - D_2^1(u) = \left(\sum_{i=1}^{j} p_{i,1} - \sum_{j=1}^{j-1} p_{i,2} \right) - \left(\sum_{i=1}^{u} p_{i,1} - \sum_{i=1}^{u-1} p_{i,2} \right)$$

$$= \sum_{j=u+1}^{j} p_{i,1} - \sum_{i=u}^{j-1} p_{i,2} \geq 0$$

for $u < j$ it becomes $\max\limits_{1 \le u \le j} D_2^1(u) = D_2^1(j)$ in (8.2)

In the same way since they become

$$\max_{1 \le u \le j+1} D_2^1(u) = D_2^1(j+1), \quad \max_{1 \le u \le j} D_2^{1'}(u) = D_2^{1'}(j), \quad \max_{1 \le u \le j+1} D_2^{1'}(u)$$
$$= D_2^{1'}(j+1).$$

under condition (a), (8.2) reduces to

$$\max[D_2^1(j) + D_3^2(j), D_2^1(j+1) + D_3^2(j+1)]$$
$$\le \max[D_2^{1'}(j) + D_3^{2'}(j), D_2^{1'}(j+1) + D_3^{2'}(j+1)] \qquad (8.3)$$

which is expressed by processing times as

$$\max\left[\sum_{i=1}^{j} p_{i,1} - \sum_{i=1}^{i-1} p_{i,2} + \sum_{i=1}^{j} p_{i,2} - \sum_{i=1}^{j-1} p_{i,3}, \right.$$
$$\left. \sum_{i=1}^{j+1} p_{i,1} - \sum_{i=1}^{j} p_{i,2} + \sum_{i=1}^{j+1} p_{i,2} - \sum_{i=1}^{j} p_{i,3} \right]$$

$$\le \max\left[\sum_{i=1}^{j-1} p_{i,1} + p_{j+1,1} - \sum_{i=1}^{j-1} p_{i,2} + \sum_{i=1}^{j-1} p_{i,2} + p_{j+1,2} - \sum_{i=1}^{j-1} p_{i,3}, \right.$$
$$\left. \sum_{i=1}^{j+1} p_{i,1} - \sum_{i=1}^{j-1} p_{i,2} - p_{j+1,2} + \sum_{i=1}^{j+1} p_{i,2} - \sum_{i=1}^{j-1} p_{i,3} - p_{j+1,3} \right].$$

By subtracting

$$\sum_{i=1}^{j+1} p_{i,1} - \sum_{i=1}^{j-1} p_{i,2} + \sum_{i=1}^{j+1} p_{i,2} - \sum_{i=1}^{j-1} p_{i,3}$$

from its both sides we have an equivalent inequality

$$\max[-p_{j+1,1} - p_{j+1,2}, -p_{j,2} - p_{j,3}]$$
$$\le \max[-p_{j,1} - p_{j,2}, -p_{j+1,2} - p_{j+1,3}],$$

which is transformed, by the identity $\max[A, B] = -\min[-A, -B]$, into

$$-\min[p_{j+1,1} + p_{j+1,2}, \ p_{j,2} + p_{j,3}] \le -\min[p_{j,1} + p_{j,2}, p_{j+1,2} + p_{j+1,3}].$$

$$\min[p_{j,1} + p_{j,2}, p_{j+1,2} + p_{j+1,3}] \le \min[p_{j+1,1} + p_{j+1,2}, \ p_{j,2} + p_{j,3}]$$
$$\qquad (8.4)$$

respectively.

Hence if (8.4) holds without equality, then (8.2) holds without equality and so $I_3(\omega) \le I_3(\omega')$ holds, where equality $I_3(\omega) = I_3(\omega')$ occurs, provided there exists

$$\max_{1 \le u \le v} D_2^1(u) + D_3^2(v) = \max_{1 \le u \le v} D_2^{1'}(u) + D_3^{2'}(v)(v \ne j, j+1)$$

not smaller than any side of (8.2). When such a $v \neq j, j+1$ does not exist we have $I_3(\omega) < I_3(\omega')$ and then job j must precede job $j+1$ for two adjacent jobs $j, j+1$ in order to decide the optimal sequence.

Since (8.4) satisfies the transitive property as verified in the same way as in the proof of Theorem 6 of Chapter 7, the conclusion of Theorem 1 follows as in the two-machine case.

Next, we consider the case where condition (b) holds. In this case, by expressing

$$I_3(\omega) = \max_{1 \leq u \leq n} [D_2^1(u) + \max_{u \leq v \leq n} D_3^2(v)],$$

$$I_3(\omega') = \max_{1 \leq u \leq n} [D_2^{1'}(u) + \max_{u \leq v \leq n} D_3^{2'}(v)]$$

since they become $D_2^{1'}(u) = D_2^1(u)$, for $u \neq j, j+1$, $D_3^{2'}(v) = D_3^2(v)$ for $v \neq j$, $j+1$ as shown before, it is sufficient to have

$$\max[D_2^1(j) + \max_{j \leq v \leq n} D_3^2(v), \ D_2^1(j+1) + \max_{j+1 \leq v \leq n} D_3^2(v)$$

$$\leq \max[D_2^{1'}(j) + \max_{j \leq v \leq n} D_3^{2'}(v), \ D_2^{1'}(j+1) + \max_{j+1 \leq v \leq n} D_3^{2'}(v)] \quad (8.5)$$

in order to have $I_3(\omega) \leq I_3(\omega')$.

Since, in case (b), we have

$$D_3^2(j) - D_3^2(v) = \left(\sum_{i=1}^{j} p_{i,2} - \sum_{i=1}^{j-1} p_{i,3} \right) - \left(\sum_{i=1}^{v} p_{i,2} - \sum_{i=1}^{v-1} p_{i,3} \right)$$

$$= \sum_{i=j}^{v-1} p_{i,3} - \sum_{i=j+1}^{v} p_{i,2} \geq 0$$

for $j < v$ we have $\max\limits_{j \leq v \leq n} D_3^2(v) = D_3^2(j)$ in (8.5). In the same way since it becomes

$$\max_{j+1 \leq v \leq n} D_3^2(v) = D_3^2(j+1), \ \max_{j \leq v \leq n} D_3^{2'}(v) = D_3'(j),$$

$$\max_{j+1 \leq v \leq n} D_3^{2'}(v) = D_3^{2'}(j+1)$$

from condition (b), (8.5) reduces to (8.3) in case (a), that is,

$$\max[D_2^1(j) + D_3^2(j), \ D_2^1(j+1) + D_3^2(j+1)]$$
$$\leq \max[D_2^{1'}(j) + D_3^{2'}(j), \ D_2^{1'}(j+1) + D_3^{2'}(j+1)].$$

Hence the conclusion of Theorem 1 follows as in case (a).

8.5. Formulation by Flow Times $T_2(i)$, $T_3(i)$

In the following two sections we show the formulation by using flow times $T_2(i)$, $T_3(i)$ that take the main parts (t, t_i, t_{ij} and the like) in dynamic programming formulation for the two-machine case into consideration and in the proof of Theorem 1.

8.6. Flow times $T_2(i)$, $T_3(i)$ and Makespan

As defined previously in Section 7.5 of Chapter 7, let $T_2(i_q)$ be a flow time of job i_q on the second machine M_2 and $T_3(i_q)$ be a flow time of job i_q on the last two machines M_2, M_3, that is, an elapsed time from the completion time of job i_q on the first machine M_1 to its completion on the third machine M_3, ($q = 1, 2, \ldots, n$) for any sequence $\omega = i_1 i_2 \ldots i_n$. Then makespan $M(\omega)$ is expressed as

$$M(\omega) = \sum_{q=1}^{n} p_{i_q,1} + T_3(i_n)$$

and since the first term on this right side is constant for any sequence ω it is sufficient to decide a sequence ω which minimizes $T_3(i_n)$.

8.7. Recurrence Relation between $T_2(i_q)$, $T_3(i_q)$ ($q = 1, 2, \ldots, n$)

By the same argument as in (7.2) in Section 7.6 of Chapter 7 (cf. Fig. 8.1), the following recurrence relations hold:

$$T_2(i_q) = p_{i_q,2} + \max[T_2(i_{q-1}) - p_{i_q,1}, 0], \quad (q = 1, 2, \ldots, n) \tag{8.6}$$

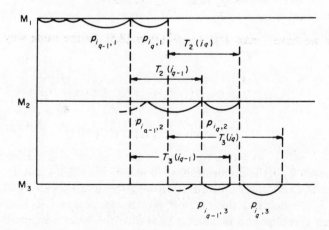

FIG. 8.1

$$T_3(i_q) = p_{i_q,3} + \max[T_3(i_{q-1}) - p_{l_q,1}, T_2(i_q)], \quad (q = 1, 2, \ldots, n) \quad (8.7)$$

where $T_2(i_0) = 0, \quad T_3(i_0) = 0$.

As is clear by substituting (8.6) into the right side of (8.7), each $T_3(i_q)$ is a nondecreasing function of $T_3(i_{q-1})$ and $T_2(i_{q-1})$ $(q = 2, 3, \ldots, n)$ and hence even if $T_3(i_{q-1})$ is made smaller, the respective $T_3(i_q), T_3(i_{q+1}), \ldots, T_3(i_n)$ do not necessarily become smaller. For this reason we cannot obtain a criterion for the three-machine case as easily as for the two-machine case. Also, the complete enumeration method for deciding the optimal sequence with minimal $T_3(i_n)$ by calculating $T_3(i_n)$ from (8.6), (8.7) for each of $n!$ possible sequences is not efficient.

8.8. Dynamic Programming-type Formulation

When an optimal scheduling policy is employed, let two jobs i, j be processed after the processing of a certain subsequence S with the last job l, then if these two jobs are processed in the order ij after S, we have, from (8.6) and (8.7) in the previous section,

$$T_2(i) = p_{i,2} + \max[T_2(l) - p_{i,1}, 0], \tag{8.8}$$

$$T_3(i) = p_{i,3} + \max[T_3(l) - p_{i,1}, T_2(i)]; \tag{8.9}$$

$$T_2(ij) \equiv T_2(j) = p_{j,2} + \max[T_2(i) - p_{j,1}, 0], \tag{8.10}$$

$$T_3(ij) \equiv T_3(j) = p_{j,3} + \max[T_3(i) - p_{j,1}, T_2(ij)]; \tag{8.11}$$

where $T_2(ij), T_3(ij)$ shows $T_2(j), T_3(j)$ respectively under the order ij (we use similar notations for the same reason) and $T_2(l) = 0 \ T_3(l) = 0$ in case job i is the first job of the sequence.

On the other hand, if two jobs i, j are processed in the order ji after S, we have similarly

$$T_2(j) = p_{j,2} + \max[T_2(l) - p_{j,1}, 0], \tag{8.12}$$

$$T_3(j) = p_{j,3} + \max[T_3(l) - p_{j,1}, T_2(j)]; \tag{8.13}$$

$$T_2(ji) \equiv T_2(i) = p_{i,2} + \max[T_2(j) - p_{i,1}, 0], \tag{8.14}$$

$$T_3(ji) \equiv T_3(i) = p_{i,3} + \max[T_3(j) - p_{i,1}, T_2(ji)]; \tag{8.15}$$

where $T_2(l) = 0, T_3(l) = 0$ in case job j is the first job of the sequence.

Since each $T_3(i_q)$ is nondecreasing function of $T_3(i_{q-1})$ and $T_2(i_{q-1})$ as described in Section 8.7 and therefore we may have $T_2(ij) > T_2(ji)$ even if $T_3(ij) \leq T_3(ji)$ holds, a definite job processed after two jobs i, j is not necessarily completed on the machine M_3 after the order ij sooner than after the order ji. This fact differs from the two-machine case.

For this fact we define the following condition (N): Condition (N) is defined if

$$T_3(ij) \leq T_3(ji)$$

holds without equality, then a definite job is completed on the machine M_3 after the order ij not later than after the order ji, and if we have equality then the successive jobs are completed at the same time after either order.

From this definition of the condition (N) the next theorem holds:

THEOREM 2. *In the present problem, where two jobs i, j are processed after any subsequence S, if an inequality*

$$T_3(ij) \leq T_3(ji) \tag{8.16}$$

holds and also the condition (N) is satisfied, then job i must precede job j after S in the optimal sequence, where when (8.16) holds with equality either ordering is optimal.

8.9. Values of $T_3(i)$, $T_3(ij)$, and $T_3(j)$, $T_3(ji)$

By substituting (8.8) into (8.9) in the former section and changing its terms we obtain

$$
\begin{aligned}
T_3(i) &= p_{i,3} + \max\left[T_3(l) - p_{i,1}, p_{i,2} + \max(T_2(l) - p_{i,1}, 0)\right] \\
&= p_{i,3} + \max\left[T_3(l) - p_{i,1}, p_{i,2} - p_{i,1} + \max(T_2(l), p_{i,1})\right] \\
&= p_{i,3} - p_{i,1} + \max\left[T_3(l), p_{i,2} + \max(T_2(l), p_{i,1})\right] \\
&= p_{i,3} - p_{i,1} + \max\left[T_3(l), T_2(l) + p_{i,2}, p_{i,1} + p_{i,2}\right].
\end{aligned} \tag{8.17}
$$

Also since it becomes, by substituting (8.8) into (8.10) in the former section

$$
\begin{aligned}
T_2(ij) &= p_{j,2} + \max\left[p_{i,2} + \max(T_2(l) - p_{i,1}, 0) - p_{j,1}, 0\right] \\
&= p_{j,2} - p_{j,1} + \max\left[p_{i,2} - p_{i,1} + \max(T_2(l), p_{i,1}), p_{j,1}\right],
\end{aligned} \tag{8.18}
$$

we obtain

$$
\begin{aligned}
T_3(ij) &= p_{j,3} + \max\left[p_{i,3} - p_{i,1} + \max(T_3(l), T_2(l) + p_{i,2}, p_{i,1} \right. \\
&\quad \left. + p_{i,2}) - p_{j,1}, p_{j,2} - p_{j,1} + \max(p_{i,2} - p_{i,1} \right. \\
&\quad \left. + \max(T_2(l), p_{i,1}), p_{j,1})\right] \\
&= p_{i,3} + p_{j,3} - p_{i,1} - p_{j,1} + \max\left[T_3(l), T_2(l) + p_{i,2}, p_{i,1} \right. \\
&\quad \left. + p_{i,2}, p_{i,1} + p_{j,2} - p_{i,3} + \max(T_2(l), p_{i,1}), p_{i,1} + p_{j,1} \right. \\
&\quad \left. + p_{j,2} - p_{i,3}\right] \\
&= p_{i,3} + p_{j,3} - p_{i,1} - p_{j,1} + \max\left[T_3(l), T_2(l) + p_{i,2}, p_{i,1} \right. \\
&\quad \left. + p_{i,2}, T_2(l) + p_{i,2} + p_{j,2} - p_{i,3}, p_{i,1} + p_{i,2} + p_{j,2} \right. \\
&\quad \left. - p_{i,3}, p_{i,1} + p_{j,1} + p_{j,2} - p_{i,3}\right].
\end{aligned} \tag{8.19}
$$

In the same way we obtain the following equations from (8.12) to (8.15) in the former Section 8.8:

$$T_3(j) = p_{j,3} - p_{j,1} + \max[T_3(l), T_2(l) + p_{j,2}, p_{j,1} + p_{j,2}]$$

$$T_3(ji) = p_{j,3} + p_{i,3} - p_{j,1} - p_{i,1} + \max[T_3(l), T_2(l) + p_{j,2}, p_{j,1}$$
$$+ p_{j,2}, T_2(l) + p_{j,2} + p_{i,2} - p_{j,3}, p_{j,1} + p_{j,2} + p_{i,2}$$
$$- p_{j,3}, p_{j,1} + p_{i,1} + p_{i,2} - p_{j,3}]. \tag{8.20}$$

Hence by substituting (8.19) and (8.20) into (8.16) in Theorem 2 and subtracting $p_{i,3} + p_{j,3} - p_{i,1} - p_{j,1}$ from both sides, we obtain the following inequality which is equivalent to (8.16) in Theorem 2; $T_3(ij) \leq T_3(ji)$:

$$\max[T_3(l), T_2(l) + p_{i,2}, p_{i,1} + p_{i,2}, T_2(l) + p_{i,2} + p_{j,2} - p_{i,3}, p_{i,1}$$
$$+ p_{i,2} + p_{j,2} - p_{i,3}, p_{i,1} + p_{j,1} + p_{j,2} - p_{i,3}]$$
$$\leq \max[T_3(l), T_2(l) + p_{j,2}, p_{j,1} + p_{j,2}, T_2(l) + p_{j,2} + p_{i,2} - p_{j,3}, p_{j,1}$$
$$+ p_{j,2} + p_{i,2} - p_{j,3}, p_{j,1} + p_{i,1} + p_{i,2} - p_{j,3}]. \tag{8.21}$$

Generally it is difficult to derive an inequality not including $T_3(l), T_2(l)$, that is, not depending on previous jobs, in order to have (8.21). Morever, since condition (N) must be satisfied it looks impossible to find an efficient criterion for the general case, such as a criterion in the two-machine case. In the following section we prove Theorem 1.

8.10. Proof by Using Flow Times

When an optimal scheduling policy is employed and two jobs i, j are processed after any subsequence S with last job l, an inequality $T_3(ij) \leq T_3(ji)$ is equivalent to (8.21) in the former section as shown above. We will thus not repeat the presentation here.

8.11. Case (a)

From condition (a) and (8.6) in Section 8.7, we have

$$T_2(k) = p_{k,2} \leq \min_i p_{i,1} \leq p_{i,1} \tag{8.22}$$

for any jobs k, i. Hence $T_2(ijr) \leq T_2(jir)$ holds since we have $T_2(ij), T_2(ji) \leq p_{r,1}$ for the following job r after three jobs (l, i, j). Hence if $T_3(ij) \leq T_3(ji)$ holds then $T_3(ijr) \leq T_3(jir)$ follows. The same thing holds for any subsequent job and so condition (N) is satisfied.

Next, since we have from (8.22) and condition (a)

$$T_2(l) + p_{i,2} \leq p_{i,1} + p_{i,2},$$
$$T_2(l) + p_{i,2} + p_{j,2} - p_{i,3} \leq p_{i,1} + p_{j,1} + p_{j,2} - p_{i,3}$$

in the parenthesis in the left side of (8.21) in Section 8.9, this side is equal to

$$\max [T_3(l), p_{i,1} + p_{i,2}, p_{i,1} + p_{j,1} + p_{j,2} - p_{i,3}].$$

As the right side of the above (8.21) is simplified similarly, (8.21) in Section 8.9 is equivalent with

$$\begin{aligned}
&\max [T_3(l), p_{i,1} + p_{i,2}, p_{i,1} + p_{j,1} + p_{j,2} - p_{i,3}] \\
&\leqq \max [T_3(l), p_{j,1} + p_{j,2}, p_{j,1} + p_{i,1} + p_{i,2} - p_{j,3}].
\end{aligned} \tag{8.23}$$

Since the term $T_3(l)$ is common to both sides, if an inequality

$$\begin{aligned}
&\max [p_{i,1} + p_{i,2}, p_{i,1} + p_{j,1} + p_{j,2} - p_{i,3}] \\
&\leqq \max [p_{j,1} + p_{j,2}, p_{j,1} + p_{i,1} + p_{i,2} - p_{j,3}]
\end{aligned} \tag{8.24}$$

holds then (8.23) and therefore $T_3(ij) \leq T_3(ji)$ holds.

By subtracting $p_{i,1} + p_{j,1} + p_{i,2} + p_{j,2}$ from both sides of (8.24) we obtain

$$\max [-p_{j,1} - p_{j,2}, -p_{i,2} - p_{i,3}] \leqq \max [-p_{i,1} - p_{i,2}, -p_{j,2} - p_{j,3}],$$

that is,

$$-\min [p_{j,1} + p_{j,2}, p_{i,2} + p_{i,3}] \leqq -\min [p_{i,1} + p_{i,2}, p_{j,2} + p_{j,3}].$$

Hence we obtain finally

$$\min [p_{i,1} + p_{i,2}, p_{j,2} + p_{j,3}] \leqq \min [p_{j,1} + p_{j,2}, p_{i,2} + p_{i,3}]. \tag{8.25}$$

If (8.25) holds without equality job i must precede job j. Since the job order by (8.25) satisfies transitive property the conclusion of the Theorem 1 follows in case (a).

8.12. Case (b)

Let job r be the following job after three jobs (l, i, j) and $C_2(ijr)$, $C_3(ijr)$ be the completion times of a job r on M_2, M_3 respectively in the case when the processing proceeds in the order ij. Then taking account of the condition (N) we consider the following two cases:

1. In case $C_2(ijr) \leq C_2(jir)$ holds, we obtain $C_3(ijr) \leq C_3(jir)$ from

$$T_3(ij) \leqq T_3(ji)[C_3(ij) \leqq C_3(ji)]$$

and (7.1) in Section 7.3 of Chapter 7.

2. In case $C_2(ijr) > C_2(jir)$ holds (Fig. 8.2), then we must have $T_2(ij) > T_2(ji)$.

Therefore, $C_1(ijr) = C_1(jir) \leq C_2(ij)$ must hold. Since inequalities

$$T_3(ij) \geq T_2(ij) + p_{j,3} \geq T_2(ij) + p_{r,2}, T_3(ji) \geq T_2(ji) + p_{i,3}$$
$$\geq T_2(ji) + p_{r,2}$$

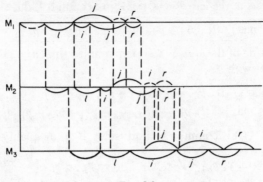

FIG. 8.2

hold from (8.7) in Section 8.7 and condition (b), $T_3(ij) \leq T_3(ji)$ yields $C_3(ijr) \leq C_3(jir)$.

The same result holds for any subsequent job and therfore condition (N) is satisfied.

Next since, in the parenthesis in the left side of (8.21) in Section 8.9 which is equivalent with $T_3(ij) \leq T_3(ji)$, inequalities

$$T_3(l) \geq T_2(l) + p_{l,3} \geq T_2(l) + p_{i,2} \geq T_2(l) + p_{i,2} + p_{j,2} - p_{i,3}.$$

$$p_{i,1} + p_{i,2} \geq p_{i,1} + p_{i,2} + p_{j,2} - p_{i,3}$$

hold from (8.7) in Section 8.7 and condition (b), the left side of (8.21) in Section 8.9 reduces to

$$\max[T_3(l), p_{i,1} + p_{i,2}, p_{i,1} + p_{j,1} + p_{j,2} - p_{i,3}]$$

Since the same thing holds for the right side of (8.21) in Section 8.9, as in the case (a), this (8.21) is equivalent with (8.23) in the former section, that is

$$\max[T_3(l), p_{i,1} + p_{i,2}, p_{i,1} + p_{j,1} + p_{j,2} - p_{i,3}]$$
$$\leq \max[T_3(l), p_{j,1} + p_{j,2}, p_{j,1} + p_{i,1} + p_{i,2} - p_{j,3}].$$

Hence the conclusion follows as in case (a).

Remark: It must be noticed that the terms $T_3(l)$, $T_2(l)$ in (8.21) in Section 8.9 could be excluded under the assumptions (a) or (b) and then we could obtain a criterion of the same type as a criterion in Theorem 3 for the two-machine case.

Exercise

1. Obtain the optimal sequence and its makespan in the 10×3 flow-shop (the order $M_1 M_2 M_3$) min-makespan problem with processing times shown in Table 8.1 and Table 8.2 respectively.

TABLE 8.1

i	1	2	3	4	5	6	7	8	9	10
$p_{i,1}$	6	7	5	8	12	5	9	6	6	7
$p_{i,2}$	1	5	4	5	5	2	4	3	2	4
$p_{i,3}$	2	2	6	4	3	1	2	1	3	6

TABLE 8.2

i	1	2	3	4	5	6	7	8	9	10
$p_{i,1}$	5	6	4	5	4	2	6	5	5	5
$p_{i,2}$	1	4	3	2	2	2	3	4	3	2
$p_{i,3}$	4	7	6	4	5	4	6	6	6	4

8.13. Limited Solution under Other Special Processing Times

In this section we investigate the case where the assumption in (a) or (b) is inverted. That is to say, the following theorem holds when condition (c):

$$\min_i p_{i,2} \geqq \max_i p_{i,1}$$

is taken for the condition (a):

$$\min_i p_{i,1} \geqq \max_i p_{i,2}$$

in Theorem 1.

THEOREM 3. *In the present three-machine problem, if we have* (C): $\min_i p_{i,2}$ $\geqq \max_i p_{i,1}$ *then an optimal sequence can be determined by the next rule:*

1. *Decide an optimal sequence* $\omega^0 = i_1^0 i_2^0 \ldots i_n^0$ *only on two machines* M_2, M_3 *by using a criterion*

$$\min[p_{i,2}, p_{j,3}] \leqq \min[p_{j,2}, p_{i,3}]$$

for two machines M_2, M_3.

2. *Decide at most* $n-1$ *sequences* $\omega_q^0 = i_q^0 i_1^0 \ldots i_n^0$ *obtained by moving the* qth job $i_q^0 (q \neq 1)$, *which satisfies* $p_{i_q^0,1} < p_{i_1^0,1}$, *to the top of the sequence* $\omega^0 \equiv \omega_1^0$. *Let* S *be the set of such* $q \neq 1$ *and* 1. *Then calculate at most* n *makespans* $M(\omega_q^0)$, $q \in S$.

3. *The sequence which gives* $\min_{q \in S} M(\omega_q^0)$ *is the optimal sequence.*

Proof. Let any sequence be $\omega = i_1 i_2 \ldots i_n$, then the following inequality holds from (8.6) in Section 8.7 and condition (c):

$$T_2(i_q) \geqq p_{i_q,2} \geqq \max_{i_q} p_{i_q,1}.$$

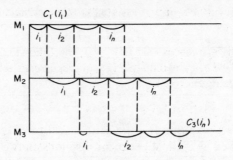

FIG. 8.3

Hence processing of every job $i_1, i_2, \ldots, i_n$ is made without idle time of M_2 (Fig. 8.3).

Therefore, makespan of ω becomes $M(\omega) = p_{i_1,1} + \{C_3(i_n) - C_1(i_1)\}$, where the minimum of the second term on the right side can be determined by optimally sequencing n jobs by using a criterion:

$$\min[\,p_{i,2}, p_{j,3}\,] \leqq \min[\,p_{j,2}, p_{i,3}\,]$$

for two machines M_2, M_3. Let this optimal sequence be $\omega^0 = i_1^0 i_2^0 \ldots i_n^0$ for which $C_3(i_n) - C_1(i_1)$ is minimal, then we can decide the desired optimal sequence by the procedures 2 and 3.

Next the following theorem holds when condition (d):

$$\min_i p_{i,2} \geq \max_i p_{i,3}$$

is taken for the condition (b):

$$\min_i p_{i,3} \geq \max_i p_{i,2}$$

in Theorem 1.

THEOREM 4. *In the present three-machine problem, if we have* (d):

$$\min_i p_{i,2} \geq \max_i p_{i,3}$$

then an optimal sequence can be determined by the following rule:

1. *Decide an optimal sequence* $\omega^0 = i_1^0\, i_2^0 \ldots o_m^0$ *on two machines* M_1, M_2 *by using a criterion*

$$\min[\,p_{i,1}, p_{j,2}\,] \leqq \min[\,p_{j,1}, p_{i,2}\,]$$

for two machines M_1, M_2.

2. *Decide at most* $n - 1$ *sequences* $\omega_q^0 = i_1^0\, i_2^0 \ldots i_n^0\, i_q^0$ *obtained by moving the* q-*th job* i_q^0 $(q \neq n)$, *which satisfies* $p_{i_q^0,3} < p_{i_n^0,3}$, *to the tail of the sequence* $\omega^0 \equiv \omega_n^0$. *Let S be the set of such* $q \neq n$ *and* n. *Then calculate at most* n *makespans* $M(\omega_q^0)$, $q \in S$.

3. *The sequence which gives* $\min\limits_{q \in S} M(\omega_q^0)$ *is the optimal sequence.*

Proof. For any sequences $\omega = i_1 i_2 \ldots i_n$ the following relation holds for every q ($q = 1, 2, \ldots, n$) by inductively using recurrence relations (8.6) (8.7) in Section 8.7 and condition (d):

$$T_3(i_q) = T_2(i_q) + p_{i_q, 3}, \quad (q = 1, 2, \ldots, n)$$

(cf. Fig. 8.4). Hence we have $M(\omega) = C_3(i_n) = C_2(i_n) + p_{i_n, 3}$, for which the term $C_2(i_n)$ is minimized by optimally sequencing n jobs on two machines M_1, M_2 by a criterion (7.18) in Theorem 3 of Chapter 7. Let this sequence be $\omega^0 = i_1^0 i_2^0 \ldots i_n^0$. Since the term $C_2(i_n)$ is minimal for the sequence ω^0 we can determine the optimal sequence by the procedures 2 and 3.

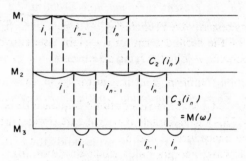

FIG. 8.4

Remark. By the rules in Theorems 3 and 4, we can determine an optimal sequence in a polynomial-time $O(n^2)$.

Exercises

1. Derive the above relation

$$T_3(i_q) = T_2(i_q) + p_{i_q, 3} \quad (q = 1, 2, \ldots, n)$$

by induction.

2. Solve the problem which is obtained by exchanging $p_{i, 1}$ and $p_{i, 2}$ for every i in Table 8.1 and the problem which is obtained by exchanging $p_{i, 2}$ and $p_{i, 3}$ for every i in Table 8.2, both in exercise 1 in Section 8.12.

8.14. Sufficient Conditions for Two Adjacent Jobs to be in a Definite Order in the Optimal Sequence

As described in Section 8.9, in order to determine the order of two adjacent jobs i, j in an optimal sequence independently of the former job l it is sufficient to derive the condition (inequalities) which does not include $T_2(l)$, $T_3(l)$ and assures the existence of the following inequality (8.26) ((8.21) in Section 8.9) as an equivalence to $T_3(ij) \leqq T_3(ji)$ and also we must assure the existence of the condition (N) (Theorem 8.2):

$$\max[T_3(l), T_2(l) + p_{i,2}, p_{i,1} + p_{i,2}, T_2(l) + p_{i,2} + p_{j,2} - p_{i,3},$$

$$p_{i,1} + p_{i,2} + p_{j,2} - p_{i,3}, p_{i,1} + p_{j,1} + p_{j,2} - p_{i,3}]$$

$$\leqq \max[T_3(l), T_2(l) + p_{j,2}, p_{j,1} + p_{j,2}, T_2(l) + p_{j,2} + p_{i,2} - p_{j,3},$$

$$p_{j,1} + p_{j,2} + p_{i,2} - p_{j,3}, p_{j,1} + p_{i,1} + p_{i,2} - p_{j,3}]. \tag{8.26}$$

One way of doing this was to assume the condition (a) or (b), as already shown in Section 8.3.

In this section we give another method which is based on the following fundamental theorem concerning the existence of the condition (N).

THEOREM 5. *In the present three-machine problem, let two jobs i, j be processed after any definite subsequence S when an optimal scheduling policy is employed. If two inequalities:*

$$T_k(ij) \leqq T_k(ji) \quad (k = 2, 3) \tag{8.27}$$

hold, then condition (N) holds, that is, job i must precede job j after S in an optimal sequence, where either ordering is optimal when equality holds in (8.27).

Proof. The conclusion follows from the fact that $T_3(i_q)$ is a nondecreasing function of $T_2(i_{q-1})$, $T_3(i_{q-1})$ and the same holds for $T_2(i_q)$ to $T_2(i_{q-1})$ for every $q (q = 2, 3, \ldots, n)$ in any sequence $i_1 i_2 \ldots i_n$.

8.15. Sufficient Inequalities not including $T_2(l)$ and $T_3(l)$

Sufficient inequalities not including $T_2(l)$ and $T_3(l)$ that are used as criteria for deciding the definite order of two adjacent jobs i, j for two machines will be itemized and named as follows:

$$\min(p_{i,1}, p_{j,2}) \leqq \min(p_{j,1}, p_{i,2}), \tag{a}$$

$$\min(p_{i,2}, p_{j,3}) \leqq \min(p_{j,2}, p_{i,3}), \tag{b}$$

$$\min(p_{i,1}, p_{j,3}) \leqq \min(p_{j,1}, p_{i,3}), \tag{c}$$

$$\min(p_{i,1} + p_{i,2}, p_{i,1} + p_{j,3}, p_{j,2} + p_{j,3}) \leqq \min(p_{j,1} + p_{j,2}, p_{j,1} + p_{i,3}, p_{i,2} + p_{i,3}), \tag{d}$$

$$\min(p_{i,1} + p_{i,2}, p_{j,2} + p_{j,3}) \leqq \min(p_{j,1} + p_{j,2}, p_{i,2} + p_{i,3}), \tag{e}$$

where (d) alone does not satisfy a transitive property.

Any sequence determined by using (a), which is optimal for two machines M_1, M_2 will be called an *a*-sequence. The *e*-sequence is interpreted as any optimal sequence on two machines $M_1 + M_2$, $M_2 + M_3$, on each of them every job i has respective processing times $p_{i,1} + p_{i,2}$, $p_{i,2} + p_{i,3}$. Moreover, any sequence which is optimal by (b) as well as (a) will be called an *ab*-sequence.

In the following we put the left-hand side of each inequality as shown below:

$A = \min(p_{i,1}, p_{j,2})$, $B = \min(p_{i,2}, p_{j,3})$, $C = \min(p_{i,1}, p_{j,3})$,

$D = \min(p_{i,1} + p_{i,2}, p_{j,1} + p_{j,3}, p_{j,2} + p_{j,3})$, $E = \min(p_{i,1} + p_{i,2}, p_{j,2} + p_{j,3})$.

The following theorem holds from Theorem 5:

THEOREM 6. *If (a) holds, then* $T_2(ij) \leq T_2(ji)$ *follows, and if (b) and (d) hold, then* $T_3(ij) \leq T_3(ji)$ *follows. Hence, if (a), (b) and (d) hold job i must precede job j in an optimal sequence which will be denoted by a notation:* $i < j$. *When all equalities hold either ordering is optimal.*

Proof. In the same way as in Section 7.14 of Chapter 7, when job order *ij* or *ji* is processed after any definite subsequence *S* with last job *l* we obtain respectively

$$T_2(ij) = p_{i,2} + p_{j,2} - p_{i,1} - p_{j,1} + \max[T_2(l), p_{i,1}, p_{i,1} + p_{j,1} - p_{i,2}],$$

$$T_2(ji) = p_{j,2} + p_{i,2} - p_{j,1} - p_{i,1} + \max[T_2(l), p_{j,1}, p_{j,1} + p_{i,1} - p_{j,2}]. \quad (8.28)$$

By substituting (8.28) into $T_2(ij) \leq T_2(ji)$ and subtracting $p_{i,2} + p_{j,2} - p_{i,1} - p_{j,1}$ from both sides it becomes

$$\max[T_2(l), p_{i,1}, p_{i,1} + p_{j,1} - p_{i,2}] \leq \max[T_2(l), p_{j,1}, p_{j,1} + p_{i,1} - p_{j,2}]. \quad (8.29)$$

Since a term $T_2(l)$ is common for both sides, if we have

$$\max[p_{i,1}, p_{i,1} + p_{j,1} - p_{i,2}] \leq \max[p_{j,1} \, p_{j,1} + p_{i,1} - p_{j,2}] \quad (8.30)$$

then (8.29) follows and $T_2(ij) \leq T_2(ji)$ holds.

By subtracting $p_{i,1} + p_{j,1}$ from every term in the parenthesis of each side of (8.30), we obtain an inequality which is equivalent with (8.30):

$$\max[-p_{j,1}, -p_{i,2}] \leq \max[-p_{i,1}, -p_{j,2}],$$

that is,

$$\min[p_{i,1}, p_{j,2}] \leq \min[p_{j,1}, p_{i,2}]. \quad (a)$$

Hence if (a) holds, then $T_2(ij) \leq T_2(ji)$ follows.

Next we derive sufficient inequalities not including $T_2(l)$ and $T_3(l)$ for $T_3(ij) \leq T_3(ji)$ to hold.

By arranging the terms in the parentheses of (8.26) in Section 8.14 which is equivalent with $T_3(ij) \leq T_3(ji)$, we obtain

$$\max[T_3(l), T_2(l) + \max(p_{i,2} \, p_{i,2} + p_{j,2} - p_{i,3}),$$

$$\max(p_{i,1} + p_{i,2}, p_{i,1} + p_{i,2} + p_{j,2} - p_{i,3}, p_{i,1} + p_{j,1} + p_{j,2} - p_{i,3})],$$

$$\leq \max[T_3(l), T_2(l) + \max(p_{j,2}, p_{j,2} + p_{i,2} - p_{j,3}),$$

$$\max(p_{j,1} + p_{j,2}, p_{j,1} + p_{j,2} + p_{i,2} - p_{j,3}, p_{j,1} + p_{i,1} + p_{i,2} - p_{j,3})] \quad (8.31)$$

Hence if the following two inequalities not including $T_2(l)$ and $T_3(l)$ hold:

$$\max[p_{i,2}, p_{i,2} + p_{j,2} - p_{i,3}] \leqq \max[p_{j,2}, p_{j,2} + p_{i,2} - p_{j,3}], \quad (8.32)$$

$$\max[p_{i,1} + p_{i,2}, p_{i,1} + p_{i,2} + p_{j,2} - p_{i,3}, p_{i,1} + p_{j,1} + p_{j,2} - p_{i,3}]$$
$$\leqq \max[p_{j,1} + p_{j,2}, p_{j,1} + p_{j,2} + p_{i,2} - p_{j,3}, p_{j,1} + p_{i,1} + p_{i,2} - p_{j,3}]. \quad (8.33)$$

then (8.31), that is, $T_3(ij) \leqq T_3(ji)$, follows.

In a similar way to the above, we can show that inequalities (8.32), (8.33) are equivalent with (b), (d) respectively. Hence, if two inequalities (b) and (d) hold, then $T_3(ij) \leqq T_3(ji)$ follows. Hence, from Theorem 5, if three inequalities (a), (b) and (d) hold, then $i < j$ follows.

Within three inequalities (a), (b) and (d), only (d) does not satisfy the transitive property. That is, the orders of any two jobs i, j determined by using (d) does not satisfy this property, because, for example, for three jobs 1, 2, 3 with respective processing times as shown in Table 8.3, the orders $1 < 2, 2 < 3$, and $3 < 1$ hold by (d).

TABLE 8.3

i	$p_{i,1}$	$p_{i,2}$	$p_{i,3}$
1	3	7	1
2	7	6	4
3	5	3	4

Therefore, we look for an inequality satisfying the transitive property, instead of (d), in the following section.

Exercise

1. Prove that inequalities (8.32), (8.33) are equivalent with (b), (d) respectively.

8.16. Sufficient Inequalities that Satisfy the Transitive Property

We list important results in the following. Some related results will be described in exercises.

THEOREM 7. *If three inequalities (a), (b) and (c) hold, then inequality (d) follows. Conversely, if (a), (b) and (d) hold, then (c) follows. Hence three inequalities (a), (b) and (c), each of them has transitive property, are equivalent with three inequalities (a), (b) and (d) that leads to an optimal order $i < j$. Therefore, abc-sequences are optimal.*

Proof. We divide and check the cases according to the values of the left sides of (a), (b) and (c), that is, A, B and C respectively.

1. In case $A = p_{i,1}$, $B = p_{i,2}$, since the term $p_{i,1} + p_{i,2}$ becomes the smallest term in (d), obviously (d) holds. In the same way, the following hold.

2. In case $A = p_{i,1}$, $B = p_{j,3}$, the term $p_{i,1} + p_{j,3}$ is the smallest.

3. In case $A = p_{j,2}$, $B = p_{j,3}$, the term $p_{j,2} + p_{j,3}$ is the smallest.

4. In case $A = p_{j,2}$, $B = p_{i,2}$, if $C = p_{i,1}$ the term $p_{i,1} + p_{i,2}$ is the smallest. If $C = p_{j,3}$ the term $p_{j,2} + p_{j,3}$ is the smallest. Hence (d) holds.

Conversely we divide and check the cases according to the values of D, A and B respectively as shown below:

1. In case $D = p_{i,1} + p_{i,2}$, if $A = p_{i,1}$, $B = p_{i,2}$, then $p_{i,1} \leqq p_{j,1}$ and $p_{i,1} \leqq p_{i,2} \leqq p_{i,3}$ hold and so (c) holds. If $A = p_{j,2}$, $B = p_{i,2}$, then $p_{i,2} = p_{j,2}$ holds. From $D = p_{i,1} + p_{i,2} \leqq \min (p_{i,2} + p_{i,3}, p_{j,1} + p_{j,2})$ we obtain $p_{i,1} \leqq p_{i,3}$ and $p_{i,1} \leqq p_{j,1}$. Hence (c) holds. Note that $B \neq p_{j,3}$.

2. In case $D = p_{i,1} + p_{j,3}$, we have $p_{j,3} \leqq p_{i,2}$ and $p_{i,1} \leqq p_{j,2}$ from $p_{i,1} + p_{j,3} \leqq p_{i,1} + p_{i,2}$ and $p_{i,1} + p_{j,3} \leqq p_{j,2} + p_{j,3}$ respectively. From $p_{j,3} \leqq p_{i,2}$ it follows $B = p_{j,3}$ and from $p_{i,1} \leqq p_{j,2}$ it follows $A = p_{i,1}$, which leads $p_{j,3} \leqq p_{i,3}$ and $p_{i,1} \leqq p_{j,1}$ respectively. Hence (c) holds.

3. In case $D = P_{j,2} + P_{j,3}$, we have $p_{j,2} \leqq p_{i,1}$ and $p_{j,3} \leqq p_{j,1}$ from $p_{j,2} + p_{j,3} \leqq p_{i,1} + p_{j,3}$ and $p_{j,2} + p_{j,3} \leqq p_{j,1} + p_{j,2}$ respectively. From $p_{j,2} \leqq p_{i,1}$ it follows $A = p_{j,2}$. If $B = p_{i,2}$, it becomes $p_{i,2} = p_{j,2}$ from A, B and then $p_{j,3} \leqq p_{i,3}$ holds from D. Also from $p_{j,3} \leqq p_{j,1}$ (c) holds. If $B = p_{j,3}$, $p_{j,3} \leqq p_{i,3}$ holds. Also from $p_{j,3} \leqq p_{j,1}$ (c) holds. Hence (c) holds. Therefore, (a), (b) and (c) are equivalent with (a), (b) and (d) and the rest of the conclusion follows directly from Theorem 6.

As described in Section 7.15 of Chapter 7, generally we use a general working rule (GWR) for any criterion for two machines.

Also we can apply effectively the above optimal orders not only to the implicit enumeration algorithms such as BAB algorithm in order to reduce the computation-time, but also to the constructions of the approximate algorithms. Cf. the Remark after Example 2 (BAB alg.) in Section 9.8 of Chapter 9 and Section 10.13 (appr. alg.) of Chapter 10.

However, if we use the restricted working rule (RWR) (Section 7.17 of Chapter 7) for both (a) and (b), then the following theorem shows that an additional inequality (c) can be omitted for the optimal order $i < j$ to hold when the order $i < j$ holds by (a), (b) respectively under the restricted working rule.

THEOREM 8. *If the order $i < j$ holds for each of two inequalities (a), (b) under the restricted working rule, then two inequalities (d), (c) follow, that is, the optimal order $i < j$ holds, which shows that the ab-sequence is optimal when the restricted working rule is used for (a) and (b).*

Proof. We divide and check the same cases as in the proof of the first part of

Theorem 7. In cases 1, 2 and 3, (d) follows, without (c), in the same way as in Theorem 7. Moreover, (c) follows as shown below:

1. In case $A = p_{i,1}$, $B = p_{i,2}$, we have $p_{i,1}, \leqq p_{j,1}$, $p_{i,1} \leqq p_{i,2} \leqq p_{i,3}$ and so (c) holds, where the set of orders decided by GWR contains an order by RWR. In the same way we can show that (c) holds in cases 2 and 3. Here the assumption can be satisfied in cases 1, 2 and 3.

Next we will show below that case 4 does not occur under the assumption of this theorem.

In case 4: $A = p_{j,2} < p_{i,1}$, $B = p_{i,2} < p_{j,3}$, where the equality cases are included in the cases $A = p_{i,1} \leqq p_{j,2}$, $B = p_{j,3} \leqq p_{i,2}$ respectively. From (a) and (b), $p_{j,2} \leqq p_{i,2}$ and $p_{i,2} \leqq p_{j,2}$ hold. Hence $p_{i,2} = p_{j,2}$ holds in this case and this value is the smallest among six processing times. Then if job number i is smaller than job number j, $p_{i,2}$ is selected by RWR for M_1, M_2 because $p_{i,2} = p_{j,2} < p_{i,1}$ holds and therefore job i must follow job j by RWR for M_1, M_2, which contradicts the assumption. Otherwise, $p_{j,2}$ is selected by RWR for M_2, M_3 because $p_{j,2} = p_{i,2} < p_{j,3}$ holds and so job j must precede job i by RWR for M_2, M_3, which contradicts the assumption. Hence case 4 does not occur under the assumption. This completes the proof.

The result in the above theorem states that, when RWR is used, a proposition, proposed by Johnson, that a sequence which is optimal for the first two machines M_1, M_2 and also optimal for the last two machines M_2, M_3 becomes optimal for three machines M_1, M_2 and M_3, is correct. Later in Theorem 10 we will show that the set of ab-sequence (obviously by GWR) contains an optimal sequence for three machines whenever this set is not empty.

Next introduce the following condition R_1:

$$p_{j,2} < p_{i,1}, \ p_{i,2} < p_{j,3}; \tag{R_1}$$

and let $\bar{R}_1$ be its negation, then the following theorem holds:

THEOREM 9. CASE I. *If (a) and (b) hold under condition $\bar{R}_1$, then (d) follows, that is, the optimal order $i < j$ follows. Hence any ab-sequence under $\bar{R}_1$ is optimal for three machines.*

CASE II. *If (a), (b) and (c) hold under condition R_1, then the optimal order $i < j$ follows. Hence, any abc-sequence under R_1 is optimal for three machines.*

Proof. Since case II obviously holds from Theorem 7, it is sufficient to prove the case I as below: Condition $\bar{R}_1$ is $p_{j,2} \geqq p_{i,1}$ or $p_{i,2} \geqq p_{j,3}$. In case $p_{j,2} \geqq p_{i,1}$, we have $A = p_{i,1}$. If $B = p_{i,2}$, then the term $p_{i,1} + p_{i,2}$ is the smallest term in (d). Hence (d) holds. Similarly if $B = p_{j,3}$, then the term $p_{i,1} + p_{j,3}$ is the smallest. Hence (d) holds. Also in case $p_{i,2} \geqq p_{j,3}$, we have $B = p_{j,3}$. If $A = p_{i,1}$, then the term $p_{i,1} + p_{j,3}$ is the smallest. If $A = p_{j,2}$, then the term $p_{j,2} + p_{j,3}$ is the smallest. Hence (d) holds. Therefore $i < j$ holds.

Theorem 9 is weaker than Theorem 7 and resulted optimal orders can be supplied to BAB algorithm as elimination criteria.

Remarks. As seen from the proof of Theorem 8, excluding case 4 is equivalent with $\bar{R}_1$. Hence Theorem 8 is included in case I of Theorem 9. In case II in the above Theorem 9, obviously the condition that R_1, (a) and (b) hold is equivalent with the following condition R_2 (cf. Fig. 8.5):

$$p_{i,2} = p_{j,2} < \min(p_{i,1}, p_{j,3}), \; p_{i,2} = p_{j,2} \leqq \min(p_{j,1}, p_{i,3}); \qquad (R_2)$$

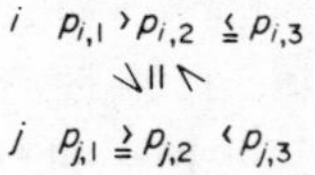

$$i \quad p_{i,1} > p_{i,2} \leqq p_{i,3}$$
$$\searrow \, \| \, \nwarrow$$
$$j \quad p_{j,1} \geqq p_{j,2} < p_{j,3}$$

FIG. 8.5. R_2.

and both (a) and (b) hold with equality, which means that either ordering of two jobs i, j is optimal by (a) and (b) in case II. By applying this fact, the following theorem holds:

THEOREM 10. *The set of ab-sequence contains an optimal sequence for three machines whenever this set is not empty.*

Proof. Any subsequence consisting of consecutive pairs of two jobs, for each case II in Theorem 9 holds, can be arranged by a criterion (c) because either ordering is optimal by (a) and (b) as shown in the above remarks. Then we obtain an optimal sequence for three machines.

Concerning an inequality (e), it must be noticed that any sequence determined by a criterion (e) becomes a good suboptimal sequence for three machines, which has been reported by Giglio and Wagner. In case II of Theorem 9, the condition that (a), (b) and (c) hold is equivalent with the condition that (a), (b) and (e) hold (Exercise 1). Some results concerning (e) are included in the exercises.

Exercises

1. Prove that, in case II of Theorem 9, conditions (a), (b) and (c) is equivalent with conditions: (a), (b) and (e). That is, if condition R_2 holds, (e) is equivalent with (c).

2. Prove that if (a), (b) and (e) hold then (c) holds. Also give an example which shows that (e) does not hold even if (a), (b) and (c) hold.

3. Generally let us introduce the following conditions R_3, R_4:

$$\left.\begin{array}{l} p_{i,1} < p_{j,2} < p_{i,2}, p_{i,1} < p_{i,3}, p_{i,1} \leqq p_{j,1} < p_{i,2}, \\ p_{j,1} < p_{j,3} \leqq \min(p_{j,2}, p_{i,3}), p_{j,1} + p_{j,2} < p_{i,1} + p_{i,2}, \end{array}\right\} \qquad (R_3)$$

$$\left.\begin{array}{l} p_{j,3} < p_{i,2} < p_{j,2}, p_{j,3} < p_{i,1} \leqq \min(p_{j,1}, p_{i,2}, p_{j,2}) \\ p_{j,3} \leqq p_{i,3} < p_{i,1}, p_{i,2} + p_{i,3} < p_{j,2} + p_{j,3} \end{array}\right\} \qquad (R_4)$$

then prove that if R_3 or R_4 holds under (a), (b) and (c) then (e) does not hold and also prove that if $\bar{R}_3$ and $\bar{R}_4$ hold under (a), (b) and (c) then (e) holds.

4. Prove that if (a), (b) and (e) hold then (c) and (d) follow, that is, *abe*-sequence is optimal for three machines.

5. Prove that if condition R_2 holds then each side of (d) and (e) is equal.

6. Let us introduce the following conditions R_5, R_6:

$$p_{i,3} = p_{j,3} \leqq \min(p_{i,2}, p_{j,2}) \quad (R_5), \; p_{i,3} = p_{j,3} < p_{i,1}, \; p_{i,3} = p_{j,3} \leqq p_{j,1} \quad (R_6),$$

then prove that if R_5 or R_6 holds then (a) is equivalent with (d). Also show that an optimal order $i < j$ holds, provided conditions R_5 and (a) hold.

7. Let us introduce the following conditions R_7, R_8:

$$p_{i,1} = p_{j,1} \leqq \min(p_{i,2}, p_{j,2}) \quad (R_7), \; p_{i,1} = p_{j,1} < p_{j,3}, p_{i,1} = p_{j,1} \leqq p_{i,3} \quad (R_8),$$

then prove that if R_7 or R_8 holds then (b) is equivalent with (d). Also prove that an optimal order $i < j$ holds, provided conditions R_7 and (b) hold.

8. Let us introduce the following condition:

$$[\min(p_{i,1}, p_{j,2}) - \min(p_{j,1}, p_{i,2})][\min(p_{i,2}, p_{j,3}) - \min(p_{j,2}, p_{i,3})] \geqq 0, \tag{S}$$

then prove that if (S) holds for any two jobs i, j we have an *ab*-sequence.

9. Prove that if condition (S) in exercise 8 and an inequality (d) hold, then (a) and (b) hold, and (d) is equivalent with (c).

8.17. Two-machine Min-Makespan Problem where Time Lags Exist

In real production where n jobs are processed by two machines M_1, M_2 in this machine order, there may exist the case where each job consists of a lot and then processing by the second machine M_2 begins after the processing of a part of the job (lot) is completed on the first machine M_1, or two machines M_1, M_2 are bottleneck machines, then there exist some intermediate nonbottleneck machines between them. In these situations they are specified by the start lags and stop lags of the processings on M_1 and M_2. In this section we treat the min-makespan problem in those cases, by slightly extending the problem as shown below:

Let n jobs be processed by two machines M_1, M_2 in this machine order and no passing be allowed. Also let every job i consist of two parts i_1 and i_2 and i_1 be processed by M_1 and M_2, while job i_2 is processed only by M_1 after i_1. Let $p_{i,1}, p_{i,2}$ be the processing times of i_1 on M_1, M_2 respectively and F_i be the processing time of i_2 on M_1.

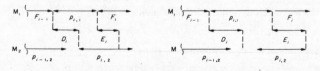

FIG. 8.6

Next let us assume that, for every job i_1, the processing of i_1 on M_2 cannot start sooner than a time D_i after the starting of the processing of i_1 on M_1 and also the completion of the processing of i_1 on M_2 cannot occur sooner than a time E_i after its completion on M_1 (cf. Fig. 8.6).

In this model, every job i_1 and job i_2 have a main part and a simple part respectively of related job i, and start lag D_i and stop lag E_i means the processing by intermediate machines, transportation time between machines or overlap processing on M_1, M_2 in lot production.

For the resolution of the min-makespan problem under the above assumptions, we can use idle time on M_2 or flow time $T_2(i)$.

In the following we give the solution by using flow time in the same way as in Section 7.14 of Chapter 7. When an optimal scheduling policy is employed, let two jobs i, j be processed after a definite subsequence S with last job l.

If job i is processed first after S, then since the start of job i on M_2 must be later than the time $\max[T_2(l), D_i]$ and its completion on M_2 must be later than the time $P_{i,1} + E_i$, we have (cf. Fig. 8.7)

$$
\begin{aligned}
T_2(i) &= \max[\max\{\max(T_2(l), D_i) + p_{i,2}, p_{i,1} + E_i\} - (p_{i,1} + F_i), 0] \\
&= p_{i,1} - F_i + \max[\max(T_2(l), D_i) + p_{i,2}, p_{i,1} + E_i, p_{i,1} + F_i] \quad (8.34) \\
&= p_{i,2} - p_{i,1} - F_i + \max[T_2(l), D_i, p_{i,1} - p_{i,2} + E_i, p_{i,1} - p_{i,2} + F_i].
\end{aligned}
$$

Then if job j is processed after job i, we obtain as above for $T_2(ij) \equiv T_2(j)$

$$
\begin{aligned}
T_2(ij) = p_{j,2} - p_{j,1} - F_j + \max[T_2(i), D_j, p_{j,1} - p_{j,2} \\
+ E_j, p_{j,1} - p_{j,2} + F_j].
\end{aligned} \quad (8.35)
$$

By substituting (8.34) into (8.35) and rearranging, we have

$$
\begin{aligned}
T_2(ij) = {} & p_{i,2} + p_{j,2} - p_{i,1} - p_{j,1} - F_i - F_j \\
& + \max[T_2(l), D_i, p_{i,1} - p_{i,2} + E_i, p_{i,1} - p_{i,2} + F_i, \\
& D_j + p_{i,1} - p_{i,2} + F_i, p_{i,1} + p_{j,1} - p_{i,2} - p_{j,2} + F_i + E_j, \\
& p_{i,1} + p_{j,1} - p_{i,2} - p_{j,2} + F_i + F_j].
\end{aligned}
$$

The above equation can be expressed as (8.36) by putting $e_i = p_{i,1} - p_{i,2}$, $T_i = \max(D_i, e_i + E_i) > 0$,

$$
\begin{aligned}
T_2(ij) = {} & p_{i,2} + p_{j,2} - p_{i,1} - p_{j,1} - F_i - F_j \\
& + \max[T_2(l), T_i, e_i + F_i, T_j + e_i + F_i, \quad (8.36) \\
& e_i + e_j + F_i + F_j].
\end{aligned}
$$

On the other hand, if two jobs i, j are processed after S in the order ji, then the equation for $T_2(ji) \equiv T_2(i)$ becomes an equation obtained by interchanging i and j in (8.36).

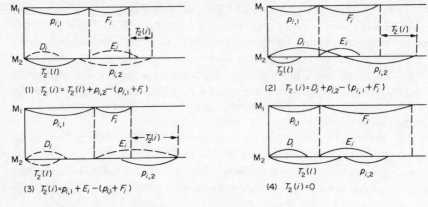

FIG. 8.7

Since the following recurrence relation holds for any sequence $i_1 i_2 \ldots i_n$:

$$T_2(i_q) = p_{iq,2} - p_{iq,1} - F_{iq} + \max[T_2(i_{q-1}), D_{iq}, p_{iq,1} - p_{iq,2}$$
$$+ E_{iq}, p_{iq,1} - p_{iq,2} + F_{iq}],$$
$$(q = 1, 2, \ldots, n)$$

where $T_2(i_0) = 0$, $T_2(i_q)$ is a nondecreasing function of $T_2(i_{q-1})$ $(q = 2, 3, \ldots, n)$. Hence, if $T_2(ij) \leq T_2(ji)$ holds, then job i must precede job j in an optimal sequence, where if equality holds either ordering is optimal.

Therefore, after some reasoning (Exercise 1), we obtain the following theorem:

THEOREM 11. *In the present problem, an optimal sequence can be determined by the following rule: if an inequality*

$$\min[T_i, T_j - (e_j + F_j)] \leq \min[T_j, T_i - (e_i + F_i)] \tag{8.37}$$

where $e_i = p_{i,1} - p_{i,2}$, $T_i = max(D_i, e_i + E_i)$ *hold, then job i precedes job j. If equality holds in* (8.37) *either ordering is optimal.*

The working rule for deciding the optimal sequence by using a criterion (8.37) is obtained by taking $T_i, T_i - (e_i + F_i)$ for $p_{i,1}, p_{i,2}$ respectively as in Sections 7.15–7.17 of Chapter 7.

Exercises

1. Complete the proof of Theorem 11.

2. Derive the following Theorem 12 from Theorem 11.

THEOREM 12. *In the present problem, an optimal sequence can be determined by the following rule: decompose the set of n jobs into two subsets J_1, J_2:*

$$J_1 = \{i | e_i + F_i \leq 0\}, \ J_1 = \{i | e_i + F_i > 0\}.$$

1. Arrange any job in J_2 after all jobs in J_1.
2. Sequence jobs in J_1 according to increasing order of T_i.
3. Sequence jobs in J_2 according to decreasing order of $T_i - (e_1 + F_i)$, where if a tie occurs in items 2 and 3 then either ordering is optimal.

   3. Prove the above Theorem 12 in the case where $F_i = 0$ and $D_i = E_i$ (start lag is equal to stop lag) for all i.
   4. Show that criterion (8.37) becomes criterion (7.18) in Section 7.11 of Chapter 7 in the case where there exist no time lags, that is, $D_i = p_{i,1}, E_i = p_{i,2}, F_i = 0$ for all i.

8.18. On the Generalizations to m Machine Permutation Scheduling

   In this section, some generalized results for the m machine permutation min-makespan problem will be itemized without proof.
   These results will be noted as in Result 1 as follows; each of them shows related theorem for the three-machines case in parentheses. First, by the definition of flow time and the similar condition (N) as that for $m = 3$ in Section 8.8, the following result holds:

Result 1 (Generalization of Theorem 2 in Section 8.8). In the present problem, when two jobs i, j are processed after any definite subsequence S with last job l if we have

$$T_m(ij) \leqq T_m(ji) \tag{8.38}$$

and condition (N) is satisfied, then job i must directly precede job j after S in an optimal sequence. If equality holds in (8.38), then either ordering is optimal.
   Then by successively substituting the recurrence relation ((7.2) in Section 7.6 of Chapter 7):

$$T_k(i_q) = p_{i_{q,k}} + \max[T_k(i_{q-1}) - p_{i_{q,1}}, T_{k-1}(i_q)] \tag{8.39}$$
$$(q = 1, 2, \ldots, n; k = 2, 3, \ldots, m)$$

we have

$$T_m(ij) = p_{i,m} + p_{j,m} - p_{i,1} - p_{j,1} + T'_m(ij),$$

where

$$T'_m(ij) = \max[V_m, \max_{m-1 \geqq k \geqq 1} W_k],$$

in which we define

$$V_m = \max\left(T_m(l), T_{m-1}(l) + p_{i,m-1}, \ldots, T_2(l) + \sum_{q=2}^{m-1} p_{i,q}, \sum_{q=1}^{m-1} p_{i,q}\right),$$

$$W_k = p_{i,k} + \sum_{q=k}^{m-1} p_{j,q} - p_{i,m} + \max\left(T_k(l), T_{k-1}(l) + p_{i,k-1}, \ldots, T_2(l)\right.$$
$$\left. + \sum_{q=2}^{k-1} p_{i,q}, \sum_{q=1}^{k-1} p_{i,q}\right)$$

where $T_u(l) = 0 \ (u \leq 1), p_{i,u} = 0 \ (u \leq 0)$.

Also $T'_m(ji)$ for the order ji has the same form as $T'_m(ij)$ except that i and j are interchanged in $T'_m(ij)$. By using an inequality $T'_m(ij) \leq T'_m(ji)$ which is equivalent with an inequality (8.38) and from Result 1 we can obtain the following result under restraints on processing times:

Result 2 (Generalization of Theorem 1) In the present problem, if the next $m - 2$ inequalities hold for a certain constant $h (h = 1, 2, \ldots, m - 1)$:

$$\min_i p_{i,k} \geq \max_i p_{i,k+1} \, (k = 1, 2, \ldots, h - 1),$$

$$\min_i p_{i,k+1} \geq \max_i p_{i,k} \, (k = h + 1, h + 2, \ldots, m - 1),$$

then an optimal sequence can be determined by the following rule: when an inequality

$$\min \left[\sum_{q=1}^{m-1} p_{i,q}, \sum_{q=2}^{m} p_{j,q} \right] \leqq \min \left[\sum_{q=1}^{m-1} p_{j,q}, \sum_{q=2}^{m} p_{i,q} \right]$$

holds without equality, then job i precedes job j. When equality holds in this inequality, then either ordering is optimal.

Remark. An optimal sequence derived from the above criterion is determined in a polynomial-time $0 (n \log n)$.

Next, under inverted restraints on processing times, we obtain the following result:

Result 3 (Generalization of Theorems 3 and 4). In the present problem, if the next $m - 2$ inequalities hold for a certain constant $h (h = 1, 2, \ldots, m - 1)$:

$$\min_i p_{i,k+1} \geqq \max_i p_{i,k} \, (k = 1, 2, \ldots, h - 1),$$

$$\min_i p_{i,k} \geqq \max_i p_{i,k+1} \, (k = h + 1, h + 2, \ldots, m - 1),$$

then an optimal sequence can be determined by the following rule:

1. By a criterion

$$\min [p_{i,h}, p_{j,h+1}] \leq \min [p_{j,h}, p_{i,h+1}]$$

for two machines M_h, M_{h+1}, determine an optimal sequence $\omega^0 = i_1^0 i_2^0 \ldots i_n^0$ for two machines M_h, M_{h+1} alone.

2. Let $\omega_{q,\gamma}^0 = i_q^0 i_1^0 \ldots i_n^0 i_\gamma^0 (q \neq \gamma; q, \gamma = 1, 2, \ldots, n; q \neq 1 \text{ or } \gamma \neq n)$ be the sequences of n jobs obtained from the sequence $\omega^0 \equiv \omega_{1,n}^0$ by shifting qth job

i_q^0 to the top and γth job i_γ^0 to the end, only in case

$$\sum_{l=1}^{h-1} p_{i,l} + \sum_{l=h+2}^{m} p_{j,l},$$

where $i = i_q^0$ and $j = i_\gamma^0$, is smaller than that for $i = i_1^0, j = i_n^0$, then calculate makespan $\mathrm{M}(\omega_{q,\gamma}^0)$ for each of at most $n(n-1)$ sequences including $\omega^0 = \omega_{1,n}^0$ and such $\omega_{q,\gamma}^0$.

3. The sequence giving the $\min_{q,\gamma} \mathrm{M}(\omega_{q,\gamma}^0)$ is the desired optimal sequence.

Next, the following Result 4 is fundamental for finding the sufficient conditions for any two adjacent jobs i, j to be a definite order in an optimal sequence.

Remark. The above optimal sequence is determined in a polynomial-time $0(n^3)$ in cases $2 \leq h \leq m-2$ and $0(n^2)$ in cases $h = 1, m-1$.

Also we can obtain condensed conditions that are weaker than the conditions in Results 2 and 3 respectively by applying a transformation method (cf. Misc. Exercise 9).

As a practical application of these conditions, if we could suitably design large permutation flow shop so that either condition is satisfied, then the related optimal sequence follows in a polynomial-time.

Result 4 (Generalization of Theorem 5). When an optimal scheduling policy is employed, let two jobs i, j be processed after a certain subsequence S with last job l, then if $m-1$ inequalities:

$$T_k(ij) \leqq T_k(ji) \, (k = 2, 3, \ldots, m)$$

hold, where, say, $T_k(ij)$ means $T_k(j)$ under the order ij after S, then job i directly precedes job j after S. When equalities hold for all these inequalities, either ordering can be taken after S.

For simplicity, in the following, this ordering of two jobs i, j in an optimal sequence, as described in Result 4, will be referred to a notation $i < j$.

Then by using (8.39) successively, we have ultimately

$$T_k(ij) = \max[T_k(l), \max_{r=0 \sim k-2} A(ij, t, r, k)], \, (k = 2, 3, \ldots, m)$$

where

$$A(ij, t, r, k) = T_{k-r-1}(l) + \max_{t=-1 \sim r} \left(p_{i, k-t-1} + \sum_{q=k-t-1}^{k-1} p_{j, q} - p_{i, k} \right.$$
$$\left. + \sum_{q=k-r-1}^{k-t-2} p_{i, q} \right),$$

and

$$T_k(ji) = \max[T_k(l), \max_{r=0 \sim k-2} A(ji, t, r, k)], \, (k = 2, 3, \ldots, m)$$

where $A(ji, t, r, k)$ is an expression obtained by exchanging i and j in $A(ij, t, r, k)$. By substituting those $T_k(ij)$, $T_k(ji)(k = 2, 3, \ldots, m)$ in an inequality in Result 4 and comparing every corresponding term in both sides, we can obtain the following inequalities:

$$\max\left[\sum_{q=k-r-1}^{k-1} p_{i,q}, \max_{t=0 \sim r-1}\left(p_{i,k-t-1} + \sum_{q=k-t-1}^{k-1} p_{j,q} - p_{i,k} + \sum_{q=k-r-1}^{k-t-2} p_{i,q} \right),\right.$$
$$\left. p_{i,k-r-1} + \sum_{q=k-r-1}^{k-1} p_{j,q} - p_{i,k} \right]$$
$$\leq \max\left[\sum_{q=k-r-1}^{k-1} p_{j,q}, \max_{t=0 \sim r-1}\left(p_{j,k-t-1} + \sum_{q=k-t-1}^{k-1} p_{i,q} - p_{j,k} \right.\right. \tag{8.40}$$
$$\left.\left. + \sum_{q=k-r-1}^{k-t-2} p_{j,q} \right), p_{j,k-r-1} + \sum_{q=k-r-1}^{k-1} p_{i,q} - p_{j,k} \right]$$

for all $r(r = 0, 1, \ldots, k-2)$ for each $k(k = 2, 3, \ldots, m)$, which leads to $T_k(ij) \leq T_k(ji)$ for each k. By subtracting

$$\sum_{q=k-r-1}^{k-1} p_{i,q} + \sum_{q=k-r-1}^{k-1} p_{j,q}$$

from both sides of (8.40), we have the following result:

Result 5 (Generalization of Theorem 6). If $(k-1)$ inequalities:

$$\min\left[\sum_{q=k-r-1}^{k-1} p_{i,q}, \min_{t=0 \sim r-1}\left(\sum_{q=k-r-1}^{k-t-2} p_{i,q} + \sum_{q=k-t}^{k} p_{j,q} \right), \sum_{q=k-r}^{k} p_{j,q} \right]$$
$$\leq \min\left[\sum_{q=k-r-1}^{k-1} p_{j,q}, \min_{t=0 \sim r-1}\left(\sum_{q=k-r-1}^{k-t-2} p_{j,q} + \sum_{q=k-t}^{k} p_{i,q} \right), \sum_{q=k-r}^{k} p_{i,q} \right]$$
$$(k = 2, 3, \ldots, m; r = 0, \ldots, k-2) \tag{8.41}$$

hold for all $r(r = 0, 1, \ldots, k-2)$ for each $k(k = 2, 3, \ldots, m)$, then $T_k(ij) \leq T_k(ji)$ follows. Hence, if $m(m-1)/2$ inequalities (8.41) for all $k(k = 2, 3, \ldots, m)$ and all $r(r = 0, 1, \ldots, k-2)$ hold, then from Result 4, $i < j$ holds.

Remarks. 1. Inequalities (d) for m machines, which correspond to an inequality (d) in the three-machine case (Section 8.15), are $(m-1)(m-2)/2$ inequalities (8.41) for $k = 3, 4, \ldots, m$ and $r = 1, 2, \ldots, k-2$ because (8.41) for $r = 0$ coincides with

$$\min(p_{i,k-1}, p_{j,k}) \leq \min(p_{j,k-1}, p_{i,k})$$

for each $k(k = 2, 3, \ldots, m)$.

2. Inequalities (8.40) ($k = 2, 3, \ldots, m; r = 0, 1, \ldots, k-2$) can be denoted as

$$\max_{u \leq r \leq v} \left(\sum_{q=u}^{r} p_{i,q} + \sum_{q=r}^{v} p_{j,q} \right) \leq \max_{u \leq r \leq v} \left(\sum_{q=u}^{r} p_{j,q} + \sum_{q=r}^{v} p_{i,q} \right) (1 \leq u < v \leq m),$$

where $u = k - r - 1$ and $v = k$.

Also, inequalities (8.41) ($k = 2, 3, \ldots, m; r = 0, 1, \ldots, k-2$) can be denoted as

$$\min_{u \leq w \leq v} \left[\sum_{q=u}^{w-1} p_{i,q} + \sum_{q=w+1}^{v} p_{j,q} \right] \leq \min_{u \leq w \leq v} \left[\sum_{q=u}^{w-1} p_{j,q} + \sum_{q=w+1}^{v} p_{i,q} \right].$$

$$(1 \leq u < v \leq m). \ (u = k - r - 1, w = k - t - 1, v = k).$$

Let us introduce the following inequalities used as criteria for deciding the definite order of two adjacent jobs i, j for two machines:

$$\min(p_{i,k}, p_{j,k+1}) \leq \min(p_{j,k}, p_{i,k+1}), \ (k = 1, 2, \ldots, m-1) \qquad (m(k, k+1))$$

$$\min(p_{i,u}, p_{j,v}) \leq \min(p_{j,u}, p_{i,v}), \qquad (2 \leq u + 1 < v \leq m) \qquad (m(u, v))$$

$$\min\left(\sum_{k=u}^{v} p_{i,k}, \sum_{k=u+1}^{v+1} p_{j,k} \right) \leq \min\left(\sum_{k=u}^{v} p_{j,k}, \sum_{k=u+1}^{v+1} p_{i,k} \right).$$

$$(1 \leq u < v \leq m-1) \qquad (m(u \sim v, u+1 \sim v+1)).$$

Then inequalities (8.41) in Result 5 are equivalent with inequalities $m(k, k+1)(k = 1, 2, \ldots, m-1)$ and (d) by the above Remark 1.

In the following, we will only list the generalized results of the Theorems 7, 8, condition R_1, Theorem 9, condition R_2, Theorem 10, respectively in Section 8.16 for the three-machine case.

Result 6 (Theorem 7). If $m(m-1)/2$ inequalities $m(k, k+1)(k = 1, 2, \ldots, m-1)$ and $m(u, v)(2 \leq u + 1 < v \leq m)$ hold, then inequalities (d) hold for $m \geq 3$ and $r \geq 1$, and (8.41) holds for $m = 2$ and $m \geq 3, r = 0$. Hence $i < j$ holds.

Inversely, if inequalities $m(k, k+1)(k = 1, 2, \ldots, m-1)$ and (d) hold, then inequalities $m(u, v)$ $(2 \leq u + 1 < v \leq m)$ hold. Therefore, inequalities $m(k, k+1)(k = 1, 2, \ldots, m-1)$ and $M(u, v)(2 \leq u + 1 < v \leq m)$ are equivalent with inequalities $m(k, k+1)(k = 1, 2, \ldots, m-1)$ and (d), that is, (8.41). This equivalence can be expressed briefly so that inequalities $m(u, v)(1 \leq u < v \leq m)$ are equivalent with inequalities (8.41).

Result 7 (Theorem 8). If $m(k, k+1)$ holds for every $k(k = 1, 2, \ldots, m-1)$ under the restricted working rule, then (d) holds. Hence we obtain $i < j$.

Condition R_1: Let us introduce the following condition R_1:

$$\exists k_0, n_0 (k_0 = 1, \ldots, m-2; n_0 = 1, \ldots, m-k_0-1); p_{j,k_0+1} < p_{i,k_0},$$

$$p_{i,k_0+n_0} < p_{j,k_0+n_0+1}, \quad (R_1)$$

then, the condition $R_1(1, m)$, which will be denoted as condition $PR_1(1, m)$, is defined as the R_1, where $k_0 = 1$ and $n_0 = m-2$, which does not include any other R_1 between machine M_1 and M_m. Then the following result holds:

Result 8 (Theorem 9)

Case I. If $m(k, k+1)$ holds for every k $(k = 1, 2, \ldots, m-1)$ under condition $\overline{PR_1(1, m)}$, then (d) follows, that is, the optimal order $i < j$ follows.

Case II. If $m(m-1)/2$ inequalities $m(k, k+1)(k = 1, 2, \ldots, m-1)$, $m(u, v)(2 \leq u+1 < v \leq m)$ hold under condition $PR_1(1, m)$, then the optimal order $i < j$ follows.

Remark. As noted at Section 8.16, optimal orders resulted from Results 6 and 8 can be applied to BAB algorithm as elimination criteria and also to approximate algorithm as the heuristics (cf. Section 10.13, Chapter 10).

Condition R_2: Let us introduce condition R_2 as

$$\forall k = k_0 + 1, \ldots, k_0 + n_0 - 1; \; p_{i,k} = p_{j,k} = p_{i,k+1}$$

$$= p_{j,k+1} < \min(p_{i,k_0}, p_{j,k_0+n_0+1}), \quad (R_2)$$

$$p_{i,k} = p_{j,k} = p_{i,k+1} = p_{j,k+1} \leq \min((p_{j,k_0}, p_{i,k_0+n_0+1}).$$

(cf. Fig. 8.8).

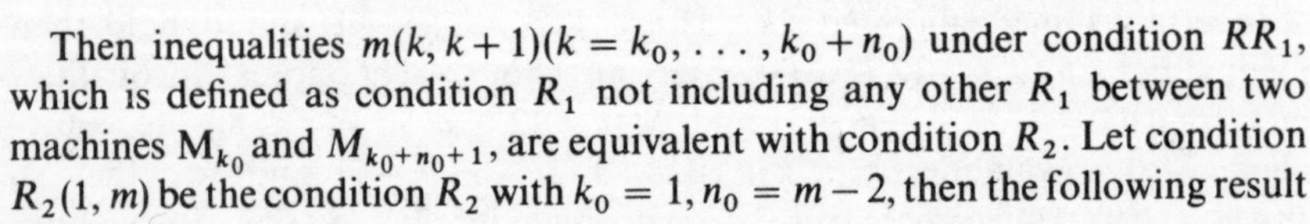

FIG. 8.8. R_2.

Then inequalities $m(k, k+1)(k = k_0, \ldots, k_0 + n_0)$ under condition RR_1, which is defined as condition R_1 not including any other R_1 between two machines M_{k_0} and $M_{k_0+n_0+1}$, are equivalent with condition R_2. Let condition $R_2(1, m)$ be the condition R_2 with $k_0 = 1, n_0 = m-2$, then the following result holds.

Result 9 (Theorem 10). Under the assumptions that case II in Result 8 occurs only as $R_2(1, m)$ and there exists an optimal sequence which is optimal by every criterion $m(u, v)(2 \leq u+1 < v \leq m)$ or equivalently by every criterion $m(u \sim v,\ u+1 \sim v+1)$ $(1 \leqq u < v \leqq m-1)$, for any $R_2(1, m)$ with a different pair of two jobs i, j, then the set of optimal sequences that are optimal by every criterion $m(k, k+1)(k = 1, 2, \ldots, m-1)$ contains an optimal sequence for m machines whenever this set is not empty.

Exercise

1. Let us introduce the condition (S) with the following $(m-2)$ inequalities:

$$[\min(p_{i,1}, p_{j,2}) - \min(p_{j,1}, p_{i,2})][\min(p_{i,k}, p_{j,k+1}) - \min(p_{j,k}, p_{i,k+1})] \geqq 0,$$

$$(k = 2, \ldots, m-1),$$

$$(S)$$

then prove that if condition (S) holds we have a sequence which is optimal by every criterion $m(k, k+1)(k = 1, 2, \ldots, m-1)$. Also show that if condition (S) and inequalities (d) hold $m-1$ inequalities $m(k, k+1)(k = 1, 2, \ldots, m-1)$ follows.

Miscellaneous Exercises

1. **Single-machine scheduling problem.** This problem is to determine a sequence of n jobs on a single machine in order to minimize a given objective function, where p_i is a processing time of job i, d_i is a due date for job i and $u_i > 0$ is a weight for job i. Derive a denoted criterion, which shows that if we have without equality job i precedes job j and if we have with equality either ordering is optimal, for the following respective objective function.

Objective function	Criterion
(1) Weighted mean completion time	$p_i/u_i \leqq p_j/u_j$
(2) Weighted mean lateness	$p_i/u_i \leqq p_j/u_j$
(3) Maximum lateness	$d_i \leqq d_j$
(4) Maximum tardiness	$d_i \leqq d_j$

2. Prove by induction the following expressions for the flow time $T_k(i_q)$ for any sequence $i_1 i_2 \ldots i_n$ in a m-machine permutation (flow shop) scheduling:

$$T_k(i_q) = \max_{1 \leqq r_1 \leqq \ldots \leqq r_{k-1} \leqq q} \left[\sum_{w=1}^{k-1} \left(\sum_{t=1}^{r_w} p_{i_t,w} - \sum_{t=1}^{r_{w-1}} p_{i_t,w+1} \right) \right] + \sum_{t=1}^{q} (p_{i_t,k} - p_{i_t,1})$$

$$= \max_{1 \leqq r_1 \leqq r_2 \ldots \leqq r_{k-1} \leqq q} \left[\sum_{t=1}^{r_1} p_{i_t,1} + \sum_{w=2}^{k-1} \sum_{t=r_{w-1}}^{r_w} p_{i_t,w} + \sum_{t=r_{k-1}}^{q} p_{i_t,k} \right] - \sum_{t=1}^{q} p_{i_t,1}.$$

3. Show the following expressions for the makespan $M(\omega)$ of any sequence $\omega = i_1 i_2 \ldots i_n$ in the problem in exercise 2:

$$M(\omega) = \max_{1 \leqq r_1 \leqq \ldots \leqq r_{m-1} \leqq n} \left[\sum_{w=1}^{m-1} \left(\sum_{t=1}^{r_w} p_{i_t,w} - \sum_{t=1}^{r_{w-1}} p_{i_t,w+1} \right) \right] + \sum_{t=1}^{n} p_{i_t,m}$$

$$= \max_{1 \leqq r_1 \leqq \ldots \leqq r_{m-1} \leqq n} \left[\sum_{t=1}^{r_1} p_{i_t,1} + \sum_{w=2}^{m-1} \sum_{t=r_{w-1}}^{r_w} p_{i_t,w} + \sum_{t=r_{m-1}}^{n} p_{i_t,m} \right].$$

4. Without loss of generality let $\omega = (1, 2, \ldots, n)$ be any sequence and $m(\omega)$ be its makespan when ω is processed on two machines

$$\sum_{k=1}^{m-1} M_k, \ \sum_{k=2}^{m} M_k$$

with respective processing times

$$\sum_{k=1}^{m-1} p_{i,k}, \ \sum_{k=2}^{m} p_{i,k}$$

for each job $i(i = 1, 2, \ldots, n)$ and $M(\omega)$ be its makespan when ω is processed on the original m machines $M_k(k = 1, 2, \ldots, m)$ with respective processing times $p_{i,k}(k = 1, 2, \ldots, m)$ for each job $i(i = 1, 2, \ldots, n)$. Also let ω_1 be an optimal sequence for the above two machines, which is determined by a criterion

$$\min\left(\sum_{k=1}^{m-1} p_{i,k}, \sum_{k=2}^{m} p_{j,k}\right) \leqq \min\left(\sum_{k=1}^{m-1} p_{j,k}, \sum_{k=2}^{m} p_{i,k}\right),$$

and ω_0 be an optimal sequence for the original m machines.

Then prove the following result by applying the expression in exercise 3.

The next relation holds for any sequence $\omega = (1, 2, \ldots, n)$:

$$m(\omega) - \sum_{k=2}^{m-1}\left(\sum_{i=1}^{n} p_{i,k}\right) \leqq M(\omega).$$

particularly for an optimal sequence ω_1 for two machines

$$\sum_{k=1}^{m-1} M_k, \sum_{k=2}^{m} M_k,$$

we have

$$m(\omega_1) - \sum_{k=2}^{m-1}\left(\sum_{i=1}^{n} p_{i,k}\right) \leqq M(\omega_0) \leqq M(\omega_1).$$

Hence, if equation

$$m(\omega_1) - \sum_{k=2}^{m-1}\left(\sum_{i=1}^{n} p_{i,k}\right) = M(\omega_1)$$

holds, a sequence ω_1 becomes optimal also for the original m machines. Also see Misc. Exercise 7.

5. Optimality conditions for the Johnson approximation method. Show the result in case $m = 3$ in exercise 4.

6. In the above case where $m = 3$, if inequalities $p_{i,2} \leqq p_{i+1,1}(i = 1, 2, \ldots, n-1)$, or inequalities $p_{i+1,2} \leqq p_{i,3}(i = 1, 2, \ldots, n-1)$ hold for the sequence $\omega_1 = (1, 2, \ldots, n)$ defined in exercise 4, then the sequence ω_1 is optimal also for three machines.

From the above result, derive a result that if $p_{i,1} \geqq p_{i,2}(i = 1, 2, \ldots, n)$ and $p_{i,2} \leqq p_{i+1,2}$ $(i = 1, 2, \ldots, n-1)$; or $p_{i,3} \geqq p_{i,2}(i = 1, 2, \ldots, n)$ and $p_{i,2} \geqq p_{i+1,2}$ hold for the sequence $\omega_1 = (1, 2, \ldots, n)$, then ω_1 is optimal also for three machines.

Further, from the first result, derive Theorem 1 that if Johnson's condition: $\min_i p_{i,1} \geqq \max_i p_{i,2}$, or $\min_i p_{i,3} \geqq \max_i p_{i,2}$ holds, then the sequence ω_1 is optimal also for three machines.

7. Equivalent sufficient optimality machine-base conditions for a sequence ω_1 in min-makespan problem with m machines $(m \geqq 3)$.

For any sequence $\omega = (1, 2, \ldots, n)$ in which number $i(1 \leqq i \leqq n)$ shows ith job in ω, the makespan $M(\omega)$ of ω is expressed by

$$M(\omega) = \max_{1 \leqq r_1 \leqq r_2 \leqq \ldots \leqq r_{m-1} \leqq n}\left[\sum_{i=1}^{r_1} p_{i,1} + \sum_{t=2}^{m-1}\sum_{i=r_{t-1}}^{r_t} p_{i,t} + \sum_{i=r_{m-1}}^{n} p_{i,m}\right]$$

$$\equiv \sum_{i=1}^{r_1^0} p_{i,1} + \sum_{t=2}^{m-1}\sum_{i=r_{t-1}^0}^{r_1^0} p_{i,t} + \sum_{i=r_{m-1}^0}^{n} p_{i,m}, \text{ (machine-based expression)}$$

where each job $r_t^0(1 \leqq t \leqq m-1)$ denotes a corner job on the tth machine along any critical path corresponding to $M(\omega)$ (cf. Chapter 7, Section 7.10).

Then, each of the following machine-base conditions 1, 2 and 3 is equivalent to the condition shown at Misc. Exercise 4:

$$m(\omega) - \sum_{i=1}^{n} \left(\sum_{t=2}^{m-1} p_{i,t} \right) = M(\omega).$$

1. $\exists r_h^0 (1 \leq h \leq m-1)$, $\exists \{r_t^0; 1 \leq t \leq m-1, t \neq h\}$;

$$\sum_{t=2}^{m-1} \sum_{i=r_{t-1}^0}^{r_t^0} p_{i,t} \leq \sum_{i=r_1^0+1}^{r_h^0} p_{i,1} + \sum_{i=r_h^0}^{r_{m-1}^0-1} p_{i,m} + \sum_{t=2}^{m-1} p_{r_h^0,t}.$$

2. $\exists \{r_t^0; 1 \leq t \leq m-1\}$; $r_1^0 = r_2^0 = \ldots = r_{m-1}^0$. In this case, those values of $r_t^0 (1 \leq t \leq m-1)$ for some such $\{r_t^0\}$ are equal to some u^0 which is a corner job on the first machine

$$\sum_{t=1}^{m=1} M_t$$

along any critical path corresponding to the makespan $m(\omega)$ of ω in the related two-machine problem defined at Misc. Exercise 4.

3. $\exists u(1 \leq u \leq n)$; $M(\omega) = M(\omega; r_1 = r_2 = \ldots = r_{m-1} = u)$, where

$$M(\omega; r_1 = r_2 = \ldots = r_{m-1} = u) \overset{\text{def.}}{=} \sum_{i=1}^{u} p_{i,1} + \sum_{t=2}^{m-1} p_{u,t} + \sum_{i=u}^{n} p_{i,m}$$

is the makespan of ω in m-machine problem when all corner jobs $r_t(1 \leq t \leq m-1)$ of any critical path are assumed to be identical and equal to a job $u(1 \leq u \leq n)$.

Therefore, if $\omega_1 = (1, 2, \ldots, n)$ defined at Misc. Exercise 4 satisfies any one of the above four equivalent conditions, then ω_1 becomes an optimal sequence in the original m-machine problem (cf. Misc. Exercise 4).

Verify the above equivalency for, say, $\omega_1 = (1, 3, 4, 2, 5, 6)$ in a problem $(n = 6, m = 3)$ given in Table 8.4 and identify ω_1 with an optimal sequence.

Note that this identification can be made in a polynomial-time $O(n \log n)$.

TABLE 8.4

i	1	2	3	4	5	6
$p_{i,1}$	2	4	2	2	2	1
$p_{i,2}$	1	2	3	3	2	1
$p_{i,3}$	3	1	2	2	1	1

8. Equivalent sufficient optimality job-base conditions for a sequence $\omega_{a,b}^{k_0}$ in a minimum class k_0 in min-makespan problem with m machines $(m \geq 3)$.

We divide $n!$ sequences of the given n jobs $\{1, 2, \ldots, n\}$ into $n(n-1)$ classes $k(k = 1 \sim n(n-1))$. Each class $k = (j_1, \ldots, j_2)$ consists of $(n-2)!$ sequences $\omega_{a,b}^k = (1, 2, \ldots, n)$, in which each number $i(1 \leq i \leq n)$ shows the ith job, having two jobs j_1, j_2 designated by k as the fixed ath job, fixed bth job $(1 \leq a < b \leq n)$ respectively where a, b are arbitrarily taken.

Then, for each class k we define two new jobs J_1^k and J_2^k where jobs J_1^k, J_2^k consist of the original $n-1$ jobs $\{1, \ldots, b-1, b+1, \ldots, n\}, \{1, \ldots a-1, a+1, \ldots, n\}$ excluding the fixed bth job (j_2), fixed ath job (j_1) respectively and have their processing times

$$\sum_{i \neq b} p_{i,t}, \sum_{i \neq a} p_{i,t}$$

respectively on the tth machine $M_t(1 \leq t \leq m)$. Therefore, J_1^k, J_2^k, and their processing times are the same for any sequence $\omega_{a,b}^k$ in that class k regardless of the values of position pair$\{a,b\}$.

Let $m_{a,b}(J_1^k J_2^k)$ be the makespan of a definite two-job sequence $J_1^k J_2^k$ processed on m machines in the same ordering as in the original m-machine problem, then an expression

$$m_{a,b}(J_1^k J_2^k) - \sum_{t=1}^{m} (k) \sum_{i \neq a,b} p_{i,t}$$

takes a constant value for any sequence $\omega_{a,b}^k$ in a definite class k for any position pair $\{a,b\}$ where (k) shows the related class k.

Also we define a minimum class k_0 as a class k giving

$$\min_k \left\{ m_{a,b}(J_1^k J_2^k) - \sum_{t=1}^m (k) \sum_{i \neq a,b} p_{i,t} \right\}.$$

Note that k_0 is determined in a polynomial-time $0(n^2)$.

Next, we have the following job-base expression of $M(\omega_{a,b}^k)$ of any sequence $\omega_{a,b}^k = (1,2,\ldots, n-1,n)$ in a class k for any $\{a,b\}$:

$$M(\omega_{a,b}^k) = \max_{1 \leq v_1 \leq v_2 \leq \ldots \leq v_{n-1} \leq m} \left[\sum_{t=1}^{v_1} p_{i,t} + \sum_{i=2}^{n-1} \sum_{t=v_{i-1}}^{v_i} p_{i,t} + \sum_{t=v_{n-1}}^m p_{n,t} \right]$$

$$\equiv \sum_{t=1}^{v_1^0} p_{1,t} + \sum_{i=2}^{n-1} \sum_{t=v_{i-1}^0}^{v_2^0} p_{i,t} + \sum_{t=v_{n-1}^0}^m p_{n,t} \quad \text{(job-base expression)},$$

where each machine $v_i^0 (1 \leq i \leq n-1)$ denotes a corner machine on the ith job-line along any critical path for $M(\omega_{a,b}^k)$. Then, under the restraint $(C_{a,b}^k)$:

$$\sum_{t=1}^{w^0-1} p_{1,t} + \sum_{t=w^0+1}^m p_{n,t} = \sum_{t=1}^{w^0-1} p_{a,t} + \sum_{t=w^0+1}^m p_{b,t} \qquad (C_{a,b}^k)$$

for at least one w^0 for $m_{a,b}(J_1^k J_2^k)$ where a machine w^0 denotes a corner machine along any critical path for $m_{a,b}(J_1^k J_2^k)$ in the related two-job m-machine problem. (Note that $(C_{a,b}^k)$ is satisfied when $\{a = 1, b = n\}$.) Then, each of the following job-base conditions 1, 2 and 3 is equivalent to the next condition for any sequence $\omega_{a,b}^k = (1,2,\ldots, n-1,n)$:

$$m_{a,b}^k \equiv m_{a,b}(J_1^k J_2^k) - \sum_{t=1}^m (k) \sum_{i \neq a,b} p_{i,t} = M(\omega_{a,b}^k).$$

(Generally $m_{a,b}^k \leq M(\omega_{a,b}^k)$ holds.)

1. $\exists v_j^0 (1 \leq j \leq n-1), \exists \{v_i^0; 1 \leq i \leq n-1, i \neq j\}$;

$$\sum_{t=1}^{v_1^0} p_{1,t} + \sum_{i=2}^{n-1} \sum_{t=v_{i-1}^0}^{v_i^0} p_{i,t} + \sum_{t=v_{n-1}^0}^m p_{n,t} \leq \sum_{i=1}^{a-1} p_{i,v_j^0} + \sum_{t=1}^{v_j^0} p_{a,t} + \sum_{i=a+1}^{b-1} p_{i,v_j^0}$$

$$+ \sum_{t=v_j^0}^m p_{b,t} + \sum_{i=b+1}^n p_{i,v_j^0}.$$

2. $\exists \{v_i^0; 1 \leq i \leq n-1\}; v_1^0 = v_2^0 = \ldots = v_{n-1}^0$. In this case, those values of $v_i^0 (1 \leq i \leq n-1)$ for some such $\{v_i^0\}$ are equal to some w^0 in $(C_{a,b}^k)$.

3. $\exists \{v_i; 1 \leq i \leq n-1, i \neq a,b, 1 \leq v_1 \leq v_2 \leq \ldots \leq v_{n-1} \leq m\}, \exists w (1 \leq w \leq m)$;

$$M(\omega_{a,b}^k) = M_{a,b}(\omega_{a,b}^k; v_i = w (i \neq a,b), \sum_{t=1}^w p_{a,t}, \sum_{t=w}^m p_{b,t})$$

$$\overset{\text{def.}}{=} \sum_{i=1}^{a-1} p_{i,w} + \sum_{t=1}^w p_{a,t} + \sum_{i=a+1}^{b-1} p_{i,w} + \sum_{t=w}^m p_{b,t} + \sum_{i=b+1}^n p_{i,w}$$

which is defined as the sum of $\sum_{i=1}^{a-1} p_{i,w}$, $\sum_{i=b+1}^n p_{i,w}$, and the makespan of $\omega_{a,b}^k$ in the intermediate $(b-a+1)$-machine problem with machines $M_t (a \leq t \leq b)$ under the restraint $v_i = w (a \leq i \leq b-1)$ for any definite $w (1 \leq w \leq m)$.

Note that those conditions are a sort of counterpart of the conditions 1–3 in the Misc. Exercise 7, in a case $\{a = 1, b = n\}$.

If any one of the above equivalent conditions holds for a sequence $\omega_{a,b}^k - (1,2,\ldots, n-1,n)$ in any definite class k for any definite position pair $\{a,b\}$ under the restraint $(C_{a,b}^k)$, then $\omega_{a,b}^k$ is a locally optimal sequence in that class k. If $k = k_0$ in the above, then $\omega_{a,b}^{k_0}$ is an optimal sequence.

Then, for a problem $(n = 4, m = 3)$ given in Table 8.5, show that $k_0 = (1, -, 3)$ and $(1, -, 4)$, and successively taking the values of $\{a, b\}$ along say a sequence of $\{a, b\}:\{a = 1, b = 4\}, \{a = 1, b = 3\}, \{a = 1, b = 2\}, \{a = 2, b = 4\}, \{a = 3, b = 4\}$, show that $\omega_{1:2}^{k_0} = (1, 3, 2, 4)$ for $k_0 = (1, -, 3), \{a = 1, b = 2\}$, containing subsequence of ω_1, satisfies the restraint $(C_{1:2}^{k_0})$ and, say, condition 2, and therefore is an optimal sequence, while ω_1 in Misc. Exercise 7 is not optimal.

Note that this fact clarifies that the above conditions extend further the range of polynomially solvable cases in our hard problem.

TABLE 8.5

i	1	2	3	4
$p_{i,1}$	1	3	2	2
$p_{i,2}$	2	5	3	1
$p_{i,3}$	4	1	1	1

9. Transformation method in the permutation scheduling problem.

The transformation method described here is applied to the hard permutation scheduling problem with normal (regular) objective function.

Suitably enlarging the processing times, due-dates, and/or the weights given in the original hard problem P_1, this method transforms the original problem P_1 not satisfying a certain existing sufficient optimality condition (A) for a specified sequence ω_{app}, constructed in a polynomial-time, into a similar problem P_2 maintaining the character of ω_{app} and satisfying the condition (A). It enables us to identify an approximate degree of an approximate sequence ω_{app} and to obtain a weaker or more general condition (B) than the original condition (A), which may extend the range of polynomially solvable cases in the hard problem.

As an example, we consider the hard m-machine $(m \geq 3)$ permutation flow-shop makespan scheduling problem P_1 which has a sufficient optimality condition (A) (Result 2 at Section 8.18):

$$\exists h(1 \leq h \leq m-1); \forall t(1 \leq t \leq h-1), \ \min_i p_{i,t} \geq \max_i p_{i,t+1},$$

$$\forall t(h+1 \leq t \leq m-1), \min_i p_{i,t+1} \geq \max_i p_{i,t}, \tag{A}$$

for a sequence ω_1 (cf. Misc. Exercise 7).

We transform P_1 in a similar problem P_2 with processing times

$$p'_{i,t} = p_{i,t} + c_t \, (c_t \geq 0), 1 \leq i \leq n, 1 \leq t \leq m.$$

Then, (A) in P_2 becomes

$$\exists h(1 \leq h \leq m-1); \forall t(1 \leq t \leq h-1), \min_i p_{i,t} + c_t \geq \max_i p_{i,t+1} + c_{t+1}, \tag{1}$$

$$\forall t(h+1 \leq t \leq m-1), \min_i p_{i,t+1} + c_{t+1} \geq \max_i p_{i,t} + c_t. \tag{2}$$

Then solve the subsequent questions (a) − (e):

(a) In (1) having the given value of c_{t+1}, show that the value of $c_t (t = h-1, h-2, \ldots, 1)$ is determined by

$$c_t = \max[\max_i p_{i,t+1} + c_{t+1} - \min_i p_{i,t}, 0]. \tag{3}$$

(b) Successively using (3) to $t = h-1, h-2, \ldots, 1$ under $c_h = 0$, obtain the value of c_1:

$$c_1 = \max\left[\max_{2 \leq u \leq h} \sum_{t=1}^{u-1} (\max_i p_{i,t+1} - \min_i p_{i,t}), 0 \right]. \tag{4}$$

(c) In the same way, show that the value of c_m is represented by

$$c_m = \max\left[\max_{h+1 \leq u \leq m-1} \sum_{t=u}^{m-1} (\max_i p_{i,t} - \min_i p_{i,t+1}), 0 \right]. \tag{5}$$

(d) On the other hand, defining the revised values of c_1 and c_m as $\max(c_1, c_m)$ of c_1 by (4) and c_m by (5) which yields $c_1 = c_m$, we can obtain an upper bound $(n-1)c_1$ of the absolute deviation $M(\omega_1) - M(\omega_0)$ where ω_0 is an optimal sequence. Then, from $c_1 = 0$ in (4) and $c_m = 0$ in (5), derive the following sufficient optimality condition (B) for ω_1:

$$\exists h(1 \leq h \leq m-1);$$

$$\min_i p_{i,1} \geq \max_i p_{i,2} + \max_{2 \leq u \leq h} \sum_{t=2}^{u-1} (\max_i p_{i,t+1} - \min_i p_{i,t}),$$

$$\min_i p_{i,m} \geq \max_i p_{i,m-1} + \max_{h+1 \leq u \leq m-1} \sum_{t=u}^{m-2} (\max_i p_{i,t} - \min_i p_{i,t+1}), \tag{B}$$

where $\sum_{t=a}^{a-1} P(t)$ means zero.

(e) Show that new condition (B) is weaker than the original condition (A) except a case $m = 3$. For the other applications of the transformation method, see References.

10. m-machine scheduling problem with time lags. Let n jobs be processed by m machines $M_1, M_2, \ldots, M_m$ in this machine order, where no passing of jobs is permitted, and processing of every job $i(i = 1, 2, \ldots, n)$ can start on M_{k+1} not sooner than $D_{i,k}$ time units after its starting on M_k and can complete on M_{k+1} not sooner than $E_{i,k}$ time units after its completion on $M_k(k = 1, 2, \ldots, m-1)$. Then if we put

$$\underline{R}_{i,k} = \max[D_{i,k}, E_{i,k} - p_{i,k+1} + p_{i,k}],$$
$$\bar{R}_{i,k+1} = \max[D_{i,k} - p_{i,k} + p_{i,k+1}, E_{i,k}]$$

the following result holds.

In the present problem, if, for a certain constant, $h(h = 1, 2, \ldots, m-1)m-2$ inequalities:

$$\min_i \underline{R}_{i,k} \geq \max_i \bar{R}_{i,k+1}, \quad (k = 1, 2, \ldots, h-1)$$

$$\min_i \bar{R}_{i,k+1} \geq \max_i \underline{R}_{i,k}, \quad (k = h+1, h+2, \ldots, m-1)$$

hold, then an optimal sequence can be determined by the following rule: if an inequality

$$\min\left[\sum_{q=1}^{m-1} \underline{R}_{i,q}, \sum_{q=2}^{m} \bar{R}_{j,q} \right] \leq \min\left[\sum_{q=1}^{m-1} \underline{R}_{j,q}, \sum_{q=2}^{m} \bar{R}_{i,q} \right]$$

holds without equality, then job i precedes job j. If equality holds, then either ordering is optimal.

Verify that the above result reduces to Theorem 11 in Section 8.17 when $m = 2$ and $F_i = 0(i = 1, 2, \ldots, n)$, and that it includes Result 2 in Section 8.18.

11. $n \times m$ ordered flow-shop (permutation) problem. An ordered flow-shop problem has the following two characteristics: (1) If we have $p_{i,k} > p_{j,k}$ for any two jobs i, j and a certain machine M_k, then $p_{i,k} \geq p_{j,k}$ holds for all machines $M_k(k = 1, 2, \ldots, m)$ and those two jobs i, j, and (2) If $p_{i,k} > p_{i,t}$ holds for a certain job i and any two machines M_k, M_t, then $p_{i,k} \geq p_{i,t}$ holds for all jobs $i(i = 1, 2, \ldots, n)$ and those two machines M_k, M_t.

In the min-makespan problem, verify the following result: If the greatest processing times are taken for the first machine M_1, or last machine M_m, then an optimal sequence can be determined by ordering n jobs in nonincreasing, or nondecreasing, order of processing times respectively.

12. In the min-mean completion time problem for $n \times m$ ordered flow shop defined above, verify the following result: An optimal sequence can be determined by ordering n jobs in nondecreasing order of processing times.

Bibliography and Comments

Section 8.3

S. M. JOHNSON, "Optimal two- and three-stage production schedules with setup times included", *Nav. Res. Log. Quart.* **1** (1954), 61–68; Chapter 2, *Industrial Scheduling*, J. F. MUTH and G. L. THOMPSON (eds.), Prentice-Hall, 1963.

Sections 8.5–8.12

I. NABESHIMA, *Scheduling Theory* (in Japanese), Morikita Shuppan, 1974, pp. 66–72.

Section 8.13

I. NABESHIMA, *op. cit.*, pp. 72–74.
For the three-machine case see
W. SZWARC, "Mathematical aspects of the 3 × n job-shop sequencing problem", *Nav. Res. Log. Quart.* **21**, No. 1 (1974), 145–153.
W. SZWARC, "A note on mathematical aspects of the 3 × n job-shop sequencing problem", *Nav. Res. Log. Quart.* **21**, No. 4 (1974), 725–726.

Sections 8.14, 8.15

I. NABESHIMA, *op. cit.*, 74–84.
I. NABESHIMA, "The order of *n* items processed on *m* machines. [III]", *J. Oper. Res. Soc. Japan*, **16**, No. 3 (1973), 163–185.
I. NABESHIMA, "Notes on the analytical results in flow shop scheduling: Part 3", *Rep. Univ. Electro-Comm.*, **28**, No. 1 (1977), 35–44.

Section 8.15

See
W. SZWARC, "Optimal two machine orderings in the 3 × n flow-shop problem", *Opns. Res.* **25**, No. 1 (1977), 70–77.

Section 8.16

The following papers are concerned with the content in this section:
I. NABESHIMA, "The order of *n* items processed on *m* machines. [III]", *J. Oper. Res. Soc. Japan*, **16**, No. 3 (1973), 163–185.
YUEH MING-I, "On the N job, M machine sequencing problem of flow-shop", *Operational Research '75*, K. B. HALEY, (ed.), North-Holland, 1975, 179–200.
F. BURNS and J. ROOKER, "Extensions and comments regarding special cases of the three machine flow-shop problem", *Nav. Res. Log. Quart.* **22**, No. 6, (1975), 811–817.
F. BURNS and J. ROOKER, "Johnson's three machine flow-shop conjecture", *Opns. Res.* **24**, No. 3 (1976), 578–580.
W. SZWARC, "Optimal two-machine orderings in the 3 × n flow-shop problem", *Opns. Res.* **25**, No. 1 (1977), 70–77.
W. SZWARC, "Precedence relations of the flow-shop problem", Working Paper, *School of Business Administration*, University of Wisconsin–Milwaukee, 1977, pp. 1–13.
I. NABESHIMA, "Notes on the analytical results in flow shop scheduling: Part 3", *Rep. Univ. Electro-Comm.* **28**, No. 1 (1977), 35–44.
R. J. GIGLIO and H. M. WAGNER, "Approximate solutions to the three-machine scheduling problem", *Opns. Res.* **12**, No. 2 (1964), 305–324.

Section 8.17

I. NABESHIMA, Sequencing on two machines with start lag and stop lag", *J. Oper. Res. Soc. Japan*, **5**, No. 3 (1963), 97–101.
The problem in the case all $F_i = 0$ has been presented in the next two papers:
L. G. MITTEN, "Sequencing *n* jobs on two machines with arbitrary time lags", *Manag. Science*, **5**, No. 3, (1959), 293–298.
S. M. JOHNSON, "Discussion: sequencing n jobs on two machines with arbitrary time lags", *Manag. Science*, **5**, No. 3 (1959), 299–303.

Section 8.18
The following papers are concerned with the content of this section:

I. NABESHIMA, "The order of n items processed on m machines", *J. Oper. Res. Soc. Japan*, **3**, No. 4 (1961), 170–175.

I. NABESHIMA, "The order of *n* items processed on *m* machines. [II]", *J. Oper. Res. Soc. Japan*, **4**, No. 1 (1961), 1–8.

YUEH MING-I, "On the *N* job, *M* machine sequencing problem of flow-shop", *Operational Research '75*, K. B. HALEY, (ed.), North-Holland, 1975, pp. 179–200.

I. NABESHIMA, "Notes on the analytical results in flow shop scheduling: Part 1", *Rep. Univ. Electro-Comm.* **27**, No. 2 (1977), 245–252; also "Part 2", *Rep. Univ. Electro-Comm.*, **27**, No. 2 (1977), 253–257; and "Part 4", *Rep. Univ. Electro-Comm.* **28**, No. 1 (1977), 45–55.

I. NABESHIMA, "Some extensions of the m machine scheduling problem", *J. Oper. Res. Soc. Japan*, **10**, Nos. 1 and 2 (1967), 1–17.

W. SZWARC, *op. cit.*, p. 3.

Exercise 1
I. NABESHIMA, "Notes on the analytical results in flow shop scheduling: Part 4", *Rep. Univ. Electro-Comm.* **28**, No. 1 (1977), 45–55.

Miscellaneous Exercises

1. W. E. SMITH, "Various optimizers for single stage production", *Nav. Res. Log. Quart.* **3**, No. 1 (1956), 59–66.

Concerning the single machine scheduling problem, refer further to the following papers and their references:

A. H. G. RINNOOY KAN, B. J. LAGEWEG and J. K. LENSTRA, "Minimizing total costs in one-machine scheduling", *Opns. Res.* **23**, No. 5 (1975), 908–927.

H. EMMONS, "A note on a scheduling problem with dual criteria", *Nav. Res. Log. Quart.* **22**, No. 3 (1975), 615–616.

L. VAN WASSENHOVE and L. GELDERS, "Four solution techniques for a general one machine scheduling problem: a comparative study", *Eur. J. Oper. Res.* **2** (1978), 281–290.

K. R. BAKER and L. E. SCHRAGE, "Finding an optimal sequence by dynamic programming: an extension to precedence-related tasks", *Opns. Res.* **26**, No. 1 (1978), 111–120.

E. L. LAWLER and B. D. SIVAZLIAN, "Minimization of time-varying costs in single machine scheduling", *Opns. Res.* **26**, No. 4 (1978), 563–569.

C. L. MONMA, "Sequencing to minimize the maximum job cost", *Opns. Res.* **28**, No. 4 (1980), 942–951.

L. VAN WASSENHOVE and L. GELDERS, "Solving a bicriterion scheduling problem", Working Paper *Katholieke Universiteit Leuven*, 78–15, Okt. 1978.

For convex objective functions in bicriterion problem, see

J. L. COHON, R. L. CHURCH and D. P. SHEER, "Generating multiobjective trade-offs: an algorithm for bicriterion problems", *Water Resources Res.* **15**, No. 5 (1979), 1001–1010.

Also, as the related multicriteria scheduling problem, see the next papers:

K. HUCKERT, R. RHODE, O. ROGLIN and R. WEBER, "On the interactive solution to a multicriteria scheduling problem", *Zeitschrift für Oper. Res.* **24** (1980), 47–60.

I. NABESHIMA, "Extended branch and bound algorithm and its application to biobjective problem", *Rep. Univ. Electro-Comm.* **28**, No. 1 (1977), 67–74.

2–4. I. NABESHIMA, "Notes on the analytical results in flow shop scheduling, Part 5", *Rep. Univ. Electro-Comm.* **28**, No. 1, 1977, 57–65. Also, "Part 11", *Rep. Univ. Electro-Comm.* **31**, No. 1 (1980), 53–64, makes a relation at Misc. Exercise 4 minute by taking account of the corner job on every machine along any critical path for M(W). Cf.

3. W. SZWARC, *op. cit.*, p. 3. Misc. Exercise 7. The other solvable cases, see "Parts 16–19" (to appear).

5. W. SZWARC, "Mathematical aspects of the 3 × *n* job-shop sequencing problem", *Nav. Res. Log. Quart.* **21**, No. 1 (1974), 145–153.

I. NABESHIMA, *op. cit.*, p. 60.

6. I. NABESHIMA, *op. cit.*, pp. 61–62.

7. I. NABESHIMA, "Notes on the analytical results in flow shop scheduling: Part 11", *Rep. Univ. Electro-Comm.* **31**, No. 1. (1980), 53–64.
This Part contains a number of sufficient optimality conditions for ω_1, that are weaker than, say, the condition at Result 2 in Section 8.18, which is a generalization of Johnson condition in $m = 3$ (Theorem 1 at Section 8.3) and a generalized condition for $m \geq 3$ of a condition for $m = 3$:

$$\forall i (1 \leq i \leq n); \, p_{i,2} \leq \min(p_{i,1}, p_{i,3})$$

presented in
F. BURNS and J. ROOKER, "Three-stage flow-shops with recessive second stage", *Opns. Res.* **26**, No. 1 (1978), 207–208.

8. I. NABESHIMA, "Notes on the analytical results in flow shop scheduling: Part 19", *Rep. Univ. Electro-Comm.* (to appear).
For a case $\{a = 1, b = n\}$, see "Part 13", *Rep. Univ. Electro-Comm.*, **31**, No. 2 (1981) 201–212. Note that the value of $m_{a,b}^k$ in each class k is a lower bound of M $(\omega_{a,b}^k)$ of any sequence $\omega_{a,b}^k$ in that class k and a class $k = (j_1, -, j_2)$ means a precedence constraint $j_1 < j_2$ in the problem.
Concerning the recent analytic and algorithmic developments in the scheduling problem with precedence constraints, refer to the following two papers and their references:
J. K. LENSTRA and A. H. G. RINNOOY KAN, "Complexity of scheduling under precedence constraints", *Opns. Res.* **26**, No. 1 (1978), 22–35.
C. L. MONMA, "Sequencing to minimize the maximum job cost", *Opns. Res.* **28**, No. 4 (1980), 942–951.

7.8. Concerning general description on the polynomially solvable cases, refer to
M. R. GAREY and D. S. JOHNSON, *Computers and Intractability: A Guide to the Theory of NP-Completeness*, Freeman, 1979, Section 4.1.
S. EILON, "Production scheduling", *OR '78*, K. B. HALEY (ed.), North-Holland, 1979, pp. 237–266, p. 260.
Also, a type of critical path which is common to all sequences and yields an optimal sequence is examined in
W. SZWARC, "Permutation flow-shop theory revisited", *Nav. Res. Log. Quart.* **25**, No. 3 (1978), 557–570.

9. I. NABESHIMA, "General formulation and applications of a transformation method for the NP-complete permutation scheduling problems", *Rep. Univ. Electro-Comm.* (to appear).
Concrete applications of this method to the m-machine ($m \geq 3$) makespan problem are found in "Parts 7 (Misc. Exercise 9)–10, 12, and 14", *Rep. Univ. Electro-Comm.* **29**, No. 1 (1978), 27–31; **29**, No. 2 (1979), 179–186; **30**, No. 1 (1979), 51–54; **30**, No. 2 (1980), 189–196 (revised); **31**, No. 2 (1981); **32**, No. 1 (1981) 23–33, respectively, and to the m-machine ($m \geq 2$) mean completion time problem, see "Part 15", **32**, No. 1 (1981) 35–41, and also to the single-machine problem, see
I. NABESHIMA, "An analysis of the SPT and EDD heuristics by transformation method in the single-machine mean weighted tardiness problem", *Rep. Univ. Electro-Comm.* **32**, No. 2 (1982) 205–212.

10. I. NABESHIMA, "Some extensions of the m machine scheduling problem", *J. Oper. Res. Soc. Japan*, **10**, Nos. 1 and 2 (1967), 1–17.

11. M. L. SMITH, S. S. PANWALKER and R. A. DUDEK, "Flowshop sequencing problem with ordered processing time matrices", *Manag. Sci.* **21**, No. 5 (1975), 544–549.

12. S. S. PANWALKER and A. W. KHAN, "An ordered flow-shop sequencing problem with mean completion time criterion", *Int. J. Prod. Res.* **14**, No. 5 (1976), 631–635.
Concerning the ordered flow-shop sequencing problem, further refer to
M. L. SMITH, S. S. PANWALKAR and R. A. DUDEK, "Flowshop sequencing problem with ordered processing time matrices: a general case", *Nav. Res. Log. Quart.* **23**, No. 3 (1976), 481–486.
S. S. PANWALKAR and A. W. KHAN, "A convex property of an ordered flow shop sequencing problem", *Nav. Res. Log. Quart.* **24**, No. 1 (1977), 159–162.

CHAPTER 9

Flow-shop Scheduling Problems: General Solutions

9.1. Introduction

As shown in Chapters 7 and 8 there exists no simple criterion for determining an optimal sequence in min-makespan problems with more than two machines. Generally, for an algorithm for determining an optimal sequence, we use branch and bound algorithms, which will be abbreviated as BAB algorithms. We can apply a BAB algorithm for job-shop problems with normal objective functions which will be presented at Section 12.21 in Chapter 12. We designed some BAB algorithms that are peculiar to the flow shop, where no passing is allowed, that is, to permutation schedules.

Historically, Z. A. Lomnicki, E. Ignall and L. Schrage developed a BAB algorithm for min-makespan problems with three machines in 1965 and it was generalized to the $m(m \geq 3)$ machines case where no passing is allowed. Nabeshima developed a BAB algorithm in 1966, for the problem with more than three machines where passing of jobs is allowed. Subsequently, a few devices were made in order to make the standard lower bound used in the former BAB algorithm more exact.

The other algorithms, backtrack programming and lexicographical search method can also be applied. BAB algorithms are also applied to the min-mean completion-time problem, min-penalty cost problem with tardiness criterion, a problem with time lags, and a problem with explicit setup times. Moreover, as shown in the next chapter, we can develop a unified multistage combinatorial algorithm for normal objective functions, as a direct application of the state transformation-process method which was presented in Section 3.8 in Chapter 3. Also we refer to some approximate algorithms for the min-makespan problem.

9.2. m Machine Min-Makespan Problem
($m \geq 3$, no Passing is Allowed)

Here the assumption that no passing is allowed does not lose generality for the three-machine case ($m = 3$).

200

In the following, we will first explain concrete procedures of the BAB algorithm. Then we will describe some problems that are related to a BAB algorithm with a standard lower bound, and also a backtrack programming, or a lexicographical search method for the present problem.

9.3. Concrete Procedures in BAB Algorithms

In any BAB algorithm, if we classify the ways of deciding a node to be branched next by the procedures of branching at some incompletely searched node defined in Section 3.9 of Chapter 3 there exist complete branching procedure and partial branching procedure. Then the former procedure can be classified into a frontier node search procedure and active new node search procedure by the different ways of deciding a node to be branched.

Definitions of a same branch, a terminal node and an intermediate node: Any BAB algorithm makes a set of all feasible solutions a root node of a related solution tree and then successively branches the node decided by a criterion. In these cases, when a node, which associates with a subset of the set of all feasible solutions, is branched into nodes that correspond to its subsets, any node constructed by one such branching of the same node is said to be laid on the *same branch*.

By successive branching, we arrive finally at a node (subset) consisting of a single feasible solution. We call such node a *terminal node* and the other nodes in the solution tree *intermediate nodes*.

Then the complete branching procedure is defined as a procedure which decomposes some intermediate node with smallest lower bound into the direct sum of subsets of the set of feasible solutions, corresponding to this intermediate node, that is to say, a procedure which branches this intermediate node completely and makes it a node which was completely searched.

In this respect, there exist two types of the complete branching procedures according to the ways of deciding an intermediate node with smallest lower bound as shown below. Let N_0 be a node which expresses all feasible solutions.

1. FRONTIER NODE SEARCH PROCEDURE (cf. Fig. 9.1)

(a) Decide lower bounds of all nodes on the same branch constructed by branching a node N_0 completely.

(b) If a node with a smallest lower bound determines a feasible solution with the value of the objective function which is equal to this lower bound, then this feasible solution becomes an optimal solution. Otherwise, branch this node completely and then decide lower bounds of all nodes created.

(c) In the solution tree generated up to date, if a node with smallest lower bound among all nodes of degree one, that is, all nodes not branched yet, determines a feasible solution as in step (b), then this is an optimal solution.

Otherwise, branch completely a node with smallest lower bound, which is laid on the newest branch and repeat step (c).

2. ACTIVE NEW NODE SEARCH PROCEDURE (cf. Fig. 9.2)

Steps (a) and (b) are the same as the former procedure 1. Then let f^* be a smallest value of the objective functions of all known feasible solutions found to date, that is, an upper bound known to date of an optimal value f_0 for an optimal solution. If we do not know any feasible solution, we put $f^* = \infty$. Subsequent steps after step (b) are as follows:

3. If a node with smallest lower bound on the same branch constructed at a former stage gives a feasible solution in the same sense as in step 2, proceed to step 5. Otherwise, proceed to step 4.

4. If this smallest lower bound is not less than f^*, proceed to step 5. Otherwise, branch a node with smallest lower bound completely and decide lower bounds of all nodes on the same branch just constructed and go back to step 3.

5. In a solution tree generated to date, let M be a set of nodes of degree one, that is, not branched yet, that have lower bounds less than f^*, then, if $M = \phi$ (empty set), a feasible solution giving f^* is an optimal solution.

Otherwise, backtrack to a nearest node $N \in M$ which can be reached through least number of branches from the present node, branch this node N completely and decide lower bounds of all nodes on the same branch just constructed. Then go back to step 3.

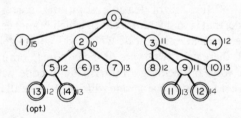

FIG. 9.1

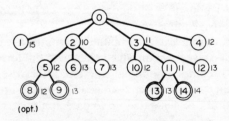

FIG. 9.2

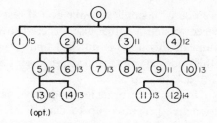

FIG. 9.3

Remarks: Figures 9.1 and Fig. 9.2 are examples of procedures 1 and 2 respectively. Figure 9.3 is another expression of the tree in Fig. 9.1. In the solution trees shown in Figs 9.1 to 9.4, a number laid outside of every node means related lower bound and every doubly circled node means terminal node, that is, related feasible solution. Also nodes are numbered in increasing order according to the order of their occurrences.

3. PARTIAL BRANCHING PROCEDURE (cf. Fig. 9.4)

This procedure is often applied in the cases when every subset of the set of all feasible solutions is decomposed into its two subsets, and when variants of the BAB algorithm are applied to the solution of integer linear programming or 0–1 programming. This procedure 3 has similar steps to the former procedure 2, except that this procedure 3 does not use the complete branching as shown below.

1. Think of examining only one node or a few nodes on the same branch constructed by branching the first node N_0. Such branching is referred to as partial branching.

2. If a node or a node with smallest lower bound respectively becomes a terminal node, proceed to step 5. Otherwise, branch this node partially and decide lower bound for every node just constructed. Proceed to step 3.

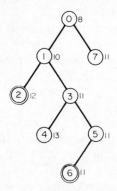

FIG. 9.4

3. If a node or a node with smallest lower bound respectively becomes a terminal node, proceed to step 5. Otherwise, proceed to step 4.

4. If a lower bound of this node is not less than f^*, proceed to step 5. Otherwise, branch this node partially and decide a lower bound for every node just constructed. Go back to step 3.

5. Let M be a set of incompletely branched nodes that has lower bounds less than f^*, in a solution tree generated up to date. If $M = \phi$ (empty set), a terminal node giving f^* becomes an optimal solution. Otherwise, backtrack to the nearest node $N \in M$ as in step 5 in procedure 2, branch this node N partially, and decide lower bound of every node just constructed. Then go back to step 3.

Remarks: The BAB algorithms for flow-shop types use mainly procedure 2, or 1 sometimes, and those for job-shop types and project scheduling use mainly procedure 3. For the EXTBAB algorithm procedures 3 or 2 are used by themselves.

9.4. BAB Algorithms for Flow Shops

Active new node search procedure for the $n \times m$ min-makespan flow shop scheduling problem, where no passing is allowed, is as follows:

1. Let a set (J_0) of all feasible sequences be a starting node (J_0) of a solution tree. Branch this node (J_0) into n nodes (subsets of a set (J_0)) $\{(J_1)\}$ according to whether the first job of the sequences is $1, 2, \ldots,$ or n and decide every lower bound $LB(J_1)$.

2. Let (J_1) be a node with a smallest lower bound among these n $LB(J_1)$'s, where if there exist two such nodes we select usually a node with a smallest job number. Then, branch this node (J_1) into $n - 1$ nodes (subsets) $\{(J_2)\}$ according to whether the second job of the sequence is one of the undefined $n - 1$ jobs and decide every lower bound $LB(J_2)$.

3. In the same way, at r stage $(r = 1, 2, \ldots, n - 1)$ $n - r + 1$ nodes $\{(J_r)\}$ are constructed by branching completely a node (J_{r-1}) with a smallest lower bound $LB(J_{r-1})$, where each node (J_r) shows the set of sequences, each of them has a definite starting subsequence consisting of r definite jobs, and every $LB(J_r)$ is decided. Then a node (J_r) with a smallest $LB(J_r)$ is branched completely into $n - r$ nodes $\{(J_{r+1})\}$ according to what is the $r + 1$th job in the sequences among undefined $n - r$ jobs.

4. Finally, we have two nodes $\{(J_{n-1})\}$ on some same branch, each of them determines a feasible sequence (a permutation). Hence the smallest among two $LB(J_{n-1})$'s becomes a least upper bound f^* to date of the minimal makespan f_0.

5. In the solution tree constructed up to date, if there exists a nearest unbranched node (J_r) from the present node, which satisfies $LB(J_r) <$

f^* ($r = 1, 2, \ldots, n-2$), then backtrack to this node (J_r) and branch this node (J_r) completely as in step 3. Then proceed to step 6.

Otherwise, a node giving f^* determines an optimal sequence.

6. Generally if $\mathrm{LB}(J_r) \geqq f^*$ holds for every node (J_r) on the same branch just constructed ($r = 2, 3, \ldots, n-1$) then go back to step 5. Otherwise, proceed to step 7 ($r = 2, 3, \ldots, n-2$). In a case $r = n-1$, we obtain a $\mathrm{LB}(J_{n-1})$ which is smaller than the then f^*. Hence this $\mathrm{LB}(J_{n-1})$ becomes a new f^*. Then go back to step 5.

7. Branch completely a node with smallest $\mathrm{LB}(J_r)$ on that same branch ($r = 2, 3, \ldots, n-2$) as in step 3, then go back to step 6.

Remark. We may apply the frontier node search procedure in the same way of complete branching as in the above procedure.

9.5. Standard Lower Bound

This lower bound is determined by considering the successive processings of the remaining jobs on every machine and minimal processing time on subsequent machines. Hence this lower bound is also called machine-base lower bound. It is expressed as below:

$$\mathrm{LB}(J_r) = \max_{k=1\sim m} \left[C_k(J_r) + \sum_{i\in J_r} p_{i,k} + \min_{i\in J_r} \sum_{q=k+1}^{m} p_{i,q} \right], \qquad (9.1)$$

$$(r = 1, 2, \ldots, n-1)$$

where J_r is a presubsequence of definite r jobs among n jobs, $C_k(J_r)$ is a completion time of this subsequence J_r on machine M_k, which is computed by the relation (7.1) at Section 7.3 in Chapter 7, and $\bar{J}_r$ shows the set of remaining $n-r$ jobs.

The reasons that (9.1) is a lower bound of the makespans of all sequences with definite presubsequence J_r, which is associated with a node J_r, are the following: Let $\mathrm{LB}_k(J_r)$ be a finishing time of the processing on machine M_m in the case when initially all jobs in $\bar{J}_r$ are processed continuously, that is, without idle time, on M_k after the time $C_k(J_r)$ and then a job $i_0^k \in \bar{J}_r$ with minimal sum of processing times on subsequent machines $\mathrm{M}_{k+1}, \mathrm{M}_{k+2}, \ldots, \mathrm{M}_m$ is processed on these machines without waiting times (Fig. 9.5), then since any sequence of all jobs in $\bar{J}_r$ may produce idle times on M_k after the time $C_k(J_r)$. Also its last job may have a sum of processing times on subsequent machines which is not smaller than the sum for a job i_0^k, every $\mathrm{LB}_k(J_r)$ ($k = 1, 2, \ldots, m-1$) becomes a lower bound. Also $\mathrm{LB}_m(J_r)$, which is defined as a finishing time of the processing on M_m in the case when all jobs in $\bar{J}_r$ are continuously processed on M_m after the time $C_m(J_r)$, is a lower bound since usually the processing of jobs in $\bar{J}_r$ makes idle times on M_m. Hence $\max\limits_{k=1, 2, \ldots, m} \mathrm{LB}_k(J_r) = \mathrm{LB}(J_r)$ becomes a lower bound.

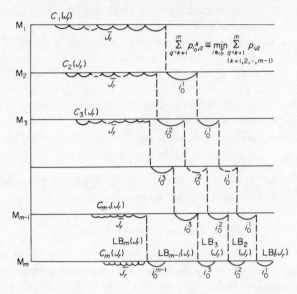

FIG. 9.5

Here it must be noticed that any definite presubsequence J_{n-1} determines a sequence ω, for which $LB(J_{n-1}) = M(\omega)$, makespan of ω, holds (Exercise 1).

EXAMPLE 1. For the present 6×3 problem with processing times shown in Table 9.1, determine an optimal sequence with minimal makespan by a BAB algorithm which uses standard lower bound (9.1).

TABLE 9.1

i	1	2	3	4	5	6
$p_{i,1}$	5	6	30	2	3	4
$p_{i,2}$	8	30	4	5	10	1
$p_{i,3}$	20	6	5	3	4	4

Solution. By using lower bound (9.1), that is,

$$LB(J_r) = \max \begin{bmatrix} C_1(J_r) + \sum_{i \in J_r} p_{i,1} + \min_{i \in J_r} \sum_{q=2}^{3} p_{i,q}, \\ C_2(J_r) + \sum_{i \in J_r} p_{i,2} + \min_{i \in J_r} p_{i,3}, \\ C_3(J_r) + \sum_{i \in J_r} p_{i,3} \end{bmatrix}, \; (r = 1, 2, \ldots, 5)$$

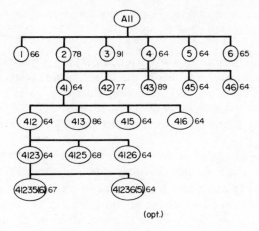

(opt.)

FIG. 9.6

we obtain a solution tree in Fig. 9.6 and an optimal sequence 412365 with makespan 64. Lower bound for every node in this solution tree is shown beside a related node.

Exercise

1. Show that $LB(J_{n-1}) = M(\omega)$ holds for the sequence ω determined by a J_{n-1}.

9.6. Efficiency of BAB Algorithm

The following are related to the efficiency of any BAB algorithm for the minimization problem.

1. *Exactness of lower bound.* If we use as large a lower bound as possible, then generally the number of nodes in the related solution tree becomes smaller (cf. Section 9.8). Also $LB(J_{n-1})$ must equal a value of a feasible sequence determined by related subsequence J_{n-1}.

2. *Easy computability of lower bound.* Generally this is opposed to exactness. Hence it is necessary to make them in harmony.

3. *Effectiveness of the branching procedure.* First it must be decided which of three procedures described in Section 9.3 to use. Then it is useful to find some effective rule for determining a node to be branched when there exist more than one node with smallest lower bound. However, usually the determination of a node to be branched among equivalent nodes is made by following the job-numbers in increasing order. Therefore, if we renumber the job-numbers according to some suboptimal sequence, then we may obtain an

optimal sequence more quickly. For this purpose we can use an approximate sequence (cf. Section 10.12 of Chapter 10).

McMahan and Burton proposed to renumber the job-numbers according to either of the following four rules in the three-machine case: (1) increasing order of $p_{i,1}$; (2) decreasing order of $p_{i,3} - p_{i,1}$; (3) decreasing order of $p_{i,3}$; (4) increasing order of $(p_{i,3} - p_{i,1})/(p_{i,1} + p_{i,2} + p_{i,3})$, where rule 1 seems to make computation time smaller than by random numbering.

4. *Utilization of analytical results.* For the min-makespan problem, for example, we can utilize the definite order of two adjacent jobs (cf. Theorem 7 or 9 in Section 8.16 and Result 6 or Result 8 in Section 8.18 in Chapter 8) in order to exclude the nodes with the opposite order (cf. Example 2 in Section 9.8). Alternatively we can consider the utilization of dominance relation (elimination criteria) which allows us to exclude some subsets (nodes) or of an upper bound for the subset at every node. Also, by utilizing the result of Theorem 1 in the next section, if the sum of the processing times on the first machine M_1 is somewhat larger than that on the last machine M_3 in the three-machine case, we can determine an optimal sequence for the original problem where ordering is M_1, M_2, M_3, by inverting the order of an optimal sequence for a problem with ordering M_3, M_2, M_1, which was obtained by the BAB algorithm. For the above case it was reported by McMahon *et al.* that the computation time becomes somewhat smaller. Also when the values of given processing times are large, we can make them smaller by applying Theorem 2 in the next section and related computation time may become less.

5. *Utilization of EXTBAB method.* For a large problem we may determine a reliable approximate sequence by applying the EXTBAB method. Generally, we have to construct any efficient approximate algorithm (cf. Sections 10.12 and 10.13, Chapter 10).

9.7. Relations between Machine Order, Processing Times, and Optimal Sequence

The following theorem holds for the optimal sequence in the case when the given ordering $M_1, M_2, \ldots, M_m$ is inverted in the n job m machine min-makespan flow shop problem where no passing is allowed.

THEOREM 1. *Let* $\omega^0 = i_1^0 i_2^0 \ldots i_n^0$ *be an optimal sequence for the original problem with ordering* $M_1, M_2, \ldots, M_m$, *then an inverted sequence* $\omega_0' = i_n^0 \ldots i_1^0 i_1^0$ *becomes an optimal sequence for the problem of the same type where ordering is* $M_m, \ldots, M_2, M_1$, *and both makespans are equal to each other.*

Proof. Let $\omega = i_1 i_2 \ldots i_{n-1} i_n$ be any sequence for the original problem and a graph G_ω be a related graph which has mn nodes corresponding with mn operations and has directed arcs determined by the precedence relation decided by given ordering $M_1, M_2, \ldots, M_m$ and a sequence ω and two dummy nodes: a node 0 as a source node and a node $mn + 1$ as a sink node, where every directed arc $(0, i)$ $(i = 1, 2, \ldots, n)$ has a null length and every directed arc (i, j) $(i \neq 0)$ has a length of processing time of an operation i. (Figure 9.7 shows a graph G_{132} of a sequence 132 for the 3×3 problem).

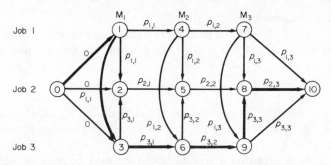

FIG. 9.7. Graph G_{132} of original problem for a sequence 132. Bold line shows a critical path.

Makespan $M(\omega)$ of ω is equal to the length of a critical path on G_ω (cf. Section 7.10 in Chapter 7). Hence, if we invert the direction of every arc in G_ω and exchange a source node and a sink node with each other, then we obtain a graph G'_ω, where the length of a critical path in G'_ω, which has an opposite direction to a critical path in G_ω, is equal to the makespan $M'(\omega')$ of a sequence $\omega' = i_n i_{n-1} \ldots i_2 i_1$ and we have $M(\omega) = M'(\omega')$. A sequence ω'_0 corresponding with an optimal sequence ω_0 for the original problem is optimal for the inverted problem.

Next, the following theorem, which shows that any optimal sequence is invariant even if every processing time is changed by a definite linear transformation, will be proved by the same reasoning as above.

THEOREM 2. *In the present problem, even if every processing time $p_{i,k}$ is transformed into $a(p_{i,k} + b)$, $a > 0$, $b > 0$ $(i = 1, 2, \ldots, n; k = 1, 2, \ldots, m)$, any optimal sequence is invariant and a solution tree by the same BAB algorithm is constant, where minimal makespan becomes $a\{M(\omega_0) + (n + m - 1)b\}$ from $M(\omega_0)$ for the processing times $p_{i,k}(i = 1, 2, \ldots, n; k = 1, 2, \ldots, m)$.*

Proof. Let $\omega = i_1 i_2 \ldots i_n$ be any sequence for the problem with processing times $p_{i,k}$, then, as in the proof of Theorem 1, length $L_\omega(P_\omega)$ of a critical path P_ω on a graph G_ω for ω is equal to the makespan $M(\omega)$. On the other hand, if we put n_k as the number of jobs on $M_k(k = 1, 2, \ldots, m)$ among the jobs (nodes) on some path P in G_ω, then only one job doubles on every pair (M_k, M_{k+1}) $(k = 1, 2, \ldots, m-1)$ which corresponds to a horizontal arc. Hence it holds

$$\sum_{k=1}^{m} n_k - (m-1) = n,$$

that is,

$$\sum_{k=1}^{m} n_k = n + m - 1$$

is constant independently of a path P.

Also the length $L_\omega(P)$ of a path P takes its maximum $M(\omega)$ when $P = P_\omega$. Since the length $L'_\omega(P)$ of a path on a graph G_ω for the problem with processing times $a(p_{i,k} + b)$ is equal to

$$L'_\omega(P) = a\{L_\omega(P) + (n + m - 1)b\},$$

it takes its maximum for $P = P_\omega$ and so a critical path P_ω for any sequence is invariant. By taking $\omega = \omega_0$, an optimal sequence for the original problem, ω_0 is invariant.

Also, since the relation of the sizes of the lower bounds used in a BAB algorithm, that include the summation, maximization and minimization, is invariant under the proposed linear transformation, the related solution tree is invariant. Also, from the above equation, minimal makespan changes to $a\{M(\omega_0) + (n + m - 1)b\}$.

Exercise

1. In Theorem 1 in Chapter 8, derive the case (b) from the case (a) and Theorem 1.

9.8. Revised Lower Bound and Composite Lower Bound

Concerning the exactness of the lower bounds, two bounds larger than the standard lower bound (9.1) in Section 9.5 are presented. One is a revised lower bound which makes the standard lower bound more exact on machine base and the other is a composite lower bound which adds new lower bound on job base to the standard lower bound.

1. Revised lower bound (RLB)

Although, in the standard lower bound, the remaining jobset $\bar{J}_r$ are continuously processed on the machine M_{k+1} $(k = 1, 2, \ldots, m-1)$ after the time $C_{k+1}(J_r)$, generally there exist idle times on M_{k+1} for the processing of the jobs in $\bar{J}_r$. Therefore, if we can include the lower bound of such idle times into our lower bound, then we can construct more exact lower bounds.

In this respect, a lower bound for these idle times can be determined when an optimal order of the jobs in $\bar{J}_r$ is processed on two machines M_k, M_{k+1}, where this optimal order is determined by a criterion for two machines M_k, M_{k+1}:

$$\min[p_{i,k}, p_{j,k+1}] \leqq \min[p_{j,k}, p_{i,k+1}], \quad (k = 1, 2, \ldots, m-1) \quad (9.2)$$

in case $\bar{J}_r$ is processed on M_k continuously after the time $C_k(J_r)$ and on M_{k+1} after the time $C_{k+1}(J_r)$ $(k = 1, 2, \ldots, m-1)$.

Let $\omega_{k+1}^k(\bar{J}_r) = i_{r+1}^k i_{r+2}^k \ldots i_n^k$ be an optimal order of $(n-r)$ jobs in $\bar{J}_r$ determined by a criterion (9.2) for two machines M_k, M_{k+1} $(k = 1, 2, \ldots, m-1)$ and the time C_{k+1} be a completion time of the order $\omega_{k+1}^k(\bar{J}_r)$ on M_{k+1} when it is processed continuously from the time $C_k(J_r)$ on M_k and after the time $C_{k+1}(J_r)$ on M_{k+1} (cf. Fig. 9.8). By putting an elapsed time from the time $C_{k+1}(J_r)$ to the above time C_{k+1} on M_{k+1} to $T_{k+1}^k(\bar{J}_r)$, we obtain the following revised lower bound $\text{RLB}(J_r)$:

$$\text{RLB}(J_r) = \max \begin{bmatrix} C_1(J_r) + \sum_{i \in \bar{J}_r} p_{i,1} + \min_{i \in \bar{J}_r} \sum_{q=2}^{n} p_{i,q}, \\[2mm] C_2(J_r) + T_2^1(\bar{J}_r) + \min_{i \in \bar{J}_r} \sum_{q=3}^{n} p_{i,q} \\[2mm] C_3(J_r) + T_3^2(\bar{J}_r) + \min_{i \in \bar{J}_r} \sum_{q=4}^{n} p_{i,q}, \\[2mm] \ldots\ldots\ldots\ldots\ldots\ldots\ldots\ldots, \\[2mm] C_{m-1}(J_r) + T_{m-1}^{m-2}(\bar{J}_r) + \min_{i \in \bar{J}_r} p_{j,m}, \\[2mm] C_m(J_r) + T_m^{m-1}(\bar{J}_r). \end{bmatrix} \quad (9.3)$$

$$(r = 1, 2, \ldots, n-1)$$

F<small>IG</small>. 9.8

The first term (a lower bound for M_1) is the same as in the standard lower bound ($k = 1$), and since every succeeding term in $RLB(J_r)$ is not smaller than that in the standard lower bound $LB(J_r)$ for the same J_r, we have

$$RLB(J_r) \geqq LB(J_r).$$
$$(r = 1, 2, \ldots, n-1)$$

for the same J_r.

Also, $RLB(J_{n-1})$ is equal to the makespan of a sequence determined by a subsequence J_{n-1}. In the calculation of $RLB(J_r)$, it is sufficient for identifying every optimal order $\omega_{k+1}{}^k(\bar{J_r})$ to decide an optimal sequence of all n jobs on two machines M_k, M_{k+1} in advance ($k = 1, 2, \ldots, m-1$).

Remark. As in the revised LB, we may utilize any optimizing criterion existing in the single-machine scheduling and two-machine flow-shop make-span scheduling problems in order to construct the lower bounds for the other problems. Cf. Section 9.12 and its reference.

Exercise

1. Check that, instead of the above definition of the time C_{k+1}, if the first $(n-r-1)$ jobs $i_{r+1}{}^k, i_{k+2}{}^k, \ldots, i_{n-1}{}^k$ are processed continuously from the time $C_k(J_r)$ on M_k and the last job i_n^k is just finished at the time C_k, which means that we decide these new C_ks according to the increasing order of $k(k = 1, 2, \ldots, m-1)$, then we can determine a larger $RLB(J_r)$.

II. *Composite lower bound* (CLB)

A lower bound constructed from standard lower bound by adding the following job-base lower bound is called a composite lower bound, where a job-base lower bound is

$$\max_{k=1, \ldots, m-1} h^{(k)}(J_r),$$

$$h^{(k)}(J_r) = C_k(J_r) + \max_{i \in \bar{J_r}} \left\{ \sum_{q=k}^{m} p_{i,q} + \sum_{j \in \bar{J_r}, j \neq i} \min(p_{j,k}, p_{j,m}) \right\}. \tag{9.4}$$

Hence composite lower bound $CLB(J_r)$ is expressed as

$$CLB(J_r) = \max \left[\begin{array}{l} \displaystyle\max_{k=1, \ldots, m} \left[C_k(J_r) + \sum_{i \in J_r} p_{i,k} + \min_{i \in J_r} \sum_{q=k+1}^{m} p_{i,q} \right], \\[2em] \displaystyle\max_{k=1, \ldots, m-1} \left[C_k(J_r) + \max_{i \in \bar{J_r}} \left\{ \sum_{q=k}^{m} p_{i,q} \right. \right. \\[1.5em] \left. \left. + \sum_{j \in J_r, j \neq i} \min(p_{j,k}, p_{j,m}) \right\} \right] \end{array} \right] \tag{9.5}$$

$$(r = 1, 2, \ldots, n-1)$$

The reason that the above $h^{(k)}(J_r)(k = 1, 2, \ldots, m-1)$ is a lower bound follows from the fact that, for any definite job i in $\bar{J}_r$, any job j in $\bar{J}_r$ preceding job i, which may be processed after job i, is processed on M_k with processing time $p'_{j,k} = \min(p_{j,k}, p_{j,m})$ and job i is processed on $M_k, M_{k+1}, \ldots, M_m$ without waiting times. Then after the job i on M_m succeeding job j in $\bar{J}_r$ is processed on M_m with processing time $p'_{j,m} = \min(p_{j,k}, p_{j,m})$ (cf. Fig. 9.9).

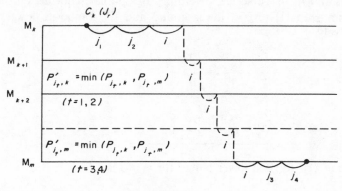

FIG. 9.9

Another definition of the job-base lower bound $\underline{h}^{(k)}(J_r)(k = 1, 2, \ldots, m-1)$ is

$$\underline{h}^{(k)}(J_r) = C_k(J_r) + \sum_{q=k}^{m} p_{ik,q} + \sum_{j \in J_r, j \neq ik} \min(p_{j,k}, p_{j,m}), \qquad (9.6)$$
$$(k = 1, 2, \ldots, m-1)$$

where

$$\sum_{q=k}^{m} p_{ik,q} = \max_{i \in J_r} \sum_{q=k}^{m} p_{i,q}.$$

which is not greater than the related $h^{(k)}(J_r)$. Hence, we can use the following simple composite lower bound:

$$\underline{\text{CLB}}(J_r) = \max[\text{LB}(J_r), \max_{k=1,\ldots,m-1} \underline{h}^{(k)}(J_r)]. \qquad (9.7)$$
$$(r = 1, 2, \ldots, n-1)$$

Obviously relation $\text{CLB}(J_r) \geqq \underline{\text{CLB}}(J_r) \geqq \text{LB}(J_r)$ holds for the same J_r. On the other hand, the relation between sizes of $\text{RLB}(J_r)$ and $\text{CLB}(J_r)$ for the same J_r is not uniquely determined. Also, any $\text{CLB}(J_{n-1})$ is equal to the makespan determined by a subsequence J_{n-1} for the same reason as for standard lower bound.

Remark. We can construct the lower bounds of another type as shown below: lower bound $\text{LB}(R_r)$ $(r = 1, 2, \ldots, n-1)$ of the makespans of all sequences that have a common subsequence R_r consisting of the last r definite jobs and/or lower bound $\mathrm{LB}(J_r, R_s$ $(r+s = 1, 2, \ldots, n-1)$ of the make-spans of all sequences that have two common subsequences J_r, R_s, where J_r consists of the first r definite jobs and R_s consists of the last s definite jobs.

EXAMPLE 2. In the present 6×3 min-makespan problem with processing times as shown in Table 9.2, determine an optimal sequence by the BAB algorithm with (1) revised lower bound and (2) composite lower bound respectively.

TABLE 9.2

i	1	2	3	4	5	6
$p_{i,1}$	6	12	4	3	6	2
$p_{i,2}$	7	2	6	11	8	14
$p_{i,3}$	3	3	8	7	10	12

Solution (1). Revised lower bound for $m = 3$ is

$$\mathrm{RLB}(J_r) = \max \begin{bmatrix} C_1(J_r) + \sum_{i \in J_r} p_{i,1} + \min_{i \in \bar{J}_r} \sum_{q=2}^{3} p_{i,q}, \\ C_2(J_r) + T_2^1(\bar{J}_r) + \min_{i \in \bar{J}_r} p_{i,3}, \\ C_3(J_r) + T_3^2(\bar{J}) \end{bmatrix},$$

$$r = 1, 2, \ldots, 5.$$

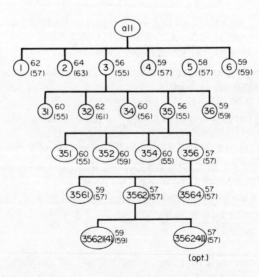

(opt.)

FIG. 9.10

In order to calculate $T^1_2(J_r), T^2_3(J_r)$, we determine, say, an optimal sequence 643152 for M_1, M_2 and an optimal sequence 235641 for M_2, M_3. Then a solution tree becomes as in Fig. 9.10 and we obtain an optimal sequence 356241 with minimal makespan 57 under the least node searching, that is, twenty nodes, in this case.

In Fig. 9.10 the number in every parenthesis shows the related standard lower bound, for the ease of comparison with every revised lower bound written above.

Solution (2). Composite lower bound for $m = 3$ is

$$
\text{CLB}(J_r) = \max
\begin{bmatrix}
C_1(J_r) + \sum_{i \in J_r} p_{i,1} + \min_{i \in J_r} \sum_{q=2}^{3} p_{i,q}, \\[2ex]
C_2(J_r) + \sum_{i \in J_r} p_{i,2} + \min_{i \in J_r} p_{i,3}, \\[2ex]
C_3(J_r) + \sum_{i \in J_r}^{3} p_{i,3}, \\[2ex]
C_1(J_r) + \max_{i \in J_r} \left\{ \sum_{q=1}^{3} p_{i,q} + \sum_{j \in J_r, \, j \neq i} \min (p_{j,1}, p_{j,3}) \right\}, \\[2ex]
C_2(J_r) + \max_{i \in J_r} \left\{ \sum_{q=2}^{3} p_{i,q} + \sum_{j \in J_r, j \neq i} \min (p_{j,2}, p_{j,3}) \right\},
\end{bmatrix}
$$

$r = 1, 2, \ldots, 5$.

In this example, the related solution tree happened to be the same as in case (1) and it happened to hold $\text{CLB}(J_r) = \underline{\text{CLB}}(J_r) = \text{RLB}(J_r)$ at every node J_r.

Remark. Application of definite order Theorems 7 and 9 in Chapter 8.

If we apply any of the above two theorems, definite orders in optimal sequence become 31, 35, 41, 51, 61 and 64. In the solution tree by $\text{RLB}(J_r)$ or $\text{CLB}(J_r)$ in Fig. 9.10, these definite orders are naturally satisfied. However, if we would use standard lower bound in the example, then we would not need to consider the nodes 314, 315 and 316 when a node 31 would be branched and so we could save the computation time.

Computationally these definite order theorems are effective if we apply them in addition to a revised lower bound.

Exercises

1. Verify the result in Theorem 1 in Section 9.7 for the original problem in Example 2.

2. Determine an optimal sequence for the present 6×3 min-makespan problem with the processing times shown in Table 9.3.

TABLE 9.3

i	1	2	3	4	5	6
$p_{i,1}$	5	3	12	2	9	11
$p_{i,2}$	9	8	10	6	3	1
$p_{i,3}$	6	2	4	12	7	3

9.9. Backtrack Programming and Lexicographical Search Method

In addition to the BAB algorithm as a solution method for the $n \times m$ min-makespan flow-shop permutation problem, there exists an algorithm by backtrack programming (BP algorithm), or equivalently a lexicographical search method (LS method). As is clear from the solution tree (Fig. 9.10) in Example 2 in Section 9.8, a tree searched by the BAB algorithm becomes a tree shown in Fig. 9.11 for three jobs $\{1, 2, 3\}$ case. In this figure, say a node 123 determined by a subsequence 12 is connected to a node 12. Although the BAB algorithm first branches a root node consisting of all feasible schedules into all nodes (J_1), that is, nodes 1, 2 and 3 for the figure, decides a lower bound for every node, also branches a node with a smallest lower bound, and then makes up a related solution tree by following the procedure of the BAB algorithm, together with examining the nodes of the search tree in the order decided by the procedure of the BAB algorithm, any BP algorithm examines, as described in Section 3.11 in Chapter 3, the nodes of the search tree in a constant direction, such as the order of the nodes: 1, 12, 123, 13, 132, 2, 21, 213, 23, ..., 312, 32, 321 for the figure.

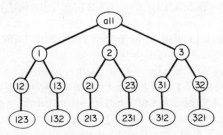

FIG. 9.11

We can regard this BP algorithm as a LS method for the reasons described below:

Let us consider the n job problem and let the n jobs be $1, 2, \ldots, n$ and express all sequences constructed by a definite presubsequence $i_1 i_2 \ldots, i_k$ of k definite jobs as the sequence $i_1 i_2 \ldots i_k i_{k+1} \ldots i_n$, where $i_q = 0 (q = k+1, \ldots, n)$ when $k < n$, then a lexicographical order of all these sequences is determined by the following dominance rule:

Dominance rule. Among the sequences with the same jobs $i_q (q = 1, 2, \ldots, k)$ for each k ($k = 1, 2, \ldots, n - 1$), a sequence with the smaller job-number i_{k+1} dominates the other jobs.

By this rule a LS method is considered to examine the needs in the search tree in the same order as by the above BP algorithm. Then this BP algorithm computes the lower bound of the makespans of all sequences at each node, makes the value of a makespan of a sequence first determined a smallest upper bound f^*, where up to this time we have $f^* = \infty$. Hence it compares a reduced f^* by a refined sequence with a lower bound of each subsequent node and prunes a subtree with a node N as its root only when we have $f^* \leq LB(N)$, where in a related LS method this pruning corresponds to the following rule: Let $\omega_k = i_1 i_2 \ldots i_{k-2} i_{k-1} i_k$ be a subsequence (a node N) with a lower bound which satisfies $f^* \leq LB(N)$ and let $\omega'_k = i'_1 i'_2 \ldots i'_{k-1} i'_k$ be the next subsequence and n_k be a maximum possible job-number for the kth job in the subsequence ω_k, then the next subsequence ω'_k to be followed after the excluded subsequence ω_k is determined by the following rule (cf. Example 3):

1. In case $k \neq n$, if $i_k \neq n_k$, then $i'_q = i_q (q = 1, 2, \ldots, k - 1)$ and i'_k is a job with the next larger job-number than i_k. If $i_q = n_q (q = k, k - 1, \ldots, r)$, then when $r \neq 1$, $i'_q = i_q (q = 1, 2, \ldots, r - 2)$ i'_{r-1} is a job with the next larger job-number than i_{r-1} and $i'_q = 0$ ($q = r, r + 1, \ldots, k$), and when $r = 1$ LS method terminates.

2. In case $k = n$, ω'_k is the next subsequence of ω_k in lexicographical order.

Remark. We can decide some dominance relation among subsequences depending upon the objective function (cf. Section 9.14). Generally the BP algorithm requires less computation time than the BAB algorithm.

EXAMPLE 3. For a present 4×5 problem with processing times shown in Table 9.4, determine an optimal sequence with minimal makespan by BP algorithm, or LS method.

Solution. In this example, we will use the last term of the standard lower bound as a lower bound for every node (subset) J_r. For $m = 5$

$$LB(J_r) = C_5(J_r) + \sum_{i \in J_r} p_{i,5},$$

TABLE 9.4

i	$p_{i,1}$	$p_{i,2}$	$p_{i,3}$	$p_{i,4}$	$p_{i,5}$
1	4	3	7	2	8
2	3	7	2	8	5
3	1	2	4	3	7
4	3	4	3	7	2

because this lower bound is effective since we have

$$\max_{q=1,\ldots,5} \sum_{i=1}^{4} p_{i,q} = \sum_{i=1}^{4} p_{i,5} = 22$$

in this example. However, $\mathrm{LB}(J_{n-1}) = \mathrm{LB}(J_3)$ is less than or equal to the makespan of the sequence determined by a subsequence $J_{n-1} = J_3$ for the above lower bound. Hence we must calculate the value of the makespan at every time we arrive at any sequence J_n. A solution tree by the BP algorithm becomes as shown in Fig. 9.12 and an optimal sequence is 3412 with makespan 33, where the number beside every intermediate node shows its lower bound. That beside every terminal node shows its makespan.

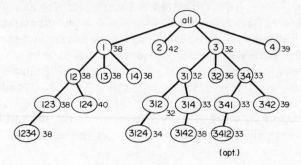

FIG. 9.12

TABLE 9.5

No.	Seq.	Comp. time on mach.					LB.	Make-span		f^*
		C_1	C_2	C_3	C_4	C_5				
1	1	4	7	14	16	24	38		<	∞
2	12	7	14	16	24	29	38		<	
3	123	8	16	20	27	36	28		<	
4	1234	11	20	23	34	38		38	<	
5	124	10	18	21	31	33	40		>	38
6	13	5	9	18	21	31	38		=	
7	14	7	11	17	24	26	38		=	
8	2	3	10	12	20	25	42		>	
9	3	1	3	7	10	17	32		<	
10	31	5	8	15	17	25	32		<	
11	312	8	5	17	25	30	32		<	
12	3124	11	19	22	32	34		34	<	
13	314	8	12	18	25	27	32		<	34
14	3142	11	19	21	33	38		38	>	
15	32	4	11	13	21	26	36		>	
16	34	4	8	11	18	20	33		<	
17	341	8	11	18	20	28	33		<	
18	3412	11	18	20	28	33		33	<	
19	342	7	15	17	26	31	39		>	33
20	4	3	7	10	17	19	39		>	

Next, if we apply the related LS method, it becomes as shown in the search table of Table 9.5 and we obtain the same result as by the above BP algorithm.

Remarks. 1. The effect of the BP algorithm seems to vary according to what we select as the lower bound.

2. If we decide the first f^* as a makespan 34 of an approximate sequence 3124 determined by a single criterion:

$$\min\left(\sum_{q=1}^{4} p_{i,q}, \sum_{q=2}^{5} p_{j,q} \right) \leqq \min\left(\sum_{q=1}^{4} p_{j,q}, \sum_{q=2'}^{5} p_{i,q} \right)$$

(cf. Section 10.12 in Chapter 10), then Nos. 2–7 in Table 9.5 are eliminated. Therefore, we can obtain an optimal sequence in less computation time.

3. This LS method requires less computation times than by the BAB algorithm with standard lower bound (cf. Reference).

Exercises

1. Solve the Example 3 by the BP algorithm with another possible lower bound.

2. Solve the problem in Exercise 2 in Section 9.8 by the BP algorithm and LS method respectively.

9.10. *m* Machine Min-Mean Completion Time Problem

In this section, some analytical results and a BAB algorithm for the $n \times m$ min-mean completion (finishing) time flow-shop permutation problem are presented. For the two-machine case ($m = 2$), without loss of generality, we can assume the above permutation scheduling, which means that no passing is allowed (cf. Section 7.2 in Chapter 7). Also any sequence minimizing mean completion time minimizes mean waiting time, mean flow time and mean lateness (cf. Section 4.3 in Chapter 4).

Let $\omega = i_1 i_2 \ldots i_n$ be any sequence and $C_{i_q} \equiv C_m(i_q)$ be the completion time of job i_q ($q = 1, 2, \ldots, n$) on the last machine M_m, then, since mean completion time is

$$\overline{C} = \sum_{q=1}^{n} C_{i_q}/n,$$

it is sufficient to minimize the sum of completion times:

$$n\overline{C} = \sum_{q=1}^{n} C_{i_q}.$$

In the following, we present a lemma which is necessary to compute the lower bound in the BAB algorithm, analytical results and a BAB algorithm.

9.11. A Lemma and Analytical Results

LEMMA. *Let* $\{a_t\}$ $(t = 1, 2, \ldots, n)$ *be a strictly decreasing sequence* $(a_1 > a_2 > \ldots > a_n)$, b_i $(i = 1, 2, \ldots, n)$ *be the constants and* $\omega = i_1 i_2 \ldots i_n$ *be any permutation of* n *numbers* $1, 2, \ldots, n$, *then a permutation which minimizes*

$$f(\omega) = \sum_{t=1}^{n} a_t b_{i_t}$$

is a permutation which satisfies $b_{i_1} \leq b_{i_2} \leq \ldots \leq b_{i_n}$.

Proof. For a permutation $\omega = i_1 i_2 \ldots i_n$, when we have inequalities $b_{i_t} \leq b_{i_{t+1}}$ $(t = 1, 2, \ldots, j-1)$ and $b_{i_j} > b_{i_{j+1}}$ for some j $(j = 1, 2, \ldots, n-1)$ let ω' be a permutation constructed by exchanging i_j and i_{j+1} in ω, then we have

$$f(\omega) - f(\omega') = a_j(b_{i_j} - b_{i_{j+1}}) + a_{j+1}(b_{i_{j+1}} - b_{i_j}) = (a_j - a_{j+1})(b_{i_j} - b_{i_{j+1}}) > 0.$$

Hence ω' which satisfies $b_{i_t} \leq b_{i_{t+1}}$ $(t = 1, 2, \ldots, j-1, j)$ must be taken for ω for our purpose. Since a criterion that if $b_{i_j} \leq b_{i_{j+1}}$ holds then i_j precedes i_{j+1} satisfies obviously the transitive property, the conclusion of the lemma follows by this criterion.

Next we show some analytical results derived from this lemma.

THEOREM 3. *When n jobs are processed continuously on a single machine, an optimal sequence which minimizes mean completion time can be determined by processing n jobs in nondecreasing order of their processing times.*

Proof. Let p_i be a processing time of job i $(i = 1, 2, \ldots, n)$, then since the sum of completion times of all jobs in any sequence $\omega = i_1 i_2, \ldots, i_n$ is

$$n\bar{C} = \sum_{p=1}^{n} C(i_p) = p_{i_1} + (p_{i_1} + p_{i_2}) + (p_{i_1} + p_{i_2} + p_{i_3}) + \ldots + (p_{i_1} + p_{i_2} + p_{i_3} + \ldots + p_{i_n})$$

$$= n p_{i_1} + (n-1) p_{i_2} + (n-2) p_{i_3} + \ldots + 2 p_{i_{n-1}} + p_{i_{n-1}}$$

$$= \sum_{t=1}^{n} (n - t + 1) p_{i_t}$$

the conclusion follows from the lemma, where $a_t = n - t + 1$ and $b_{i_t} = p_{i_t}$.

THEOREM 4. *In the present $n \times m$ problem $(m \geq 2)$, if the following $m-1$ inequalities hold for a certain constant $h(h = 0, 1, \ldots, m-1)$:*

$$\min_i p_{i,k} \geq \max_i p_{i,k+1} \quad (k = 1, 2, \ldots, h) \tag{9.8}$$

$$\min_i \sum_{q=2}^{h+2} p_{i,q} \geqq \max_i \sum_{q=1}^{h+1} p_{i,q} \qquad (9.9)$$

$$\min_i p_{i,k} \geqq \max_i p_{i,k+1} \quad (k = h+2, \ldots, m-1) \qquad (9.10)$$

We have an optimal sequence by the following rule:

1. When $h \neq m-1$, let $\omega^0 = i_1^0 i_2^0 \ldots, i_n^0$ be a sequence constructed by arranging n jobs on the machine M_{h+2} in nondecreasing order with the processing times $p_{i,h+2}$ $(i = 1, 2, \ldots, n)$, then an optimal sequence is a sequence with least mean completion time among n sequences $\omega_p^0 = i_p^0, i_1^0, \ldots, i_n^0$ $(p = 1, 2, \ldots, n)$ determined by shifting only one job i_p^0 in ω^0 to the top of the sequence ω^0.

2. When $h = m-1$, an optimal sequence is determined by arranging n jobs in nondecreasing order with the processing times $p_{i,1}$ $(i = 1, 2, \ldots,)$ on the first machine M_1.

Remark. Conditions (9.8), (9.9) and (9.10) reduce to (9.9) and (9.10) for $h = 0$, (9.8) and (9.9) for $h = m-2$, and (9.8) for $h = m-1$.

1. *Proof.* When $h \neq m-1$, from the conditions the processing of any sequence $\omega = i_1 i_2 \ldots, i$ on M_{h+2} is made continuously without idle times of M_{h+2} as shown in Fig. 9.13 and we can obtain the following expression of the sum of completion times for the sequence ω:

$$\sum_{p=1}^{n} C(i_p) \equiv \sum_{p=1}^{n} C_m(i_p) = C_m(i_1) + (C_{h+2}(i_1) + p_{i_2,h+2} + \sum_{q=h+3}^{m} p_{i_2,q})$$

$$+ (C_{h+2}(i_1) + \sum_{t=2}^{3} p_{it,h+2} + \sum_{q=h+3}^{m} p_{i_3,q}) + \ldots + (C_{h+2}(i_1)$$

$$+ \sum_{t=2}^{n} p_{it,h+2} + \sum_{q=h+3}^{m} p_{i_n,q}) \qquad (9.11)$$

$$= C_m(i_1) + (n-1)C_{h+2}(i_1) + \sum_{t=2}^{n} (n-t+1)p_{it,h+2}$$

$$+ \sum_{q=h+3}^{m} \sum_{t=2}^{n} p_{it,q}.$$

Now if we fix the first job i_1, then the terms $C_m(i_1)$, $(n-1)C_{h+2}(i_1)$ and the last term in the right side of (9.11) are constant. Hence it is sufficient to minimize the third term in order to minimize the sum of the completion times, (9.11). Then this is achieved, from the lemma, by arranging the jobs $i_t (t = 2, 3, \ldots, n)$ in nondecreasing order of the processing times $p_{i_t,h+2}$ $(t = 2, 3, \ldots, n)$.

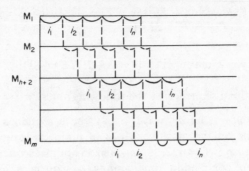

FIG. 9.13

Therefore, by first arranging n jobs in nondecreasing order of $p_{i, h+2}$ ($i = 1, 2, \ldots, n$), the conclusion follows.

2. When $h = m - 1$, from the condition (9.8) as shown in Fig. 9.14, the sum of completion times for the above sequence ω becomes as below by the same computation as for the single machine case:

$$\sum_{p=1}^{n} C(i_p) = \sum_{t=1}^{n} (n - t + 1)p_{it, 1} + \sum_{q=2}^{m} \sum_{t=1}^{n} p_{it, q}.$$

Since the second term on the right side is constant, it is sufficient to minimize the first term by arranging n jobs in nondecreasing order of $p_{i, 1}$'s ($i = 1, 2, \ldots, n$) for our purpose.

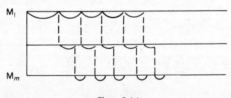

FIG. 9.14

Remark. We can determine an optimal sequence in a polynomial-time $0\,(n^2)$ in the special case of Theorem 4.

9.12. A BAB Algorithm

1. *Procedure of a BAB algorithm.* The BAB algorithm for the min-makespan problem in Section 9.4 is applied also in the present problem. Its outline is as follows:

A root node (J_0) of the solution tree shows the set of all sequences. A node (J_0) is branched into n nodes $\{(J_1)\}$ where every node (J_1) is assigned each job J_1 among n jobs as the first job in the sequences contained in this (J_1).

Then a node (J_1) with smaller lower bound $LB(J_1)$ is branched into $n-1$ nodes $\{(J_2)\}$ that are constructed according to which job in the remaining $n-1$ jobs is assigned as the second job of the sequences, where J_2 shows a definite subsequence of the specified two jobs. Every node (J_2) expresses the set of sequences with common subsequence J_2. Then a node (J_2) with smallest lower bound $LB(J_2)$ is branched. In the same way, active new node search procedure is applied.

2. *Lower bound of the sum $n\bar{C}$ of the completion times of all jobs.* First, when any sequence $i_{r+1}i_{r+2}\ldots i_n$ of $n-r$ remaining jobs in the set $\bar{J}_r$ is processed after the completion time $C_1(J_r)$ of the definite subsequence J_r on the first machine M_1, the value of $n\bar{C}$ computed under the assumption that every job $i_{r+t}(t=1, 2, \ldots, n-r)$ is processed on the subsequent machines $M_2, M_3, \ldots, M_m$ without waiting times is not greater than the real value. That value of $n\bar{C}$ becomes as shown below, where a job l_r is the last job of J_r:

$$
\begin{aligned}
n\bar{C} = & \sum_{i \in J_r} C_m(i) + \{C_1(l_r) + p_{i_{r+1},1} + \sum_{q=2}^{m} p_{i_{r+1},q}\} + \{C_1(l_r) + p_{i_{r+1},1} \\
& + p_{i_{r+2},1} + \sum_{q=2}^{m} p_{i_{r+2},q}\} + \ldots + \{C_1(l_r) + p_{i_{r+1},1} \\
& + p_{i_{r+2},1} + \ldots + p_{i_n,1} + \sum_{q=2}^{m} p_{i_n,q}] \\
= & \sum_{i \in J_r} C_m(i) + (n-r)C_1(l_r) + \sum_{t=1}^{n-r} (n-r-t+1)p_{i_{r+t},1} \\
& + \sum_{t=1}^{n-r} \sum_{q=2}^{m} p_{i_{r+t},q}
\end{aligned}
$$

where the first two terms and the last term in the right side are constant regardless of the sequence. Here the third term is minimized, from the lemma, by arranging the $p_{i_{r+t},1}$ $(t=1, 2, \ldots, n-r)$ in nondecreasing order. Let this sequence be $i_{r+1}^1 i_{r+2}^1 \ldots i_n^1$, then a bound of $n\bar{C}$ becomes

$$
\sum_{i \in J_r} C_m(i) + (n-r)C_1(l_r) + \sum_{t=1}^{n-r} (n-r-t+1)p_{i_{r+t},1}^1 + \sum_{i \in J, q=2}^{m} p_{i,q}.
$$

This corresponds to the case $h = m-1$ in Theorem 4.

Next, the value of $n\bar{C}$ computed under the assumption that any sequence $i_{r+1} i_{r+2} \ldots i_n$ of the jobs in $\bar{J}_r$ is processed on the second machine M_2, after the time

$$
S_2(\bar{J}_r) \equiv \max[C_2(l_r), C_1(l_r) + \min_{i \in \bar{J}_r} p_{i,1}]
$$

continuously without idle times of M_2 and then every job i_{r+t} $(t=1, 2, \ldots, n-r)$ is processed on subsequent machines $M_3, M_4, \ldots M_m$ without waiting times is not greater than the real value. Hence, for the same reason as for the above lower bound, we obtain another lower bound

$$\sum_{i \in J_r} C_m(i) + (n-r)S_2(\bar{J}_r) + \sum_{t=1}^{n-r} (n-r-t+1)p^2_{i_{r+t},2} + \sum_{i \in J, q=3}^{m} p_{i,q}$$

where

$$S_2(\bar{J}_r) = \max [C_2(l_r), C_1(l_r) + \min_{i \in J_r} p_{i,1}].$$

and a sequence $i^2_{r+1,2} i^2_{r+2,2} \ldots i^2_{n,2}$ is a sequence determined by arranging $p_{i,2}, i \in \bar{J}_r$, in nondecreasing order. This corresponds to the case $h = 0$ in Theorem 4. In the same way for M_3, M_4, $\ldots$, M_m respectively we obtain the following lower bound $LB(J_r)$ $(r = 1, 2, \ldots, n-1)$ of the sum of the completion times:

$$LB(J_r) = \sum_{i \in j_r} C_m(i) + \max \begin{bmatrix} (n-r)C_1(l_r) \\ + \sum_{t=1}^{n-r} (n-r-t+1)p^1_{i_{r+t},1} + \sum_{i \in \bar{J}, q=2}^{m} p_{i,q}, \\ (n-r)S_2(\bar{J}_r) \\ + \sum_{t=1}^{n-r} (n-r-t+1)p^2_{i_{r+t},2} + \sum_{i \in \bar{J}, q=3}^{m} p_{i,q}, \\ (n-r)S_3(\bar{J}_r) \\ + \sum_{t=1}^{n-r} (n-r-t+1)p^3_{i_{r+t},3} + \sum_{i \in J, q=4}^{m} p_{i,q}, \\ \cdots\cdots\cdots\cdots\cdots\cdots\cdots\cdots\cdots\cdots \\ (n-r)S_{m-1}(\bar{J}_r) \\ + \sum_{t=1}^{n-r} (n-r-t+1)p^{m-1}_{i_{r+t},m-1} + \sum_{i \in J_r} p_{i,m}, \\ (n-r)S_m(\bar{J}_r) \\ + \sum_{t=1}^{n-r} (n-r-t+1)p^m_{i_{r+t},m}. \end{bmatrix} \quad (9.12)$$

$$(r = 1, 2, \ldots, n-1)$$

where a job l_r is the last job of the definite sequence J_r, a job i_{r+t}^k $(t = 1, 2, \ldots, n-r)$ is the tth job when $n-r$ jobs i in $\bar{J}_r$ are arranged in nondecreasing order of $p_{i,k}, i \in \bar{J}_r$.

Also each start time $S_k(\bar{J}_r)$ of the processing of the jobs in $\bar{J}_r$ on M_k is determined by the recurrence relation:

$$S_k(\bar{J}_r) = \max [C_k(l_r), S_{k-1}(\bar{J}_r) + \min_{i \in J_r} p_{i,k-1}] \quad (k = 2, 3, \ldots, m) (9.13)$$

where $S_1(\bar{J}_r) = C_1(l_r)$.

In particular, the $LB(J_{n-1})$ is equal to the sum $n\bar{C}$ of the completion times for a sequence determined by a subsequence J_{n-1}.

Remarks: 1. We can use the completion time $C_k(l_r)$ of a definite subsequence J_r, where a job l_r is the last job in J_r, instead of $S_k(J_r)$ $(k = 2, 3, \ldots, m)$ in the above lower bound. However, since $C_k(l_r) \leqq S_k(J_r)$ holds, we obtain a smaller lower bound.

2. For the two-machine case $(m = 2)$, the proposed lower bound (9.12) reduces to the lower bound due to Ignall and Schrage:

$$LB(J_r) = \sum_{i \in J_r} C_m(i) + \max \begin{bmatrix} (n-r)C_1(l_r) + \displaystyle\sum_{t=1}^{n-r} (n-r-t+1)p^1_{i_{r+t},1} + \sum_{i \in J_r} p_{i,2}, \\ \\ (n-r)\max\{C_2(l_r),\ C_1(l_r) + \min_{i \in J_r} p_{i,1}\} \\ \\ + \displaystyle\sum_{t=1}^{n-r} (n-r-t+1)p^2_{i_{r+t},2}. \end{bmatrix}$$

$$(r = 1, 2, \ldots, n-1)$$

3. As in the above lower bound (9.12), we may construct a lower bound by utilizing the situation in the (polynomially) solvable special case.

Exercises

1. For the 3×2 flow-shop problem with processing times shown in Table 9.6, determine an optimal sequence which minimizes the mean completion time.
2. Solve the problem given in exercise 1 by backtrack programming algorithm and lexicographical search method respectively.

TABLE 9.6

i	1	2	3
$p_{i,1}$	2	10	1
$p_{i,2}$	11	3	8

9.13. *m*-Machine Min-Penalty Cost by Tardiness Problem

In the $n \times m$ flow-shop problem where ordering is $M_1, M_2, \ldots, M_m$ and no passing is allowed, let $C_i \equiv C_m(i)$ be a completion time on M_m, of every job i $(i = 1, 2, \ldots, n)$, then the tardiness of job i is defined as $T_i = \max(C_i - d_i, 0)$, where d_i is a due-date of job i (cf. Section 4.3 in Chapter 4).

In the following, we consider the next two types as an objective function f concerning the tardiness of every job:

1.

$$f = \sum_{i=1}^{n} g_i(T_i),$$

where each $g_i(T_i)$ is a nondecreasing function and $g_i(0) = 0$, *that is*, $g_i(T_i)$ means a penalty cost by tardiness. In particular, it reduces to the weighted sum of tardiness when $g_i(T_i) = w_i T_i$, where w_i is a nonnegative constant, for every job i, that is, we have the min-weighted mean tardiness problem. Also, when all w_i are equal to one we have the min-mean tardiness problem.

2. $f = f(T_1, T_2, \ldots, T_n)$ where f is not decomposable to the type 1 and is a nondecreasing function of every $T_i (i = 1, 2, \ldots, n)$ and $f(0, 0, \ldots, 0) = 0$. In particular, when an operation f is a maximization, f becomes the maximum tardiness and then we have the min-maximum tardiness problem.

Remark. Concerning the lateness $L_i = C_i - d_i$ for every job i, note that a sequence which minimizes the mean completion time treated in the former sections also minimizes the mean lateness.

9.14. Backtrack Programming and Lexicographical Search Method

As an algorithm which can be well applied to any objective functions 1 or 2 described in Section 9.13, we give a backtrack programming algorithm (BP algorithm), or equivalently a lexicographical search method (LS method). When we applied these algorithms for the min-makespan problem in Section 9.9, a lower bound at every node, that is, subsequence, examined in lexicographical order, was successively compared with the then upper bound f^* of an optimal value. For the present problem the elimination of node (subsequence) is made by using the following dominance relation due to Gupta, in addition to the above comparison.

1. DOMINANCE RELATION

Let σ be any presubsequence, σi be a subsequence determined by arranging a job i after the subsequence σ and $C(\sigma i, m)$ be a completion time of the sequence σi on the last machine M_m, then the following recurrence relation holds as already shown in Section 7.3 in Chapter 7:

$$C(\sigma i, m) = \max \left[C(\sigma i, m-1), C(\sigma, m) \right] + p_{i,m} \tag{9.14}$$

where $C(\phi, m) = 0$.

LEMMA. *For a subsequence σ and a sequence ω, if*

$$f(\sigma) \geq f(\omega)$$

holds, then for any subsequent sequence π we have

$$f(\sigma\pi) \geq f(\omega)$$

where, say, $f(\sigma)$ is a value of the objective function f for the subsequence σ.

Proof. f is a nondecreasing function of every T_i, that is, every $C_i(i = 1, 2, \ldots, n)$, and the value of f increases when the number of jobs increases. Therefore

$$f(\sigma\pi) \geq f(\sigma)$$

holds. Then the conclusion follows from the assumption.

COROLLARY. *If $f(\omega) = 0$ holds, then a sequence ω is an optimal sequence.*

Proof. The conclusion is obvious from min $f = 0$.

THEOREM 5. *For a subsequence σ and a sequence ω, if*

$$f(\sigma i) \geq f(\omega) \tag{9.15}$$

holds for a job i not contained in σ, then, for any subsequent sequence π where $\pi \cap \sigma = \phi$, we have the dominance relation

$$f(\sigma\pi) \geq f(\omega). \tag{9.16}$$

Hence, if (9.15) holds it is not necessary to consider any sequence including presubsequence σ.

Proof. If $\pi = i\pi'$ holds, (9.16) follows from (9.15) since the value of $f(\sigma\pi)$ is larger than $f(\sigma i)$ from $T_j \geq 0$ for every job j in π'. Also when $\pi = j\pi'i\pi''$ holds, if $f(\sigma j) \geq f(\omega)$ holds then (9.16) follows from the lemma. Even if $f(\sigma j) < f(\omega)$ holds, since $C(\sigma j \pi' i, m) \geq C(\sigma i, m)$ holds from (9.14), generally T_i for the sequence $\sigma\pi$ is larger than T_i for the sequence σi. Hence $f(\sigma\pi) \geq f(\sigma i) \geq f(\omega)$ follows because f is a nondecreasing function of T_i.

COROLLARY. *If*

$$f(i) \geq f(\omega)$$

holds, then for any sequence ω' we have

$$f(\omega') \geq f(\omega).$$

Proof. Since ω' contains a job i the conclusion follows immediately from Theorem 5.

2. A BP ALGORITHM AND AN LS METHOD

Although the procedures are the same as in Section 9.9, we use $f(\sigma)$ as a lower bound of the values of f for any sequence with a subsequence σ. Then if $f(\sigma) \geq f^*$ holds for a subsequence σ which is not a sequence, where $\sigma = \sigma'kji$, then, from the dominance relation (9.16) in Theorem 5, where σ corresponds to $\sigma'kj$, we backtrack the search tree up to a node $\sigma'k(j+1)$ in case $j \neq n$, and in case $j = n$ we backtrack to a node $\sigma'(k+1)$. Also if we obtain $f^* = 0$ then a sequence giving $f^* = 0$ is an optimal sequence.

EXAMPLE 4. *Min-weighted mean tardiness problem.* As an example of the type 1, for the present 4×5 problem with processing times, due-dates and weights as shown in Table 9.7, an optimal sequence minimizing weighted mean tardiness

$$f = \sum_{i=1}^{n} w_i T_i / n$$

will be determined by the BP algorithm and the LS method respectively.

TABLE 9.7

i	$p_{i,1}$	$p_{i,2}$	$p_{i,3}$	$p_{i,4}$	$p_{i,5}$	d_i	w_i
1	4	3	7	2	8	28	2
2	3	7	2	8	5	33	3
3	1	2	4	3	7	17	4
4	3	4	3	7	2	20	5

Solution. It is sufficient to minimize

$$F = nf = \sum_{i=1}^{n} w_i T_i.$$

As an initial value of F^* we use the value 66 of F for a sequence 4321 which corresponds to the last node in the search tree. Then a solution tree by the BP

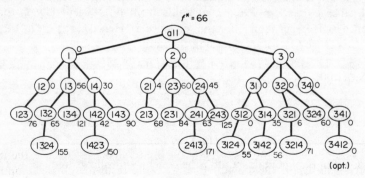

FIG. 9.15

algorithm becomes as shown in Fig. 9.15. Here $F(\sigma i) = nf(\sigma i)$ is used as a lower bound and we backtrack when $LB(\sigma i) \geq F^*$ because dominance relation (9.16) holds in this case. Since we have $F = 0$ (minimum) at node 3412 the procedure terminates and an optimal sequence is 3412 with $f_0 = 0$. Also the result by the LS method is shown in Table 9.8.

TABLE 9.8

No.	σ	i	C_1	C_2	C_3	C_4	C_5	$nf(\sigma i)$	$\begin{smallmatrix}\leq\\>\end{smallmatrix}$	f^*
1	ϕ	1	4	7	14	16	24	0	<	66
2	1	2	7	14	16	24	29	0	<	
3	12	3	8	16	20	27	36	76	>	
4	1	3	5	9	18	21	31	56	<	
5	13	2	8	16	20	29	36	65	<	
6	132	4	11	20	23	36	36	155	>	
7	13	4	8	13	21	28	33	121	>	
8	1	4	7	11	17	24	26	30	<	
9	14	2	10	18	20	32	37	42	<	
10	142	3	11	20	24	35	44	150	>	
11	14	3	8	13	21	27	32	90	>	
12	ϕ	2	3	10	12	20	25	0	<	
13	2	1	7	13	20	22	30	4	<	
14	21	3	8	15	24	27	33	68	>	
15	2	3	4	12	16	23	32	60	<	
16	23	1	8	15	23	25	40	84	>	
17	2	4	6	14	17	27	29	45	<	
18	24	1	10	17	24	29	37	63	<	
19	241	3	11	19	28	32	44	171	>	
20	24	3	7	16	21	30	37	125	>	
21	ϕ	3	1	3	7	10	17	0	<	
22	3	1	5	8	15	17	24	0	<	
23	31	2	8	15	18	24	30	0	<	
24	312	4	11	19	22	29	31	55	<	
25	31	4	8	12	18	25	27	35	<	55
26	314	2	11	19	27	35	40	56	>	
27	3	2	4	11	13	21	26	0	<	
28	32	1	8	14	21	23	31	6	<	
29	321	4	11	18	24	31	33	71	>	
30	32	4	7	15	18	30	32	60	>	
31	3	4	4	8	11	18	20	0	<	
32	34	1	8	11	18	20	28	0	<	
33	341	2	11	18	20	28	33	$0 = f_0$	<	

Remark. The differences l_i ($i = 1, 2, 3, 4$) of the sum of processing times from the due-date for every job i become as below:

$$l_1 = 24 - 28 = -4, \; l_2 = 25 - 33 = -8, \; l_3 = 17 - 17 = 0,$$

$$\text{and } l_4 = 19 - 20 = -1.$$

Hence if we first take into consideration the sequences that have the most severe job 3 at the top in common, then we could easily determine an optimal sequence 3412. Moreover, if we renumber the jobs according to the decreasing order of l_i we can directly obtain an optimal sequence. The above technique may be useful for the problem concerning due-dates.

EXAMPLE 5. *Min-maximum tardiness problem.* Again the data in Table 9.7 are used. An optimal sequence minimizing $f = \max_i T_i$ which is an objective function of type 2 will be determined by the BP algorithm. As a lower bound for a node σi, we use the most simple lower bound $\mathrm{LB}(\sigma i) = \max_{j \in \sigma i} T_j$ as in Example 4. Also we use the dominance relation (9.16), and an initial $f^* = 13$ is decided as the value of f for a sequence 4321. Then the solution tree becomes as in Fig. 9.16 with an optimal sequence 3412 ($f_o = 0$) since $f = 0$ (minimum) holds at node 3412. In the same way we can determine an optimal sequence 3412 by applying the LS method. Also we can determine this optimal sequence more quickly by renumbering the job numbers as described in the remark after Example 4.

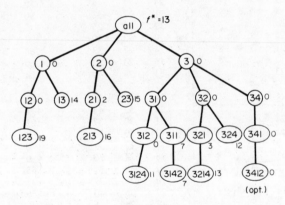

FIG. 9.16

Exercise

1. Solve example 5 by the LS method.

9.15. A BAB Algorithm and its Lower Bound

For both the min-mean tardiness problem and the min-maximum tardiness problem we can apply the BAB algorithm. This BAB algorithm creates every node by the same rule as for the min-makespan problem described in Section 9.4. A related lower bound is constructed as follows.

First we give a lemma and a theorem necessary to construct the lower bound.

LEMMA. *When $C_1 \leqq C_2$ and $d_1 \leqq d_2$ hold, let us define*

$$P = \max(C_1 - d_1, 0) + \max(C_2 - d_2, 0),$$
$$Q = \max(C_2 - d_1, 0) + \max(C_1 - d_2, 0);$$

or

$$P = \max[\max(C_1 - d_1, 0), \max(C_2 - d_2, 0)],$$
$$Q = \max[\max(C_2 - d_1, 0), \max(C_1 - d_2, 0)];$$

then $P \leqq Q$ holds.

Proof. 1. If $C_1 \leqq d_1$ and $C_2 \leqq d_2$ hold, then $P \leqq Q$ follows from $P = 0$ and $Q \geqq 0$.

2. If $C_1 \leqq d_1$ and $C_2 > d_2$ hold, then $P \leqq Q$ holds as is clear from Fig. 9.17.

3. If $C_1 > d_1$ and $C_2 \leqq d_2$ hold, then $P \leqq Q$ holds as is clear from Fig. 9.18.

4. If $C_1 > d_1$ and $C_2 > d_2$ hold, (a) when $C_1 > d_2$, $P \leqq Q$ holds as is clear from Fig. 9.19, and (b) when $C_1 \leqq d_2$, $P \leqq Q$ holds as is clear from Fig. 9.20.

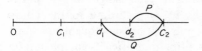

FIG. 9.17   FIG. 9.18

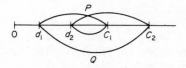
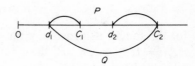

FIG. 9.19   FIG. 9.20

THEOREM 6. *In the assignments of k C_i's $(i = 1, 2, \ldots, k)$ to k d_j's $(j = 1, 2, \ldots, k)$, the minimum of*

$$\sum_{i=1}^{k} \max(C_i - d_i, 0),$$

or

$$\max_i \max(C_i - d_i, 0)$$

is achieved when $C_1 \leqq C_2 \leqq \ldots \leqq C_k$ and $d_1 \leqq d_2 \leqq \ldots \leqq d_k$ hold.

Remark. Note that two conditions in Theorem 6 correspond to the SPT rule (shortest processing time order) and EDD rule (earliest due-date order) in the single-machine scheduling problem.

Proof. If $d_l > d_m$ holds under $C_l \leqq C_m$ for any l, m, then the following inequalities must hold from the lemma:

$$\max (C_l - d_l, 0) + \max (C_m - d_m, 0) \geqq \max (C_l - d_m, 0) + \max (C_m - d_l, 0),$$
$$\max [\max (C_l - d_l, 0), \max (C_m - d_m, 0)] \geqq \max [\max (C_l - d_m, 0),$$
$$\max (C_m - d_l, 0)].$$

Hence $d_l \leqq d_m$ must hold under $C_l \leqq C_m$ for the minimum of any expression in the theorem. Consequently, the conclusion follows.

Now we proceed to construct the *lower bound* $\text{LB}(J_r)$ for every node (J_r) $(r = 1, 2, \ldots, n-1)$.

Let $f(J_r)$ be the sum of tardinesses or maximum tardiness for all jobs in a definite subsequence J_r. Now the remaining jobs in $\bar{J}_r$ are processed on one machine $M_k (k = 1, 2, \ldots, m)$ continuously after the time $C_k(J_r)$; completion time of J_r on M_k. In order to complete as early as possible, each tth job $(t = 1, 2, \ldots, n-r)$ of the sequence of $\bar{J}_r$ on M_k, it is sufficient to arrange all jobs i in $\bar{J}_r$ in nondecreasing order of their processing times $p_{i, k}$. Let $i^k_{r+1} i^k_{r+2} \ldots i^k_n$ be a sequence of all jobs in $\bar{J}_r$ according to the above arrangement. Then by processing its tth job i^k_{r+t} on subsequent machines $M_{k+1}, M_{k+2}, \ldots, M_m$, $k \neq m$, without waiting time after its completion on M_k, and by taking

$$\min_{i \in \bar{J}_r} \sum_{q=k+1}^{m} p_{i, q}$$

for the sum of its processing times on M_{k+1}, $M_{k+2}, \ldots, M_m$ for every job $i^k_{r+t} (t = 1, 2, \ldots, n-r)$, the completion time of the tth job i^k_{r+t} on the last machine becomes

$$C^k_t \equiv C_k(J_r) + \sum_{u=1}^{t} p^k_{i_{r+u}, k} + \min_{i \in \bar{J}_r} \sum_{q=k+1}^{m} p_{i, q} \quad (t = 1, 2, \ldots, n-r)$$

and this is a lower bound of the actual completion time of the tth job in any sequence of $\bar{J}_r$, where obviously $C^k_1 < C^k_2 < \ldots < C^k_{n-r}$ holds. Next, let $d_1 \leqq d_2 \leqq \ldots \leqq d_{n-r}$ be the nondecreasing order of the due-dates d_i of jobs i in $\bar{J}_r$, then, from Theorem 6, $f(\bar{J}_r)$, the value of f for all jobs in $\bar{J}_r$, becomes minimal when

$$T^k_i = \max (C^k_i - d_i, 0); \ i = 1, 2, \ldots, n-r$$

holds. Hence, we obtain the following lower bound $\text{LB}(J_r)$, where

$$\underset{t=1,\ldots,n-r}{f} \ (T^k_t) = \sum_{t=1}^{n-r} T^k_t, \text{ or } \max_{t=1,\ldots,n-r} T^k_t (k = 1, 2, \ldots, m):$$

$$
\mathrm{LB}(J_r) = f(J_r) + \max \left[
\begin{array}{l}
\displaystyle \operatorname*{f}_{t=1,\ldots,\,n-r}\left(\max\left[C_1(J_r) + \sum_{u=1}^{t} p^1_{i_{r+u},1} \right.\right. \\[3mm]
\left.\left. \qquad\qquad + \min_{i\varepsilon J_r} \sum_{q=2}^{m} p_{i,q} - d_t,\, 0 \right] \right), \\[6mm]
\displaystyle \operatorname*{f}_{t=1,\ldots,\,n-r}\left(\max\left[C_2(J_r) + \sum_{u=1}^{t} p^2_{i_{r+u},2} \right.\right. \\[3mm]
\left.\left. \qquad\qquad + \min_{i\varepsilon J_r} \sum_{q=3}^{m} p_{i,q} - d_t,\, 0 \right] \right), \\[4mm]
\cdots\cdots\cdots\cdots\cdots\cdots\cdots\cdots\cdots\cdots\cdots\cdots\cdots\cdots\cdots \\[3mm]
\displaystyle \operatorname*{f}_{t=1,\ldots,\,n-r}\left(\max\left[C_{m-1}(J_r) + \sum_{u=1}^{t} p^{m-1}_{i_{r+u},m-1} \right.\right. \\[3mm]
\left.\left. \qquad\qquad + \min_{i\varepsilon J_r} p_{i,m} - d_t,\, 0 \right] \right), \\[6mm]
\displaystyle \operatorname*{f}_{t=1,\ldots,\,n-r}\left(\max\left[C_m(J_r) + \sum_{u=1}^{t} p^m_{i_{r+u},m} - d_t,\, 0 \right] \right).
\end{array}
\right]
$$

$$ r = 1, 2, \ldots, n-1 \tag{9.17} $$

d_t in (9.17) shows the tth value in nondecreasing order of all due-dates d_i, $i \in \bar{J}_r$. Also, the lower bound $\mathrm{LB}(J_{n-1})$ is equal to the value of f for a sequence determined by J_{n-1}.

Exercises

1. In the same way as in the min-makespan problem in Section 9.8, we can construct a revised lower bound which is more exact than (9.17). Construct this revised lower bound.

2. Solve the problem in Example 4 in Section 9.14, where all weights $w_i = 1$ hold, by the BAB algorithm.

3. Solve the problem in Example 5 in Section 9.14 by the BAB algorithm.

Bibliography and Comments

Section 9.4
The procedure of the BAB algorithm for the problem was developed by
Z. A. LOMNICKI, "A branch-and-bound algorithm for the exact solution of the three machine scheduling problem", *Opnl. Res. Quart.* **16**, No. 1 (1965), 89–100.
E. IGNALL and L. SCHRAGE, "Application of the branch and bound technique to some flow-shop scheduling problems", *Opns. Res.* **13**, No. 3 (1965), 400–412.

Section 9.5
The standard lower bound for the three-machine case was presented in
Z. A. LOMNICKI, *op. cit.*
E. IGNALL and L. SCHRAGE, *op. cit.*

234   *Mathematical Aspects of Scheduling and Applications*

Section 9.6
For the effect of the approximate sequence and 4, see
G. B. MCMAHON and P. Q. BURTON, "Flow-shop scheduling with the branch-and-bound method", *Opns. Res.*, **15**, No. 3 (1967), 473–481.
For the dominance relation see, for example,
W. SZWARC, "Elimination methods in the $m \times n$ sequencing problem", *Nav. Res. Log. Quart.* **18**, No. 3 (1971), 295–305.
For the other types of the lower bound see
I. NABESHIMA, "On the bound of makespans and its application to m machine scheduling problem", *J. Oper. Res. Soc. Japan*, **9**, Nos. 3–4 (1967), 98–136.

Section 9.7
For Theorem 1 see
Z. A. LOMNICKI, *op. cit.*
For Theorem 2 see
E. IGNALL and L. SCHRAGE, *op. cit.*

Section 9.8
The revised lower bound was developed by
I. NABESHIMA, *op. cit.*
The composite lower bound was developed by
A. P. G. BROWN and Z. A. LOMNICKI, "Some applications of the branch-and-bound algorithm to the machine scheduling problem", *Opnl. Res. Quart.* **17**, No. 2 (1966), 173–186.
G. B. MCMAHON and P. Q. BURTON, *op. cit.*
Also refer to the next papers and their References:
B. J. LAGEWEG, J. K. LENSTRA and A. H. G. RINNOOY, KAN, "A general bounding scheme for the permutation flow-shop problem", *Opns. Res.*, **26**, No. 1 (1978), 53–67.
W. SZWARC, "Permutation flow-shop theory revisited", *Nav. Res. Log. Quart.* **25**, No. 3 (1978), 557–570.

Section 9.9
This lexicographical search method was developed by
J. N. D. GUPTA, "A general algorithm for the $n \times M$ flow shop scheduling problem", *Int. J. Prod. Res.* **7**, No. 3 (1969), 241–247.

Sections 9.10, 9.11 and 9.12
The content of these sections is found in
I. NABESHIMA, *Scheduling Theory* (in Japanese), Morikitä Shuppan, 1974, Section 4.3.
Also refer to
W. TOWNSEND, "A branch-and-bound method for sequencing problems with linear and exponential penalty functions", *Opnl. Res. Quart.* **28**, No. 1 (1977), 191–200.

Section 9.11
The lemma is found in
G. H. HARDY, J. E. LITTLEWOOD and G. POLYA, *Inequalities*, Cambridge University Press, 1952.
Theorem 3 was developed by
W. E. SMITH, "Various optimizer for single stage production", *Nav. Res. Log. Quart.* **3**, Nos. 1 and 2 (1956), pp. 59–66.

Section 9.14
This lexicographical search method was developed by
J. N. D. GUPTA, "Optimal flowshop scheduling with due dates and penalty costs", *J. Oper. Res. Soc. Japan*, **14**, No. 1 (1971), pp. 35–46.

Section 9.15
The content of this section is found in
I. NABESHIMA, *Scheduling Theory* (in Japanese), Morikita Shuppan, 1974, Section 4.4.

CHAPTER 10

Flow-shop Scheduling Problems: Unified Algorithms and Approximate Solutions

10.1. Introduction

We continue our discussions of flow-shop scheduling problems under different scenarios. However, in this chapter we exploit the state space transformations discussed extensively earlier to develop dynamic programming-type formulations for more generalized objective functions. Also, we discuss some approximate algorithms for min-makespan problem.

10.2. Unified Multistage Combinatorial Algorithms for Setup-time Imbedded Processing Times

In Chapter 9 we considered individual objective functions in the $n \times m$ flow-shop problem where no passing is allowed and applied the BAB algorithm, the BP algorithm and the LS method respectively. On the other hand, there exists a BAB algorithm on a disjunctive graph for the job-shop problem with any normal objective function, which can be applied also to the flow-shop problem. This BAB algorithm will be described in Section 12.21 of Chapter 12.

In the present flow-shop problem we can consider mean intermediate waiting time, or equivalently mean in-process inventory time, and mean idle time, in addition to any normal objective function defined in Section 4.3 in Chapter 4.

As an algorithm which can treat in a unified way these objective functions, we give a multistage combinatorial algorithm constructed from a formulation by the state transformation process described in Section 3.8 in Chapter 3. This algorithm takes the form of a multistage decision process by considering all permutations (states) for each combination of any k jobs at stage $k (k = 1, 2, \ldots, n)$. Since any presubsequence of an optimal sequence need not follow an optimal order of the jobs contained in this presubsequence, hence, by using the principle of domination in the state transformation process, only the permutations (states) that have the possibility of yielding an optimal sequence

235

at the final stage are transformed into the next stage. This transformation corresponds to the fundamental state equation. Consequently, the formulations presented in Sections 10.3 and 10.11 are examples of dynamic programming-type formulation for the scheduling problem.

10.3. A Formulation by the State Transformation Process

We decide the elements of the state transformation process in an n stage decision process as follows:

At state k $(k = 1, 2, \ldots, n)$, let S_k be a combination of any k jobs in n jobs and $\{S_k\}$ be a set of $\binom{n}{k}$ combinations S_k. For every S_k, let $P(S_k)$ be a permutation, or subsequence, of k jobs in S_k and let $\{P(S_k)\}$ be a set of $k!$ permutations $P(S_k)$. Also, we define $f(S_k)$ as a set of $P(S_k)$ capable of yielding the desired optimal sequence of n jobs. Particularly, for stage 1, they become $P(S_1) = j_1, f(S_1) = j_1$ for each $S_1 = j_1$. Now, let $F(P_i(S_k))$ $(i = 1, 2)$ be the value of the objective function F for any two subsequences $P_i(S_k)$ $(i = 1, 2)$ respectively, then, as shown in the following Section 10.4, there exists a simple function $g(F, P(S_k))$ for each objective function F, such that an inequality $g(F, P_1(S_k)) \leq g(F, P_2(S_k))$ yields a desired inequality $F(P_1(S_k)) \leq F(P_2(S_k))$.

Next, the principle of domination in this case becomes as shown below:

Principle of domination. I. For each combination S_k at stage k $(k = 2, 3, \ldots, n-1)$, the definition that a subsequence $P_1(S_k)$ dominates a subsequence $P_2(S_k)$ means that if $P_1(S_k)$ cannot yield an optimal sequence $P_2(S_k)$ also cannot. Equivalently by comparing two subsequence $P_1(S_k)$, $P_2(S_k)$, it is not necessary to consider any subsequence or sequence including $P_2(S_k)$ as its presubsequence, if we have the following m inequalities:

$$g(F, P_1(S_k)) \leq g(F, P_2(S_k)) \tag{10.1}$$

$$T_q(P_1(S_k)) \leq T_q(P_2(S_k)) \tag{10.2}$$

$$(q = 2, 3, \ldots, m)$$

where $T_q(P(S_k))$ is a flow time, already used in the analysis in Chapter 7, defined as the flow time of the last job of $P(S_k)$ during the processing on machines $M_2, M_3, \ldots, M_q$. Namely, it is an elapsed time from the completion time C_1 to the completion time C_q in Fig. 10.1.

The reason for the above inequalities (10.1) and (10.2) is that, since the value of F is not greater for $P_1(S_k)$ from (10.1) and $P_1(S_k)$ completes on every machine $M_q(q = 2, 3, \ldots, m)$ not later than $P_2(S_k)$ from (10.2), any sequence of n jobs containing $P_1(S_k)$ as a presubsequence has a value of F not greater than for the same sequence constructed from $P_2(S_k)$ as above. Hence, at stage k it is sufficient to consider $P_1(S_k)$ alone.

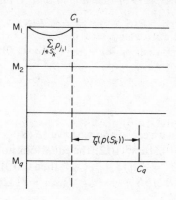

FIG. 10.1

II. For each combination S_n at stage n, the definition that a sequence $P_1(S_n)$ dominates a sequence $P_2(S_n)$ is obvious if we have an inequality (10.1); that is, $g(F, P_1(S_n)) \leqq g(F, P_2(S_n))$, which means that the value of F for $P_1(S_n)$ is not greater than for $P_2(S_n)$.

From the above definitions, we have for each $S_k, f(S_k) = G[\{P(S_k)\}]$ $\equiv ND\{P(S_k)\}$, where $ND\{P(S_k)\}$ is a set of subsequence $P(S_k)$ not dominated by any other $P(S_k)$. And we have $S'_k = S_k$, and $S_k - i$ is a set of $(k-1)$ jobs after excluding one job i from S_k and therefore equal to some S_{k-1}. Next, the operation H necessary to construct the fundamental state equation is defined as below in this case:

Operation H. Let a job i be each job in S_k, then an operation H is defined as an operation which constructs a direct sum of the sets $\{\{P(S_k - i)\}i\}$ of subsequences with every job i as its last job. That is, equation

$$\{P(S_k)\} = \underset{\substack{i \in S'_k \\ (S_k - i)}}{H} (\{P(S_k - i)\}, i) = \sum_{i \in S_k} \{\{P(S_k - i)\}i\} \qquad (10.3)$$

$$(k = 2, 3, \ldots, n)$$

holds. Since the restraint (R) is satisfied directly from the definition of H, we obtain the following fundamental state equation:

$$f(S_k) = G[\sum_{i \in S_k} \{f(S_k - i)i\}] \quad (k = 2, 3, \ldots, n) \qquad (10.4)$$

EXAMPLE 1. Examples of (10.3) and (10.4).

An example of (10.3) is shown in Fig. 10.2 for the case $k = 3$ and $S_3 = \{1, 2, 3\}$.

$$S_3 \qquad i \qquad \{P(S_3 - i)\} \qquad \{P(S_3 - i)\}i$$

$$\{1, 2, 3\} \quad \rightarrow \quad \begin{cases} 1 \rightarrow & \{23, 32\} \quad \rightarrow \quad \{231, 321\} \\ 2 \rightarrow & \{13, 31\} \quad \rightarrow \quad \{132, 312\} \\ 3 \rightarrow & \{12, 21\} \quad \rightarrow \quad \{123, 213\} \end{cases} \quad = \{P(S_3)\}$$

FIG. 10.2

Also, a S_2 is associated with each i and we have $\{P(S_3 - i)\} = \{P(S_2)\}$. Let, for each of these S_2, from (10.1) and (10.2), the equations hold $i = 1$, $f(S_2) = \{32\}$; $i = 2$, $f(S_2) = \{13, 31\}$; $i = 3$, $f(S_2) = \{12\}$, then (10.4) becomes, for example, as shown in Fig. 10.3, where $S_3 - i = S_2$. $f(S_3) = \{132, 123\}$ is a subset of the

set $\sum\limits_{i \in S_3} \{f(S_2)i\} = \{321, 132, 312, 123\}$, which was constructed by using the

dominance relations (10.1) and (10.2), and is a set of the subsequences $P(S_3)$ for $S_3 = \{1, 2, 3\}$ that can be the first three positions of the optimal sequence.

$$i \qquad \{P(S_2)\} \qquad f(S_2) \qquad f(S_2)i \qquad\qquad f(S_3)$$

$$\begin{array}{lllll} 1 \rightarrow & \{23, 32\} & \rightarrow & \{32\} & \rightarrow \{321\} \\ 2 \rightarrow & \{13, 31\} & \rightarrow & \{13, 31\} & \rightarrow \{132, 312\} \\ 3 \rightarrow & \{12, 21\} & \rightarrow & \{12\} & \rightarrow \{123\} \end{array} \Bigg\} \quad \rightarrow \quad \{132, 123\}$$

FIG. 10.3

Calculation of the value of flow time $T_q(i) = T_q(f(S_k - i)i)$ on $M_2, \ldots, M_q$ of the last job i of $f(S_k - i)i \equiv f(S_{k-1})i$ is made by the recurrence relation:

$$T_q(i) = p_{i, q} + \max[T_q(l) - p_{i, 1}, T_{q-1}(i)] \ (q = 2, 3, \ldots, m) \qquad (10.5)$$

where $T_1(i) = 0$, l is the last job of $f(S_k - i) \equiv f(S_{k-1})$, $T_q(l) = T_q(f(S_k - i))$, and $T_q(l) = 0$ when job i is the first job.

Remark. The above formulation remains valid under dominance condition (10.1) even in a single-machine case ($m = 1$).

10.4. Simple Function $q(F, P(S_k))$ for each Objective Function F

By defining each element as described in the former section, we can determine the optimal sequence with minimal F by successively using (10.4) in the former section for $k = 2, 3, \ldots, n$. In this case, we must decide the function $g(F, P(S_k))$ for each $P(S_k)$ in order to apply (10.1) for checking an inequality: $F(P_1(S_k)) \le F(P_2(S_k))$ for each pair $P_1(S_k), P_2(S_k)$ in $\{P(S_k)\}$ for every S_k at stage $k(k = 1, 2, \ldots, n)$.

In the following, we put $F_k = F(P(S_k))$ and $g_k = g(F, P(S_k))$, and let $S_k = \{1, 2, \ldots, k\}$ and $P(S_k) = 1 \ 2 \ldots k$ for simplicity.

I. *Makespan.* Since the first term of

$$F_k = \sum_{i=1}^{k} p_{i,1} + T_m(k)$$

is constant, we have $g_k = T_m(k) \equiv T_m(P(S_k))$. Hence (10.1) is included in (10.2) and the value of g_k is calculated by using (10.5).

II. *Weighted mean completion time.* It is sufficient to minimize the weighted sum $F = \sum_{i=1}^{n} u_i C_i (u_i > 0)$. Since we have

$$F_k = u_1\{p_{1,1} + T_m(1)\} + u_2\left\{\sum_{j=1}^{2} p_{j,1} + T_m(2)\right\} + \ldots + u_k\left\{\sum_{j=1}^{k} p_{j,1} + T_m(k)\right\}$$

$$= \sum_{i=1}^{k} u_i p_{i,1} + \sum_{i=1}^{k-1} \left\{p_{i,1} \cdot \sum_{t=i+1}^{k} u_t\right\} + \sum_{i=1}^{k} u_i T_m(i),$$

and its first term is constant, we have

$$g_k = \sum_{i=1}^{k-1} \left\{p_{i,1} \cdot \sum_{t=i+1}^{k} u_t\right\} + \sum_{i=1}^{k} u_i T_m(i).$$

Between g_{k-1} for the partial order $P(S_{k-1}) = 1\,2\,3 \ldots (k-1)$ and g_k for the order (subsequence) $P(S_k) = 1\,2\,3 \ldots (k-1)k$, the following recurrence relation holds:

$$g_k = g_{k-1} + u_k\left\{\sum_{i=1}^{k-1} p_{i,1} + T_m(k)\right\}.$$

By the relation g_k at stage k is calculated by g_{k-1} at stage $k-1$.

In particular for the mean completion time, or equivalently for the mean waiting time and the mean lateness respectively, F_k and g_k, become respectively

$$F_k = \sum_{i=1}^{k} p_{i,1} + \sum_{i=1}^{k-1} (k-i)p_{i,1} + \sum_{i=1}^{k} T_m(i) = \sum_{i=1}^{k} (k-i+1)p_{i,1} + \sum_{i=1}^{k} T_m(i),$$

$$g_k = \sum_{i=1}^{k-1} (k-i)p_{i,1} + \sum_{i=1}^{k} T_m(i), \; g_k = g_{k-1} + \sum_{i=1}^{k-1} p_{i,1} + T_m(k).$$

Also weighted mean lateness, where

$$F = \sum_{j=1}^{n} u_j(C_j - d_j) = \sum_{j=1}^{n} u_j C_j - (\text{const.})$$

can be treated in the same way as above.

III. *Mean intermediate waiting time.* It is sufficient to minimize the sum

$$F = \sum_{i=1}^{n} \sum_{q=2}^{m} w_{i,q}$$

of intermediate waiting times $w_{i,q}$ ($i = 1, 2, \ldots, n$; $q = 2, 3, \ldots, m$), where the first job of the order has no such times. Then since this sum $W(i)$ for any job i becomes (cf. Fig. 10.4)

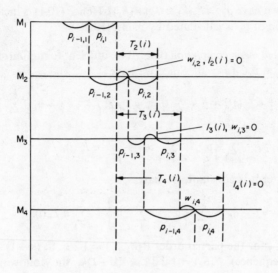

FIG. 10.4

$$W(i) = \sum_{q=2}^{m} w_{i,q} = (T_2(i) - p_{i,2}) + (T_3(i) - T_2(i) - p_{i,3}) + (T_4(i) - T_3(i) - p_{i,4})$$

$$+ \ldots + (T_m(i) - T_{m-1}(i) - p_{i,m}) = T_m(i) - \sum_{q=2}^{m} p_{i,q},$$

we have

$$F_k = \sum_{i=1}^{k} W(i) = \sum_{i=1}^{k} T_m(i) - \sum_{i=1}^{k} \sum_{q=2}^{m} p_{i,q}.$$

Since its second term on the right side is constant, we obtain

$$g_k = \sum_{i=1}^{k} T_m(i)$$

and the recurrence relation between g_k and g_{k-1} defined in II is

$$g_k = g_{k-1} + T_m(k).$$

For the other objective functions, associated F_k, g_k and/or the recurrence relation between g_k and g_{k-1} are shown in the following exercises.

Exercises

1. For the machine idle times, derive the following expressions:

$$F_k = k \sum_{i=1}^{k} p_{i,1} - \sum_{q=2}^{m} \cdot \sum_{i=1}^{k} p_{i,q} + \sum_{q=2}^{m} T_q(k),$$

$$g_k = \sum_{q=2}^{m} T_q(k) = \sum_{q=2}^{m} T_q(P(S_k)) \quad (k = 2, 3, \ldots, n).$$

2. For the weighted mean tardiness, derive the following for the weighted sum F of tardinesses:

$$F_k = \sum_{i=1}^{k} u_i \max \left[\sum_{j=1}^{i} p_{j,1} + T_m(i) - d_i, 0 \right],$$

$$g_k = F_k,$$

$$g_k = g_{k-1} + u_k \cdot \max \left[\sum_{j=1}^{k} p_{j,1} + T_m(k) - d_k, 0 \right].$$

3. For the maximum lateness and the maximum tardiness respectively, derive the following F_k respectively:

$$F = \max_{i=1,\ldots,n} L_i = \max_{i=1,\ldots,n} (C_i - d_i),$$

$$F = \max_{i=1,\ldots,n} T_i = \max_{i=1,\ldots,n} \max[L_i, 0] = \max_{i=1,\ldots,n} \max[C_i - d_i, 0].$$

Also derive for both F_k

$$g_k = \max_{i=1,\ldots,k} \left[\sum_{j=1}^{i} p_{j,1} + T_m(i) - d_i \right],$$

$$g_k = \max \left[g_{k-1}, \sum_{j=1}^{k} p_{j,1} + T_m(k) - d_k \right].$$

10.5. Relation between Min-Makespan Problem and Min-Other Objective Problems

As shown in the former section, among m conditions (10.1), (10.2) necessary for the order $P_1(S_k)$ to dominate the order $P_2(S_k)$ at every stage $k(k = 1, 2, \ldots, n-1)$, condition (10.1) is included in condition (10.2) for the min-makespan problem, which we call problem I, and both conditions (10.1) and (10.2) are necessary for another objective function case, which we call problem II. Hence the family $\{f(S_k)\}$ of the sets $f(S_k)$ that can yield the optimal sequence of problem I are included in the $\{f(S_k)\}$ associated with problem II. Consequently, at the last stage n, the sequence $f(S_n - i)i$ with least $T_m(S_n)$ among the set $\{f(S_n - i)i\}$ for problem II is an optimal sequence for problem I. That is to say, we can determine the optimal sequences for both problem II and problem I whenever we solve problem II.

10.6. Unified Multistage Combinatorial Algorithm

We obtain a unified multistage combinatorial algorithm of the dynamic programming type applicable to any objective function described above. This algorithm follows the fundamental state equation established in Section 10.3 and then takes the form of the following n stage decision process:

Stage 1. For each job $S_1 = j_1$, decide $f(S_1) = j_1$ and associated values of g_1 and $T_q(q = 2, 3, \ldots, m)$ and then store each ordered set $(f(S_1), g_1, T_2, T_3, \ldots, T_m)$ for the data at stage 2.

Stage $k(k = 2, 3, \ldots, n - 1)$. For each combination $S_k = (j_1, j_2, \ldots, j_k)$ of k jobs among n jobs, decompose an order (subsequence) set $\{P(S_k)\}$ into k subsets: $\{P(S_k - j_1)\}j_1, \{P(S_k - j_2)\}j_2, \ldots, \{P(S_k - j_k)\}j_k$ where, for example, $\{P(S_k - j_1)\} = \{P(S_{k-1})\}$, $S_{k-1} = (j_2, j_3, \ldots, j_k)$ and $i = j_1$. Then decide every $f(S_k - j_t)j_t(t = 1, 2, \ldots, k)$ from the respective subset defined above by using the results determined at the former stage. Next decide $f(S_k)$ for each S_k from dominance conditions (10.1) and (10.2) by comparing the values of g_k and $T_q(P(S_k))(q = 2, 3, \ldots, m)$ respectively. These are calculated by applying the respective recurrence relation for g_k and $T_q(q = 1, 2, \ldots, m)$. Then store each ordered set $(f(S_k), g_k, T_2, T_3, \ldots, T_m)$ for the data at the next stage.

Stage n. By following the above procedure, except that only one inequality (10.1) is used as the dominance condition in this stage, the set $f(S_n)$ for a unique combination S_n gives a set of optimal sequences.

The flow chart of this multistage combinatorial algorithm is shown in Fig. 10.5.

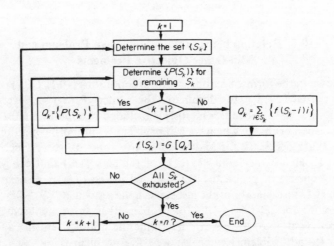

FIG. 10.5

10.7. Application to Parallel Scheduling

By the above combinatorial algorithm, we decide the set of optimal orders, $f(S_k)$, for every combination S_k of k jobs among n jobs at every stage $k(k = 1, 2, \ldots, n)$.

Although the usual scheduling problem is oriented to a single station, for example single shop, we can imagine the parallel scheduling problem which seems to minimize the maximum F among the minimal values of a given objective function at q identical stations. Here n jobs are dispersed into these q stations so that every station accepts at least one job. For this parallel scheduling problem we can apply the results at the first $(n - q + 1)$ stages in the above algorithm. Namely, by computing the value of F for every decomposition $(n_1, n_2, \ldots, n_q)$, $n_1 + n_2 + \ldots + n_q = n, n_j \geq 1 (j = 1, 2, \ldots, q)$ we can determine an optimal parallel scheduling by following a decomposition giving minimal F. An example will be given in the following section.

10.8. Numerical Examples of Min-Mean Intermediate Waiting-time Problem and Related Parallel Scheduling

In the 4×3 problem with processing times as shown in Table 10.1 relations

$$g_k = \sum_{i=1}^{k} T_3(i),$$

$$g_k = g_{k-1} + T_3(k)$$

TABLE 10.1

i	1	2	3	4
$p_{i,1}$	3	12	5	2
$p_{i,2}$	8	10	9	6
$p_{i,3}$	2	4	6	12

hold for the order $P(S_k) = 1\ 2\ 3 \ldots k$ and suborder $P(S_{k-1}) = 1\ 2\ 3 \ldots (k-1)$ as presented in III in Section 10.4. Then every set S_k, $f(S_k)(g_k, T_2, T_3)$ at stage $k(k = 1, 2, 3)$ becomes as follows:

Stage 1. 1, 1 (10, 8, 10); 2, 2 (14, 10, 14); 3, 3 (15, 9, 15); 4, 4 (18, 6, 18).

Stage 2. (1, 2), 12(24, 10, 14).   (2, 3), 32(29, 10, 14).

(1, 3), 13(28, 12, 18,), 31(31, 14, 16).   (2, 4), 42(32, 10, 14).

(1, 4), 14(34, 12, 24), 41(35, 11, 17).   (3, 4), 43(37, 10, 19).

Stage 3. (1, 2, 3), 321(41, 15, 17), 132(42, 10, 14). (1, 3, 4), 431(55, 15, 18).

(1, 2, 4), 412(49, 10, 14).   (2, 3, 4), 324(50, 14, 26),

                                             432(51, 10, 14).

Stage 4.   Here some explanations will be made. We look for $f(S_4), S_4 = (1, 2, 3, 4)$, with minimal g_4. First, g_4 for the order $f(S_4 - i)i$ for every $i(i = 1, 2, 3, 4)$ is computed.

(1) $i = 1$, $S_4 - i = (2, 3, 4)$.

Since $f(S_4 - i) = \{324(50, 14, 26), 432(51, 10, 14)\}$ from the result at Stage 3, we have $i(S_4 - i)i = \{3241, 4321\}$. Then, for 3241 we have $T_2(1) = 19$, $T_3(1) = 25$, $g_4 = 75$ and $3241(75)$. Similarly, for 4321 we obtain $T_2(1) = 15$, $T_3(1) = 17$, $g_4 = 68$ and $4321(68)$. In the same way we obtain as below:

(2) $i = 2$. $4312(72)$.
(3) $i = 3$. $4123(69)$.
(4) $i = 4$. $3214(72), 1324(68)$.

Hence, the set of optimal sequences becomes $f(S_4) = \{4321(68), 1324(68)\}$ and the associated minimal mean intermediate waiting time is

$$\left(68 - \sum_{i=1}^{4} \sum_{q=2}^{3} p_{i,q}\right)\bigg/ 4 = 2.075.$$

Next we consider a parallel scheduling for two identical flow shops under the above situation. Since $n - q + 1 = 3$, we perform the algorithm up to stage 3. Then $(f(S_{n_1}), f(S_{n_2}))$ and $\max(F_{n_1}/n_1, F_{n_2}/n_2)$ for every decomposition $(n_1, n_2), n_1 + n_2 = 4, n_1 \geq 1, n_2 \geq 1$, becomes as below, where F_{n_1}, F_{n_2} means the respective sum of intermediate waiting times.

(1, 324) max (0, 1) = 1.   (2, 431) max (0, 4) = 4.
(3, 412) max (0, 7/3). 7/3   (4, 321) max (0, 2/3) = 2/3.
(12, 43) max (0, 2) = 2.   (13, 42) max (3/2, 0) = 3/2.
(14, 32) max (3, 0) = 3.

Hence, an optimal parallel scheduling is (4, 321).

Exercises

1. Solve a min-mean completion time problem with processing times in Table 10.1 and a related parallel scheduling problem for two identical flow shops.

2. Solve a min-machine-idle-time problem in the same situation as in exercise 1.

10.9. Unified Multistage Combinatorial Algorithm where Explicit Setup Times Exist

In the following sections we give a unified combinatorial algorithm for the case where processing times do not include setup times, that is, setup times for each job depend on the prior job and on the processing machine in the flow-shop problem where no passing is allowed. This case is somewhat complicated, but a formulation by the state transformation process is possible as shown in the following sections and exercises.

10.10. Setup Times

Setup times for the processing of any job i on any machine M_k consist of the transportation time $t_{ji,k}$ and arrangement time $a_{ji,k}$, where job j is a job prior to job i, and when job i is the first job in the sequence we assume that $a_{ji,k} = 0(k = 1, 2, \ldots, m)$, and also we assume that $t_{ji,1} = 0$ for the processing of job i on the first machine M_1. That is to say, the start time of the processing of job i on machine $M_k(k = 2, 3, \ldots, m)$ is not earlier than the completion time of job i on machine M_{k-1} plus transportation time $t_{ji,k}$ of job i to the machine M_k and also is not earlier than the completion time of job j, prior to job i, on machine M_k plus arrangement time $a_{ji,k}$ for processing job i on M_k. Namely, it is the start time of job i on M_k. It is not earlier than both the time AT and the time CT on M_k as shown in Fig. 10.6.

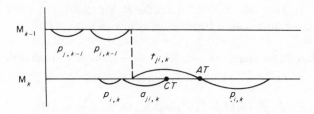

FIG. 10.6

10.11. A Formulation by the State Transformation Process

The main difference from the formulation for the case where processing times include setup times is that, at stage $k(k = 1, 2, \ldots, n)$, the set of all orders of any k jobs among n jobs is decomposed into n subsets, each of them contains the orders that have a common job $i(i = 1, 2, \ldots, n)$ as their last job respectively. Also in this case since every different job is successively ordered from the top of the sequence the formulation becomes a n stage decision process. The elements of the state transformation process are defined as follows:

At stage $k(k = 1, 2, \ldots, n)$, let S_k^i be a special kind of combination of k jobs among n jobs which consists of a definite job $i(i = 1, 2, \ldots, n)$ and a combination of the other definite $(k-1)$ jobs $(j_1, j_2, \ldots, j_{k-1})$. From this definition, S_k is denoted by S_k^i, and the number of all S_k^i is $n \cdot \binom{n-1}{k-1} = k \cdot \binom{n}{k}$. Let $\{S_k^i\}$ be a set of all S_k^i.

In practice, in order to construct every S_k^i, first a job i is defined, then every $k-1$ job $(j_1, j_2, \ldots, j_{k-1})$ is combined with this job i.

For each combination S_k^i, let $\{P(S_k)^i\}$ be a set of all orders (subsequences) $P(S_k)^i$ of k jobs in S_k^i that have job i as their last job and $f(S_k)^i$ be a set of $P(S_k)^i$ capable of yielding an optimal sequence.

Then, for each S_1^i ($k = 1$), we have

$$S_1^i = \{i\}, \qquad P(S_1)^i = i$$

and

$$f(S_1)^i = G[\{P(S_1)^i\}] = i.$$

Next, for each S_k^i ($k = 2, 3, \ldots, n$), as in the earlier section (Section 10.4) we can decide a simple function $g(F, P(S_k)^i)$ associated with each objective function F such that if

$$g(F, P_1(S_k)^i) \leqq g(F, P_2(S_k)^i)$$

holds, it follows

$$F(P_1(S_k)^i) \leqq F(P_2(S_k)^i)$$

where $F(P_t(S_k)^i)$ is a value of F for the order $P_t(S_k)^i$ ($t = 1, 2$) in $\{P(S_k)^i\}$. Then the principle of domination becomes as below in this case:

I. For each S_k^i at stage k ($k = 2, 3, \ldots, n-1$), if $(m+1)$ inequalities

$$g(F, P_1(S_k)^i) \leqq g(F, P_2(S_k)^i), \tag{10.6}$$

$$F_q(P_1(S_k)^i) \leqq F_q(P_2(S_k)^i), \quad (q = 1, 2, \ldots, m) \tag{10.7}$$

hold, then an order $P_1(S_k)^i$ dominates an order $P_2(S_k)^i$, where $F_q(P(S_k)^i)$ means a flow time of an order $P(S_k)^i$ on the first q machines $M_1, M_2, \ldots, M_q$ as shown in Fig. 10.7.

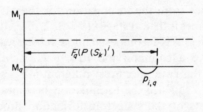

$$M_1$$

$$\longleftarrow F_q(P(S_k)^i) \longrightarrow$$

$$M_q$$

$$P_{i,q}$$

FIG. 10.7

II. For each S_n^i at stage n ($k = n$), if (10.6) for $k = n$ holds, then an order $P_1(S_n)^i$ dominates an order $P_2(S_n)^i$. Let $S_k' = i$.

Next, an operation H is defined, for each S_k^i, as an operation which makes a direct sum of all orders $\{P(S_k^i - i)^j\}^i$ that have job i as their last job, where

$\{P(S_k^i - i)^j\}$ is the set of all orders of $(k-1)$ jobs in a combination $S_k^i - i$ $= S_{k-1}^j$ that have every job j in $S_k^i - i$ as their last job, that is,

$$\{P(S_k)^i\} = \sum_{j \in S_k^i - i} \{\{P(S_k^i - i)^j\}i\}. \quad (k = 2, 3, \ldots, n). \qquad (10.8)$$

Hence restraint (R) is satisfied for each $k(k = 2, 3, \ldots, n)$ and so the fundamental state equation

$$f(S_k)^i = G\left[\sum_{j \in S_k^i - i} \{f(S_k^i - i)^j i\}\right] \qquad (10.9)$$

$$(k = 2, 3, \ldots, n)$$

follows. Then the set $f(S_n)$ of optimal sequences is determined only by (10.6) and we have

$$f(S_n) = G\left[\sum_{i=1}^{n} f(S_n)^i\right]. \qquad (10.10)$$

EXAMPLE 2. Examples of (10.8) and (10.9). Figure 10.8 shows an example of (10.8) for $n = 5$, $k = 4$ and $i = 1$.

Next, in Figure 10.8 let $P(S_k^i - i)^j = P(S_{k-1})^j$ and let us assume that, for example, we have $f(S_{k-1})^2 = \{432\}, f(S_{k-1})^3 = \{243\}$ and $f(S_{k-1})^4 = \{234, 324\}$, for $S_k^i = \{2, 3, 4, 1\}$, from the former stage, then (10.9) becomes as shown in Fig. 10.9 when $f(S_k)^i = \{2431, 2341\}$.

i	$S_k{}^i$	j	$\{P(S_k{}^i - i)^j\}$	$\{P(S_k{}^i - i)^j\}i$	
		2	$\{342, 432\}$	$\{3421, 4321\}$	
	$\{2, 3, 4, 1\} \rightarrow$	3	$\{243, 423\}$	$\{2431, 4231\}$	$= \{P(S_k)^i\}$
		4	$\{234, 324\}$	$\{2341, 3241\}$	
$1 \rightarrow$		2	$\{352, 532\}$	$\{3521, 5321\}$	
	$\{2, 3, 5, 1\} \rightarrow$	3	$\{253, 523\}$	$\{2531, 5231\}$	$= \{P(S_k)^i\}$
		5	$\{235, 325\}$	$\{2351, 3251\}$	
	$\{2, 4, 5, 1\} \rightarrow$		$\{\ldots\ldots\ldots\ldots\ldots\ldots\ldots\ldots\}$	$\ldots\ldots\ldots\ldots$	
	$\{3, 4, 5, 1\} \rightarrow$		$\{\ldots\ldots\ldots\ldots\ldots\ldots\ldots\ldots\}$	$\ldots\ldots\ldots\ldots$	

FIG. 10.8. Example of (10.8) ($n = 5$, $k = 4$, $i = 1$).

i	$S_k{}^i$	j	$f(S_{k-1})^j$	$f(S_{k-1})^j i$	$f(S_k)^i$
1	$\{2, 3, 4, 1\} \rightarrow$	2	$\{432\}$	$\{4321\}$	
		3	$\{243\}$	$\{2431\}$	$\rightarrow \{2431, 2341\}$
		4	$\{234, 324\}$	$\{2341, 3241\}$	

FIG. 10.9. Example of (10.9) ($i = 1$, $S_k^i = \{2, 3, 4, 1\}$, $n = 5$, $k = 4$).

Remark. The above formulation holds for a single machine case ($m = 1$) under the dominance conditions (10.6) and (10.7) ($q = 1$).

For more details, refer to the exercises.

Exercises

1. Practical dominance conditions. Let $P(S_k)^i = f(S_k^i - i)^j i = 12 \ldots (k-3)lji$ be any order at stage $k(k = 2, 3, \ldots, n-1)$, $E_q(i) = E_q(P(S_k)^i)$ be a flow time of job i on $M_2, M_3, \ldots, M_q$ (see Fig. 10.10)

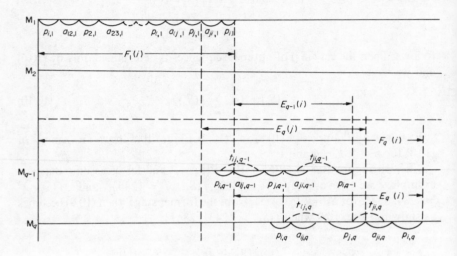

FIG. 10.10. E_q and F_q.

Then we have

$$F_q(i) = E_q(i) + F_1(i)$$
$$= E_q(i) + \left(\sum_{r=1}^{k-3} p_{r,1} + p_{l,1} + p_{j,1} + p_{i,1} + \sum_{r=1}^{k-4} a_{r,r+1,1} + a_{k-3,l,1} + a_{lj,1} + a_{ji,1} \right).$$

Next let us define

$$a_1(P(S_k)^i) = \sum_{r=1}^{k-4} a_{r,r+1,1} + a_{k-3,l,1} + a_{lj,1} + a_{ji,1},$$

then show that the dominance conditions (10.7) is equivalent to the inequalities

$$E_q(P_1(S_k)^i) + a_1(P_1(S_k)^i) \leqq E_q(P_2(S_k)^i) + a_1(P_2(S_k)^i)$$
$$(q = 1, 2, \ldots, m)$$

where $E_1(P_t(S_k)^i) = 0$ ($t = 1, 2$).

2. Show that the following recurrence relations hold for $E_q(i)$ and $a_1(i) = a_1(P(s_k)^i)$ respectively:

$$E_q(i) = \max[E_q(j) + a_{ji,q} - a_{ji,1} - p_{i,1}, E_{q-1}(i) + t_{ji,q}] + p_{i,q},$$
$$(q = 2, 3, \ldots, m)$$
$$a_1(i) = a_1(j) + a_{ji,1}.$$

3. $g(F, P(S_k)^i)$ for each objective function F. For simplicity, let $S_k^i = \{1, 2, \ldots, k-1, k\}$, $P(S_k)^i = 12 \ldots (k-1)k$, $P(S_k^i - 1)^j = 12 \ldots (k-1)$ and $F_k^i = F(P(S_k)^i)$, $g_k^i = g(F, P(S_k)^i)$, $g_{k-1}^i = g(F, P(S_k^i - i)^j)$, then show the following expressions and relations for the respective objective functions:

(1) Makespan.

$$F_k^i = E_m(P(S_k)^i) + \sum_{r=1}^{k} p_{r,1} + a_1(P(S_k)^i),$$

$$g_k^i = E_m(P(S_k)^i) + \sum_{r=1}^{k-1} a_{r,r+1,1}.$$

Inequality (10.6) is included in the inequalities (10.7), or equivalent inequalities in exercise 1.

(2) Weighted mean completion time, that is, weighted sum F of completion times.

$$F_k^i = \sum_{j=1}^{k} u_j p_{j,1} + \sum_{j=1}^{k-1} \left\{ p_{j,1} \cdot \sum_{t=j+1}^{k} u_t \right\} + \sum_{j=1}^{k} u_j E_m(j) + \sum_{j=1}^{k} u_j a_1(j),$$

$$g_k^i = \sum_{j=1}^{k-1} \left\{ p_{j,1} \cdot \sum_{t=j+1}^{k} u_t \right\} + \sum_{j=1}^{k} u_j E_m(j) + \sum_{j=1}^{k} u_j a_1(j),$$

$$g_k^i = g_{k-1}^i + u_k \left\{ \sum_{j=1}^{k-1} p_{j,1} + E_m(k) + a_1(k) \right\}.$$

Especially for mean completion time, that is, sum of completion times,

$$F_k^i = \sum_{j=1}^{k} p_{j,1} + \sum_{j=1}^{k-1} (k-j) p_{j,1} + \sum_{j=1}^{k} E_m(j) + \sum_{j=1}^{k} a_1(j),$$

$$g_k^i = \sum_{j=1}^{k-1} (k-j) p_{j,1} + \sum_{j=1}^{k} E_m(j) + \sum_{j=1}^{k} a_1(j),$$

$$g_k^i = g_{k-1}^i + \sum_{j=1}^{k-1} p_{j,1} + E_m(k) + a_1(k).$$

The above is almost the same for weighted mean lateness.

(3) Mean intermediate waiting time, that is, sum F of waiting times $w_{j,q}$, where $w_{j,q}$ means, for $q = 1$, the waiting time of each job $j(j = 1, 2, \ldots, n)$ after the completion time of the prior job $j-1(j \geq 2)$ on $M_1(q = 1)$ and, for $q \geq 2$, the waiting time of each job $j(j = 1, 2, \ldots, n)$ for its processing on every machine $M_q(q = 2, 3, \ldots, m)$.

$$F_k^i = \sum_{j=1}^{k} W(j) = \sum_{j=1}^{k} a_{j-1,j,1} + \sum_{j=1}^{k} E_m(j) - \sum_{j=1}^{k} \sum_{q=2}^{m} p_{j,q},$$

$$g_k^i = \sum_{j=1}^{k} a_{j-1,j,1} + \sum_{j=1}^{k} E_m(j) = a_1(P(S_k)^i) + \sum_{j=1}^{k} E_m(j),$$

$$g_k^i = g_{k-1}^i + \sigma_{k-1,k,1} + E_m(k).$$

(4) Machine idle time.

$$F_k^i = a_1(k) + \sum_{q=2}^{m} \{E_q(k) + a_1(k)\} + (m-1) \sum_{j=1}^{k} p_{j,1} - \sum_{q=2}^{m} \sum_{j=1}^{k} p_{j,q},$$

$$g_k^i = a_1(P(S_k)^i) + \sum_{q=2}^{m} \{E_q(P(S_k)^i) + a_1(P(S_k)^i)\}.$$

When $k \neq n$, inequality (10.6) is included in the inequalities (10.7), that is, equivalent inequalities in exercise 1. And when $k = n$

$$g_n^i = ma_1(P(S_n)^i) + \sum_{q=2}^{m} E_q(P(S_n)^i).$$

(5) Weighted mean tardiness, that is, weighted sum F of tardinesses.

$$F_k^i = \sum_{j=1}^{k} u_j \max\left[\sum_{t=1}^{j} p_{t,1} + a_1(j) + \dot{E}_m(j) - d_{j,}0 \right],$$

$$g_k^i = F_k^i, g_k^i = g_{k-1}^i + u_k \max\left[\sum_{t=1}^{k} p_{i,1} + a_1(k) + E_m(k) - d_{k,}0 \right].$$

(6) Maximum lateness and maximum tardiness. We have respectively

$$F_k^i = \max_{j=1,\ldots,k} \left\{ \sum_{t=1}^{j} p_{t,1} + a_1(j) + E_m(j) - d_j \right\},$$

$$F_k^i = \max_{j=1,\ldots,k} \left[\sum_{t=1}^{j} p_{t,1} + a_1(j) + E_m(j) - d_{j,}0 \right].$$

For both

$$g_k^i = \max_{j=1,\ldots,k} \left\{ \sum_{t=1}^{j} p_{t,1} + a_1(j) + E_m(j) - d_j \right\},$$

$$g_k^i = \max\left[g_{k-1}^i, \sum_{t=1}^{k} p_{t,1} + a_1(k) + E_m(k) - d_k \right].$$

4. Multistage combinational algorithm. Verify the following flow chart in Fig. 10.11 for this algorithm.

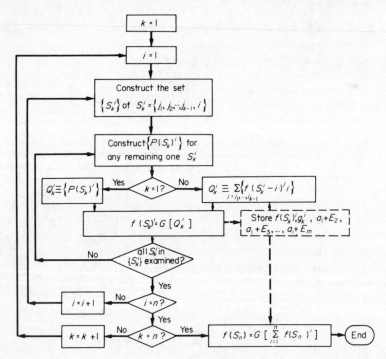

FIG. 10.11. Flow chart.

5. By referring to Section 10.7, give the procedure in parallel scheduling for the present problem.

10.12. Approximate Algorithms for Min-Makespan Problem

Generally speaking, if we have any BAB algorithm, BP algorithm or LS method as an optimum seeking solution method, then we can apply a heuristic algorithm giving reliable approximate solutions, that is, an EXTBAB algorithm. See Section 3.10 in Chapter 3. For the individual problem, however, we can develop various approximate algorithms by using analytical results obtained by using the special structure of the respective problem.

In the following sections we consider approximate algorithms for the min-makespan problem in a flow shop where no passing is allowed.

There exist three types of approximations, as follows:

1. In order to construct an approximate sequence, the positions of n_k jobs are determined at stage k. Usually the case $n_k = 1 (k = 1, 2, \ldots, n)$ is considered.
2. The order of two (adjacent) jobs in a specified sequence is systematically changed to make the makespan smaller.
3. The set of n jobs is decomposed into r subsets and then optimal or approximate subsequences of every subset are constructed reasonably.

In the methods, although, for example, there exist sorting methods, that apply merging, pairing, or exchanging, and Chain Monte Carlo method, decomposition methods and an approximate algorithm by multiple criteria, we concentrate on an application of a specified function which determines the position of every job on an approximate sequence. This method has a deep connection with analytical results as described in the following section.

10.13. Application of a Specified Function to Construct an Approximate Sequence

In a single-machine sequencing problem, there exists a specified function $g(i)$ which determines the position of every job i for an optimal sequence for the respective objective functions. For example, by arranging n jobs in nondecreasing order of $g(i) = P_i/u_i$ for weighted mean completion time and weighted mean lateness, and in nondecreasing order of $g(i) = d_i$ for maximum lateness and maximum tardiness, an optimal sequence can be determined.

Also in the flow-shop case, generation of an optimal sequence for two machines by a criterion:

$$\min(p_{i,1}, p_{j,2}) \leqq \min(p_{j,1}, p_{i,2})$$

can be done as shown below instead of using the working rule. See Theorem 5 at section 7.11 in Chapter 7.

Arrange n jobs in nondecreasing order of

$$g(i) = (\text{sign of } p_{i,1} - p_{i,2})/\min(p_{i,1}, p_{i,2}),$$

where the sign of $p_{i,1} - p_{i,2}$ is $+1$ for the case $p_{i,1} > p_{i,2}$, -1 for the case $p_{i,1} \leqq p_{i,2}$.

Hence, in case

$$\min_i p_{i,1} \geqq \max_i p_{i,2},$$

or

$$\min_i p_{i,3} \geqq \max_i p_{i,2}$$

holds for three machines, since we can determine an optimal sequence by a criterion:

$$\min[p_{i,1} + p_{i,2}, p_{j,2} + p_{j,3}] \leqq \min[p_{j,1} + p_{j,2}, p_{i,2} + p_{i,3}],$$

an optimal sequence can be determined in this case by arranging n jobs in nondecreasing order of

$$g(i) = (\text{sign of } p_{i,1} - p_{i,3}) / \min_{1 \leqq q \leqq 2} (p_{i,q} + p_{i,q+1}). \tag{10.11}$$

For the general case where no restrictions on processing times exist in the three-machine sequencing problem, the above generation of an approximate sequence by (10.11) is called the Johnson approximation by Giglio and Wagner and this method produces good suboptimal sequences and is superior to the other methods such as rounding by linear programming, Monte Carlo method and so on.

If we generalize this Johnson approximation to the m machine case ($m \geqq 3$), by referring to Result 2 in Section 8.18 in Chapter 8, an approximate sequence can be determined by arranging n jobs in nondecreasing order of

$$g(i) = (\text{sign of } p_{i,1} - p_{i,m}) / \min_{1 \leqq q \leqq 2} \left(\sum_{t=q}^{q+m-2} p_{i,t} \right). \tag{10.12}$$

Gupta uses the following function as a similarity of (10.11):

$$g(i) = (\text{sign of } p_{i,1} - p_{i,m}) / \min_{1 \leqq q \leqq m-1} (p_{i,q} + p_{i,q+1}).$$

Generation of an approximate sequence by the above function $g(i)$ ($i = 1, 2, \ldots, n$) is not so complex and efficient in relation to the sorting method, as noted by Page.

Also Palmer presented a function:

$$g(i) = \sum_{q=1}^{m} (m - 2q + 1) p_{i,q}.$$

Also in case there exist no restrictions on the processing times in Result 6 in Section 8.18 in Chapter 8, the sufficient conditions for job i to precede job j for any two adjacent jobs i and j in an optimal sequence were $m(m-1)/2$

inequalities:

$$\min[p_{i,k}, p_{j,k+1}] \min[p_{j,k}, p_{i,k+1}], \qquad m(k, k+1)$$

$$(k = 1, 2, \ldots, m-1)$$

$$\min[p_{i,u}, p_{j,v}] \leqq \min[p_{j,u}, p_{i,v}], \quad (2 \leqq u+1 < v \leqq m) \quad m(u,v)$$

that is, together $\min(p_{i,u}, p_{j,v}) \leqq \min(p_{j,u}, p_{i,v})$. $m(u,v)$ ($1 \leqq u < v \leqq m$). Then we put $g_k(i) = $ (sign of $p_{i,u} - p_{i,v}$)/$\min(p_{i,u}, p_{i,v})$, ($k = 1, 2, \ldots, m(m-1)/2$) for every k determined successively in increasing order of $u(u = 1, 2, \ldots, m-w)$ for each value $w = v - u$ which increases from I to $m - 1$, that is, $w = v - u = 1, 2, \ldots, m-1$.

Hence, we can construct an approximate sequence by arranging n jobs in nondecreasing order of a weighted mean $g(i)$ of those $M = m(m-1)/2$ $g_k(i)$, where $g(i)$ is defined as

$$g(i) = \sum_{k=1}^{M} u_k g_k(i) \bigg/ \sum_{k=1}^{M} u_k, \quad u_k \geqq 0 \quad (k = 1, 2, \ldots, M). \qquad (10.13)$$

The above weights may be decided according to the larger and smaller sizes of the sums of the processing times on every machine.

In addition to the above weighted mean, we may decide $g(i)$ as a mode or a median of the values of a certain $\gamma g_k(i)$ ($\gamma \leqq M$). As another method we can construct an approximate sequence by arranging n jobs in nondecreasing order of the weighted means of the position rankings by every $g_k(i)$. Also as an approximate sequence by the BAB algorithm, we can determine the kth job i_k in the approximate sequence by a job which minimizes a certain function $g_k(i)$ for the remaining jobs i. For example, if we decide $g_k(i)$ as a lower bound $LB(J_{k-1}i)$, where J_{k-1} is a subsequence of $k-1$ jobs already arranged and $J_{k-1}i$ means a subsequence of k jobs with last job i after J_{k-1} and $J_0 i = i$, then an approximate sequence determined by this is just a sequence obtained first by the active new node search procedure in the BAB algorithm.

EXAMPLE 3. In the present 4×5 problem with processing times in Table 10.2, determine an approximate sequence by (10.12).

TABLE 10.2

i	$p_{i,1}$	$p_{i,2}$	$p_{i,3}$	$p_{i,4}$	$p_{i,5}$
1	4	3	7	2	8
2	3	7	2	8	5
3	1	2	4	3	7
4	3	4	3	7	2

Solution. Since $g(1) = -1/16$, $g(2) = -1/20$, $g(3) = -1/10$, $g(4) = 1/16$, we have an approximate sequence 3124 with makespan 34. Here an optimal sequence is 3412 with minimal makespan 33.

Exercise

1. Approximate algorithm by multiple criteria. We can decide an approximate sequence as a sequence with minimal makespan among p sequences determined by each of p criteria:

$$\min\left(\sum_{k=1}^{q} p_{i,k}, \sum_{k=m+1-q}^{m} p_{j,k}\right) \leqq \min\left(\sum_{k=1}^{q} p_{j,k}, \sum_{k=m+1-q}^{m} p_{i,k}\right)$$

$$(q = 1, 2, \ldots, p)$$

where $p \leqq m - 1$. Apply this algorithm to Example 3 by taking $p = m - 1$.

Remark. For the other approximate algorithms using multiple criteria and two-job exchange method respectively, see Reference.

Miscellaneous Exercises

1. Generalized problem. The main problems considered in the early days of research on the sequencing problem were min-makespan problem in the two-machine flow shop treated in Section 7.11 in Chapter 7 and another is a problem, where time lags exist, treated in Section 8.17 in Chapter 8. Then a generalized problem including both problems as special cases becomes as follows:

Let there exist m bottleneck machines $M_1, M_2, \ldots, M_m$ and each intermediate machine $M_{k,k+1}$ between every two adjacent bottleneck machines M_k, M_{k+1} $(k = 1, 2, \ldots, m - 1)$ and let $p_{i,k}$ and $H_{i,k}$ be the processing times of each job i $(i = 1, 2, \ldots, n)$ on $M_k (k = 1, 2, \ldots, m)$ and $M_{k,k+1}$ $(k = 1, 2, \ldots, m - 1)$ respectively. The following conditions are assumed for this problem:

(1) Every job is processed by $2m - 1$ machines $M_1, M_{12}, M_2, M_{23}, M_3, \ldots,$ $M_{m-1}, M_{m-1,m}, M_m$ in this identical order.

(2) The sequence of n jobs on every machine is the same, that is, no passing is allowed.

(3) Each of $m - 1$ intermediate machines can process more than one job simultaneously, but m bottleneck machines cannot.

(4) The other conditions in the usual sequencing problem hold. If there exist no intermediate machines, the generalized problem reduces to the usual m machine problem.

Also for the problem where time lags exist, that is, where every job i is processed on M_{k+1} not sooner than $D_{i,k}$ time units after the start time of this job on M_k and completes on M_{k+1} not sooner than $E_{i,k}$ time units after the completion time of this job on M_k $(k = 1, 2, \ldots, m - 1)$, show that this problem reduces to the generalized problem by putting

$$H_{i,k} = \max[D_{i,k} - p_{i,k}, E_{i,k} - p_{i,k+1}]$$

$$(k = 1, 2, \ldots, m - 1)$$

and then explain the meanings of the cases $H_{i,k} \geq 0$ and $H_{i,k} < 0$ respectively.

2. Lower bound in the BAB algorithm for the generalized problem. For the generalized problem we use the same procedure in the BAB algorithm as for the min-makespan problem (cf. Section 9.4 of chapter 9).

Show that we can use the following lower bound for the min-makespan problem:

$$\mathrm{LB}(J_r) = \max \begin{bmatrix} C_1(J_r) + \sum_{i \in J_r} p_{i,1} + \min_{i \in J_r} \sum_{q=2}^{m} (H_{i,q-1} + p_{i,q}), \\ C_2(J_r) + \sum_{i \in J_r} p_{i,2} + \min_{i \in J_r} \sum_{q=3}^{m} (H_{i,q-1} + p_{i,q}), \\ \cdots\cdots\cdots\cdots\cdots\cdots\cdots\cdots\cdots\cdots\cdots\cdots\cdots\cdots \\ C_{m-1}(J_r) + \sum_{i \in J_r} p_{i,m-1} + \min_{i \in J_r} (H_{i,m-1} + p_{i,m}), \\ C_m(J_r) + \sum_{i \in J_r} p_{i,m} \end{bmatrix}$$

$$r = 1, 2, \ldots, n - 1$$

where the notations have the same meanings as in the standard lower bound in Section 9.5 of Chapter 9.

3. Consider a revised lower bound and a composite lower bound respectively for the generalized problem.

4. Consider lower bounds in the BAB algorithms and/or the BP algorithms for minimizing the other objective functions in the generalized problem and a special m machine sequencing problem, where time lags exist, respectively.

5. The BAB algorithm for the min-makespan problem where explicit setup times exist. For the problem treated in Section 10.9, the same procedure in the BAB algorithm as in Section 9.4 of Chapter 9 is applied. Then show that we can use the following lower bound for the min-makespan problem under the same notations:

$$
LB(J_r) = \max
\begin{bmatrix}
C_1(J_r) + \min_{i \in J_r} a_{j,i,1} + \sum_{i \in J_r} p_{i,1} + \min_{k=r+1,\ldots,n} \sum_{j=\bar{J}_r-j_k} \min_{i \in J_r} a_{ji,1} \\
\quad + \sum_{k=2}^{m} \left\{ \min_{\substack{j \in \{j_r, \bar{J}_r\} \\ i \in J_r}} t_{ji,k} + \min_{i \in J_r} p_{i,k} \right\}, \\[4mm]
C_2(J_r) + \min_{i \in J_r} a_{j,i,2} + \sum_{i \in J_r} p_{i,2} + \min_{k=r+1,\ldots,n} \sum_{j \in \bar{J}_r-j_k} \min_{i \in J_r} a_{ji,2} \\
\quad + \sum_{k=3}^{m} \left\{ \min_{\substack{j \in \{j_r, \bar{J}_r\} \\ i \in J_r}} t_{ji,k} + \min_{i \in J_r} p_{i,k} \right\}, \\[4mm]
\cdots\cdots\cdots\cdots\cdots\cdots\cdots\cdots\cdots\cdots\cdots\cdots\cdots\cdots \\[2mm]
C_{m-1}(J_r) + \min_{i \in J_r} a_{j,i,m-1} + \sum_{i \in J_r} p_{i,m-1} + \min_{k=r+1,\ldots,n} \sum_{j \in \bar{J}_r-j_k} \min_{i \in J_r} a_{ji,m-1} \\
\quad + \min_{\substack{j \in \{j_r, \bar{J}_r\} \\ i \in J_r}} t_{ji,m} + \min_{i \in J_r} p_{i,m}, \\[4mm]
C_m(J_r) + \min_{i \in J_r} a_{j,i,m} + \sum_{i \in J_r} p_{i,m} + \min_{h=r+1,\ldots,n} \sum_{j \in \bar{J}_r-j_k} \min_{i \in J_r} a_{ji,m}
\end{bmatrix}
$$

$$r = 1, 2, \ldots, n-1$$

where in particular a job j_r is the last job of a definite subsequence J_r and $\bar{J}_r = \{j_{r+1}, j_{r+2}, \ldots, j_n\}$. Also $\bar{J}_r - j_k$ is a subset of $\bar{J}_r$ after the exclusion of a job j_k. Every fourth term becomes zero for $r = n-1$ since $\bar{J}_r - j_k$ is empty in this case. Also when $r = n-1$, since $j \neq i$ a job j in $\{j_r, \bar{J}_r\}$ becomes a job j_{n-1}.

6. The min-makespan problem with no wait in process. In the min-makespan problem in the flow shop with no wait in process, let the ordering be $M_1, M_2, \ldots, M_m$, then an example of a Gant chart in this case becomes as shown in Fig. 10.12.

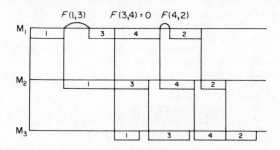

FIG. 10.12

Let the order of two adjacent jobs i, j be ij and $F(i, j)$ be an elapsed time from the completion time of job i on M_1 to the start time of job j on M_1, then show the following expression of $F(i, j)$:

$$F(i,j) = \max_{2 \le k \le m} \left[\sum_{q=2}^{k} p_{i,q} - \sum_{q=1}^{k-1} p_{j,q}, 0 \right].$$

7. For the problem in the above exercise 6, show that the makespan of any sequence $i_1 i_2 \ldots i_n$ is expressed by

$$\sum_{q=1}^{n} p_{i_q, 1} + \sum_{q=1}^{n-1} F(i_q, i_{q+1}) + \sum_{k=2}^{m} p_{in, k}.$$

8. The problem defined in exercise 6 becomes equivalent to a traveling-salesman problem, for which every cost between any two cities is suitably determined. Determine these costs between any two cities.

Bibliography and Comments

Sections 10.1–8
The contents of these sections may be found in I. NABESHIMA, *Scheduling Theory* (in Japanese), Morikita Shuppan, 1974, Section 4.7.

Sections 10.9–11
The contents of these sections also appear in *ibid.*, Section 4.8.

Section 10.12
For the sorting methods see
E. S. PAGE, "An approach to the scheduling of jobs on machines", *J. Roy. Statist. Soc.* **23**, No. 2 (1961), 484–492.
For the Chain Monte Carlo method see
E. S. PAGE, "On Monte Carlo methods in congestion problems: searching for an optimum in discrete situation", *Opns. Res.* **13**, No. 2 (1965), 291–299.
For the decomposition methods see
S. ASHOUR, "A decomposition approach for the machines scheduling problem", *Int. J. Prod. Res.* **6**, No. 2 (1967), 109–122.
S. ASHOUR "A modified decomposition algorithm for scheduling problem", *Int. J. Prod. Res.* **8**, No. 3 (1970), 281–284.
J. N. D. GUPTA, "Flow-shop scheduling by heuristic decomposition", *Int. J. Prod. Res.* **11**, No. 2 (1973), 105–111.
For the heuristic rules, see
J. R. KING and A. S. SPACHIS, "Heuristics for flow-shop scheduling", *Int. J. Prod. Res.* **18**, No. 3 (1980), 345–357.

Section 10.13
The Johnson approximation was developed first by
R. J. GIGLIO and H. M. WAGNER, "Approximate solution to the three-machine scheduling problem", *Opns. Res.* **12**, No. 2 (1964), 305–324.
See also the following two papers for the above approximation.
W. SZWARC and G. K. HUTCHINSON, "Johnson's approximate method for the $3 \times n$ job shop problem", *Nav. Res. Log. Quart.* **24**, No. 1 (1977), 153–157.
I. NABESHIMA, "Notes on the analytical results in flow shop scheduling: Part 5", *Rep. Univ. Electro-Comm.* **28**, No. 1 (1977), 57–65.
The Gupta's function is found in
J. N. D. GUPTA, "A functional heuristic algorithm for the flow shop scheduling problem", *Opnl. Res. Quart.* **22**, No. 1 (1971), 39–47.
The efficiency of the function $g(i)$ was stated in
E. S. PAGE, "An approach to the scheduling of jobs on machines", *J. Roy. Statist. Soc.* **23**, No. 2 (1961), 484–492.
Also see

VON G. LIESEGANG and A. SCHIRMER, "Heuristische Verfahren zur Maschinenbelegungsplanung bei Reihenfertigung", *Zeitschr. für Oper. Res.*, Band 19 (1975), pp. 195–211.
The Palmer's method is found in
D. S. PALMER, "Sequencing jobs through a multi-stage-process in the minimum total time—a quick method of obtaining a near optimum", *Opnl. Res. Quart.* **16**, No. 1 (1965), 101–107.
Also, as the statistic estimations of an optimal schedule value, see
D. G. DANNENBRING, "Procedures for estimating optimal solution values for large combinatorial problems", *Manag. Sci.* **23**, No. 12 (1977), 1273–1283.
B. L. GOLDEN and F. B. ALT, "Interval estimation of a global optimum for large combinatorial problems", *Nav. Res. Log. Quart.* **26**, No. 1, (1979), 69–77.
Exercise
The method in exercise 1 is found in
H. G. CAMPBELL, R. A. DUDEK and M. L. SMITH, "A heuristic algorithm for the *n* job. *m* machine sequencing problem", *Manag. Sci.* **16**, No. 10 (1970), B630-B637.
For the other approximate algorithms using multiple criteria see
I. NABESHIMA, "The order of *n* items processed on *m* machines [III]", *J. Oper. Res. Soc. Japan*, **16**, No. 3 (1973), 163–185.
S. MIYAZAKI, N. NISHIYAMA and F. HASHIMOTO," An adjacent pairwise approach in the mean flow-time scheduling problem", *J. Oper. Res. Soc. Japan*, **21**, No. 2 (1978), 287–299.
S. MIYAZAKI, and N. NISHIYAMA, "Analysis for minimizing weighted mean flow-time in flow-shop scheduling", *J. Oper. Res. Soc. Japan*, **23**, No. 2 (1980), 118–131.
For the two-job exchange method see
Y. MING-I, "On the *n* job, *m* machine sequencing problem of flow-shop," *OR '75*, K. B. HAREY (ed.), North-Holland, 1976, pp. 179–200.
I. NABESHIMA, "Notes on the analytical results in flow shop scheduling: Part 14", *Rep. Univ. Electro-Comm.* **32**, No. 1 (1981), 23–33.

Miscellaneous Exercises

The following papers or books are concerned with the exercise:
1, 2. I. NABESHIMA, "Some extension of the *m* machine scheduling problem", *J. Oper. Res. Soc. Japan* **10**, Nos. 1–2 (1967), 1–17.
5. I. NABESHIMA, *Scheduling Theory* (in Japanese), Morikita Shuppan, 1974, Section 4.6.
6, 7, 8. S. S. REDDI and C. V. RAMAMOORTHY, "On the flowshop sequencing problem with no wait in process", *Opnl. Res. Quart.* **23**, No. 3 (1972), 323–331.
D. A. WISMER, "Solution of the flowshop-scheduling problem with no intermediate queues", *Opns. Res.* **20**, No. 3 (1972), 689–697.
Concerning the scheduling problem with no wait in process, further refer to
S. S. REDDI and C. V. RAMAMOORTHY, "A scheduling problem", *Opnl. Res. Quart.* **24**, No. 3 (1973), 441–446.
S. K. GOYAL, "Job-shop sequencing problem with no wait in process", *Int. J. Prod. Res.* **13**, No. 2 (1975), 197–206.
S. S. PANWALKAR and C. R. WOOLLAM, "Flow-shop scheduling problems with no in-process waiting: a special case", *J. Oper. Res. Soc.* **30**, No. 7 (1979), 661–664; "Ordered flowshop problems with no in-process waiting: further results," *ibid.*, **31**, No. 11 (1980), 1039–1043.
Related papers are:
S. K. DUTTA and A. A. CUNNINGHAM, "Sequencing two-machine flow-shops with finite intermediate storage", *Manag. Sci.* **21**, No. 9 (1975), 989–996.
S. S. REDDI, "Sequencing with finite intermediate storage", *Manag. Sci.* **23**, No. 2 (1976), 216–217.

CHAPTER 11

Flow-shop Scheduling under Sequence Dependence Conditions

11.1. Sequence Dependent Setup Times

In Chapter 10 we gave a brief introduction to scheduling problems involving sequence dependent setup times. The complications that arise when we explicitly consider setup times that are dependent on job sequence were outlined. In this chapter we want to explore these more realistic albeit complicated situations for flow-shop scheduling problems. We begin by considering two-machine scheduling problems and then extend our treatment to the multidimensional cases involving three or more machines. As we will note, our results are novel having not been similarly approached elsewhere.

Let us concern ourselves for the moment with the two-machine flow-shop scheduling problem. Further, let us consider the two distinct scheduling problems that result from the classic two-machine scheduling problem when one machine is assumed to have setup times that are dependent on job sequence. For both problems, the objective is to determine a job sequence for each machine (schedule) that minimizes the total elapsed time to complete all jobs (makespan). A minimal makespan schedule will be hereafter referred to as an optimal schedule.

Attention is focused on these two particular problems because they are closely related to both the classic two-machine scheduling problem and the traveling-salesman problem discussed extensively in Chapter 1. Therefore, there is a large potential carryover of both solution properties and solution methods from these latter problems to the former ones. In particular, we can readily show that the class of schedules for which the job sequence on each machine is identical (permutation schedules) contains an optimal schedule for the classic two-machine problem. Also, as we have shown, two essentially equivalent dynamic programming (DP) formulations for the TSP, or equivalently the single-machine scheduling problem involving sequence dependent setup times can be developed. These formulations are well suited for handling relatively small problems (14 or fewer jobs). For larger problems one has to recourse to ingenious formulations or combinations of techniques. These considerations, however, suggest investigating, for each of these problems,

258

both the optimality of permutation schedules and the suitability of DP for finding such a schedule.

The solution method we employ here for these two scheduling problems consists of two related parts. In the first part, it is shown that the class of permutation schedules contains an optimal schedule for both of these problems. In the second part, a DP formulation is developed for each of these problems. The computational requirements of each formulation are shown to be comparable to those of the DP formulation of the TSP. We note that we can develop algorithms of the branch and bound (B&B) variety for these problems. We therefore discuss the relative merits of the DP and branch and bound (B & B) approaches to each of these problems for various problem sizes. The DP approach is shown to have a distinct advantage in both cases for problems of small size.

11.2. Problem Definition

We begin by restricting our attention to the two distinct two-machine static flow-shop scheduling problems that can be defined when exactly one of the machines is characterized by sequence dependent setup times. A machine on which setup times are dependent on job sequence will be called a type D machine while a machine on which setup times are independent of job sequence will be called a type I machine. Using this notation, the two problems considered here will be separately referred to as problem type ID and problem type DI. As noted previously, the objective for each problem type is to determine a schedule that minimizes makespan. We note that since no constraints such as due dates, etc., are imposed, all $(n!)^2$ possible schedules are feasible.

Restricting attention to the static version of each of these problem types imposes the assumptions that (1) all n jobs to be scheduled are simultaneously available at schedule time zero and (2) all machines are idle at this time and immediately available for work. For purposes of this chapter, a flow shop is defined by the assumptions that (1) each job is processed exactly once on each machine, (2) the processing of each job on machine 1 must precede its processing on machine 2 and (3) machine 2 cannot start setup for any job until the job is completed by machine 1. These assumptions are required in order to prove the optimality of permutation schedules for both problem types.

In order to complete the problem definition, notation for representing the total job times for the set of n jobs to be scheduled is required for both type I and type D machines. For a machine of type I, define the $n \times 1$ vector of total sequence independent job times $p = (p_j), j = 1, 2, \ldots, n$, where p_j is the combined setup and processing time of job j on this machine. For a machine of type D, define the $(n + 1) \times n$ matrix of total sequence dependent job times $SP = (s_{ij})$, $i = ps, 1, 2, \ldots, n$ and $j = 1, 2, \ldots, n$, where s_{ij} is the combined setup and processing time of job j on this machine if it immediately follows job i. Note that in forming this matrix an imaginary $(n+1)$st job is added to represent the preliminary state (ps) of the machine. It is assumed that a return to the ps is not required upon completion of the n jobs, so there is no column of SP corresponding to this imaginary job. For a type I machine, the combined setup and processing time of job j will be denoted by $p_j, j = 1, 2, \ldots, n$.

11.3. Optimality of Permutation Schedules

The optimality of permutation schedules for each problem type is established by the following theorems:

THEOREM 1. *The class of permutation schedules contains an optimal schedule for any static flow-shop scheduling problem of type ID.*

Proof. Due to the static nature of job arrivals, only schedules with no idle time on machine 1 until completion of the last job there need be considered. Let sequence 1 and sequence 2 be the job sequences associated with machine 1 and machine 2, respectively. Suppose for some schedule, sequence 1 is different from sequence 2. Then somewhere in sequence 1 there must be a job j^β that directly precedes a job j^α, where j^β follows j^α (possibly with intervening jobs) in sequence 2. Since machine 1 is of type I, the positions of jobs j^β and j^α in sequence 1 can be reversed without changing the flow time of any job. Hence, this reversal of job order in sequence 1 cannot cause an increase in makespan. Repeating this argument for each such pair of jobs j^β and j^α for a particular sequence 2, and then extending it to all $n!$ possible sequences 2s gives the desired result.

Machine 1	$\cdots$ j^β j^α $\cdots$
	$\cdots$ j^α j^β $\cdots$

THEOREM 2. *The class of permutation schedules contains an optimal schedule for any static flow-shop scheduling problem of type DI.*

Proof. Again only schedules with no idle time on machine 1 until completion of the last (nth) job there need be considered. Suppose for some schedule, sequence 2 is different from sequence 1. Then somewhere in sequence 2 there must be a job j^α that directly follows a job j^β, where j^α precedes j^β (possibly with intervening jobs) in sequence 1. Since machine 2 is of type I, reversing the positions of jobs j^β and j^α in sequence 2 simply interchanges their flow times.

Machine 1	j^α $\cdots$ j^β $\cdots$

Machine 2	$\cdots$ j^β j^α

The flow times of all other jobs remain unchanged. Hence, this reversal of job order in sequence 2 cannot cause an increase in makespan. Repeating this argument for each such pair of jobs j^α and j^β for a particular sequence 1, and then extending it to all $n!$ possible sequences 1s gives the desired result.

11.4. Dynamic Programming Formulations for ID and DI

11.4.1. *Sequence Dominance Conditions*

A DP formulation of the problem of finding an optimal permutation schedule (hence any optimal schedule) can be developed for both problem type ID and problem type DI. A concept of sequence dominance can be defined for these two problems. The associated set of sequence dominance conditions provides the basis for a forward recursion DP formulation of problem type ID.

We begin by noting that a permutation schedule is completely described by a particular permutation of the job numbers $1, 2, \ldots, n$. We refer to any such permutation as a *full sequence*. Next, consider a sequence of $r (1 < r < n)$ jobs that corresponds to the first r positions of a full sequence. We refer to any such sequence as a *presequence* of size r. For any presequence ρ_r, and $m = 1, 2$, let $T_m(\rho_r)$ be the time that the job in position r of ρ_r is completed on machine m. Let ρ_r^α and ρ_r^β be two different presequences of r jobs that contain the same r jobs and end with the same job. If

$$T_1(\rho_r^\alpha) \le T_1(\rho_r^\beta) \tag{11.1}$$

and

$$T_2(\rho_r^\alpha) \le T_2(\rho_r^\beta), \tag{11.2}$$

then ρ_r^α is said to dominate ρ_r^β. Let π be any permutation of the $(n-r)$ jobs not contained in ρ_r^α and ρ_r^β. Conditions (11.1) and (11.2) insure that $(\rho_r^\beta \pi)$ cannot have a smaller makespan than $(\rho_r^\alpha \pi)$. Thus, all full sequences starting with ρ_r^β can be eliminated from further consideration. Conditions (11.1) and (11.2) are the sequence dominance conditions for problem types ID and DI.

11.5. Forward DP Recursion for Problem Type ID

Consider problem type ID. Since machine 1 is of type I, (11.1) must hold as an equality. Thus, ρ_r^α dominates ρ_r^β if the completion time on machine 2 (flow time) of the job in position r under ρ_r^α is less than or equal that under ρ_r^β. We now exploit the foregoing results to develop a forward recursion DP formulation in the presequence completion time for problem type ID. The formulation is a direct extension of the DP formulation for the traveling-salesman problem discussed in Chapter 1.

Let J = the set of all n jobs,
    j_l = a single job, and
    $J_k = \{j_1, j_2, \ldots, j_k\}$ be a subset of k $(0 \le k \le n-1)$
    jobs from $\{J - j_l\}$.

Suppose that the first $(k+1)$ jobs of some optimal full sequence have been completed, with the remaining $(n-k-1)$ jobs yet to be done. Regard the first k jobs as some set of jobs J_k, and the $(k+1)$st job as some job j_l. For any J_k and j_l, define $f(\text{ps}; J_k; j_l)$ to be the minimum time required to complete the k jobs of J_k (in some order) and then job j_l, where machine 2 starts from the preliminary state, ps. Then $f(\text{ps}; J_k; j_l)$ is given by

$$f(\text{ps}; J_k; j_l) = \min_{j_p \in J_k} [f(\text{ps}; \{J_k - j_p\}; j_p)$$
$$+ I(j_l | \rho_{k-1}^p j_p) + s_{j_p j_l}] \text{ for } k = 1, 2, \ldots, n-1 \quad (11.3)$$

where ρ_{k-1}^p is the associated optimal presequence of the $(k-1)$ jobs of $\{J_k - j_p\}$ and $I(j_l | \rho_{k-1}^p j_p)$ is the idle time incurred on machine 2 immediately preceding job j_l when the presequence $(\rho_{k-1}^p j_p)$ is used. Note that $I(j_l | \rho_{k-1}^p j_p)$ is given by

$$I(j_l | \rho_{k-1}^p j_p) = \max \left[\sum_{j \in \{J_k, j_l\}} p_j - f(\text{ps}; \{J_k - j_p\}; j_p), 0 \right].$$

Let j_m be a choice of j_p that corresponds to the minimum in (11.3). If $(f_k^* j_l)$ is an optimal presequence associated with $f(\text{ps}; J_k; j_l)$ then $(f_k^* j_l)$ is given by $(\rho_{k-1}^m j_m j_l)$. The recursive procedure of (11.3) may be initiated by use of the known relation

$$f(\text{ps}; J_0; j_l) = p_{j_l} + s_{\text{ps} j_l} \text{ for } k = 0,$$

where $J_0 = \phi$, the null set. Once $f(\text{ps}; J_{n-1}; j_l)$ and an associated optimal full sequence $(p_{n-1}^* j_l)$ have been obtained for each of the n possible jobs j_l, a solution to the problem is given by

$$\min_{j_l \in J} f(\text{ps}; J_{n-1}; j_l).$$

Consider relation (11.1). It can be readily seen that it establishes $f(\text{ps}; J_k; j_l)$ by use of the sequence dominance conditions (11.1) and (11.2). For each $j_p \in J_k$,

$$f(\text{ps}; \{J_k - j_p\}; j_p) + I(j_l | \rho_{k-1}^p j_p) + s_{j_p j_l} = T_2(\rho_{k-1}^p j_p j_l).$$

Thus, the minimization in (11.3) selects a presequence $(\rho_{k-1}^m j_m j_l)$ from the k presequences $(\rho_{k-1}^p j_p j_l)$ that dominates the remaining $(k-1)$ presequences. Since the relations $T_1(\rho_{k-1}^m j_m j_l) = T_1(\rho_{k-1}^p j_p j_l)$ and $T_2(\rho_{k-1}^m j_m j_l) \le$

$T_2(\rho^p_{k-1}j_p j_l)$ must hold for each of the $(k-1)$ presequences $(\rho^p_{k-1}j_p j_l)$ corresponding to a job $j_p \in \{J_k - j_m\}$, each of these presequences is dominated by the presequence $(\rho^m_{k-1}j_m j_l)$ and therefore can be eliminated from further consideration.

11.6. Computational Aspects

It is instructive to compare the computational requirements (storage and time) of this DP formulation of an n job problem of type ID to those of the DP formulation of an $(n + 1)$ city TSP. It can be readily seen that the calculation of $I(j_l|\rho^p_{k-1}j_p)$ required for (11.3) is essentially the only computational difference between these two formulations. The computer storage requirements of each problem solved at stage k $(0 \le k \le n - 1)$, and hence at stage k itself, are identical for both formulations. For each problem solved at stage k, $I(j_l|\rho^p_{k-1}j_p)$ must be calculated for each of the k alternatives compared. Thus, the computation-time requirements of the former formulation are slightly greater than those of the latter.

11.7. Backward DP Recursion for Problem Type DI

A forward recursion DP formulation in the presequence completion time analogous to the preceding development would not be valid for problem type DI. Since machine 1 is of type D, (11.1) does not necessarily hold as an equality. Thus, ρ^α_r may or may not dominate ρ^β_r if the flow time of the job in position r under ρ^α_r is less than or equal that under ρ^β_r. Assume f (ps; $J_k; j_l$) is defined for problem type DI as it was before for problem type ID, where now machine 1 starts from the preliminary state. A forward recursion relation analogous to (11.3) would not be valid because f (ps; $J_k; j_l$) cannot, in general, be expressed in terms of the minimum completion time f (ps; $\{J_k - j_p\}; j_p$) for some job $j_p \in J_k$ and the idle time and job time that result on machine 2 from appending job j_l to the end of the associated presequence $(\rho^p_{k-1}j_p)$.

Fortunately, we can develop a background recursion DP for this problem. Let J and j_l be defined as before. Assume initially that the search for an optimal full sequence is to be restricted to those full sequences that have job j_l in sequence position n. We will refer to the DP formulation of the problem of finding an optimal full sequence ending with job j_l as the DP formulation of problem type DI with specified last job j_l. Consider next a sequence of r jobs $(1 \le r \le n)$ that corresponds to the last r positions of a full sequence. We will refer to any such sequence as a *postsequence* of size r. The time required to complete a *postsequence*, given the identity of the job immediately preceding it and the time at which machine 2 is available to start it will be referred to as the *postsequence time*. The DP formulation of problem type DI with specified last job j_l utilizes a backward recursion in the postsequence time. Let

j_i = a single job different from j_l,
$J_k = \{j_1, j_2, \ldots, j_k\}$ be a subset of $k (0 \le k \le n-2)$ jobs from $\{J - j_l - j_i\}$.

For $k = n - 1$, let
$j_i = $ ps and
$J_{n-1} = \{J - j_l\}$.

Consider the last $(k + 1)$ jobs of some optimal full sequence with a specified last job. Regard this last job as some job j_l, and the remaining k jobs as some set of jobs J_k. Let the immediate predecessor of these $(k + 1)$ jobs be job j_i, which will be referred to as the preliminary job. Define the integer valued state variable L to be the length of time between the completion of the preliminary job j_i on machine 1 and its completion on machine 2. For a specified j_l, and any J_k and j_i, define $f(j_i; J_k; j_l|L)$ to be the minimum time required to complete the jobs of J_k (in some order) and then job j_l, with job j_i as the preliminary job, given the value of L. We define L as follows: $L \ge p_{j_i}$ for $k = 0, 1, \ldots, n-3$; $L = p_{j_i}$, for $k = n - 2$ and $L = 0$ for $k = n - 1$. Then $f(j_i; J_k; j_l|L)$ is given by

$$f(j_i; J_k; j_l|L) = \min_{j_p \in J_k} [sp_{j,j_p} + f(j_p; \{J_k - j_p\}; j_l|L'(j_p))]$$
$$\text{for } k = 1, 2, \ldots, n - 1 \tag{11.4}$$

where $L'(j_p) = \max (1 - s_{j,j_p}, 0) + p_{j_p}$.

The state variable $L'(j_p)$ is the length of time between the completion of job j_p on machine 1 and its completion on machine 2 if job j_p immediately follows the preliminary job j_i.

The recursive procedure of (11.4) can be considerably simplified by the two properties of $f(j_i; J_k; j_l|L)$ established by the following theorem.

THEOREM 3. *Consider $f(j_i; J_k; j_l|L)$ for $k = 0, 1, \ldots, n - 3$. If $(\rho_k^* j_l)$ is an optimal postsequence associated with $f(j_i; J_k; j_l|p_{j_i})$, then an optimal postsequence associated with $f(j_i; J_k; j_l|L)$ for any $L \ge p_{j_i}$ is given by $(\rho_k^* j_l)$. Furthermore,*

$$f(j_i; J_k; j_l|L) = \begin{cases} f(j_i; J_k; j_l|p_{j_i}), \text{ if } p_{j_i} \le L \le [f(j_i; J_k; j_l|p_{j_i}) - C] \\ L + C, \text{ if } L > [f(j_i; J_k; j_l|p_{j_i}) - C] \end{cases} \tag{11.5}$$

where

$$C = \sum_{j \in \{J_k, j_l\}} p_j.$$

Proof. For any postsequence $(\rho_k j_l)$ following j_i, let $\text{PT}_2(\rho_k j_l|L)$ be the postsequence time given the value of L. Let $(\rho_k' j_l)$ be any postsequence different from all optimal postsequences associated with $f(j_i, J_k; j_l|p_{j_i})$. Note that there can be no postsequence $(\rho'_k j_l)$ different from $(\rho^*_k j_l)$ unless $k \geq 2$. It must be shown that, for $k = 2, 3, \ldots, n - 3$.

$$PT_2(\rho^*_k j_l | L) \leq PT_2(\rho'_k j_l | L) \text{ for all } L \geq p_{j_i}. \tag{11.6}$$

Consider the case $L = p_{j_i}$. Note that

$$PT_2(\rho^*_k j_l | p_{j_k}) = f(j_i; J_k; j_l | p_{j_i}).$$

From the definitions of $(\rho^*_k j_l)$ and $(\rho'_k j_l)$,

$$PT_2(\rho^*_k j_l | p_{j_i}) < PT_2(\rho'_k j_l | p_{j_i}). \tag{11.7}$$

The postsequence $(\rho^*_k j_l)$ can be shifted to the right on machine 2, leaving an interval of time $[PT_2(\rho^*_k j_l | p_{j_i}) - C]$ between the start of the first job of $(\rho^*_k j_l)$ on machine 1 and its start on machine 2. Similarly, the postsequence $(\rho'_k j_l)$ can be shifted to the right on machine 2, leaving an interval of time $[PT_2(\rho^\alpha_k j_l | p_{j_i}) - C]$ between the start of the first job of $(\rho^\alpha_k j_l)$ on machine 1 and its start on machine 2. It follows from the definition of $PT_2(\rho^*_k j_l | p_{j_i})$ from (11.7) that

$$p_{j_i} \leq [PT_2(\rho^*_k j_l | p_{j_i}) - C] < [PT_2(\rho^\alpha_k j_l | p_{j_i}) - C].$$

In order to establish (11.6), the following three cases must be considered:

Case 1.

$$p_{j_i} \leq L \leq [PT_2(\rho^*_k j_l | p_{j_i}) - C].$$

Here

$$PT_2(\rho^*_k j_l | L) = PT_2(\rho^*_k j_l | p_{j_i})$$

and

$$PT_2(\rho^\alpha_k j_l | L) = PT_2(\rho^\alpha_k j_l | p_{j_i}).$$

Therefore,

$$PT_2(\rho^*_k j_l | L) < PT_2(\rho^\alpha_k j_l | L) \text{ by (11.7).}$$

Case 2.

$$[PT_2(\rho^*_k j_l | p_{j_i}) - C] < L < [PT_2(\rho^\alpha_k j_l | p_{j_i}) - C].$$

Here

$$PT_2(\rho^*_k j_l | L) = PT_2(\rho^*_k j_l | p_{j_i}) + \{L - [PT_2(\rho^*_k j_l | p_{j_i}) - C]\} = L + C$$

and

$$PT_2(\rho^\alpha_k j_l | L) = PT_2(\rho^\alpha_k j_l | p_{j_i}).$$

Therefore,

$$PT_2(\rho^*_k j_l | L) < PT_2(\rho^\alpha_k j_l | L) \text{ since } L + C < PT_2(\rho^\alpha_k j_l | p_{j_i}).$$

Case 3.

$$[PT_2(\rho^\alpha_k j_l | p_{j_i}) - C] \leq L.$$

Here

$$PT_2(\rho^*_k j_l | L) = PT_2(\rho^*_k j_l | p_{j_i}) + L - [PT_2(\rho^*_k j_l | p_{j_i}) - C] = L + C$$

and

$$PT_2(\rho_k^\alpha j_l | L) = PT_2(\rho_k^\alpha j_l | p_{j_i}) + \{L - [PT_2(\rho_k^\alpha j_l | p_{j_i}) - C]\} = L + C.$$

Therefore,

$$PT_2(\rho_k^* j_l | L) = PT_2(\rho_k^\alpha j_l | L).$$

Combining the results of cases 1, 2 and 3 gives (11.6). Therefore, $(\rho_k^* j_l)$ is optimal for any $L \geq p_{j_i}$. Since $(\rho_k^* j_l)$ is optimal for any $L \geq p_{j_i}$, it follows that

$$f(j_i; J_k; j_l | L) = PT_2(\rho_k^* j_l | L) \text{ for } L \geq p_{j_i}. \tag{11.8}$$

Equation (11.5) follows directly from (11.8) and the results of cases 1, 2 and 3.

11.8. Implications of Theorem 3

Let us consider the importance of Theorem 3 in our formulation. As a consequence of this theorem only $f(j_i; J_k; j_l | p_{j_i})$ and an associated optimal postsequence $(\rho_k^* j_l)$ must be obtained. Therefore, the recursive procedure of (11.4) can be replaced by

$$f(j_i; J_k; j_l | p_{j_i}) = \min_{j_p \in J_k} [sp_{j_i j_p} + f(j_p; \{J_k - j_p\}; j_l | L^\alpha(j_p))]$$

$$\text{for } k = 1, 2, \ldots, n-1. \tag{11.9}$$

where

$$L^\alpha(j_p) = \max(p_{j_i} - sp_{j_k j_p}, 0) + p_{j_p}.$$

Note that (11.5) provides a simple means of evaluating $f(j_p; \{J_k - j_p\}; j_l | L^\alpha(j_p))$ for any $L^\alpha(j_p) > p_{j_p}$. Let $(\rho_{k-1}^p j_l)$ be the optimal postsequence of the $(k-1)$ jobs of $\{J_k - j_p\}$ and job j_l associated with $f(j_p; \{J_k - j_p\}; j_l | p_{j_p})$, and let j_m be a choice of j_p that corresponds to the minimum in (11.9). An optimal postsequence $(\rho_k^* j_l)$ associated with $f(j_i; J_k; j_l | p_{j_i})$, and hence with $f(j_i; J_k; j_l | L)$ for any $L \geq p_{j_i}$, is then $(j_m \rho_{k-1}^m j_l)$. The recursive procedure of (11.9) is initiated by use of the known relation

$$f(j_i; J_0; j_l | p_{j_i}) = \max(sp_{j_i j_i}, p_{j_i}) + p_{j_l} \text{ for } k = 0.$$

The case $k = n - 1$ in (11.9) gives an optimal full sequence with specified last job j_l. This completes the DP formulation of problem type DI with specified last job j_l.

A DP formulation of problem type DI is obtained from the above formulation by successively designating each of the n jobs to be the last job j_l. Once $f(\text{ps}; J_{n-1}; j_l | 0)$ and an associated optimal full sequence $(\rho_{n-1}^* j_l)$ have been obtained for each of the n possible jobs j_l, a solution to the problem is given by

$$\min_{j_l \in J} f(\text{ps}; J_{n-1}; j_l | 0).$$

11.9. Computational Aspects

Once again let us compare the computational requirements of this DP formulation of an n job problem of type DI to those of the DP formulation of an n city TSP. Consider the computational requirements of the DP formulation of an n job problem of type DI with specified last job j_l and those of the DP formulation of an n city TSP. Because Theorem 3 renders separate consideration of different values of L unnecessary, there is a strong computational similarity between these two formulations. The computer storage requirements of each problem solved at stage $k (0 \leq k \leq n-1)$, and hence at stage k itself, are identical for both formulations. For each problem solved at stage k, $L'(j_p)$ must be calculated for each of the k alternatives compared, and (11.5) must be used to determine $f(j_p; \{J_k - j_p\}; j_l | L'(j_p))$ for any of the k alternatives for which $L'(j_p) > p_{j_p}$. Thus, the computation time requirements of the former formulation are only slightly greater than those of the latter. Consequently, since this DP formulation of an n job problem of type DI requires that all n possible last jobs j_l be considered, its computation time requirements are on the order of n times as large as those of the DP formulation of an n city TSP. The computer storage requirements of both formulations are the same.

11.10. Discussion of the Dynamic Programming Approach

The computational limitations for the DP formulation of the TSP, and thus for the DP formulations of problem types ID and DI, are primarily imposed by computer storage considerations rather than by computation time considerations. The limits on problem size n for the DP formulation of the TSP have received some attention and were discussed in Chapter 1. Because of the similarities in formulations, we estimate the largest problems of type ID and type DI solvable are $n = 14$ and $n = 15$, respectively. However, by employing branch and bound procedures to fathom the state space, one can increase the size of solvable problems considerably.

Several B&B approaches to machine scheduling problems reported in the literature can, with appropriate modifications, be employed to solve problems of types ID and DI. Some discussion of these approaches and comparison of them with the DP approach of this chapter is appropriate. B&B algorithms for the generalized machine scheduling problem based on the equivalence of this problem to the problem of finding a minimaximal path in a disjunctive graph exist. These algorithms can be modified to incorporate the notion of a preliminary state and to restrict consideration to permutation schedules only, both of which are necessary in treating problem types ID and DI. It is important to note, however, that if the notion of a preliminary state is incorporated, the associated disjunctive graph cannot be defined for a problem of either type unless the job in sequence 1 is specified. Thus, this modification necessitates that these algorithms consider n different problems, one corresponding to each possible first job, in order to solve an n job problem of either type. Similar B & B algorithms for the classic three-machine scheduling problem are possible. Such algorithms are based on building increasingly larger presequences of jobs by successive branching operations, and associating a lower bound with each new presequence created. Appropriate modifications of these lower bounds to enable these algorithms to treat problem types ID and DI can be constructed.

Consider the B & B counterparts to the DP algorithms developed in this chapter for problem types ID and DI that are obtained by appropriately modifying the B & B algorithms discussed above. The computer storage requirements of each of these algorithms are both minimal for any problem size n and invariant between different problems of the same size as a result of using the newest active node search procedure in implicitly enumerating all permutation schedules. The computation-time requirements of each of these algorithms thus have the number of nodes that must be created in order to obtain and validate an optimal schedule. This number can be excessive even for small problem sizes. Furthermore, this number can vary considerably between different problems of the same size. Therefore, the computation-time requirements of each of these algorithms have the undesirable property of being problem dependent. This is not the case for the DP algorithms for problem types ID and DI. Their computational requirements do not vary between different problems of the same size. Recall the comparisons made previously between the computational requirements of the DP algorithms for problem types ID and DI and those of the DP algorithm for the TSP. DP is usually recommended over B & B for smaller TSPs because of the assurance that no problem of a given size can result in excessive computation time requirements. This same assurance can likewise be given for the DP algorithms developed in this chapter for problem types ID and DI. However, we cannot give a similar assurance for their B & B counterparts due to the problem-dependent nature of their computational requirements.

On the basis of computer-time assurances, it can be concluded that the DP algorithm for problem type ID is preferable to its B & B counterparts for problems involving approximately 14 or fewer jobs. This same conclusion must be drawn somewhat more cautiously for the DP algorithm for problem type DI because of the necessity to explicitly consider the different problems that result from each possible specification of a last job. However, as noted previously, the graph theoretic-based B & B counterparts must in an analogous fashion explicitly consider each possible specification of a first job. Thus, on the basis of computer-time assurances, the DP algorithm for problem type DI appears to be preferable to these B & B counterparts.

For problems of both types involving larger numbers of jobs, it should be noted that the B & B approach may provide an optimal schedule, while both the B & B and the DP approaches can be employed to give "good" schedules. The B & B algorithms considered here would be capable of solving some particular problems whose size exceeds the known limits on their DP counterpart. Since each of these B & B algorithms produces successively improving schedules, a "good" schedule is generally available in the event the algorithm must be terminated prematurely for a particular problem. Also, it appears that the method of successive approximations can be used to overcome the dimensionality problem inherent in the DP approach to provide "good" schedules for larger problems of both types. It is envisioned that this method would be applied in conjunction with the DP algorithm for each problem type in much the same manner as was employed in Buzzacott and Dutta (1971) in conjunction with a DP algorithm for a variant of the single-machine scheduling problem.

11.11. Optimal Schedules for Problem Types DII, IDI and IID

Let us now turn our attention to the multidimensional versions of the preceding problems. Consider the three-machine problem. The most interesting cases are the following problem types: DII, IDI and IID. Why?

We wish to consider the properties of optimal schedules for these problem types. To do so, we begin by posing the following question: How can one determine for one of these problem types whether or not the class of permutation schedules provides an optimal schedule for any problem of this type? In response to this question, the following two conditions are given:

Condition 11.1. The process of making the job sequences on the first and second machines the same does not increase the completion time of *any* job on the second machine.

Condition 11.2. The process of making the job sequences on the second and third machine the same does not increase the completion time of the *last* job on the third machine.

Now consider *any* problem type involving three machines. Denote these machines as machine 1, machine 2 and machine 3, respectively. Likewise, denote their associated job sequences as sequence 1, sequence 2, and sequence 3, respectively. Assume that these three job sequences are not all identical. Let one of these job sequences be considered fixed. If Condition 11.1 and Condition 11.2 *both* hold, then the other two job sequences can be made the same as the fixed job sequence without increasing the completion time of the *last* job on machine 3, and hence without increasing F_{max}. Thus, if *both* of these conditions hold, any arbitrary schedule can be replaced by the permutation schedule defined by the fixed job sequence without increasing F_{max}. This argument can be repeated using each of the $(n!)$ possible fixed sequences. Therefore, Conditions 11.1 and 11.2 together are sufficient, but not necessary, to insure that only permutation schedules must be considered for this particular problem type.

Conditions 11.1 and 11.2 together provide a means for investigating the properties of optimal schedules for problem types DII, IDI and IID. Note that in order to determine if these two conditions hold for certain problems of a given type, one must first select that one of the three machines on which the job sequence is considered to be fixed. Then, both conditions must be shown to hold for an arbitrary choice of this job sequence. To proceed formally, we would need to determine for each of these problem types whether or not the elements of the associated matrix SP and vectors P must satisfy certain special conditions in order for *both* conditions to hold. If no such conditions are required, then the class of permutation schedules must contain an optimal schedule for any problem of the given type. We will not, however, concern ourselves with such details in this presentation but leave them as an exercise to the reader.

11.12. Dominance Conditions for Problem Types DII, IDI, and IID

In Section 11.7 it was shown that a forward recursion dynamic programming formulation analogous to that of problem type ID cannot be developed for problem type DI. Proceeding in a similar manner, we can demonstrate that this is also the case for problem types DII, IDI and IID. Let us denote the three machines associated with each of these problem types as machine 1, machine 2 and machine 3, respectively. We first present the sequence dominance conditions for each of these problem types. These are

$$T_1(\rho_r) \le T_1(\rho_r'), \tag{11.10}$$

$$T_2(\rho_r) \le T_2(\rho_r'), \tag{11.11}$$

and

$$T_3(\rho_r) \le T_3(\rho_r'), \tag{11.12}$$

where ρ_r and ρ_r' are assumed to contain the same r jobs and end with the same job. Consider any one of these three problem types. Regardless of whether or not relation (11.12) holds for two particular presequences ρ_r and ρ_r', we cannot guarantee that both relations (11.10) and (11.11) will also hold. Thus, we cannot determine if the presequence ρ_r dominates the presequence ρ_r' by simply comparing the flow time under each presequence of the job in position r. Therefore, we conclude that, as was the case with type DI, a valid forward recursion dynamic programming formulation in the presequence time cannot be developed for problem types DII, IDI, or IID.

11.13. Backward Dynamic Programming Formulations

The introduction of a *second state* variable M enables a backward recursion dynamic programming formulation of problem type DI developed in section 11.7 to be extended to problem types DII, IDI and IID. The state variable M is associated with machine 3, whereas the state variable L is associated with machine 2. It serves to indicate the time, subsequent to the availability time of machine 2, at which machine 3 becomes available.

We now proceed to give a backward recursion dynamic programming formulation of problem type DII. The preliminary notation introduced in Section 11.2 will also be used in connection with this formulation. We will refer to the dynamic programming algorithm that we will develop to determine an optimal permutation schedule ending with job j_l and its associated duration as our dynamic programming formulation of problem type DII with specified last job j_l. This formulation, like the one developed for problem type DI, utilizes a backward recursion in the *postsequence* time. We note that here, the postsequence time of a particular postsequence depends on the identity of the job immediately preceding it, as well as the time at which *both* machine 2 and machine 3 become available to begin it.

Consider an arbitrary postsequence of size $(k + 1)$ containing the k jobs of some set J_k in a particular order and then job j_l. Let some job j_i be the job immediately preceding this postsequence. As in Section 11.7, we will refer to job j_i as the preliminary job. Let the integer valued state variable L be defined as in Section 11.7. In addition, let us define the integer valued state variable M as

$M \equiv$ the length of time between the completion of the preliminary job j_i on machine 2 and its completion on machine 3.

Note that the completion time of job j_i on machine 3 is the time at which machine 3 becomes available to start the first job of our arbitrary postsequence. Now, for a given job j_l and any set J_k and job j_i, let us define

$f(j_i; J_k; j_l | L, M) \equiv$ the minimum time required to complete the k jobs of J_k (in some order) and then job j_l, with job j_i as the preliminary job, given the values of L and M.

We note that $L \geq p_{j_i}^2$ and $M \geq p_{j_i}^3$ for $0 \leq k \leq n - 3$, and that $L = p_{j_i}^2$ and $M = p_{j_i}^3$ for $k = n - 2$; we will define $L = 0$ and $M = 0$ for $k = n - 1$. Let $(\rho_k^*(l) j_l)$ be an optimal postsequence of the k jobs of J_k and job j_l associated with $f(j_i; J_k; j_l | l, p_{j_i}^3)$, where l is some particular value of L. Consider $f(j_i; J_k; j_l | l, M)$ for any $M \geq p_{j_i}^3$. Since machine 3 is of type I, it can be shown that the postsequence $(\rho_k^*(l) j_l)$ is optimal for any $M \geq p_{j_i}^3$, and that $f(j_i; J_k; j_l | l, M)$ can be expressed as a simple function of $f(j_i; J_k; j_l | l, p_{j_i}^3)$, l, and M. These two results are given below as a theorem. Since the proof of this theorem is virtually identical to that of Theorem 3, it will be omitted.

THEOREM 4. *Consider* $f(j_i; J_k; j_l | L, M)$ *for* $L = l$ *and any* $M \geq p_{j_i}^3$, *where* $0 \leq k \leq n - 3$. *If* $(\rho_k^*(l) j_l)$ *is an optimal postsequence associated with* $f(j_i; J_k; j_l | l, p_{j_i}^3)$, *then an optimal postsequence associated with* $f(j_i; J_k; j_l | l, M)$ *for any* $M \geq p_{j_i}^3$ *is given by* $(\rho_k^*(l) j_l)$. *Furthermore,* $f(j_i; J_k; j_l | l, M)$ *can be expressed as*

$$f(j_i; J_k; j_l | l, M) = \begin{cases} f(j_i; J_k; j_l | l, p_{j_i}^3), \text{ if} \\ \qquad p_{j_i}^3 \leq M \leq [f(j_i; J_k; j_l | l, p_{j_i}^3) - CC - l] \\ \\ l + M + CC, \qquad if \\ \qquad M > [f(j_i; J_k; j_l | l, p_{j_i}^3) - CC - l] \end{cases}$$

where
$$CC = \sum_{j \in \{J_k, j_l\}} p_j^3. \tag{11.13}$$

However, the value of $f(j_i; J_k; j_l | l, p_{j_i}^3)$, as well as the identity of an associated optimal postsequence $(\rho_k^*(l) j_l)$, do not necessarily remain the same for different values of l of the state variable L. This property of $f(j_i; J_k; j_l | L, M)$ is clearly illustrated by considering the following problem of type DII involving $n \geq 5$ jobs. Let SP^1, P^2, and P^3 be partially specified as

$$SP^1 = \begin{array}{c} \\ ps \\ 1 \\ 2 \\ 3 \\ 4 \\ 5 \\ \\ \\ \\ \end{array} \begin{array}{cccccccc} 1 & 2 & 3 & 4 & - & - & - \\ \cdot & \cdot & \cdot & \cdot & \cdot & \cdot & \cdot \\ \infty & 6 & 7 & 7 & \cdot & \cdot & \cdot \\ 7 & \infty & 5 & 8 & \cdot & \cdot & \cdot \\ 6 & 4 & \infty & 5 & \cdot & \cdot & \cdot \\ \cdot & \cdot & \cdot & \cdot & \cdot & \cdot & \cdot \\ 6 & 5 & 7 & \cdot & \cdot & \cdot & \cdot \\ \cdot & \cdot & \cdot & \cdot & \cdot & \cdot & \cdot \\ \cdot & \cdot & \cdot & \cdot & \cdot & \cdot & \cdot \\ \cdot & \cdot & \cdot & \cdot & \cdot & \cdot & \cdot \end{array},$$

$$P^2 = \begin{array}{c} 1 \\ 2 \\ 3 \\ 4 \\ 5 \\ \cdot \\ \cdot \\ \cdot \end{array} \begin{bmatrix} 5 \\ 8 \\ 3 \\ 5 \\ 4 \\ \cdot \\ \cdot \\ \cdot \end{bmatrix}, \text{ and } P^3 = \begin{array}{c} 1 \\ 2 \\ 3 \\ 4 \\ 5 \\ \cdot \\ \cdot \end{array} \begin{bmatrix} 6 \\ 6 \\ 4 \\ 4 \\ 6 \\ \cdot \\ \cdot \end{bmatrix}$$

Assume that the specified last job j_l is job 4, and that the state variable L is restricted to the interval $p_{j_i}^2 \le L \le p_{j_i}^2 + 5$. Here we obtain results such as the following:

Stage $k = 2$:

$f(3; \{1, 2\}; 4|3, 4) = 28$ with postsequence (214),
$f(3; \{1, 2\}; 4|4, 4) = 28$ with postsequence (214),
$f(3; \{1, 2\}; 4|5, 5) = 29$ with postsequence (214),
$f(3; \{1, 2\}; 4|6, 4) = 30$ with either postsequence (214) or postsequence (124),
$f(3; \{1, 2\}; 4|7, 4) = 30$ with postsequence (124),
$f(3; \{1, 2\}; 4|8, 4) = 31$ with postsequence (164).

Stage $k = 3$:

$f(5; \{1, 2, 3\}; 4|4, 6) = 33$ with either postsequence (2134) or postsequence (2314),

$f(5; \{1, 2, 3\}; 4|5, 6) = 33$ with either postsequence (2134) or postsequence (2314),

$f(5; \{1, 2, 3\}; 4|6, 6) = 34$ with postsequence (2134), postsequence (2314), or postsequence (1234),

$f(5; \{1, 2, 3\}; 4|7, 6) = 34$ with postsequence (1234),

$f(5; \{1, 2, 3\}; 4|7, 6) = 35$ with postsequence (1234), postsequence (1324), or postsequence (3214),

$f(5; \{1, 2, 3\}; 4|9, 6) = 35$ with postsequence (1324).

This example demonstrates that, for any given last job j_l, preliminary job j_i, and set of jobs J_k, both the value of $f(j_i; J_k; j_l | l, p_{j_i}^3)$ and the identity of an associated optimal postsequence $(\rho_k^*(l)j_l)$ must be determined separately for each different value of the state variable L considered. Recall that $f(j_i; J_k; j_l | L, M)$ is defined for any $L \ge p_{j_i}^2$ when $0 \le k \le n - 3$. However, it is apparent that computational considerations required us to limit our attention to some closed interval $p_{j_i}^2 \le L \le p_{j_i}^2 + c_1$. Here c_1 is a constant whose value must be specified for each given problem. We will discuss the constant c_1 later in Section 11.15.

Now that we have defined $f(j_i; J_k; j_l | L, M)$ and studied its properties, we can continue the development of our dynamic programming formulation of problem type DII with specified last job j. Applying the principle of optimality gives us the following backward recursion relations:

$$f(j_i; J_k; j_l | L, M) = \min_{j_p \in J_k} [sp_{j_i j_p}^1 + f(j_p; \{J_k - j_p\}; j_l | L'(j_p), M'(j_p))]$$
$$\text{for } 1 \le k \le n - 2 \tag{11.14}$$

and

$$f(\text{pis}; J_{n-1}; j_l | 0, 0) = \min_{j_p \in J_{n-1}} [sp_{psj_p}^1 + f(j_p; \{J_{n-1} - j_p\}; j_l p_{j_p}^2, p_{j_p}^3)]$$
$$\text{for } k = n - 1, \tag{11.15}$$

where $p_{j_i}^2 \leq L \leq p_{j_i}^2 + c_1$ and $M \geq p_{j_i}^3$ for $1 \leq k \leq n-3$, and $L = p_{j_i}^2$ and $M = p_{j_i}^3$ for $k = n-2$.

11.14. Reducing Dimensionality

This formulation can be made more compact by considering the properties of the state variables and exploiting the results of Theorem 4. We proceed to do so. The state variable $L'(j_p)$, defined as in Section 11.7 is given by

$$L'(j_p) = \max (L - sp_{j_i j_p}^1, 0) + p_{j_p}^2. \tag{11.16}$$

The state variable $M'(j_p)$ represents the length of time between the completion of job j_p on machine 2 and its completion on machine 3 if job j_p immediately follows the preliminary job j_i. It is given by

$$M'(j_p) = \max [L + M - \max (L, sp_{j_i j_p}^1) - p_{j_p}^2, 0] + p_{j_p}^3. \tag{11.17}$$

However, due to Theorem 4, only $f(j_i; J_k; j_l | L, p_{j_i}^3)$ and an associated optimal postsequence must be obtained for each value of L considered. Thus, we can replace the more general backward recursion relation (11.14) by the following one:

$$f(j_i; J_k; j_l | L, p_{j_i}^3) = \min_{j_p \in J_k} [sp_{j_i j_p}^1 + f(j_p; \{J_k - j_p\}; j_l | L'(j_p), M'(j_p))] \tag{11.18}$$
$$\text{for } 1 \leq k \leq n-2,$$

where $p_{j_i}^2 \leq L \leq p_{j_i}^2 + c_1$ for $1 \leq k \leq n-3$ and $L = p_{j_i}^2$ for $k = n-2$. Here, $L'(j_p)$ is given by (11.16) and $M'(j_p)$ is given by

$$M'(j_p) = \max [L + p_{j_i}^3 - \max (L, sp_{j_i j_p}^1) - p_{j_p}^2, 0] + p_{j_p}^3. \tag{11.19}$$

In addition, we observe that equation (11.13) provides a simple means of evaluating $f(j_p; \{J_k - j_p\}; j_l | L'(j_p), M'(j_p))$ for any $M'(j_p) \geq p_{j_p}^3$. Consider $f(j_i; J_k; j_l | l, p_{j_i}^3)$, where l is a particular value of l. Let $(\rho_{k-1}^{(p)} (l'_p) j_l)$ denote the optimal postsequence of the $(k-1)$ jobs of $J_k - j_p$ and job j_l associated with $f(j_p; \{J_k - j_p\}; j_l | l'_p, p_{j_p}^3)$, where $l'_p = \max (l - sp_{j_i j_p}^1, 0) + p_{j_p}^2$. If a choice of j_p that corresponds to the minimum in (11.18) for the case $L = l$ is j_m, then an optimal postsequence $(\rho_k^*(l) j_l)$ associated with $f(j_i; J_k; j_l | l, p_{j_i}^3)$ is given by $(j_m \rho_{k-1}^{(m)} (l'_m) j_l)$. Finally, we note that the validity of relation (11.18) can be argued in the same manner as the validity of relation (11.19) was argued in Section 11.8.

The recursive procedure given by (11.18) and (11.15) is initiated through the use of the known relation

$$f(j_i; J_o; j_l | L, p_{j_i}^3) = \max [\max (sp_{j_i j_i}^1, L) + p_{j_i}^2, L + p_{j_i}^3] + p_{j_i}^3 \tag{11.20}$$
$$\text{for the case } k = 0,$$

where $p_{j_i}^2 \leq L \leq p_{j_i}^2 + c_1$. From (11.15) we obtain an optimal full sequence ending with the specified last job j_l and its corresponding duration. This completes our dynamic programming formulation of problem DII with specified last job j_l. However, job j_l can be any one of the n jobs of S. Thus, by repeating our dynamic programming formulation of problem type DII with specified last job j_l for each of the n possible last jobs j_l, we have the desired dynamic programming formulation of problem type DII. Once f(ps; J_{n-1}, $j_l | 0, 0$) and an associated optimal full sequence (ρ^*_{n-1} j_l) have been obtained for each of the n possible jobs j_l, a solution to the problem is given by the minimization

$$\min_{j_l \in s} f(\text{ps}; J_{n-1}; j_l | 0, 0). \tag{11.21}$$

11.15. Selection of Value for c_1

In developing our formulation of problem type DII, we have arbitrarily restricted the state variable L to the interval $p^2_{j_i} \leq L \leq p^2_{j_i} + c_1$ when $0 \leq k \leq n - 3$. In order to use this formulation for solving a particular n job problem, we must specify a value for the constant c_1. Therefore, we will now consider the selection of c_1.

Let us define the delay time of a job on machine 2 to be the length of time between its completion on machine 1 and its start on machine 2. Then, for any $L \geq p^2_{j_i}$, the time length $(L - p^2_{j_i})$ represents the delay time of job j_i on machine 2. By considering $f(j_i; J_k; j_l | L, M)$ for $p^2_{j_i} \leq L \leq p^2_{j_i} + c_1$ when $0 \leq k \leq n - 3$, we are excluding from further consideration any schedule with job j_i in position $(n - k - 1)$, the jobs of J_k (in some order) in positions $(n - k)$ through $(n - 1)$, and job j_i in position n for which the delay time of job j_i on machine 2 is greater than c_1. For any given n job problem, let W denote the maximum delay time incurred by a job on machine 2 under any of the $n!$ possible permutation schedules. Furthermore, let d_j represent the delay incurred by job j ($j = 1, 2, \ldots, n$) on machine 2 under an optimal permutation schedule for the given problem. There will be some problems of type DII for which the maximum of its associated d_j values is equal to its associated value of W. Therefore, for any particular problem of type DII, we *should* specify the constant c_1 to be the value of W associated with this particular problem.

Note that since the value of W will vary between different problems of size n, the value of c_1 should do likewise. Due to this property, we will refer to c_1 as being *problem dependent*. In other words, a value of c_1 that is sufficiently large to permit the solution of a given n job problem by our dynamic programming algorithm may or may not be sufficiently large to permit the solution of a different n job problem by this same algorithm. Unfortunately, the value of W for any particular n job problem cannot be obtained without enumerating all $n!$ permutation schedules and determining the delay time of each of the n jobs on machine 2 under each of these schedules. Since this is essentially equivalent to solving the given problem by enumeration, we must assume that the value of W for a particular problem cannot be determined. However, a lower bound on this value can be obtained by using equation (11.16) and the fact that $L \geq p_{j_i}^2$ for $0 \leq k \leq n-3$ and $L = p_{j_i}^2$ for $k = n-2$.

Consider equation (11.18) for any k, $1 \leq k \leq n-2$. For any given least job j_l and preliminary job j_i, job j_p can be any one of the $(n-2)$ remaining jobs. In addition, for a given last job j_l, the preliminary job j_i can be any one of the $(n-1)$ other jobs. Finally, any one of the n jobs can be the specified last job j_l. Thus, the value of W for a particular n job problem, and hence the value of c_1 for this problem, is bounded below by

$$\max_{i \in S} \left[\max_{j \in \{S-i\}} (p_i^2 - sp_{ij}^1) \right]. \qquad (11.22)$$

The value of c_1 for a particular problem must be "sufficiently large" so that we are reasonably confident that it is at least equal to the value of W associated with this problem. The lower bound given by (11.22) and an examination of the particular problem provide the basis for specifying the value of c_1.

11.16. Computational Requirements

Consider the computational requirements of our dynamic programming formulation of an n job problem of type DII with specified last job j_l. Let the successive stages of the recursive procedure given by (11.20), (11.18) and (11.15) be indexed by k, the number of the jobs in the set J_k. Since each of the $(c_1 + 1)$ possible values of L must be considered separately, there are $(c_1 + 1)$ $(n-1)\binom{n-2}{k}$ different problems of the form $f(j_i: J_k; j_l | L, p_{j_i}^3)$ to be solved at stage k $(0 \leq k \leq n-2)$. There is only one problem to be solved at stage $(n-1)$. Let us assume that the particular value of L associated with a given problem at stage k can be identified without explicitly storing it. Then, for each problem at stage k $(0 \leq k \leq n-2)$, the identity of job j_i, the identity of $\rho_k^*(l)$, and the corresponding value $f(j_i; J_k; j_l | l, p_{j_i}^3)$ must be stored. Since an optimal full sequence ending with the specified last job j_l and its associated duration are obtained at stage $(n-1)$, no information must be stored at this stage. Therefore, the computer storage requirements at stage $(0 \leq k \leq n-2)$ of our formulation of an n job problem of type DII with specified last job j_l are exactly $(c_1 + 1)$ times as large as those of our formulation of an n job problem of type DI with specified last job j_l. As the result of specifying an appropriate value of c_1, the computer storage requirements of this formulation, and hence those of our formulation of problem type DII, can very easily be prohibitive for particular problems involving a moderately small $(n \leq 10)$ number of jobs. Even for relatively small values of c_1, the limits imposed on problem size n by the storage requirements of this formulation of problem type DII will be significantly smaller than those determined in Section 11.9 for our formulation of problem type DI. The computation time requirements of our formulation of an n job problem of type DII with specified last job j_l are essentially $(c_1 + 1)$ times as great as those of our comparable formulation of problem type DI. It is important to note that, since the value of c_1 is problem dependent, the computational requirements of our formulation of problem type DII are also problem dependent. In conclusion, it is apparent that the computational requirements of our dynamic programming formulation of problem type DII far exceed those of our dynamic programming formulation of problem type DI.

11.17. Extensions

The backward recursion dynamic programming formulation of problem type DI given in Section 11.7 can also be extended to problem types IDI and IID by the addition of the state variable M. Consider the backward recursion dynamic programming formulation that we have just developed for problem type DII. By simply interchanging the roles of machine 1 and machine 2, i.e. by making the appropriate substitutions of p_j^1 for sp_{ij}^1 and sp_{ij}^2 for p_j^2 in equations (11.15), (11.16), (11.18), (11.19) and (11.20), we obtain the corresponding formulation of problem type IDI. Since machine 3 is of type I, a theorem analogous to Theorem 4 holds here. In addition, both the value of $f(j_i; J_k; j_l | l, p_{ji}^3)$ and the identity of an associated optimal postsequence $(\rho_k^*(l)_l)$ must be determined separately for each value l of the state variable L considered. Thus, since the properties of $f(j_i; J_k; j_l | L, M)$ are the same for both formulations, the above discussion of the computational requirements of our formulation of problem type DII also applies to this formulation of problem type IDI.

In a manner analogous to the foregoing, by simply interchanging the roles of machine 1 and machine 3, i.e. by making the appropriate substitutions of p_j^1 for sp_{ij}^1 and sp_{ij}^3 for p_j^3 in equations (11.14), (11.15), (11.16), (11.17) and (11.20), we obtain the corresponding formulation of problem type IID. However, due to the fact that machine 3 is now of type D, a theorem analogous to Theorem 3.2 does not hold here. Thus, both the value of $f(j_i; J_k; j_l | l, m)$ and the identity of an associated optimal postsequence $(\rho_k^*(l, m)j_l)$ must be determined separately for each pair of values (l, m) of the state variables L and M considered. A second constant c_2 is required to establish the range of the state variable M that is to be considered when $0 \le k \le n - 3$. It is apparent that the computational requirements of this formulation of problem type IID far exceed those of our formulation of problem type DII.

Exercises

Problem 1

Consider a type ID problem in which the arrival times of jobs 1, 2 and 3 are 0, 3 and 7, respectively. Define p^1 and SP^2 as

$$P^1 = \begin{bmatrix} 3 \\ 3 \\ 2 \end{bmatrix} \quad \text{and} \quad SP^2 = \begin{matrix} \text{ps} \\ \\ \\ \\ \end{matrix} \begin{bmatrix} \infty & 2 & 2 & 3 \\ 0 & \infty & 2 & 2 \\ 0 & 1 & \infty & 3 \\ 0 & 2 & 3 & \infty \end{bmatrix}$$

Show that for this problem, the schedule with sequence 1 as (1,2,3) and sequence 2 as (2,1,3) yields a smaller F_{max} value than any permutation schedule.

Problem 2

Consider the following type DII problem with SP^1, P^2 and P^3 given as

$$SP^1 = \begin{matrix} \text{ps} \\ \\ \\ \\ \end{matrix} \begin{bmatrix} \infty & 2 & 2 & 2 \\ 0 & \infty & 1 & 2 \\ 0 & 4 & \infty & 3 \\ 0 & 2 & 2 & \infty \end{bmatrix}, \quad P^2 = \begin{bmatrix} 3 \\ 2 \\ 1 \end{bmatrix} \quad \text{and} \quad p^3 = \begin{bmatrix} 1 \\ 3 \\ 1 \end{bmatrix}$$

(a) Show that the schedule with job sequence (1,2,3) on the first machine and job sequence (2,1,3) on the second and third machine gives a smaller F_{max} value than any permutation schedule.

(b) What do you conclude about the optimality of permutation schedules?

(c) Under special conditions on the elements of SP^1 and P^2 Condition 11.1 holds for problem type DII. Derive these conditions.

Problem 3

Consider any problem of type IID. Assume that the job sequence on the third machine is fixed.

(a) Applying the result derived in the text for problem type II, show that the job sequence on the first machine can be made the same as the job sequence on the second machine without increasing the completion time of any job on the second machine?

(b) What can you conclude from your results?

Problem 4

In the following problem of type IID, suppose we define the variables P^1, P^2 and SP^3 as

$$P^1 = \begin{bmatrix} 1 \\ 3 \\ 4 \end{bmatrix}, \quad p^2 = \begin{bmatrix} 3 \\ 3 \\ 2 \end{bmatrix} \quad \text{and} \quad SP^3 = \begin{matrix} \text{ps} \\ \\ \\ \\ \end{matrix} \begin{bmatrix} \infty & 2 & 2 & 3 \\ 0 & \infty & 2 & 2 \\ 0 & 1 & \infty & 3 \\ 0 & 2 & 3 & \infty \end{bmatrix}$$

(a) Show that the schedule with job sequence (1,2,3) on the first and second machines and the job sequence (2,1,3) on the third machine yields a smaller F_{max} value than any permutation schedule.

(b) What do you conclude from this result?

(c) Derive the special conditions on the elements of P^2 and SP^3 under which Condition 11.2 holds for this problem.

Problem 5

Assume one is scheduling a static flow shop scheduling problem of type IID. If

$$\min_j p_j^2 \geq \max_{i,j} sp_{ij}^3$$

and

$$[p_j^2 - \min_t sp_{tr}^3] + sp_{rj}^3 \leq sp_{rj_1}^3 + sp_{j_1 j_2}^3 + \ldots + sp_{j_k j}^3$$

for all possible sequence $(j_1, j_2 \ldots, j_k)$ of k jobs $(1 \leq k \leq n-2)$ where $j_l \neq r, j, l = 1, 2, \ldots, k$, for each job $r (r \neq \text{ps}, j)$ for a given job j. For each job j, show that the class of permutation schedules contains an optimal schedule for this problem.

Problem 6

(a) Assume one is scheduling a static flow-shop scheduling problem of type IID. If

$$\min_{i,j} sp_{ij}^3 \geq \max_j p_j^2.$$

Show that the class of permutation schedules contains an optimal schedule for this problem.

(b) Consider the following static flow-shop scheduling problem of type DII. If

$$\min_{i,j} sp_{ij}^1 \geq \max_j p_j^2.$$

Show that the class of permutation schedules contains an optimal schedule for this problem.

Problem 7

Consider the following 5-job problem of type DI. Define SP^1 and p^2 as

$$SP^1 \begin{array}{c} \text{ps} \\ 1 \\ 2 \\ 3 \\ 4 \\ 5 \end{array} \begin{array}{ccccc} 1 & 2 & 3 & 4 & 5 \\ \begin{bmatrix} 5 & 7 & 4 & 8 & 6 \\ \infty & 6 & 6 & 6 & 8 \\ 7 & \infty & 4 & 6 & 8 \\ 6 & 6 & \infty & 5 & 7 \\ 6 & 7 & 5 & \infty & 7 \\ 7 & 8 & 5 & 7 & \infty \end{bmatrix} \end{array} \quad \text{and} \quad P^2 = \begin{array}{c} 1 \\ 2 \\ 3 \\ 4 \\ 5 \end{array} \begin{bmatrix} 7 \\ 3 \\ 8 \\ 4 \\ 5 \end{bmatrix}$$

Show that a forward dynamic programming recursion approach yields a value of 34 as opposed to the true minimum time of 32. What do you conclude from this?

Problem 8

Suppose one is scheduling a static flow shop of problem type IDI. Develop a backward recursion dynamic programming formulation for this problem by using an approach similar to that of problem type DI.

Problem 9

Develop a dynamic programming formulation for problem type IID.

Problem 10

Branch and bound algorithms for flow-shop scheduling problems were discussed in Chapter 9 for minimum makespan problems under various conditions where passing of jobs is not allowed as well as those where it is allowed. This suggests that it is possible to extend these notions to other scenarios. For each of the problem types involving sequence dependent setup times listed below, develop an equivalent branch and bound algorithm. Compare the computational requirements of the B&B algorithms with their DP counterparts.

(i) DI   (iv) IDI
(ii) ID   (v) DII
(iii) IID

Bibliography and Comments

Section 11.1

That the class of schedules for which the job sequence on each machine is identical (permutation schedules) in the classic two-machine problem and contains an optimal schedule was first shown by

S. M. JOHNSON, "Optimal two and three stage production schedules with set up times included", *Naval Research Logistics Quarterly*, 1, (1954), 61–68.

As noted in Chapter 1 two essentially equivalent DP formulations for the TSP or equivalently the single-machine scheduling problem with sequence dependent setup times were first developed by

R. E. BELLMAN (1962) and M. HELD and R. M. KARP (1962), *op. cit.*

The topic of this chapter has important practical motivations. One example may be found in paper production. Another is paint manufacture. For the modeling of the paper-production problem as a single as opposed to the more realistic two-machine problem, see J. F. PIERCE and D. J. HATFIELD, "Production sequencing by combinatorial programming", Chapter 17 of *Operations Research and Management Information Systems*, J. F. PIERCE (ed), Tech. Assoc. of Pulp and Paper Industry, 1966.

Section 11.2

The set of assumptions which define the classic two-machine scheduling problem are well documented in previous chapters. See in particular:
S. M. JOHNSON (1954), *op. cit.*

Section 11.3

Being able to show the optimality of permutation schedules is a logical first step in developing efficient scheduling algorithms.

The proofs of Theorems 1 and 2 parallel those given by:
R. W. CONWAY, W. L. MAXWELL and L. W. MILLER, *Theory of Scheduling*, Addison-Wesley, Reading, Mass., 1967.

However, in each instance, their proof is only concerned with showing that the two-job sequences under consideration can be made the same without increasing F_{max}. Their proofs do not make the important distinction between guaranteeing a nonincrease in the completion time of *any* job and guaranteeing a nonincrease in the completion time of only the *last* job on the second of the two machines under consideration.

The square bracket notation $[i]$ means the job that is in position i of the permutation schedule; $[i] = 2$ identifies this job as job 2.

Section 11.4

This concept of sequence dominance is distinct from that employed by previous writers because of the presence in our case of sequence dependent setup times. For traditional concepts see R. D. SMITH and R. A. DUDEK, "A general algorithm for solution of the n-job, m-machine sequencing problem of the flow shop", *Operations Research*, 15 (1967), 71–82.

Sections 11.5 through 11.10

These discussions were presented in
B. D. CORWIN and A. O. ESOGBUE, "Two machine flow shop scheduling problems with sequence dependent set up times: a dynamic programming approach", *Naval Research Logistics Quarterly*, 21, No. 3 (1974), 515–524.

For an excellent application of the successive approximation techniques and dynamic programming algorithm to a variant of the single-machine scheduling problem see A. BUZZACOTT and S. K. DUTTA, "Sequencing many jobs on a multipurpose facility", *Naval Research Logistics Quarterly*, 18, No. 1 (1971), 75–82.

Sections 11.11 through 11.17

The extension to the three-machine problem and other multidimensional cases was given in:
A. O. ESOGBUE and B. D. CORWIN, "A dynamic programming treatment of some multidimensional machine flow shop scheduling problems involving sequence dependent set up times", 46th Joint National Meeting of ORSA and TIMS, San Juan, Puerto Rico, October 1974.
and
B. D. CORWIN, "Some flow shop scheduling problems involving sequence dependent set up times", Ph.D. Dissertation, Dept. of Operations Research, Case Western Reserve University, Cleveland, Ohio, 1969.

Note that in Section 11.13 it is necessary to introduce the superscripts in order to specify the machine in question. For example, $p_{j_i}^2$ and $p_{j_i}^3$ refer to machines 2 and 3 respectively.

CHAPTER 12

The Job-shop Scheduling Problem

12.1. Introduction

The sequencing problem, in which each of n jobs is processed by m machines, is to determine a processing order of all operations, that is, a sequence, on every machine in order to minimize a specified objective function under given ordering for every job and the other assumptions as described in Chapter 4.

In the job-shop case where ordering of every job is not the same, what differs from the flow-shop case, where ordering of any job is the same, is the fact that all feasible operations decided by given orderings must be taken into account in order to determine the next operation to be processed at each time any operation completes on any machine. From this fact it is very difficult to analyze the job-shop case and obtain any analytical result as given for the flow-shop case in Chapters 7 and 8. Hence, mostly general solution methods for determining an optimal schedule are presented. These are developed based on a Gantt chart or some graphs (networks) and classified into the following types:

1. Solution method for the $n \times 2$ min-makespan problem as an extension of the Johnson result in the two-machine flow-shop problem (Chapter 7).

2. Graphical solution method for the $2 \times m$ min-makespan problem and an attempt at its generalization.

3. An approach to the solution of the min-makespan problem by integer linear programming.

4. BAB algorithms for the min-makespan problem by using similar procedures to an active schedule generation procedure (Chapter 4), where any BAB algorithm has a common branching procedure for every operation in the set of conflicting operations, to be processed, and different lower bound.

5. BAB algorithms for any normal objective function by using disjunctive graphs for the job-shop problem and for the general multiproject scheduling problem with limited resources. This include the general job-shop problem as a special case (cf. Remark).

In this final chapter we explain these general solution methods, from which approximate methods can be derived by applying suitable heuristics and/or search rules.

Remark. The job shop considered in this chapter has each machine of the same type. As its generalization, the general job-shop problem assumes an ordering of the PERT network type for every job to be processed by one machine among multiple machines of the same kind and for some operations to be processed in parallel. Then this general job-shop problem is included in the multiproject scheduling problem with limited resources (cf. Chapter 3).

12.2. The $n \times 2$ Min-Makespan Problem

As an extension of the result by Johnson minimizing the makespan in the two-machine flow-shop case, Jackson treated the case where the set of n jobs is decomposed into the following four types in a job shop:

{A}: Set of jobs with ordering M_1.
{B}: Set of jobs with ordering M_2.
{AB}: Set of jobs with ordering M_1, M_2.
{BA}: Set of jobs with ordering M_2, M_1.

Then an optimal schedule is obtained by the following theorem:

THEOREM 1. *For the present $n \times 2$ min-makespan problem, an optimal schedule is determined by the following rule:*

1. *On the machine M_1, arrange in the order* {AB}, {A}, {BA}.
2. *On the machine M_2, arrange in the order* {BA}, {B}, {AB}.
3. *All jobs in* {AB} *are arranged by a criterion for two machines M_1, M_2 in the flow-shop problem. That is, (7.18) at Section 7.11 in Chapter 7.*
4. *All jobs in* {BA} *are arranged by a criterion for two machines M_2, M_1 in the flow-shop, that is, if a criterion*

$$\min[p_{i,2}, p_{j,1}] \leqq \min[p_{j,2}, p_{i,1}]$$

holds without equality, then job i precedes job j. If equality holds either ordering is optimal.

Proof. Since (7.18) at Section 7.11 in Chapter 7 holds for any $i \in$ {AB} and any $j \in$ {A} because $p_{i,1} > 0$, $p_{i,2} > 0$, $p_{j,1} > 0$, and $p_{j,2} = 0$ hold, any job in {AB} must precede any job in {A}. Also the order of all jobs in {AB} is obviously determined by this criterion (7.18). Jobs in {B} are processed on M_2 continuously without idle time of M_2 in any order. When any job $i \in$ {AB} is processed on M_2, the greater the committed time t_l for M_2 by the previous job l, the smaller the idle time of M_2 in the processing of job i. Hence, on M_2 we have the order {B}, {AB}. Next, on M_2, the order {BA}, {B} is determined by a criterion, described in the theorem, for the same reason as for the order {AB}, {A} on M_1, and jobs in {BA} are optimally ordered by the same criterion. Then by considering the smaller idle times on M_1 and M_2, ultimately the conclusion of the theorem follows.

EXAMPLE. 1. An optimal schedule for the present problem with the processing times for each type in Table 12.1 becomes as shown in Fig. 12.1.

TABLE 12..1

i	{A}	1 2	{B}	3 4	{AB}	5 6	{BA}	7 8
$p_{i,1}$		2 1		0 0		4 9		3 3
$p_{i,2}$		0 0		1 1		2 3		4 2

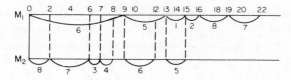

FIG. 12.1

Exercise

1. Show that, in an optimal schedule determined by Theorem 1, any idle time does not occur on at least one of two machines M_1, M_2.

12.3. Graphical Solution of the $2 \times m$ Min-Makespan Problem

For this problem, historically, in 1955 Akers and Friedman showed, by using Boolean algebra, a necessary and sufficient condition for the sequences on every machine to be a feasible sequence (Section 4.6 in Chapter 4) and, moreover, gave a necessary and sufficient condition for a feasible sequence to be a potentially optimal sequence (Section 4.9 in Chapter 4). Subsequently, in 1956, Akers gave a graphical solution by expressing any feasible schedule (sequence) as a path in a rectangle in the $X - Y$ plane and then Szwarc applied dynamic programming to determine an optimal path identifying an optimal schedule. Also theoretical study for this graphical solution methods and its generalization to the $n \times m$ min-makespan problem was made by Hardgrave and Nemhauser. Recently Turksen and Shankar decomposed the $n \times m$ problem into $\binom{n}{2} 2 \times m$ problems and transformed the latter to the set of Boolean equations for deciding an optimal schedule from dominant schedules.

In the following Sections 12.4 and 12.5 a graphical solution will be described.

12.4. Graphical Representation of the Schedule

First, a rectangular representation of the orderings of two jobs and their processing times will be explained by the following example.

EXAMPLE 2. For the present 2×5 problem, let each ordering and processing times be

Job	Ordering
1	$M_2^3 \ M_1^3 \ M_3^2 \ M_4^7 \ M_5^4$
2	$M_1^4 \ M_2^4 \ M_4^3 \ M_3^2 \ M_5^3$

where the numbers given on the right side show processing times associated with related machines. Then these orderings and processing times are represented by a rectangle in the first quadrant of the two-dimensional $T_1 - T_2$ plane in the following way (cf. Fig. 12.2):

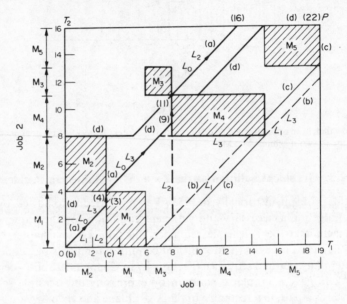

FIG. 12.2

1. Jobs 1 and 2 are represented on the T_1 axis and T_2 axis respectively. Then, on an interval

$$\left[0, \sum_{q=1}^{5} p_{1,q} \right]$$

in T_1 axis, is shown the order of machines of lengths with respective processing times of job 1 along with the ordering for job 1, from the origin 0. Similar representations of the ordering for job 2 and its related processing times are made on the T_2-axis as shown in Fig. 12.2. Then a rectangle with vertices O and

$$P\left(\sum_{q=1}^{5} p_{1,q}, \ \sum_{q=1}^{5} p_{2,q} \right)$$

is depicted.

2. We show a rectangle M_k with the intervals on T_1 and T_2 axes corresponding to each machine M_k ($k = 1, 2, 3, 4, 5$) as its width and its length respectively, and every rectangle M_k ($k = 1, 2, 3, 4, 5$) has oblique lines, that is, is shaded. Then we have a rectangle in Fig. 12.2 corresponding to Example 2.

Remark. Even if there exist a machine which processes some jobs more than once and/or does not process some jobs, a rectangle by the above paragraphs 1 and 2 can be given.

Then, each (feasible) schedule corresponds to a stepwise straight line (a path) which satisfies the conditions in the following theorem:

THEOREM 2. *For a rectangle corresponding to the present* $2 \times m$ *problem, each (feasible) schedule corresponds to a stepwise straight line (a path) which satisfies the following conditions:*

1. *It starts from an origin* O $(0, 0)$ *and ends at a point* $P(P_1, P_2)$, *where* P_1 *and* P_2 *are the sums of the processing times of jobs* 1 *and* 2 *respectively.*
2. *It consists of the segments either at a 45-degree angle to the right (processing both jobs), horizontal (processing job* 1 *alone), or vertical (processing job* 2 *alone).*
3. *It must not cross any of the shaded rectangles*

Proof. First consider any path consisting of the segments of three types in condition 2. Here a segment at a 45-degree angle is chosen, because of its equal projected segments on both axes which means the processing of both jobs during the equal times of the projected segments. If a path crosses a shaded rectangle M_k, then there exists a segment at a 45-degree angle in M_k, which means that a machine M_k processes two jobs simultaneously. This is a contradiction. Therefore, condition 3 must be satisfied.

Next, the reason that the segments are restricted to three types in 2 is obvious from Theorem 5 in Section 4.6 in Chapter 4 (cf. exercise 1). Also since any of two jobs must be completed, condition 1 must be satisfied.

From this theorem the length of any path, that is, a makespan of the corresponding schedule, f, is defined as below:

$$f = \text{(sum of the special lengths of 45-degree segments)}$$
$$+ \text{(sum of the lengths of horizontal segments)}$$
$$+ \text{(sum of the lengths of vertical segments)}, \qquad (12.1)$$

where a length of a 45-degree segment between two points (t_1, t_2), $(t_1 + t, t_2 + t)$ is defined as t, that is, $1/\sqrt{2}$ times its geometrical length, as shown in Fig. 12.3, and the lengths of horizontal and vertical segments are their geometrical lengths.

If we consider the lengths of the 45-degree segments as the lengths on a horizontal axis, then the sum of the first two terms in (12.1) becomes the total

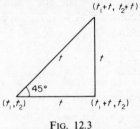

FIG. 12.3

processing times of job 1 and so is constant. Hence a path with the least sum of the vertical segments becomes a shortest path corresponding to an optimal schedule. Consequently, it is sufficient for finding an optimal schedule to determine a shortest path in a related rectangle.

Exercises

1. In Theorem 2, prove that the segments on any path are restricted to the three types described in condition 2, by using Theorem 5 in Section 4.6, of Chapter 4.

2. Show that a path with the least sum of the horizontal segments becomes a shortest path corresponding to an optimal schedule.

12.5. Construction of the Path

The paths can be constructed by the following rule:

1. Proceed from the point $O\,(0, 0)$ in the 45-degree direction until a shaded rectangle M_k is hit. Let this point be a point (t_1, r_{2k}) on a bottom edge, where a point (r_{1k}, r_{2k}) is the coordinate of a left lower vertex of M_k (cf. Fig. 12.4 (a)).

2. In this case, a branching to two directions is considered, as described below:

   (i) From the point (t_1, r_{2k}), proceed to the right until a point $(r_{1k} + p_{1,k}, r_{2k})$ is reached. By making this point as a new starting point, repeat 1. This case corresponds to processing the job 1 first by machine M_k.

   (ii) Another way is to go back to a point $(r_{1k}, r_{2k} - t_1 + r_{1k})$. Then from this point, proceed vertically to a point $(r_{1k}, r_{2k} + p_{2,k})$. By making this point as a new starting point, repeat no. 1. This case corresponds to processing the job 2 first by machine M_k.

By the above (i) or (ii) we resolve a conflict at machine M_k. As another case at no. 1, when a 45-degree segment from the origin hits the left edge of a shaded rectangle M_k at a point (r_{1k}, t_2), the procedure is the same as shown in Fig. 12.4 (b). Also if this 45-degree segment hits at vertex (r_{1k}, r_{2k}), then proceed to the right or upwards.

3. If any line hits the upper or right edge of the outer rectangle, then proceed to a terminal point P along this edge. This completes a path.

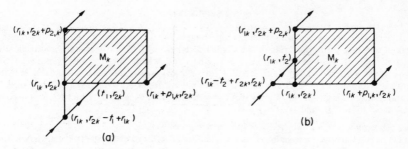

(a)

(b)

Fig. 12.4

By this rule all paths for example 2 become four paths L_0, L_1, L_2 and L_3 in Fig. 12.2. L_0 is expressed by a bold line and the others are by broken lines. By Theorem 5 in Section 4.6 of Chapter 4, all schedules, that is, all feasible sequences, can be determined by excluding the sequences including the job-order $\bar{u}v(u = M_2, v = M_1$ and $u = M_3, v = M_4)$ from all sequences. Hence the number of all schedules for example 2 amounts to $2^5 - 2 \times 2^3 + 2 = 18$. However, by the above rule it is sufficient to consider only four schedules (paths), from which an optimal schedule (a shortest path) can be determined. The reason for this fact is shown in the following Theorem 3:

THEOREM 3. *There exists a shortest path (an optimal schedule), connecting the origin with the terminal point P, among all paths constructed by the above rule.*

This theorem is proved by induction on the number N of the shaded rectangles hit by the path constructed by the above rule. For more details, refer to Hardgrave and Nemhauser's paper.

Then the lengths of the four paths L_0, L_1, L_2 and L_3 become 22, 23, 28, 24 respectively. Hence a shortest path is a path L_0. In Fig. 12.2 the length of each partial path, which starts from the origin and ends at an endpoint of each segment on a path L_0, is shown in parentheses.

A Gantt chart classified by jobs for an optimal schedule corresponding to a shortest path L_0 becomes as in Fig. 12.5.

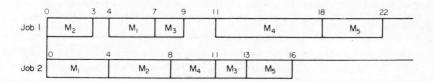

Fig. 12.5. Optimal schedule of Example 2.

Exercises

1. *Existence area of a shortest path* Let a path (a) in Fig. 12.2 be a path which starts from the origin, selects a left upper route of the shaded rectangle each time it intersects, and ends at a terminal point P. Also let a path (b) in Fig. 12.2 be a path which otherwise always selects a right lower route. Then show that a shortest path L_0 exists in an area D_1 bounded by (a) and (b). Next, let two paths (c) and (d) in Fig. 12.2 be defined in the similar manner as above by starting from a point P and ending at the origin. Then show that L_0 exists in an area D_2 bounded by (c) and (d) and so in an intersection of D_1 and D_2.

2. *Determination of a shortest path by dynamic programming.*

Let us call the origin, a right lower vertex, a left upper vertex of every shaded rectangle, and the terminal point P as nodes, and let $w_1, w_2, \ldots$ be a sequence of node numbers determined from the terminal point to the origin in nonincreasing order of abscissae of all nodes, where, in case of a tie, in decreasing order of ordinates. For Example 2 they become as in Fig. 12.6.

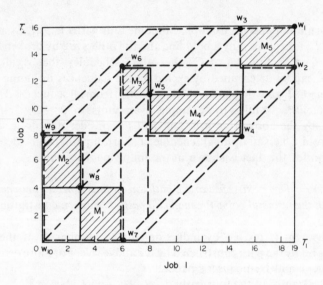

FIG. 12.6

Next let $w_i(t_{1i}, t_{2i})$ and $w_j(t_{1j}, t_{2j})$ be the coordinates of any two nodes w_i and w_j respectively. Then we define that w_i is adjacent to w_j when $t_{1i} \leq t_{1j}, t_{2i} \leq t_{2j}$ hold and, moreover, there exists at least one step-wise straight line consisting of one or two segments with the following properties:
1. The line links two nodes w_i and w_j.
2. The line uses 45-degree segments as much as we can and if necessary uses a horizontal or a vertical segment.
3. None of the other nodes lie on the line.
4. The line does not cross any shaded rectangle. This line is called a direct link.

Let $\pi(w_i)$ be the set of nodes, to which a node w_i is adjacent. Then, for the nodes in Fig. 12.6, show that they become

$$\pi(w_1) = \phi \text{ (empty)}, \ \pi(w_2) = \{w_1\},$$

$$\pi(w_3) = \{w_1\}, \ \pi(w_4) = \{w_2, w_3\}, \ \pi(w_5) = \{w_2, w_3\}, \ \pi(w_6) = \{w_2, w_3\}, \ \pi(w_7) = \{w_4, w_5, w_6\},$$

$$\pi(w_8) = \{w_4, w_5, w_6\}, \ \pi(w_9) = \{w_3, w_4, w_5, w_6\}, \ \pi(w_{10}) = \{w_7, w_8, w_9\}.$$

3. Let us define a distance of two pairwise adjacent nodes as the length of a vertical segment contained in a direct link (cf. exercise 2) between these two nodes, then show that, when a node

$w_i(t_{1i}, t_{2i})$ is adjacent to a node $w_j(t_{1j}, t_{2j})$, a distance $d(w_i, w_j)$ between w_i and w_j is expressed by the following equation:

$$d(w_i, w_j) = \max[(t_{2j} - t_{2i}) - (t_{1j} - t_{1i}), 0].$$

4. As is clear from the definition of the direct link in exercise 2, the set of paths consisting of direct links from the origin to the terminal point contains the set of paths obtained by the rule in Section 12.5,

Let $L(w_i)$ be the set of paths L consisting of direct links from a node w_i to the terminal point and $|L|$ be the sum of the lengths of vertical segments in a path L. Then by defining $f(w_i)$ to be

$$f(w_i) = \min_{L \in L(w_i)} |L|,$$

show the following recurrence relation:

$$f(w_i) = \min_{wj \in \pi(wi)} [d(w_i, w_j) + f(w_j)], \quad w_i \neq w_1$$
$$f(w_1) = 0.$$

Next by using the above relation, solve Example 2, where a length of a shortest path, that is, a makespan of an optimal schedule is given by $f(w_{10})$ + (sum of the processing times of job 1).

5. The formulation in the above exercises 2–4 is more efficient for the case where the sum of processing times of job 1 is greater than that of job 2. If necessary by exchanging the job number, solve a 2×4 problem with respective ordering and processing times: job 1, $M_1^2\,M_2^7\,M_4^3\,M_3^2$; job 2, $M_1^4\,M_2^4\,M_3^4\,M_4^5$; by using dynamic programming.

12.6. Approaches by Integer Linear Programming

Since 1959 several attempts were made to solve the job-shop problem with makespan criterion mostly, by integer linear programming, to be abbreviated as ILP. This uses 0–1 variables as the main variables. In these attempts, efficiency differs according to the method of expressing the constraints, so that every machine can process at most one job at a time, and so on, and by the way of defining the 0–1 variables. However, since the number of constraints and/or variables become very large even for small size problems in any formulation by ILP, those attempts are not very effective.

Historically there exist the formulations by Wagner, Bowman and Manne by using the cutting plane method. Among them Manne's formulation has a comparatively small number of variables and constraints. Then there exist the solution methods of Greenberg and Balas, where implicit enumeration is used.

The definitions of fundamental 0–1 variables are the following:

Wagner: $x_{ij}^{(k)} = \begin{cases} 1, \text{ provided a job } i \text{ is the } j\text{th job processed on the machine } M_k, \\ 0, \text{ otherwise.} \end{cases}$

Bowman: $x_{A,t} = \begin{cases} 1, \text{ provided a job } x \text{ is processed by machine A at time } t \\ (t = 1, 2, \ldots, T), \\ 0, \text{ otherwise.} \end{cases}$

Manne: $y_{ij}^{(k)} = \begin{cases} 1, \text{ provided a job } i \text{ is processed on the machine } M_k \text{ prior to a job } j, \\ 0, \text{ otherwise.} \end{cases}$

$$\left.\begin{array}{l} \text{Greenberg} \\ \text{Balas} \end{array}\right\} \quad \text{same as in Manne.}$$

The latter three definitions of 0–1 variables correspond to which one of the two disjunctive arcs is selected for every pair of disjunctive arcs on a disjunctive graph. This will be explained later in Section 12.14.

12.7. Standard Formulation by ILP

The constraint that both job i and job j cannot be processed simultaneously on the same machine M_k is expressed by the following disjunctive inequalities, by putting the start times of their processings to t_i and t_j respectively,

$$t_i - t_j \geqq p_{j,k}, \text{ or } t_j - t_i \geqq p_{i,k} \qquad (12.2)$$

where $p_{j,k}$, $p_{i,k}$ are the processing times of job j, job i, respectively, and the first inequality shows that job j precedes job i on the machine M_k and the second one shows the opposite precedence relation.

If we use a flow network which has all operations as its nodes and precedence relation among nodes, determined by orderings, as described in Section 12.13, then each inequality in (12.2) is expressed by a disjunctive arc and a pair of jobs $\{i, j\}$ is called a conflict set, as described in Section 12.17 for example. However, Manne transforms (12.2) into the following linear inequalities in order to formulate choosing between the two as by (12.2) in the form of ILP by defining the above 0–1 variables $y_{ij}^{(k)}$:

$$0 \leqq y_{ij}^{(k)} \leqq 1, \, y_{ij}^{(k)} \text{ is an integer}, \qquad (12.3)$$

$$(T + p_{j,k}) y_{ij}^{(k)} + (t_i - t_j) \geqq p_{j,k}, \qquad (12.4)$$

$$(T + p_{i,k}) (1 - y_{ij}^{(k)}) + (t_j - t_i) \geqq p_{i,k}, \qquad (12.5)$$

where a large positive number T is taken to be larger than an estimated start time of the processing of the final operation so that $|t_i - t_j| \leq T$ holds (cf. exercise 1).

Also concerning the ordering for each job, say the condition that an operation i processed by machine M_k precedes the next operation j can be expressed by

$$t_i + p_{i,k} \leqq t_j \qquad (12.6)$$

Then, in order to minimize the makespan, we add the following constraint for the last operation l of each job:

$$t_l + p_{l,k} \leqq t, \qquad (12.7)$$

where the last operation l is processed on the machine M_k.

Hence our objective is expressed by

$$t \rightarrow \min. \qquad (12.8)$$

Consequently our problem leans to solving an ILP of mixed type, where integer variables are 0–1 variables, which minimizes a variable t in (12.8) under the constraints (12.3)–(12.7).

Greenberg performed a similar formulation to the above ILP and solved it by a BAB algorithm of Land and Doig type.

Exercises

1. Prove that a constraint (12.2) is replaced by the constraints (12.3), (12.4), and (12.5), by showing that $y_{ij}^{(k)} = 0, 1$ correspond to the first inequality, and the second inequality in (12.2) respectively.

2. In the present problem where every job among n jobs is processed only once by each of m machines, show that, in the ILP formulation due to Manne, the number of variables and constraints are $mn(n + 1)/2$ and $mn(3n - 1)/2$ respectively.

3. Show that a constraint (12.2) can be replaced by the following constraints, where M is a sufficiently large number:

$$t_i + y_{ij}^{(k)} p_{i,k} \leqq t_j + y_{ji}^{(k)} M,$$
$$t_j + y_{ji}^{(k)} p_{j,k} \leqq t_i + y_{ij}^{(k)} M,$$
$$y_{ij}^{(k)} + y_{ji}^{(k)} = 1,$$
$$y_{ij}^{(k)}, y_{ji}^{(k)} \geqq 0, \text{ integers.}$$

12.8. BAB Algorithms by Following Active Schedule Generation Procedure

In order to obtain the BAB algorithm constructing partial schedules in the time-progressing direction, by following the active schedule generation procedure (cf. Section 4.15 in Chapter 4), it is sufficient to branch into γ nodes according to which operation among γ conflict operations is selected every time there occurs a period during which the processings of multiple operations on the same machine exist, and to determine the lower bound at every node. We resolve the conflict by branching a node with the smallest lower bound and then follow the active new node search procedure.

In the following Sections 12.9 to 12.11, a BAB algorithm which uses the same procedure as the active schedule generation procedure, due to Brooks and White, Florian *et al.* and Ashour *et al.*, is described. Also in later Sections 12.12 to 12.15, we show another similar BAB algorithm, due to Florian *et al.*, obtained by considering the associated disjunctive graph.

12.9. BAB Algorithm by Active Schedule Generation Procedure

Although it is appealing to use a machine block table as in the active schedule generation procedure in Section 4.15 in Chapter 4, we give a BAB algorithm, due to Ashour *et al.*, which reconsiders the operation completion timetable every time respective conflict is resolved by selecting an operation giving the smallest lower bound. It uses active new node search procedure. This will be denoted as the BAB algorithm I.

12.10. BAB Algorithm I

This algorithm consists of the following steps:

Step 1.
1.1. Put conflict level L, that is, the number L of conflicts already resolved, to $L = 0$ and let the upper bound of minimal makespan be $f^* = \infty$ say.
1.2. Make a completion timetable C^0 expressing the earliest completion times of all operations, in disregard of the conflicts.
1.3. Let the first schedule period $[S, T]$ be $S = 0$ and $T = \min_{iq} C^0(iq)$ where $C^0(iq)$ is a completion time of an operation iq in the table C^0.

Step 2. Search an overlapping processing (conflict) between an operation iq such that $C^L(iq) = T$ and the operations iq such that $C^L(iq) \geq T$, as follows:
2.1. For every operation iq on each machine, if

$$T \leq C^L(iq) - p_{iq}, \text{ that is, } T + p_{iq} \leq C^L(iq)$$

holds, where p_{iq} is a processing time of the operation iq, there is no conflict and then proceed to step 7.
2.2. If, for more than one operation iq on the same machine,

$$T > C^L(iq) - p_{iq}, \text{ that is, } T + p_{iq} > C^L(iq)$$

holds, then a conflict exists. Put $L = L + 1$ and proceed to step 3.

Step 3. For every operation iq constructing a conflict at level L, where every node iq is branched from the node in the solution tree, alter the completion timetable C^L and compute every lower bound $LB^L(iq)$, defined in Section 12.11.

Step 4. Find a node with the smallest lower bound:

$$LB^L = \min_{iq} LB^L(iq),$$

among the nodes of order one (not yet branched) at level L.

Step 5. By comparing the smallest lower bound LB^L at level L with f^*, if $LB^L < f^*$, proceed to step 6. Otherwise, proceed to step 8.

Step 6. A node with LB^L is determined. If there exist more than one node with LB^L, select one of them by a specified rule.

Step 7. Change the schedule period $[S, T]$ in the following way:
7.1. If the present T is not the greatest in the completion timetable C^L

corresponding to a node with LB^L, change this T to S and the next large completion time in C^L to T. Return to step 2.

7.2. On the other hand, if the present T is the greatest in C^L, then change $f^* = T$ and proceed to step 8.

Step 8. Backtrack the solution tree by one branch and change the level to $L = L - 1$.

8.1. If there exists at least one node of order one, satisfying $LB^L(iq) < f^*$, alter the schedule period $[S, T]$ such that $T = \min_{iq \in \{S^L\}} C^{L-1}(iq)$ where $\{S^L\}$ is the set of conflict operations at level L, and S is the next smaller element in the completion timetable C^{L-1}, and then return to step 4.

8.2. On the other hand, if all nodes of order one satisfy $LB^L(iq) \geq f^*$, proceed to step 9.

Step 9 (Examination of an optimal schedule).

9.1. If $L > 1$, return to step 8.

9.2. On the other hand, if $L = 1$, then f^* is a minimal makespan and the completion timetable at a node giving f^* shows an optimal schedule.

Remark. The time T in the active schedule generation procedure (Section 4.15) corresponds to the T in the period $[S, T]$ in the above BAB algorithm I.

12.11. Lower Bound in BAB Algorithm I

The lower bound $LB^L(iq)$ computed at step 3 in the BAB algorithm I can be determined, based on the following theorem due to Florian *et al.*:

THEOREM 4. *Let S_k be the set of the not yet scheduled operations to be processed by the machine M_k, which processes the last operation of at least one job, then in order to minimize the total elapsed time of all operations in S_k, it is sufficient to process these operations in nondecreasing order of their earliest starting times ES, by beginning from the earliest processable operation and processing every operation not sooner than its ES.*

The reason for the rule in this theorem is obvious, since the last operation in S_k can be processed by this rule at the earliest time. Then a lower bound for a partial schedule up to the operation iq_1 (a node iq_1) is given by the following formula:

$$LB^L(iq_1) = \max\left[\max_{i \in J} Cl^L(il), \max_{q \neq l} \left\{ \min_{iq \in R} ES^L(jq) + \sum_{jq \in R} p_{jq} \right\} \right], \quad (12.9)$$

where J is the set of all jobs, $C_l^L(i^l)$ shows an earliest completion time of the class of all not yet scheduled operations on the machine M_l processing the last operation *il* of job $i \in J$, which can be computed by applying the rule in the above Theorem 4. Also the second term in the bracket of (12.9) shows the maximum, over the machines $M_q (q \neq l)$ not processing the last operation *il* of any job $i \in J$, of the sum of the earliest starting time, counted from the then completion timetable C^L, of the class of operation *jq* processed by M_q in the set *R* of all not yet scheduled operations and the sum of the processing times of all operations *jq* in *R*.

Concerning the lower bound (12.9) the following theorem holds (cf. exercise 1).

THEOREM 5. *The lower bound defined by a formula* (12.9) *includes the lower bounds obtained by the following two methods:*

1. *We regard the maximum of the earliest completion times of all jobs as a lower bound, where an earliest completion time of job i is a time, computed by adding the sum of processing times of all not yet scheduled operations of job i to an earliest starting time among these operations.*
2. *We regard the maximum of the earliest completion times on all machines as a lower bound, where an earliest completion time on machine M_k is a time, computed by adding the sum of processing times of all not yet scheduled operations to be processed on M_k to an earliest starting time among these operations.*

Remarks: 1. An example where, in a formula (12.9), the value C_1 of the first term is smaller than the value C_2 of the second term is shown in Fig. 12.7. This time a conflict $\{11, 21\}$ was resolved by dominating an operation 21.

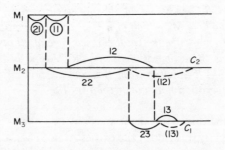

FIG. 12.7

2. Concerning the problem minimizing any normal objective function $f(C_1, C_2, \ldots, C_n)$, except the makespan, we can use $f(C_1, C_2, \ldots, C_n)$, as its lower bound at the completion timetable C^L where C_i is determined as an earliest completion time $C^L(il)$ of the last operation of job $i (i = 1, 2, \ldots, n)$ (cf. Section 12.22).

EXAMPLE 3. The 3×3 problem has the following orderings and processing times put at the upper right sides of the respective machine notations, where in parentheses the associated operation is shown:

Job	Ordering			
1	M_1^2	M_2^6	M_3^1	
	(11)	(12)	(13)	
2	M_3^4	M_2^2	M_1^3	M_2^5
	(23)	(22(1))	(21)	(22(2))
3	M_1^3	M_3^2		
	(31)	(33)		

Then an optimal scheduling minimizing the makespan is determined by the BAB algorithm I as described below:

Explanation of the solution

A solution tree by BAB algorithm I appears as in Fig. 12.8 and a node 12 at level 3 shows an optimal schedule with minimal makespan 17. Every node in the solution tree shows a dominating operation and an associated lower bound (12.9) by its side. Summary of the results at every stage in the BAB algorithm I

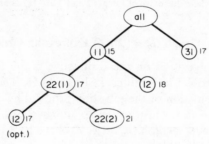

FIG. 12.8

TABLE 12.2

L	[S, T]	c	$LB^L(iq)$	LB^L	f^*
1	[0, 2]	11	5	15	∞
1		31	17		
	[2, 4]	φ			
	[4, 5]	φ			
2	[5, 6]	22(1)	17	17	
2		12	18		
	[6, 7]	φ			
	[7, 9]	φ			
3	[9, 12]	12	17	17	
3		22(2)	21		
	[12, 13]	φ			
	[13, 17]	φ			17

is shown in Table 12.2, where C shows the operations constructing the associated conflict and ϕ shows the empty conflict set. The Gantt chart of an optimal schedule is shown in Fig. 12.9.

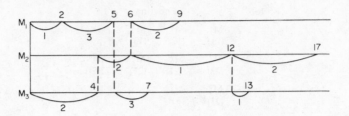

FIG. 12.9. An optimal schedule of example 3.

Exercises

1. Prove Theorem 5.

2. Determine the optimal schedules minimizing the objective functions (1) and (2) respectively in Example 3 by using the BAB algorithm I.
(1) Mean completion time.
(2) Mean tardiness, where due-dates of jobs 1, 2 and 3 are 18, 23 and 5 respectively.

12.12. Graph $G_0 = (X, Z)$ Expressing Orderings

A similar BAB algorithm on the disjunctive graph for the above BAB algorithm I is described in Sections 12.12 to 12.14. The first two sections concern the representation of the job-shop problem by a disjunctive graph. This type of representation also relates to later sections.

First we can consider a graph $G_0 = (X, Z)$ of the PERT flow diagram type, with every operation as its node along the ordering of every job. Here, X is the set of nodes $i(i = 1, 2, \ldots, N;$ N is the total number of operations) corresponding to every operation, a dummy start node 0, and a dummy terminal node $N + 1$ and Z is the set of (directed) arcs (i, j). Expressing each operation by the corresponding node number, we have $(i, j) \in Z$ when an operation j directly follows an operation i under orderings, $i = 0$ and j is the first operation of every job, or i is the last operation of every job and $j = N + 1$. Also the length $l(i, j)$ of every arc (i, j) is defined to be 0 or p_i, processing time of operation i, according to $i = 0$ or $i \neq 0$ respectively.

Remark. If we take into account the normal objective functions as a whole, it will be better to add every dummy terminal node between the last node for every job and a dummy terminal node for all jobs, already defined.

For example, a graph G_0 for the 3×3 problem in Example 3 in Section 12.11 can be expressed in three ways: (a), (b), (c), where every line corresponds to the

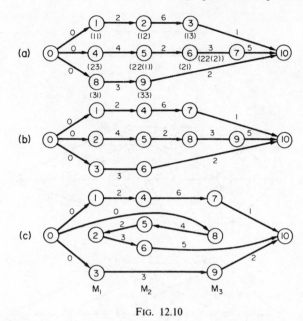

FIG. 12.10

jobs 1, 2 and 3 from the top and, on each line, all operations are arranged according to ordering; (a) and (b) differ from each other only in setting the node numbers, but (c) arranges the operations according to the order of machines: M_1, M_2, M_3. In the following we use the graph G_0 of the type like (a).

12.13. Disjunctive Graph Representation by Limited Machine Availability

As shown in Section 12.7, an assumption that each machine can process only one job (operation) at any time is expressed by the following inequalities:

$$t_i - t_j \geq p_j, \quad \text{or} \quad t_j - t_i \geq p_i. \tag{12.10}$$

As another representation of (12.10), differing from introducing a 0-1 variable, a class $\{i, j, k\}$ is associated with a pair of disjunctive arcs on G_0 described as below:

For any pair of nodes $\{i, j, k\}$ corresponding to any two operations i, j to be processed by machine $M_k (k = 1, 2, \ldots, m)$, a pair of arcs between two nodes i, j, as shown in Fig. 12.11 (a) or (b), is added in the graph G_0. Each arc is called a disjunctive arc. For example, in Example 3 we have (a) or (b) in Fig. 12.12 by adding every pair of disjunctive arcs to the graph G_0, (a) in Fig. 12.10. A graph of this type is called a disjunctive graph. As obviously seen, the selection of the first inequality $t_i - t_j \geq p_j$ in (12.10) is equivalent to the selection of a

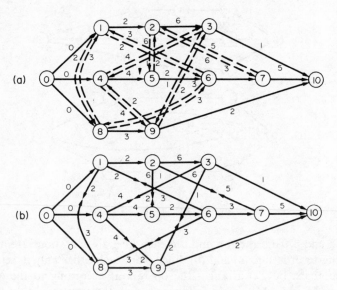

FIG. 12.11

FIG. 12.12. Disjunctive graph for example 3.

disjunctive arc (j, i), and the same holds for the second inequality $t_j - t_i \geq p_i$ in (12.10) to a disjunctive arc (i, j).

Exercises

1. Generally let $L_{ij} = [t_i + C_{ij}, t_i + f_{ij}]$, $L_{ji} = [t_j + C_{ji}, t_j + f_{ji}]$ be two intervals of positive length, where $C_{ij}, f_{ij}, C_{ji}, f_{ji}$ are known constants, $C_{ij} < f_{ij}, C_{ji} < f_{ji}$ and t_i, t_j are the starting times of two tasks i, j respectively, that is, potentials, then when $L_{ij} \cap L_{ji} = \phi$ holds two tasks i, j are said to be subjected to a constraint of interval disjunction. Show that this constraint is equivalent to
$$t_i - t_j \geq a_{ji}, \quad \text{or} \quad t_j - t_i \geq a_{ij} \, (a_{ij} + a_{ji} > 0).$$

2. In particular, considering (12.10) by an interval disjunction, show that $L_{ij} = [t_i, t_i + p_i]$ and $L_{ji} = [t_j, t_j + p_j]$ hold.

12.14. BAB Algorithm on Disjunctive Graphs by following an Active Schedule Generation Procedure

First some terminologies are necessary to construct the BAB algorithm.

1. When a disjunctive arc (i, j) is selected from every remaining pair of disjunctive arcs $\{(i, j), (j, i)\}$ at node i, which means that an operation i is forced

to precede all other jobs *j* remaining on the same machine as for *i*, we say that
an operation i is scheduled.

2. A *cut C* after an operation was scheduled is the set of the first not yet
scheduled operation (if it exists) of every job, where it includes a terminal node
in case all operations of some job have been already scheduled. Hence if an
operation *j* is contained in the cut all operations prior to *j* in the ordering are
already scheduled. Also the initial cut C_0 contains all initial operations and the
terminal cut C^*, when all pairs of disjunctive arcs have been resolved, consists
of the terminal node. The cut at every stage corresponds to the node in the
solution tree by the BAB algorithm. Figure 12.13 shows an example of the cut.

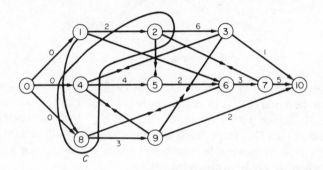

FIG. 12.13. Cut {2, 4, 8} after 1 was scheduled in Fig. 12.12 (b)

3. For the then cut $C \neq C^*$ we compute the earliest completion time among
the nodes in *C*, where the earliest completion time of a node *i* is computed
along the critical path calculation by excluding the remaining unresolved pairs
of disjunctive arcs. Let an operation *j* give this earliest completion time, that is,

j satisfy $t_j + p_j = \min_{i \in C} (t_i + p_i)$ where t_i, p_i are the earliest starting time,
processing time respectively of an operation *i*, and *j* be processed by machine
M_k, then the *generating set* G_c of the cut *C* consists of all the operations in *C*
that use machine M_k. This set G_c makes the next family of cuts $\{C^{+1}\}$, where
C^{+1} is called a *descendant cut* of cut *C*, that is, a descendant node of the present
node by cut *C*, which follows the cut *C*. The descendant cut C^{+1} of cut *C* is
determined by excluding any one operation *i* in G_c and including an operation
directly following the operation *i*. Consequently, the number of C^{+1} is equal to
the number of the operation *i* in the generating set G_c of the cut *C*, $|G_c|$. Every
C^{+1} corresponds to every node obtained by branching the present node with
cut *C* into $|G_c|$ nodes, in the related solution tree.

EXAMPLE 4. In the disjunctive graph (Fig. 12.12) of Example 3, since the
initial cut is $C_0 = \{1, 4, 8\}$ and the completion times of the operations 1, 4, and

8 become 2, 4, and 3 respectively, then the earliest completion time is 2 for an operation $j = 1$. Since the operation in C_0 using the same machine as the operation 1 is an operation 8 we have the generating set $G_{c_0} = \{1, 8\}$ of C_0. Hence there exist two descendant cuts C^{+1} of C_0, that is, they are $C^{+1} = \{2, 4, 8\}$ for $i = 1$ and $C^{+1} = \{1, 4, 9\}$ for $i = 8$. Then the part, until this stage, of the solution tree becomes as shown in Fig. 12.14. Nodes were generated in increasing order of node numbers and node 2 corresponding to an operation 1 corresponds to the graph in Fig. 12.13.

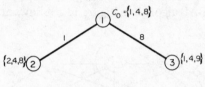

FIG. 12.14

Then a BAB algorithm in this section, which will be called BAB algorithm II, starts from the initial cut C_0. Compute the lower bound, by (12.9) at the former section 12.11, for the partial schedule at each of $|G_c|$ nodes corresponding to the descendant cuts C^{+1} respectively to decide a smallest LB, and similarly by following the active new node search procedure we can obtain an optimal schedule when we arrive at the terminal cut C^*.

In this BAB algorithm, the following theorem holds:

THEOREM 6. *In the process of repeating the above descendant cuts we can obtain a (feasible) schedule without meeting any circuit in the disjunctive graph. Hence we can determine an optimal schedule by the BAB algorithm II.*

Proof. If an operation j follows an operation i in the partial schedule associated with any node in the solution tree, then any already decided disjunctive arc is invariant and j never precedes i even if any disjunctive arc is introduced by the descendant cut generation procedure. Hence no circuit occurs and a schedule is determined at the terminal cut. Different paths in the solution tree lead to different schedules. Then an optimal schedule can be obtained by the principle of the BAB algorithm.

FIG. 12.15. Solution tree for example 3 by BAB algorithm II.

EXAMPLE 5. By solving the former Example 3, a disjunctive graph of which is shown in Fig. 12.12, using the BAB algorithm II, its solution tree becomes as shown in Fig. 12.15, where node numbers show the order of their generations and, on every node, the related cut C and an operation j making G_c are shown. Then we obtain obviously the same optimal schedule as in Example 3.

Exercises

1. Show that the earliest completion time among the nodes in $C \neq C^*$, defined at paragraph 3, corresponds to the time T in Section 12.10.

2. Show the concrete procedure of the BAB algorithm II as in Section 12.10.

12.15. BAB Algorithm by Resolving the Pairs of Disjunctive Arcs on a Disjunctive Graph

In the following Sections 12.15 to 12.21, we give another BAB algorithm based on a disjunctive graph which has a procedure to resolve the pairs of disjunctive arcs, not following the active schedule generation procedure.

12.16. Representation by Graph $G_0 = (X, Z)$

First let the job k include N_k operations and its ordering be the order of N_k operations:

$$\sum_{l=1}^{k} N_{l-1} + 1, \ \sum_{l=1}^{k} N_{l-1} + 2, \ \ldots, \ \sum_{l=1}^{k+1} N_{l-1}$$

$$\left(k = 1, 2, \ldots, n; \ N_0 = 0, N = \sum_{k=1}^{n} N_k \right).$$

Also let A_q be the set of all operations processed by the machine M_q ($q = 1, 2, \ldots, m$). Then any two operations in A_q cannot be processed simultaneously and inversely any two operations not processable simultaneously are contained in some $A_q (q = 1, 2, \ldots, m)$.

Next, a graph $G_0 = (X, Z)$ decided by the given orderings is constructed as below in this case (cf. Section 12.12): X is the set of $N + 2$ nodes, where a node 0 and a node $N + 1$ show a dummy start node and a dummy terminal node respectively, and every node i shows a respective operation i ($i = 1, 2, \ldots, N$). Z is the set of (directed) arcs expressing the orderings, where arc $(i, j) \in Z$ means that $i = 0$ and

$$j = \sum_{l=1}^{k} N_{l-1} + 1 \text{ (the first operation of every job } k)$$

$$(k = 1, 2, \ldots, n),$$

$$i = \sum_{l=1}^{k} N_{l-1} + t \text{ and } j = \sum_{l=1}^{k} N_{l-1} + t + 1$$

$$(t = 1, 2, \ldots, N_k - 1; k = 1, 2, \ldots, n),$$

or $\quad i = \sum_{l=1}^{k+1} N_{l-1} \text{ and } j = N + 1 \ (k = 1, 2, \ldots, n).$

As the length of every arc (i, j), the processing time p_i, where $p_0 = 0$, of the operation i is defined.

12.17. Conflict Set

In any pair $\{i, j\}; i, j \in A_q (q = 1, 2, \ldots, m)$, the operation i and the operation j cannot be processed simultaneously by the machine M_q. Hence we call such a pair $\{i, j\}$ conflict set. This is a special case of the conflict set defined for the general case in Section 12.25.

Then, as already explained, the following theorem holds:

THEOREM 7. *In the (feasible) schedule, the following inequalities hold for any conflict set $\{i, j\}$, and vice versa:*

$$t_j \geqq t_i + p_i, \quad \text{or} \quad t_i \geqq t_j + p_j. \tag{12.11}$$

12.18. Disjunctive Graph

As already shown, a pair of arcs (i, j), (j, i) with respective lengths p_i, p_j corresponds to each conflict set $\{i, j\}$, which will be abbreviated as CS: $\{i, j\}$ in the following. Such a pair is called a disjunctive pair of arcs and each arc is called a disjunctive arc. Then a graph G_0 combined with all disjunctive pairs of arcs is called a disjunctive graph.

To select one inequality from (12.11) corresponds one to one to selecting one disjunctive arc from a related disjunctive pair of arcs. The latter selection is called a resolution of the disjunctive pair of arcs.

12.19. Complete Selection of Disjunctive Arcs and Schedules

Let W be the set of all disjunctive pairs of arcs, then the selection of each disjunctive arc from every disjunctive pair of arcs $\{(i, j), (j, i)\} \in W$ is called the complete selection of disjunctive arcs. There exist $2^{|W|}$ complete selections. The relation between a complete selection of disjunctive arcs and a schedule is shown by the following theorem:

THEOREM 8. *If a graph $G_n (n = 1, 2, \ldots, 2^{|W|})$ obtained from a graph G_0 combined with all disjunctive arcs by a certain complete selection of disjunctive* *arcs does not include any circuit, then the graph G_n corresponds one to one to a schedule.*

Proof. If the graph G_n does not include any circuit, the earliest start time t_i of every node (operation) $i(i = 1, 2, \ldots, N)$ is determined uniquely by a critical path computation on this graph G_n. Arrangement of all operations by these t_i satisfies the given orderings and does not allow any simultaneous processing. Hence we have a schedule. Also since each disjunctive arc in the same disjunctive pair of arcs gives the opposite processing order of two operations contained in the related CS (conflict set), a G_n without any circuit corresponds one to one to a schedule.

EXAMPLE 6. Figure 12.16 shows an example of a schedule corresponding to a graph G_n by a complete selection of disjunctive arcs in the disjunctive graph (Fig. 12.12) for the 3×3 job shop problem in Example 3. Each job number is shown in the Gantt chart.

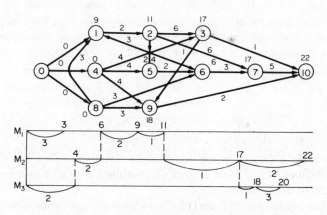

FIG. 12.16. An example of G_n and related schedule.

Exercise

1. Show that a schedule depicted in Fig. 12.16 is a nonactive schedule (cf. Section 4.13).

12.20. Formulations of Two Types

There exist the formulations of two types, that is, problem P_1 and Problem P_2, according to whether the complete selection of disjunctive arcs is applied or the partial selection of disjunctive arcs, defined below, is applied. First let V_n ($n = 1, 2, \ldots, 2^{|W|}$) be the set of disjunctive arcs obtained by every complete section of disjunctive pairs of arcs corresponding to all CS: $\{i, j\}$, then, by

Theorem 8 in the previous section, a graph $G_n = (X, Z \cup V_n)$ without any circuit corresponds one to one to a schedule. Hence the job-shop problem minimizing a normal objective function f is equivalent to the following problem P_1:

PROBLEM P_1. Determine a graph G_n without circuit giving minimal f among all such graphs G_n.

Hence, in problem P_1, it is sufficient to consider some finite sequence of critical path problems in the family $\{G_n\}$. Some algorithms such as the BAB algorithms were developed by Balas. In these algorithms it is necessary to check the circuit and/or some sophisticated procedures in selecting the disjunctive arc, and at each stage at least one disjunctive arc is changed to its twin disjunctive arc. Next, on the other hand, let $\{S_u\}$ be the family of the subsets S_u of any V_n in $\{V_n\}$. That is, for each S_u we have, for the disjunctive pair of arcs $\{(i,j), (j,i)\}$ corresponding to every CS: $\{i,j\}$, $\{i,j\} \in S_u$ and $(j, i) \notin S_u$, $(i, j) \notin S_u$ and $(j, i) \in S_u$, or $(i, j) \notin S_u$ and $(j, i) \notin S_u$. We call S_u the partial selection of disjunctive arcs. Since some S_u can be each V_n as a subset of V_n, the present job shop problem becomes equivalent to some finite sequence of the following problems P_2, where the first S_u is set to an empty set:

PROBLEM P_2. For some graph $G_u = (X, Z \cup S_u)$, determine the value of every $t_i (i = 0, 1, \ldots, N+1)$, for each $(i,j) \in Z \cup S_u$, under the constraints: $t_j \geq t_i + p_i, t_i \geq 0$. It is sufficient to look for a S_u, where $Z \cup S_u = Z \cup v_n$, which gives minimal f. The BAB algorithms for solving the problem P_2 were developed by Charlton and Death, and Nabeshima. In these BAB algorithms some remaining disjunctive pairs of arcs are expected to be resolved after the critical path computation on a graph G_n at each stage, and then a schedule with $Z \cup S_u = Z \cup V_n$ is reached somewhat quickly after simple computation at each stage. Although these algorithms introduce one disjunctive arc in the S_u at each stage, no circuit occurs (cf. Theorem 9 in the next section).

In the following section, a BAB algorithm called BAB algorithm III based on the problem P_2 will be described as an example of the algorithms obtained by resolving the disjunctive pairs of arcs. Readers interested in the algorithms based on the problem P_1 should refer to references at the end of this chapter.

12.21. BAB Algorithm by Partial Selection of Disjunctive Arcs

The procedure of the BAB algorithm III based on the problem P_2 is the following, where it uses the partial branching procedure and does not produce any circuit as shown in Theorem 9 and the node shows the node in the solution tree and f shows the normal objective function:

Step 1. Set $S_u = \phi$ (node (1)) and perform the critical path computation on a graph $G_u \equiv G_0$ by using the recurrence relation

$$t_j = \max_{(i,\,j) \in Z} (t_i + p_i)$$

and determine the solution (values of all t_i and f). Set $f^* = \infty$ say and proceed to step 2.

Step 2. If the solution resolves all CS, which means that the solution satisfies (12.11) in Section 12.17 for every CS: $\{i, j\}$, then this solution gives an optimal schedule. Otherwise, proceed to step 3.

Step 3. If there exists at least one CS: $\{i, j\}$ not satisfying (12.11) in Section 12.17 for the solution $\{t_i\}$ by a critical path computation on the graph $G_u = (X, Z \cup S_u)$, then the solution f gives a lower bound LB(S_u) of minimal value f_0 of f.
  (a) If LB$(S_u) \geqq f^*$, proceed to step 5.
  (b) If LB$(S_u) < f^*$, then, among all CS: $\{i, j\}$ not satisfying (12.11), add a disjunctive arc (i, j) with least t_i and satisfying $t_i < t_j$ (if $t_i = t_j$, use $p_i \leq p_j$) to S_u. Let us set $S_u = S_u \cup \{(i, j)\}$. In this case a new graph $G_u = (X, Z \cup S_u)$ does not produce any circuit (Theorem 9). Obtain the solution on the new G_u (next node). Proceed to step 4.

Step 4.
  (a) If the solution does not resolve all CS, return to step 3.
  (b) If the solution at node (n) resolves all CS, $G_n = (X, Z \cup S_u)$ gives a schedule. By setting $f^* = \min (f^*, f)$, proceed to step 5.

Step 5. Backtracking in the solution tree is necessary. That is, backtrack to the nearest node $(n - k)$ with LB(S_u) smaller than f^* and having one disjunctive arc not yet examined, and proceed to step 6. If such a node does not exist, then a schedule giving f^* is an optimal schedule.

Step 6. Exclude each disjunctive arc already introduced into the passed node, including the node (n), in the case of backtracking from S_u for the former node (n) and add the remaining twin disjunctive arcs at node $(n - k)$ to S_u. Then a new S_u at node $(n - k)$ is decided. Obtain the solution on a graph $G_u = (X, Z \cup S_u)$ without any circuit (Theorem 9). Return to step 4.

THEOREM 9. *Every graph $G_u = (X, Z \cup S_u)$ determined at each stage of the BAB algorithm III does not contain any circuit.*

Proof. The first graph $G_0 = (X, Z)$ where $S_u = \phi$ does not contain any circuit because it's connected only by given orderings. Let us assume that the graph $G_u = (X, Z \cup S_u)$ at any stage does not contain any circuit. Then for CS: $\{i, j\}$ generating a disjunctive pair of arcs which makes up a circuit by its disjunctive arc (i, j) or disjunctive arc (j, i) together with the arcs in the graph G_u, let $t_j > t_i$ hold in G_u (Fig. 12.17) (the same for the case $t_j < t_i$), then obviously $t_j > t_i + p_i$ holds. Hence such CS: $\{i, j\}$ satisfies (12.11) in Section 12.17. Therefore, any CS: $\{i, j\}$ which does not satisfy (12.11) in G_u does not generate the circuit together with the arcs of G_u.

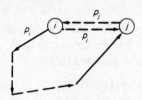

FIG. 12.17. Case $t_j > t_i$.

Remarks: 1. We can apply the EXTBAB method to each of the BAB algorithms I, II and III for deciding a reliable approximate schedule.

2. The proposed BAB algorithm III is a special case of the BAB algorithm for the multiproject scheduling problem with limited resources which will be discussed in Section 12.29.

EXAMPLE 7. We solve the 3×3 job shop problem with the makespan criterion in Example 3 by the above BAB algorithm III. The solution tree becomes as in Fig. 12.18, where node 5 gives an optimal schedule $S_u = \{(1, 8), (5, 2), (2, 7)\}$ which is equivalent to $V_n = \{(1, 8), (5, 2), (2, 7), (1, 6), (8, 6), (4, 3), (4, 9), (9, 3)\}$ and $f_0 = 17$. Also if we apply EXTBAB algorithm ($\alpha = 30\%$), it terminates at node 3 and the PRE of an approximate schedule at node 3 is smaller than $(18 - 14) \times 100/14 = 28.6\%$.

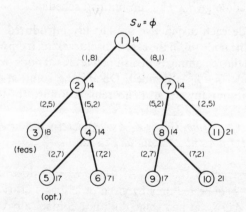

FIG. 12.18. Solution for exercise 3 by BAB algorithm III.

Exercises

1. Solve the 3×2 min-makespan flow shop problem with the following ordering and processing times by the BAB algorithm III: job 1, $M_1^7 M_2^{11}$; job 2, $M_1^{10} M_2^5$; job 3, $M_1^9 M_2^8$.

2. Determine the optimal schedule minimizing the following objective functions (1) and (2) respectively in Example 3 by using the BAB algorithm III. (1) Mean completion time. (2) Mean tardiness, where due-dates of jobs 1, 2 and 3 are 18, 23 and 5 respectively.

12.22. Generalization of the Sequencing Problem: The Multiproject Scheduling Problem with Limited Resources

As a generalization of the sequencing problem, namely the job-shop scheduling problem and further general job-shop scheduling problems with many machines of the same kind and/or with ordering of network type, we consider the multiproject scheduling problem with limited resources (cf. Section 3.6 in Chapter 3).

Although usually planning techniques used such as PERT and CPM assume unlimited resources (manpower, material, equipment, funds and so on), in practice we must perform the activities under limited availability of each resource at each period. The multiproject scheduling problem with limited resources consists of n projects, each of which has given precedence relation of PERT type among activities, and of m limited resources, some or all of them are required for each activity by specified amounts, and minimizes a normal objective function.

This problem can be formulated and solved by using integer linear programming, by BAB algorithms based on related disjunctive graphs, and by the horizon-varying algorithm along selected paths, and so on (cf. references).

In the following Sections 12.23 to 12.31, we develop a BAB algorithm, which can minimize any normal objective function, by basing it on related disjunctive graphs, as a generalization of the BAB algorithm III for the job shop scheduling problem.

12.23. Solution Based on Disjunctive Graphs

As shown in Section 12.20, there exist formulations of two types for the solution of the job-shop problem by basing it on a related disjunctive graph. For the present general problem, as before, BAB algorithms of two types can be developed. Briefly describing them, one is formulated on the disjunctive graph constructed by orderings and by conflict sets of the activities that require the same resource and the other is formulated on the other disjunctive graph constructed by orderings and by all pairs of activities that require the same resource. Since the former is a generalization of the BAB algorithm III for the job-shop problem, we will describe this BAB algorithm.

12.24. Problem Statement

Let there exist n projects h ($h = 1, 2, \ldots, n$), N activities i ($i = 1, 2, \ldots, N$) as a whole. Let the respective precedence relation of the PERT type be given for each project. Some or all of m resources r ($r = 1, 2, \ldots, m$) are required by each activity, b_r is the availability of resource r ($r = 1, 2, \ldots, m$) per unit time, $a_{r,i}$ is the requirement of resource r ($r = 1, 2, \ldots, m$) by activity i ($i = 1, 2, \ldots, N$) per unit time, where we assume that $a_{r,i} \leq b_r$ holds for every r and every i and $\sum_{i \in X_r} a_{r,i} > b_r$ holds for every r where X_r is the set of activities requiring the resource r, and p_i is the duration of activity i. Also as the objective function we take any normal objective function $f = f(C(1), C(2), \ldots, C(n))$ which is a nondecreasing function of the completion time $C(h)$ of every project h ($h = 1, 2, \ldots, n$) (cf. Section 4.3 in Chapter 4).

Then the problem is to determine the start time t_i of each activity i ($i = 1, 2, \ldots, N$) minimizing the given normal objective function f under the given precedence relations and given resource constraints.

Remark. For the job-shop scheduling problem, we have $b_r = 1$ for every r (machine M_r) and $a_{r,i} = 1$ for every r and i (operation i).

12.25. Conflict Set

We define a graph $G_0 = (X, Z)$ constructed only by given precedence relations between activities as below:

$G_0 = (X, Z)$ is a network of PERT flow diagram type, where X is the set of $N + n + 2$ nodes which consists of N nodes corresponding to each of N activities, a dummy node 0 (source), n dummy nodes $N + h$ ($h = 1, 2, \ldots, n$) (sink of each project h), and a dummy node $N + n + 1$ (a sink of the whole project) and Z is the set of (directed) arcs (i, j) determined by the given precedence relations and the dummy nodes defined above. That is, we have $(i, j) \in Z$ when the activity i directly precedes the activity j by the given precedence relations, $i = 0$ and j is the first activity of each project, or $i = N + h$ ($h = 1, 2, \ldots, n$) and $j = N + n + 1$. With every $(i, j) \in Z$ is associated the duration p_i of the activity i, where $p_0 = 0$ and $p_{N+h} = 0$ ($h = 1, 2, \ldots, n$). If the first activity j of some project starts a_j time later than the time origin shown by the node 0, then we can associate the time a_j with the arc $(0, j)$.

A sequence of node numbers (activity numbers): $1, 2, \ldots, N$, is associated with the nodes along the increasing order of their levels from the top node 0, where the level of a node is defined as the largest number of the arcs on some path among the paths connecting the top node 0 with this node. Here for the nodes with identical level we number them from the left to the right according to the increasing order of project numbers (cf. Fig. 12.19 in Section 12.27).

Next the family of conflict sets $\{T_{r,w}\}$ is defined as below:

$$T_{r,w} = \left\{ i \,|\, i \in X_r, \sum_{i \in T_{r,w}} a_{r,i} > b_r, \text{condition } \alpha \right\}.$$

Condition α is the condition that for each pair of nodes (activities) $\{i, j\}$ in $T_{r,w}$ there exists no path from i to j, or from j to i, in the graph G_0 and that every $T_{r,w}$ does not contain the other $T_{r,w}$ for any r as its proper subset.

That is to say, each conflict set $T_{r,w}$ is the minimal set of activities that are impossible to be processed simultaneously. Consequently, they conflict with each other under the given availability b_r of every resource r ($r = 1, 2, \ldots, m$).

Obviously the following theorem holds by the definition:

THEOREM 10. *In any feasible schedule of our problem, satisfying the given precedence relations and the given resource constraints, for each conflict set* $T_{r,w}$ ($w = 1, 2, \ldots, w_r$; $r = 1, 2, \ldots, m$),

$$t_j \geqq t_i + p_i, \text{ or } t_i \geqq t_j + p_j \tag{12.12}$$

must hold for at least one pair of activities (nodes) $\{i, j\}$ *in* $T_{r,w}$.

Exercise

1. Prove Theorem 10.

12.26. Disjunctive Graphs Based on Conflict Sets of Activities

With each pair of activities $\{i, j\}$ in the conflict sets $T_{r,w}$ ($w = 1, 2, \ldots, w_r$; $r = 1, 2, \ldots, m$) is associated a pair of arcs $\{(i, j), (j, i)\}$ in the graph G_0. We call each arc a disjunctive arc, with them are associated duration p_i for (i, j) and duration p_j for (j, i). Also we call this pair of arcs disjunctive pairs of arcs. By combining some or all of these disjunctive pairs of arcs with the graph G_0 we have the disjunctive graph based on the conflict sets of activities.

12.27. Formulation by Disjunctive Graph

Let $\lambda_{r,w}$ be the total number of disjunctive pairs of arcs corresponding to all pairs $\{i, j\}$ in a conflict set $T_{r,w}$ ($w = 1, 2, \ldots, w_r$; $r = 1, 2, \ldots, m$), then $\lambda_{r,w}$ $= \binom{k}{2}$ when this $T_{r,w}$ contains k activities (nodes). From Theorem 10, if the $T_{r,w}$ contains more than two nodes any other pair $\{i, j\}$ in $T_{r,w}$, except one pair, may be processed simultaneously, that is, may not satisfy (12.12) in Section 12.25. Then let W_l ($l = 1, 2, \ldots, L$) be the set of disjunctive pairs of arcs associated with each one pair $\{i, j\}$ in every $T_{r,w}$, then by combining each W_l with the graph G_0 we have the respective disjunctive graph $D_l = (X, Z \cup W_l)$

$(l = 1, 2, \ldots, L)$. In this case since each W_l is constructed by selecting only one pair $\{i, j\}$ from each conflict set $T_{r, w}$, we call each W_l a complete selection from the family of conflict sets $\{T_{r, w}\}$. Figure 12.19 is an example of the disjunctive graph D_l by complete selection from the family of conflict sets, where $n = 3, N = 19, m = 3$, doubly circled nodes show dummy nodes, conflict sets are

$$T_{1, 1} = \{4, 5\}, \lambda_{1, 1} = 1; T_{1, 2} = \{5, 6\}, \lambda_{1, 2} = 1; T_{1, 3} = \{4, 10\}, \lambda_{1, 3} = 1;$$
$$T_{1, 4} = \{4, 6, 8\}, \lambda_{1, 4} = 3;$$

$$T_{2, 1} = \{7, 9, 11\}, \lambda_{2, 1} = 3; T_{3, 1} = \{8, 13\}, \lambda_{3, 1} = 1; T_{3, 2} = \{10, 19\}, \lambda_{3, 2} = 1$$

and related complete selection W_l is a set of disjunctive pairs of arcs corresponding to one pair $\{i, j\}$ in each $T_{r, w}$ $(r = 1, 2, 3; w_1 = 4, w_2 = 1, w_3 = 2)$: $\{4, 5\}, \{5, 6\}, \{4, 10\}, \{6, 8\}, \{7, 11\}, \{8, 13\}, \{10, 9\}$, cf. Numerical example in Section 12.31.

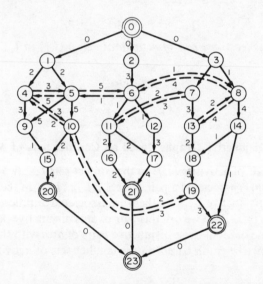

FIG. 12.19. Example of disjunctive graph D_l.

Next, by selecting only one disjunctive arc from a disjunctive pair of arcs $\{(i, j), (j, i)\}$ associated with each pair $\{i, j\}$ in the W_l, we obtain the set V_n of disjunctive arcs of the same number as of conflict sets. The graph $G_n = (X, Z \cup V_n)$ $(n = 1, 2, \ldots, n_0)$ gives the feasible schedule, provided it includes no circuit. We call each $V_n (n = 1, 2, \ldots, n_0)$ the complete selection of disjunctive arcs from the family of conflict sets.

Hence our problem reduces to the following problem I:

PROBLEM I. Determine a graph $G_n = (X, Z \cup V_n)$ which has no circuit and gives minimal value of the given objective function f among all graphs G_n ($n = 1, 2, \ldots, n_0$). This means that it is sufficient to examine a finite sequence of critical path problems on respective graphs G_n among the family $\{G_n\}$, by the definition of f.

The solution method based on the problem I may require some device for avoiding any circuit or some circuit check procedure. Each critical path computation becomes complex because of the large number of arcs in the related graph G_n including a complete selection of disjunctive arcs, V_n.

In order to avoid these weaknesses, we consider, in the following, a special partial selection of disjunctive arcs from the family of conflict sets, S_q.

Here the family of partial selection, $\{S_q\}$, is the family of subsets S_q of all V_n in $\{V_n\}$. If $\{i, j\} \subset T_{r, w} (w = 1, 2, \ldots, w_r; \ r = 1, 2, \ldots, m)$ then we have $(i, j) \in S_q$ and $(j, i) \notin S_q$, $(i, j) \notin S_q$ and $(j, i) \in S_q$, or $(i, j) \notin S_q$ and $(j, i) \notin S_q$. Since some S_q can be any V_n, by the definition of f, it is sufficient to examine a finite sequence of the following problem II:

PROBLEM II. Determine a S_q such that the associated graph $G_q = (X, Z \cup S_q)$ has no circuit (this is possible as shown below) and then determine every earliest start time t_{N+h} ($h = 1, 2, \ldots, n$) under the constraints: $t_j \geq t_i + p_i$, $t_i \geq 0$ ($i = 0, 1, 2, \ldots, N + n + 1$) for every arc (i, j) in $Z \cup S_q$. This means that we consider a finite sequence of critical path problems on respective graphs G_q and an optimal S_q is a S_q, where $Z \cup S_q = Z \cup V_n$ holds for some V_n, which gives minimal value of the given objective function f.

12.28. BAB and EXTBAB Algorithms by Partial Selection of Disjunctive Arcs

The BAB algorithm, described below, adds successively the disjunctive arc (i, j) selected from the set of pairs of nodes $\{i, j\}$ in $\{T_{r, w}\}$, ordered by some prescribed rule, to the first $S_1 = \phi$ (empty set) without occurrence of any circuit. That is to say, a disjunctive arc $(i, j) \notin S_q$ associated with some conflict set $T_{r, w}$, which does not satisfy (12.12) in Section 12.25, that is, does not satisfy the given resource constraints, in the graph $G_q = (X, Z \cup S_q)$ at each stage is added to the then S_q by some prescribed rule. In this case, since there exist some disjunctive arcs (i, j), not contained in the then S_q, that satisfy (12.12), this BAB algorithm has a distinctive feature of reaching a feasible schedule in a short time. It uses partial branching procedure and is easily extended to an EXTBAB algorithm.

12.29. BAB Algorithm

As preparations for the BAB algorithm, the identification of the family of conflict sets $\{T_{r, w}\}$ and the order of all pairs of nodes $\{i, j\}$ contained in $\{T_{r, w}\}$ are decided as below:

1. Let the set $A_r = \{a_{r,i}\}$ for each r $(r = 1, 2, \ldots, m)$, then according to the increasing order of k $(k = 2, 3, \ldots, |A_r|)$ we decide the combination $T_{r,w}$ of k activities which satisfies $\sum_{i \in T, w} a_{r,i} > b_r$ such that no two activities in $T_{r,w}$ connect with each other under the given precedence relation and each $T_{r,w}$ includes no other $T_{r,w}$ for the smaller value of k. Obviously all $T_{r,w}$ thus determined constitute all conflict sets.

2. First for each $T_{r,w}$, arrange every pair $\{i,j\}$ in $T_{r,w}$ in nonincreasing order (arbitrary for the tie) of the sum $i + j$ (this is the case $\lambda_{r,w} > 1$). We call the first pair with the largest sum a dominant pair of this conflict set $T_{r,w}$. Then arrange all conflict sets $\{T_{r,w}\}$ in nondecreasing order (arbitrary for the tie) of the sums $i + j$ for associated dominant pairs, and in each $T_{r,w}$ arrange all pairs $\{i,j\}$ in it in nonincreasing order (arbitrary for the tie) of the sums $i + j$.

Remark. The above heuristic rules reflect the fact that if a disjunctive arc from the pair $\{i,j\}$ with the smaller sum $i + j$ is first introduced in the set S_q, this pair of nodes $\{i,j\}$ is close to the source node 0 by the definition of node numbers and then there exists high possibility of dissolving the conflict sets including the pairs $\{i,j\}$ with the larger sum $i + j$. Also any disjunctive arc from the pair $\{i,j\}$ with the larger sum $i + j$ in the same conflict set $T_{r,w}(\lambda_{r,w} > 1)$ is expected to have a possibility to shorten the increment of the value of the objective function provided it is introduced in the then S_q since the associated pair of nodes $\{i,j\}$ is closer to the sink node.

Then the BAB algorithm for our problem is composed of the following steps:

Step 1. Let $f^* = \infty$ say and $S_1 = \phi$ $(G_1 = G_0)$. Solve problem II by using $t_j = \max_{(i,j) \in Z \cup S_1} (t_i + p_i)$ repeatedly (node (1) in the solution tree). Proceed to step 2.

Step 2. If the solution (value of the earliest start time t_i of every node i and value of f) satisfy (12.12) in Section 12.25 for at least one $\{i,j\}$ in every $T_{r,w}$ (satisfy all resource constraints), this solution gives an optimal schedule. Otherwise, proceed to step 3.

Step 3. Generally, if the solution of problem II for S_q does not satisfy all resource constraints, the value of f gives a lower bound $LB(S_q)$ at a node in the solution tree, associated with S_q (Theorem 14).

1 If $LB(S_q) \geq f^*$, proceed to step 5.

2. Otherwise, determine a $\{i,j\}$ with the largest sum $i + j$ in the first $T_{r,w}$ among the family $\{T_{r,w}\}$ that do not satisfy (12.12) in Section 12.25. Then if i or j is on the critical path of G_q, or i and j belong to the same project and i or j is on its critical path, add a disjunctive arc (i,j), when i is on it, to S_q, otherwise if

$$(t_i + p_i) - t_j \leq (t_j + p_j) - t_i \qquad (12.13)$$

holds, add a disjunctive arc (i, j) to S_q, where when equality holds in (12.13), (12.13) is replaced by $i < j$.

Remark. As the other criteria, a disjunctive arc (i, j) to be added to S_q is determined simply only by (12.13), $TF_i \leq TF_j$ (total float), or $a_{r,i} \geq a_{r,j}$, where the tie will be dissolved by another criterion.

Next, solve the problem II for the new $G_{q+1} = (X, Z \cup S_{q+1})$, where $S_{q+1} = S_q \cup \{(i, j)\}$ and proceed to step 4.

Step 4.
1. If the solution of problem II satisfy all resource constraints, it gives a feasible schedule. Set $f^* = \min(f^*, f)$ and proceed to step 5.
2. Otherwise, return to step 3.

Step 5. If there exists, in the then solution tree, the set of nodes that have $LB(S_q)$ smaller than f^* and are not yet examined all $2\lambda_{r,w}$ disjunctive arcs (that is, not completely branched), then backtrack the tree to the nearest node (n) in this set and proceed to step 6.

Otherwise, the feasible schedule giving f^* becomes an optimal schedule.

Step 6. From the set S_q for the previous solution node, exclude every disjunctive arc introduced in every passed solution node including the node (n) in case of backtracking. Next if the twin disjunctive arc (j, i) of the disjunctive arc (i, j) introduced at the solution note (n) is not yet examined, add this arc (j, i) to S_q, otherwise (this occurs in case $\lambda_{r,w} > 1$), from the other pairs $\{i, j\}$ in the same $T_{r,w}$, a new disjunctive arc (i, j) is added to S_q in the same way as in no. 2 in step 3. Then solve problem II under this new S_{q+1} and return to step 4.

12.30. Justification of Proposed BAB Algorithm and Remarks

The justification of the BAB algorithm developed in the previous section is clarified by the following theorems.

THEOREM 11. *The graph $G_q = (X, Z \cup S_q)$ associated with each node in the solution tree by the above BAB algorithm includes no circuit.*

Proof. The first graph $G_1 = (X, Z \cup S_1)$, where $S_1 = \phi$, includes no circuit because it is connected only by precedence relation. Next we assume that the graph $G_q = (X, Z \cup S_q)$ at any stage includes no circuit. For the pair $\{i, j\}$ in some $T_{r,w}$ which constructs a circuit by its disjunctive arc (i, j) or the twin disjunctive arc (j, i) with the arcs in the graph G_q, let us say $t_i < t_j$ in G_q (Fig. 12.20) (the same for the case $t_i > t_j$), then obviously we have $t_j > t_i + p_i$. Hence (12.12) in Section 12.25 holds for such a pair $\{i, j\}$. Consequently, any pair $\{i, j\}$ in any $T_{r,w}$, which does not satisfy (12.12) in Section 12.25 in the G_q, does not produce the disjunctive arc constructing any circuit with the arcs in the G_q.

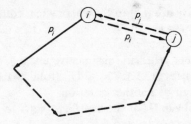

FIG. 12.20. Case $t_i < t_j$.

Next, before stating some theorems on the above BAB algorithm, a definition of the following terminology will be given. The terminology that the feasible schedule contained in the node in the solution tree associated with graph $G_q = (X, Z \cup S_q)$ means that this feasible schedule satisfies the precedence relation and also is specified to satisfy the resource constraint for each $T_{r,w}$ associated with each disjunctive arc in the set S_q.

Then the following theorems justifying the proposed BAB algorithm hold, the proofs of them will be left as an exercise for the reader.

THEOREM 12. *Node* (1) *in the solution tree, where* $S_1 = \phi$, *contains all feasible schedule and the value of the objective function f at node* (1) *is a lower bound of f for all feasible schedules.*

THEOREM 13. *When a node* (N) *in the solution tree is (completely) branched into the* $2\lambda_{r,w}$ *nodes for a conflict set* $T_{r,w}$ *which does not satisfy* (12.12) *in Section 12.25, any schedule contained in the node* (N) *is included in at least one new node in case* $\lambda_{r,w} > 1$, *or in one new node in case* $\lambda_{r,w} = 1$.

THEOREM 14. *The value of f at each node in the solution tree is a lower bound of the value of f associated with any schedule contained in this node. Also if* S_l *includes* S_k, *then a lower bound at the node associated with* S_l *is not smaller than that associated with* S_k.

THEOREM 15. *The proposed BAB algorithm terminates after a finite number of steps and a feasible schedule giving the then least upper bound* f^* *is an optimal schedule with minimal objective value* f^*.

Some remarks on the proposed BAB algorithm.

1. In practical applications, instead of constructing all conflict sets at the beginning, it is sufficient to construct the specified subfamily of conflict sets by examining the feasibility by (12.12) in Section 12.25 in the increasing order of the values of t_i at the nodes, in case of checking the (12.12) in steps 2 and 4.

2. Since it takes at least 80/10 hours in the case when a project requires 80

units of a resource with availability $b = 10$ per hour, we can use the following expression as exact lower bound of the total elapsed time (makespan) of f for the graph $G_q = (X, Z \cup S_q)$, where $S_q = \{(i_l, j_l), l = 1, 2, \ldots, n\}$:

$$LB(S_q) = \max\left[v_q, t_j + \max_r \{ (1/b_r) \sum_{i, t_i \geq t_j} a_{r,i} \cdot p_i \}, LB(S_{q-1}) \right], \quad (12.14)$$

where v_q is the length of the critical path in G_q, $t_j = \max_l t_{j}$, and $LB(S_{q-1})$ is a lower bound at the previous node in the solution tree. As another lower bound we can use that due to Zaloom.

3. Let d_{ij} be the elapsed time from the start time of activity (node) i to that of activity (node) j. Then when d_{ij} includes setup times depending on j, the above BAB algorithm taking d_{ij} for p_i may produce the circuit (cf. reference).

Exercises

1. Prove each of the Theorems 12–15.
2. Give an example for the statement in the above Remark 3.

12.31. Numerical Examples by BAB Algorithm and Related EXTBAB Algorithm

We consider three projects with the total nineteen activities subject to precedence relation and resource constraints shown in Table 12.3, where $P(i)$ is the set of activities directly preceding activity i and $r(a_{r,i})b_r$ shows that activity i requires $a_{r,i}$ units of resource r with availability b_r ($r = 1, 2, 3$).

TABLE 12.3

						Project					
	1				2				3		
i	$P(i)$	p_i	$r(a_{r,i})b_r$	i	$P(i)$	p_i	$r(a_{r,i})b_r$	i	$P(i)$	p_i	$r(a_{r,i})b_r$
1	–	2		2	–	3		3	–	1	
4	1	3	1(4)6	6	2	1	1(2)6	7	3	3	2(4)8
5	1	5	1(5)6	11	6	2	2(3)8	8	3	4	1(1)6 / 3(6)12
9	4,5	1	2(2)8	12	6	3	3(1)12	13	7	2	3(7)12
10	5	2	1(3)6 / 3(3)12	16	11	2	3(1)12	14	8	1	
15	9,10	4		17	11,12	4	2(2)8	18	13,14	5	
								19	18	3	3(10)12

These three resources are the principal resources. The graph $G_0 = (X, Z)$ only by precedence relation becomes as shown in Fig. 12.21. Also the family of

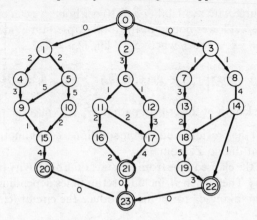

FIG. 12.21

conflict sets, $\{T_{r,w}\}$ becomes as follows: $T_{1,1} = \{4, 5\}$, $T_{1,2} = \{5, 6\}$, $T_{1,3} = \{4, 10\}$, $T_{1,4} = \{4, 6, 8\}$, $T_{2,1} = \{7, 9, 11\}$, $T_{3,1} = \{8, 13\}$, $T_{3,2} = \{10, 19\}$. Then, by the rule 2 in Section 12.29, the order of the pairs $\{i, j\}$ in $\{T_{r,w}\}$ becomes as follows:

$$\{4, 5\}, \{5, 6\}, \{4, 10\}, \{6, 8\}, \{4, 8\}, \{4, 6\}, \{9, 11\}, \{7, 11\}, \{7, 9\}, \{8, 13\},$$
$$\{10, 19\}. \tag{12.15}$$

EXAMPLE 8. *min-makespan problem.* We look for a schedule minimizing $t_{23} = \max[t_{20}, t_{21}, t_{22}]$. By examining the pair $\{i, j\}$ which includes the disjunctive arc (i, j) not contained in each S_q according to the order of (12.15), the solution tree becomes as in Fig. 12.22. An optimal schedule is a feasible

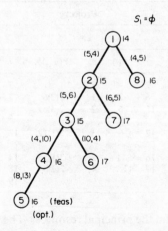

FIG. 12.22

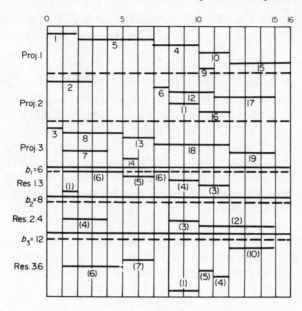

FIG. 12.23

schedule at node 5, in the solution tree, with $S_5 = \{(5, 4), (5, 6), (4, 10), (8, 13)\}$ and minimal makespan 16. Its bar chart is shown in Fig. 12.23.

EXAMPLE 9. *Min-mean completion time problem.* We look for a schedule minimizing $3f = t_{20} + t_{21} + t_{22}$. The solution tree becomes as in Fig. 12.24.

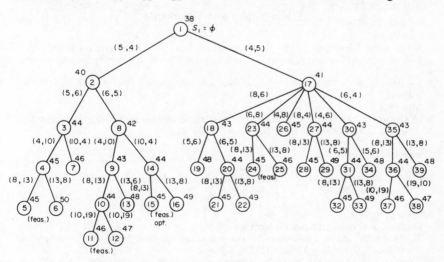

FIG. 12.24

An optimal schedule is a feasible schedule at node 15, in the solution tree, with $S_{15} = \{(5, 4), (6, 5), (10, 4), (8, 13)\}$ and minimal mean completion time $45/3 = 15$.

EXAMPLE 10. *Reliable approximate schedules by EXTBAB algorithm.* We look for the approximate schedules of $\alpha = 15\%$, that is, with percentage of relative error less than or equal to 15%, in Examples 8 and 9 respectively, where $1/(1 + 15/100) = 20/23$. In Example 8, since we have $20f^*/23 = 13.8$ for the first feasible schedule (node 5, $f^* = 16$), nodes $4-1$ in Fig. 12.22 are excluded and then we have this feasible schedule as the desired approximate schedule. Next in Example 9, since we have $20f^*/23 = 40$ for the first feasible schedule (node 5, $f^* = 46$), ultimately this feasible schedule becomes the desired approximate schedule.

Remark. The proposed EXTBAB algorithm has been effectively applied to a practical example of manpower scheduling in a construction company (cf. reference). Also there are heuristic models for an approximate schedule.

Exercises

1. Solve Example 9 by the BAB algorithm which determines a disjunctive arc (i, j) to be introduced only by (12.13) at step 3, no. 2 in Section 12.29, or by $\text{TF}_i \leq \text{TF}_j$ respectively.

2. Solve the min-maximum tardiness problem by the BAB algorithm under the constraints in Table 12.3 and the due-dates $d_1 = 15, d_2 = 8$ and $d_3 = 10$ for the projects 1, 2 and 3 respectively.

Bibliography and Comments

Section 12.1

For the general descriptions of the job-shop scheduling problem, refer to the books and papers at Bibliography and Comments, Section 4.1, in Chapter 4. Also, for the priority dispatching rules, see

S. S. PANWALKAR and W. ISKANDER, "A survey of scheduling rules", *Opns. Res.* **25**, No. 1 (1977), 45–61.

Also refer to

M. YAMAMOTO, "An approximate solution of machine scheduling problems by decomposition method", *Int. J. Prod. Res.* **15**, No. 6 (1977), 599–608.

Section 12.2

For the $n \times 2$ min-makespan problem see

J. R. JACKSON, "An extension of Johnson's results on job lot scheduling", *Nav. Res. Log. Quart.* **3**, No. 3 (1956), 201–203.

Sections 12.3–12.5

For the $2 \times m$ min-makespan problem see

S. B. AKERS, Jr. and J. FRIEDMAN, "A non-numerical approach to production scheduling problems", *Opns. Res,* **3**, No. 4 (1955), 429–442.

W. SZWARC, "Solution of the Akers–Friedman scheduling problem", *Opns. Res.* **8**, No. 6 (1960), 782–788.

W. W. HARDGRAVE and G. L. NEMHAUSER, "A geometric model and a graphical algorithm for a sequencing problem", *Opns. Res.* **11**, No. 6 (1963), 889–900.

I. B. TURKSEN and R. SHANKAR, "Some extensions of Akers and Friedman production scheduling problem", *Symp. on the Theory of Scheduling and Its Applications*, S. E. ELMAGHRABY (ed.), Springer, 1973, pp. 426–431.

For the exercises 2–4 of section 12.5, see Szwarc's paper. For the general treatment of the shortest path problem see Chapter 1.

Section 12.6
The following paper treats the ILP formulation:

H. M. WAGNER, "An integer linear-programming model for machine scheduling", *Nav. Res. Log. Quart.* **6**, No. 2 (1959), 131–140.

E. H. BOWMAN, "The schedule-sequencing problem", *Opns. Res.* **7**, No. 5 (1959), 621–624.

A. S. MANNE, "On the job-shop scheduling problem", *Opns. Res.* **8**, No. 2 (1960), 219–223.

H. H. GREENBERG, "A branch-bound solution to the general scheduling problem", *Opns. Res.* **16**, No. 2 (1968), 353–361.

E. BALAS, "Discrete programming by the filter method", *Opns. Res.* **15**, No. 5 (1967), 915–957.

Section 12.7
Manne, *op. cit.*, pp. 219–223.

For the exercises see

Greenberg, *op. cit.*, pp. 353–361.

A. H. LAND and A. DOIG, "An automatic method of solving discrete programming problems", *Econometrica*, **28** (1960), 497–520.

Sections 12.9–12.11
G. H. BROOKS and C. R. WHITE, "An algorithm for finding optimal or near optimal solution to the production scheduling problem", *J. Ind. Eng.* **16**, No. 1 (1965), 34–40.

M. FLORIAN, P. TREPANT and G. McMAHON, "An implicit enumeration algorithm for the machine sequencing problem", *Manag. Sci.* **17**, No. 12 (1971), B782–B792.

S. ASHOUR and S. R. HIREMATH, "A branch-and-bound approach to the job-shop scheduling problem", *Int. J. Prod. Res.* **11**, No. 1 (1973), 47–58.

As the methods for improving the lower bound see

P. BRATLEY, M. FLORIAN and P. ROBILLARD, "On sequencing with earliest starts and due dates with application to computing bounds for the $(n/m/G/F_{max})$ Problem", *Nav. Res. Log. Quart.* **20**, No. 1 (1973), 57–67.

M. FLORIAN, C. TILQUIN and G. TILQUIN, "An implicit enumeration algorithm for complex scheduling problems", *Int. J. Prod. Res.* **13**, No. 1 (1975), 25–40.

G. McMAHON and M. FLORIAN, "On scheduling with ready times and due dates to minimize maximum lateness", *Opns. Res.* **23**, No. 3 (1975), 475–482.

Section 12.10
ASHOUR and HIREMATH, *op. cit.*, pp. 47–58.

Sections 12.12–12.14
FLORIAN, TREPANT and McMAHON, *op. cit.*, B782-B792.

Sections 12.12–12.13
B. ROY, *Cheminement et Connexité dans le graphes-Applications aux Problèmes d'Ordonnancement*, METRA, No. 1, 1962.

B. G. SUSSMANN, "Scheduling problems with interval disjunctions", *Zeitschrift für Opns. Res.* **16** (1972), 165–178.

For the exercises, see Sussmann's paper.

Sections 12.15–12.16
I. NABESHIMA, "General scheduling algorithms with applications to parallel scheduling and multiprogramming scheduling", *J. Oper. Res. Soc. Japan*, **14**, No. 2 (1971), 72–99.

I. NABESHIMA, *Scheduling Theory* (in Japanese), Morikita Shuppan, 1974, pp. 216–228.

Section 12.20
E. BALAS, "Machine sequencing via disjunctive graphs: an implicit enumeration algorithm", *Opns. Res.* 17, No. 6 (1969), 941–957.
E. BALAS, "Machine sequencing: disjunctive graphs and degree-constrained subgraphs", *Nav. Res. Log. Quart.* 17, No. 1 (1970), 1–10.
J. M. CHARLTON, and C. C. DEATH, "A method of solution for general machine-scheduling problems", *Opnl. Res. Quart.* 18, No. 4 (1970), 689–707.

Section 12.21
For the heuristic methods related to BAB algs. I ∼ III, see
A. S. SPACHIS and J. R. KING, "Job-shop scheduling heuristics with local neighbourhood search", *Int. J. Prod. Res.* 17, No. 6 (1979), 507–526.

Sections 12.22–12.31
I. NABESHIMA, *Scheduling Theory* (in Japanese), Morikita Shuppan, 1974, pp. 231–277.

Section 12.22
On the early review see, for example,
W. S. HERROELEN, "Resource-constrained project scheduling—the state of the art", *Opnl. Res. Quart.* 23, No. 3 (1972), 261–275.
E. W. DAVIS, "Project scheduling under resource constraints—historical review and categorization of procedures", *AIIE Trans.* 5, No. 4 (1973), 297–313.
For the formulations by ILP see
A. A. B. PRITSKER, L. J. WATTERS and P. M. WOLFE, "Multiproject scheduling with limited resources: a zero-one programming approach", *Manag. Sci.* 16, No. 1 (1969), 93–108.
M. L. FISHER, "Optimal solution of scheduling problems using Lagrange multipliers: Part I", *Opns. Res.* 21, No. 5 (1973), 1114–1127.
M. L. FISHER, "Optimal solution of scheduling using Lagrange multipliers: Part II", *Symp on the Theory of Scheduling and Its Applications*, S. E. ELMAGHRABY (ed.), Springer, 1973, pp. 294–318.
F. B. TALBOT and J. H. PATTERSON, "An efficient integer programming algorithm with network cuts for solving resource-constrained scheduling problem", *Manag. Sci.* 24, No. 11 (1978), 1163–1174.
For the formulations by disj. graph and the related BAB algorithms see
E. BALAS, "Project scheduling with resource constraints", *Applications of Mathematical Programming Techniques*, E. M. L. BEALE (ed.), The Eng. Univ. Press, 1970, Section 5 (Disj. Graph).
I. NABESHIMA, "Algorithms for multiproject scheduling with resource constraints and related parallel scheduling", *Rep. Univ. Elec.-Comm.* 23, No. 1 (1972), 29–50 (BAB Alg.).
S. GORENSTEIN, "An algorithm for project (job) sequencing with resource constraints", *Opns. Res.* 20, No. 4 (1972), 835–850 (BAB Alg.).
G. E. BENNINGTON and L. F. MCGINNIS, "An improved feasibility test for Gorenstein's algorithm", *Opns. Res.* 22, No. 5 (1975), 1117–1119.
For the horizon-varying algorithms see the next two papers:
E. W. DAVIS and G. E. HEIDORN, "An algorithm for optimal project scheduling under multiple resource constraints", *Manag. Sci.* 17, No. 12, 1971, B803-B816.
This transforms the one project problem into the shortest-path problem by applying a solution method for the assembly-line balancing problem.
J. H. PATTERSON and W. D. HUBER, "A horizon-varying, zero–one approach to project scheduling", *Manag. Sci.* 20, No. 6 (1974), 990–998.
A BAB algorithm which branches to each feasible subset of activities is presented by
N. A. J. HASTING, "On resource allocation in project networks", *Opnl. Res. Quart.* 23, No. 2 (1972), 217–221.
R. J. WILLIS and N. A. J. HASTING, "Project scheduling with resource constraints using branch-and-bound methods", *Opnl. Res. Quart.* 27, No. 2, i (1976), 341–349.

A backtrack programming algorithm is presented by
I. NABESHIMA, "A backtrack programming algorithm and reliable heuristic programs for general scheduling problem", *Rep. Univ. Elec.-Comm.* **24**, No. 1 (1973), 23–36.

Sections 12.24–12.31
I. NABESHIMA, "Algorithms for multiproject scheduling with resource constraints and related parallel scheduling", *Rep. Univ. Elec.-Comm.* **23**, No. 1 (1972) 29–50.
Concerning general description on the disjunctions see
J. CALIER, "Disjunctions dans les Ordonnancements," *R.A.I.R.O.* **9**, No. 2 (1975), 83–100.

Section 12.30
Zaloom's lower bound is found in
V. ZALOOM, "On the resource constrained project scheduling problem", *AIIE Transactions*, **3**, No. 4 (1971), 302–305.
Concerning the lower bound see also
K. R. BAKER, *Introduction to Sequencing and Scheduling*, Wiley, 1974, pp. 270–277.
For the Remark 3 and exercise 2 see
I. NABESHIMA, "Branch and bound algorithm for multiproject scheduling with resource constraints where explicit setup times exist", *Rep. Univ. Elec.-Comm.* **26**, No. 1 (1975), 41–49.

Section 12.31

A practical application of the EXTBAB algorithm is found in
I. NABESHIMA and S. MARUYAMA, "Computational experience on multi-project scheduling with resource constraints", *Rep. Univ. Elec.-Comm.* **26**, No. 1 (1975), 51–64.

For the heuristic models see
J. MOSHMAN, J. JOHNSON and M. LARSEN, "RAMPS. A technique for resource allocation and multi-project scheduling", *Proc. SJCC* (1963), 17–27.
J. D. WIEST, "Heuristic programs for decision making", *Harvard Business Review*, Sept.–Oct. 1966.
J. D. WIEST and F. K. LEVY, *A Management Guide to PERT/CPM*, Prentice-Hall, 1969, Chapter 7 (second edition, 1977).
E. W. DAVIS, and J. H. PATTERSON, "A comparison of heuristic and optimum solutions in resource-constrained scheduling", *Manag. Sci.* **21**, No. 8 (1975), 944–955.

Author Index

323

Subject Index